On the Cover:

Grilled Pacific Swordfish

Photo by John Rizzo

Food preparation and styling by Lori McKean

THE MENU

SAN FRANCISCO BAY AREA

A Menu Guide
to the Top 200 Restaurants
in the San Francisco Bay Area

Narsai David

David Thomas Publishing

For Veni and Danny
and their unending patience

ISBN 0-9628274-2-8

PRINTED IN THE UNITED STATES OF AMERICA

Printed on Recycled Paper

Cover design by Heather Kier and Ron Miller
Illustrations by Heather Kier
"The Menu" logo design by Courtney Barnes
and Heather Kier
Typesetting by R&R Pre-Press
Layout by Heather Kier and Ginny Reschke

THE MENU is available at bookstores and gift shops everywhere. Bulk discounts are available for corporate giving, conventions and fund-raising. For more information, see order form in the back of this book, or contact:

448 South First Street, Suite 200
Hillsboro, Oregon 97123
(503) 640-6951

Table of Contents

Restaurants by Cuisine

Afghanistan	24
American	26
Asian	62
Bar & Grill	64
Burmese	68
Cajan-Creole	70
Californian	72
Cambodian	136
Caribbean	138
Chinese	140
Continental	172
French	186
Indian	222
Indonesian	224
International	226
Italian	232
Italian-Oriental	316
Mediterranean	320
Mexican	346
Middle Eastern	356
Moroccan	360
Japanese	362
Persian	374
Seafood	378
Vegetarian	424

Introduction	11
Publisher's Note	15
Features Guide	16
Index by Cuisine	430
Geographical Index	434
Alphabetical Index	438
Gift Order Form	443
Reader Survey & Corporate Giving/Fund-raising	*Inside Back Cover*

San Francisco is a great restaurant city. With over 3,000 restaurants in the city, and as many more in the surrounding area, choosing 200 proved to be a tough assignment. The ethnic diversity of San Francisco is exciting and is best reflected in its restaurants. There are 100-year-old restaurants in the Financial District; Chinatown and Fisherman's Wharf have been an attraction from the beginning; Italian and French have been prominent in San Francisco's restaurant history. But there are probably more Vietnamese, Thai, Cambodian and Burmese restaurants in San Francisco than anywhere in the country. The free liberal spirit of San Francisco attracts creative people from all corners of the earth. And it seems that restaurants are among the first businesses of every new immigrant group.

I have attempted to select a cross-section of the best food in the various areas around the bay. From the time we started this project, a few restaurants on our list have already retired. Of course more have opened to take their place. I have tried to include all of my favorites and am already trying restaurants for the next edition. The list will be forever changing and it is exciting to be part of the change.

Centered in the triangle of the wine producing regions of Napa, Sonoma and Livermore, San Francisco has some of the most sophisticated diners anywhere. Their knowledge of wine and its importance to fine dining are unequaled.

Only a few years ago, we were trying to define "California Cuisine" as a new creation. It is clearly a new approach, but its roots are as ancient as the first piece of meat roasted over an open fire. California chefs insist on the freshest ingredients and then prepare them to show off their subtleties.

Sometimes the experiments are not so subtle. Witness the growing interest in chile peppers. Although indigenous to the Americas, chiles went around the world before becoming important to California Cuisine.

Their comeback was heralded by the interest in Hunan and Mandarin cuisine, followed in short order by Mexican cooking which soon became "Southwest" cuisine. The incredibly hot Thai peppers, which are tempered with coconut cream and basil in cooking, were a mere stepping stone to the hottest pepper on earth, the Scotch Bonnet. Known in the Caribbean as Habanero, it is 100 times as hot as the everyday Jalapeño. It's hard to imagine why anyone would even try to cook with it. But that curiosity and willingness to experiment are really what California Cuisine is all about. We have a generation of chefs that are not bound by any tradition to the use of particular ingredients or techniques. Long before tofu and ginger root were even imagined in other parts of the country, they had been adopted as an integral part of local cooking. Exotic spices such as lemon grass, galangal and turmeric are available fresh in the market, and are not limited in use to the Asian cuisines that spawned them.

The amazing market basket that is produced by California is the envy of the world. Every imaginable fruit, nut or vegetable can be, and usually is, grown here. As soon as there is a large enough demand for virtually anything, someone will produce it. I recently spoke with a citrus nurseryman who had just grafted 500 Persian lime trees for a farmer. The fruit is somewhat like a cross between a lemon and a lime. It is very highly regarded in the Middle East and in a few years will be available fresh in California.

Laura Chenel went to France to work in a small goat cheese plant some years ago. She came home to the Napa Valley to produce California goat cheese. One success led to another and soon she was producing some of the best goat cheese of all, from the most delicate fresh cheeses to a hard, dry aged cheese. She built a larger plant in Santa Rosa and ranchers created goat herds to supply her needs. In only a decade a goat cheese industry has developed in the state with many producers of their own "farmstead" cheeses. A tiny production of sheep's milk cheese has just been started in the Sonoma Valley.

I have often felt that California Wine actually led the way for California Cuisine. In the mid 1960's, Robert Mondavi built the first new winery in Napa in a generation. Jack & Jamie Davies rebuilt Schramsberg on the site of a historic winery, abandoned since Prohibition, and limited their production to a California Champagne. They were "pioneers" of the new wave of producers. There are over 750 wineries now, competing for international recognition. California wines are now some of the finest in the world. Appreciation of fine wine is, by definition, associated with fine dining. So it was inevitable that the creativity of restaurants and wineries should evolve together.

Today, California Cuisine in the broadest sense is served in Italian, French, Chinese, Japanese, Greek, Lebanese, Saudi Arabian and even American restaurants.

Narsai David
Editor

Everyone's a critic. No experience more perfectly echoes that sentiment than dining out. It never fails — whenever someone finds out that I publish restaurant guides, they immediately proceed to tell me about their favorite places to eat. My mouth waters as they describe, in vivid detail, the dish they ordered, as well as what everyone else in their party ordered. In other words, they describe the restaurant's menu.

It follows that a great way to choose a restaurant would be to read its menu, provided the place is well recommended. That is why Narsai has chosen to let the menus speak for themselves, without a lot of additional editorial copy. The fact that he personally recommends each of these restaurants as one of the best 200 in the Bay Area is editorial enough.

Two important items must be noted:

1. NO ONE PAID TO BE IN THIS BOOK.
   Neither Narsai David nor the publisher, nor any of their associates accept paid advertising of any kind for *THE MENU* book. There are no fees charged to any of the restaurants featured in the book, nor is inclusion in the book subject to any favors, trade outs, book purchases, or any such promotional fees whatsoever.
2. MENUS CHANGE.
   Most all of the restaurants in this book change their menu frequently, many even daily. We have tried to feature menus that accurately reflect the style and approach of the chef. And, as you might expect, prices also change.

Putting this book together was no small task. My heartfelt thanks go out to Deanna Demaree, Cordy Jensen, Ginny Reschke, Heather Kier, Ron Miller, Courtney Barnes, John Rizzo, Lori McKean, Bob Dennis, Cindy Schumock, Mike Flake, and especially Narsai David.

Following our success with *THE MENU* in the Pacific Northwest, we are currently expanding into many new cities. Along the way we are continually striving to improve our product. To do so, we need your feedback. To that end, you will find a tear-out Reader Survey inside the back cover. Please take a moment to fill it out and mail it (pre-paid) to my attention. I would love to hear from you.

Here's hoping that, as a fellow food lover, you not only find *THE MENU* to be a useful handbook of your favorite places, but also a tempting map to new gastronomical discoveries.

Tom Demaree
Publisher

The following table will answer the most often asked questions about the services offered by a particular restaurant. Please keep in mind that just as menus and prices change, so do amenities. It is always best to confirm those features important to you when making your reservation.

A few explanatory notes:

Types of Cuisine — The restaurants are grouped alphabetically by type of cuisine, starting with *Afghanistan*, all the way through *Vegetarian*. The cuisine category is referenced at the top right of each two page spread. Index by Cuisine can be found on page 430.

Geographic Location — The address of the restaurant is located at the bottom of the left page on each menu. When there are additional locations, the best known or original location address is given, followed by the statement: (call for additional locations). Restaurants located in San Francisco are listed by their district or neighborhood, all others by their city name. Geographical index begins on page 434.

Hours — Dinner hours are listed at the bottom of the right page on each menu. A quick reference icon appears at the bottom right showing which meals a restaurant serves.
(Example: Ⓑ Ⓛ Ⓓ = Breakfast, Lunch, Dinner, ●●Ⓓ = Dinner *only*.)
For breakfast or lunch hours, please call the restaurant.

100% Non-Smoking — At press time many restaurants who do not presently offer 100% non-smoking were considering it. Those restaurants that do accommodate smoking guests always offer non-smoking areas as well.

Wheelchair access — Most all of the restaurants without full wheelchair access are still able and happy to accommodate the special needs of any of their guests.

Dress — The dress code rule for the Bay Area is: "Let's not have a dress code rule." It is common in San Francisco to see a guest in a jacket and tie seated next to someone in a tee-shirt and jeans. The three categories of dress referred to are only an indication of how *most* people dress for dinner. If you have a question, call ahead.

Personal Checks — Proper I.D. is required.

Features Guide

Restaurant	Pg.	Wheelchair Access	100% Non-Smoking	Visa/Master Card	American Express	Discover	Diners Club	Checks Accepted	Beer & Wine	Full Bar	Live Entertainment	Sunday Brunch	Breakfast	Lunch	Dinner	High Chairs	Take Out	Valet Parking	Private Parties	Informal Dress	Casual Dress	Dressy	Reserv. Recom.	Reserv. Required	Reserv. Not Taken
231 Ellsworth	72	●	●	●				●	●	●				●	●		●			●			●	●	
A. Sabella's	378	●		●	●			●	●	●	●	●		●	●	●		●		●			●		
Academy Grill, The	232	●		●	●				●	●				●	●		●			●			●	●	●
Acquerello	234		●	●	●	●	●	●	●						●					●			●	●	
Albona	236		●	●	●			●	●						●	●	●			●			●	●	
Alejandro's	412	●		●	●	●	●	●	●	●				●	●		●			●			●		
Alexander Lanzone	238	●		●	●	●	●		●	●				●	●	●	●			●				●	
Alfreds	414			●	●	●	●		●	●				●	●			●	●				●	●	
Alioto's	380	●		●	●	●	●		●	●				●	●	●				●			●		
Ali's	356	●	●	●	●	●			●	●	●	●			●	●		●		●			●		
Amolio's	186			●	●	●	●		●	●					●	●	●			●			●		
Angkor Palace	136	●		●	●				●						●		●			●			●		
Aqua	382	●	●	●	●				●	●				●	●			●	●			●	●	●	
Asta	26	●		●	●	●	●	●	●	●				●	●		●			●			●		
Atrium	74	●		●	●	●	●		●	●				●	●	●	●			●			●		
Auberge du Soleil	76	●	●	●	●	●	●	●	●	●			●	●	●	●		●	●				●	●	
Balboa Cafe	78			●	●	●	●		●	●	●		●	●	●					●			●		
Bay Wolf	320		●	●					●	●				●	●	●				●			●	●	
Beethoven	172			●	●				●	●					●	●				●			●		
Bella Voce (Fairmont)	240	●		●	●		●		●	●					●	●		●	●	●			●		
Benihana	362	●		●	●	●	●		●	●				●	●				●	●			●		
Bentley's	384	●		●	●	●	●		●	●	●	●		●	●				●	●			●		
Bette's Oceanview Diner	28	●						●	●				●	●	●		●			●	●				●
Big Four, The	174			●	●	●	●		●	●	●		●	●	●	●		●	●				●	●	
Bistro Clovis	188	●		●					●					●	●					●			●		
Bistro Roti	190	●		●	●	●	●		●	●	●	●		●	●	●				●			●		
Bix	80	●		●	●	●	●		●	●	●			●	●				●	●			●	●	
Blue Fox, The	242			●	●	●	●	●	●	●					●			●	●				●	●	
Bontà	244	●	●	●				●							●	●	●			●			●		
Brandy Ho's	140			●	●	●	●	●						●	●	●	●			●			●		
Brasserie Chambord	192	●		●	●	●	●		●	●	●	●	●	●	●	●			●	●			●		
Brasserie Savoy	82	●		●	●	●	●		●	●					●	●		●	●		●		●		
Brava Terrace	84	●	●	●					●	●			●	●	●	●				●			●		
Buca Giovanni	246			●	●	●	●	●							●					●			●		
Buck Eye Roadhouse	30	●	●	●		●	●		●	●		●	●	●	●					●			●		
Buena Vista Cafe	64								●	●		●	●	●	●					●					●
Cadillac Bar	346	●		●	●	●	●		●	●	●			●	●	●	●			●			●		
Café Jacqueline	194	●	●	●	●	●	●	●							●					●					●
Café Mozart	86		●	●	●	●	●	●	●						●					●			●	●	
Cafe Oritalia	316	●		●					●	●	●			●	●	●				●					●
Café Pastoral	88	●	●	●				●	●				●	●	●	●				●			●		
Caffe Esprit	90	●		●				●				●		●		●	●			●			●		
Caffe Macaroni	248	●	●					●	●						●	●	●			●			●		
Caffé Roma	250	●		●					●	●		●	●	●	●	●			●	●	●		●		
Calzone's Pizza Cucina	252	●		●	●	●			●	●			●	●	●	●				●			●		

RESTAURANT	PG.	Wheelchair Access	100% Non-Smoking	Visa/Master Card	American Express	Discover	Diners Club	Checks Accepted	Beer & Wine	Full Bar	Live Entertainment	Sunday Brunch	Breakfast	Lunch	Dinner	High Chairs	Take Out	Valet Parking	Private Parties	Informal Dress	Casual Dress	Dressy	Reserv. Recom.	Reserv. Required	Reserv. Not Taken
Campton Place	32	◆		◆	◆	◆	◆	◆	◆	◆		◆	◆	◆	◆	◆		◆	◆		◆		◆	◆	
Capp's Corner	254	◆		◆				◆	◆	◆				◆	◆	◆	◆		◆		◆		◆		
Carnelian Room	176	◆		◆	◆	◆	◆		◆	◆	◆			◆	◆		◆		◆			◆	◆		
Casa Madrona	34		◆	◆	◆			◆		◆	◆		◆	◆	◆	◆		◆	◆		◆		◆		
Cava 555	226	◆		◆	◆	◆		◆	◆	◆		◆	◆		◆	◆		◆		◆		◆			
Chateau Souverain	92	◆	◆	◆	◆			◆		◆	◆	◆	◆	◆		◆			◆		◆	◆	◆		
Chevys	348	◆		◆				◆	◆			◆	◆	◆	◆	◆		◆		◆		◆			
Chez Panisse	322	◆	◆	◆	◆	◆		◆	◆			◆	◆		◆		◆		◆					◆
Chez Panisse Café	324		◆	◆	◆	◆		◆	◆			◆	◆	◆		◆		◆		◆					◆
China Moon Cafe	142	◆		◆	◆				◆			◆	◆		◆		◆		◆			◆		
Cho-Cho	364	◆		◆	◆	◆	◆	◆	◆	◆		◆	◆	◆	◆		◆		◆		◆			
Christopher's Café	94	◆		◆	◆				◆	◆		◆	◆	◆		◆		◆		◆				
Ciao	256	◆		◆	◆	◆	◆		◆	◆		◆	◆	◆	◆	◆		◆		◆	◆	◆		
Circolo	258	◆		◆	◆		◆		◆	◆	◆		◆	◆		◆	◆		◆		◆	◆	◆		
Cliff House	386	◆		◆	◆		◆		◆	◆	◆	◆	◆	◆	◆	◆		◆		◆		◆			
Corona Bar & Grill	350	◆		◆	◆	◆	◆		◆	◆	◆		◆	◆	◆	◆		◆		◆		◆		
Cypress Club	36	◆		◆	◆	◆			◆	◆			◆	◆		◆	◆		◆		◆			
Domaine Chandon	96	◆	◆	◆	◆	◆	◆	◆	◆			◆	◆			◆			◆		◆	◆		
Donatello	260	◆		◆	◆		◆	◆	◆	◆	◆		◆			◆	◆		◆		◆	◆		
Elite Cafe, The	70	◆		◆		◆			◆	◆		◆		◆	◆	◆			◆			◆			
Embarko	38	◆		◆	◆	◆			◆	◆			◆	◆	◆		◆		◆		◆		◆		
Ernie's	196			◆	◆	◆	◆	◆	◆	◆			◆	◆		◆	◆		◆		◆	◆		
Etrusca	262	◆		◆	◆	◆	◆		◆	◆		◆	◆	◆		◆	◆		◆		◆	◆		
Faz	326	◆		◆	◆				◆	◆	◆		◆	◆	◆	◆		◆		◆		◆		
Fior d' Italia	264	◆		◆	◆	◆	◆		◆	◆	◆		◆	◆	◆	◆	◆		◆		◆	◆	◆	
Fishermen's Grotto	388	◆		◆	◆	◆	◆		◆	◆			◆	◆	◆	◆		◆	◆		◆			
Fleur de Lys	198		◆	◆		◆			◆	◆			◆			◆	◆			◆		◆		◆
Fog City Diner	98	◆		◆		◆	◆		◆	◆			◆	◆	◆		◆			◆		◆		
Fornelli	266	◆		◆	◆	◆			◆	◆	◆		◆	◆		◆		◆		◆	◆		◆	
Fournou's Ovens	100	◆		◆	◆	◆	◆		◆	◆		◆	◆	◆	◆	◆	◆	◆	◆	◆			◆	
Fourth Street Grill	102	◆		◆					◆				◆	◆	◆				◆		◆		◆	
French Laundry, The	200	◆	◆					◆	◆					◆				◆		◆				◆
French Room (Clift)	104	◆		◆	◆	◆	◆	◆	◆	◆	◆	◆			◆	◆	◆	◆	◆			◆		◆
Fringale	106	◆		◆					◆	◆			◆	◆		◆		◆		◆				◆
Garden Court, The	178	◆		◆	◆		◆		◆	◆		◆	◆	◆	◆	◆						◆	◆	
Gaylord India	222			◆	◆	◆	◆		◆	◆		◆		◆	◆	◆	◆		◆			◆	◆	
Gira Polli	268	◆	◆	◆				◆	◆					◆		◆		◆		◆		◆		
Great Eastern	144			◆	◆				◆				◆	◆	◆	◆		◆		◆			◆	◆
Greens	424	◆	◆	◆				◆	◆			◆	◆	◆	◆	◆		◆	◆	◆		◆		
Guaymas	352			◆	◆		◆		◆	◆		◆		◆	◆				◆		◆		◆	
Harbor Village	146	◆		◆	◆		◆		◆	◆	◆		◆	◆			◆	◆	◆		◆		◆	
Harris'	416	◆		◆	◆	◆	◆		◆	◆	◆		◆	◆		◆	◆	◆		◆		◆		
Hayes Street Grill	390	◆		◆	◆	◆	◆	◆	◆	◆			◆	◆				◆		◆		◆		
Helmand, The	24			◆					◆	◆	◆		◆	◆	◆	◆	◆		◆	◆	◆	◆	◆	
Hong Kong East Ocean	148	◆		◆	◆				◆	◆			◆	◆	◆	◆		◆		◆		◆		

Features Guide

Restaurant	PG.	Wheelchair Access	100% Non-Smoking	Visa/Master Card	American Express	Discover	Diners Club	Checks Accepted	Beer & Wine	Full Bar	Live Entertainment	Sunday Brunch	Breakfast	Lunch	Dinner	High Chairs	Take Out	Valet Parking	Private Parties	Informal Dress	Casual Dress	Dressy	Reserv. Recom.	Reserv. Required	Reserv. Not Taken
Hong Kong Flower Lounge	150	◆		◆	◆			◆	◆	◆				◆	◆	◆	◆		◆		◆		◆		
House of Nanking	152		◆						◆					◆	◆		◆		◆	◆					◆
House of Prime Rib	418	◆		◆	◆		◆		◆	◆					◆	◆	◆	◆	◆		◆		◆		
Hunan Village	154	◆		◆	◆	◆			◆					◆	◆	◆	◆		◆		◆				◆
Hyde Street Bistro	270	◆	◆	◆					◆	◆				◆	◆	◆	◆	◆			◆		◆		
Il Fornaio	272	◆		◆	◆	◆			◆	◆		◆	◆	◆	◆	◆	◆	◆			◆		◆		
Jackson Fillmore Trattoria	274	◆		◆	◆				◆						◆		◆				◆		◆		
Jack's	228			◆				◆	◆	◆				◆	◆		◆						◆	◆	
Joe LoCoco's	276	◆		◆	◆		◆		◆	◆	◆			◆	◆	◆		◆			◆		◆	◆	
Kansai	366	◆		◆	◆		◆		◆	◆				◆	◆	◆	◆	◆			◆		◆		
Khan Toke Thai House	422		◆	◆					◆		◆				◆		◆		◆		◆		◆		
Khayyam's	374	◆		◆					◆	◆				◆	◆	◆	◆		◆		◆		◆		
Kyoya (Sheraton Palace)	368	◆		◆	◆		◆		◆	◆				◆	◆	◆	◆	◆	◆		◆		◆		
L' Avenue	40	◆	◆	◆	◆			◆	◆	◆	◆				◆			◆	◆		◆		◆		
L' Entrecôte de Paris	328	◆		◆	◆		◆		◆	◆	◆	◆		◆	◆	◆	◆	◆	◆		◆		◆	◆	
L' Olivier	202	◆		◆	◆	◆	◆		◆	◆				◆	◆		◆	◆	◆		◆		◆		
La Fiammetta	278			◆	◆				◆						◆	◆		◆			◆		◆	◆	
La Folie	204	◆		◆	◆	◆	◆		◆	◆					◆			◆	◆		◆		◆		
La Pergola	280		◆	◆	◆				◆						◆		◆		◆		◆				◆
Lalime's	330	◆	◆	◆				◆	◆						◆						◆		◆		
Lark Creek Inn, The	42	◆		◆	◆		◆		◆	◆		◆		◆	◆	◆	◆		◆		◆		◆		
Lascaux Bar & Rotisserie	332	◆		◆	◆			◆	◆	◆	◆	◆		◆	◆			◆			◆		◆		
Le Castel	206			◆	◆			◆	◆	◆					◆			◆	◆			◆	◆		
Le Central	208			◆	◆	◆			◆	◆				◆	◆		◆				◆		◆		
Le Trou	210		◆					◆	◆						◆		◆				◆		◆		
MacArthur Park	44	◆		◆	◆		◆		◆	◆				◆	◆	◆	◆	◆			◆		◆		
Madrona Manor	108	◆	◆	◆	◆	◆	◆	◆	◆			◆	◆		◆	◆	◆		◆			◆		◆	
Mandalay	68	◆		◆		◆			◆	◆				◆	◆	◆	◆				◆		◆		
Mandarin, The	156	◆		◆	◆		◆		◆	◆				◆	◆	◆	◆				◆		◆		
Masa's	212	◆	◆	◆	◆	◆	◆	◆	◆	◆					◆			◆	◆			◆			◆
Masons (Fairmont)	110	◆		◆	◆	◆	◆		◆	◆	◆				◆	◆		◆	◆			◆	◆		
Max's Opera Cafe	46	◆		◆	◆				◆	◆	◆			◆	◆	◆					◆				◆
Maykadeh Persian Cuisine	376	◆		◆	◆		◆		◆					◆	◆	◆					◆		◆		
McCormick & Kuleto's	392	◆		◆	◆	◆	◆		◆	◆	◆	◆		◆	◆	◆	◆	◆			◆		◆		
Meadowood	180	◆	◆	◆	◆	◆	◆	◆	◆	◆	◆	◆	◆	◆	◆			◆			◆	◆	◆		
Milly's	426	◆	◆	◆					◆	◆				◆	◆	◆		◆			◆		◆		
Miss Pearl's Jam House	138	◆		◆		◆	◆		◆	◆	◆	◆		◆	◆	◆	◆	◆			◆		◆		
Modesto Lanzone's	282	◆		◆	◆	◆	◆		◆	◆					◆		◆	◆	◆		◆	◆	◆		
Monsoon	62	◆	◆	◆					◆	◆				◆	◆		◆	◆			◆		◆		
Mo's	48	◆							◆					◆	◆	◆		◆							◆
Mustards Grill	50	◆		◆		◆	◆		◆	◆				◆	◆	◆					◆		◆		
Napa Valley Wine Train	112	◆	◆	◆	◆	◆	◆		◆	◆	◆	◆	◆	◆	◆				◆		◆		◆		
New Asia	158	◆		◆					◆	◆			◆	◆	◆	◆	◆		◆		◆		◆		
Nob Hill (Mark Hopkins)	114	◆		◆	◆				◆	◆	◆		◆	◆	◆			◆				◆	◆		
North Beach	284			◆	◆	◆	◆		◆	◆				◆	◆	◆	◆	◆			◆		◆		

Features Guide

RESTAURANT	PG.	Wheelchair Access	100% Non-Smoking	Visa/Master Card	American Express	Discover	Diners Club	Checks Accepted	Beer & Wine	Full Bar	Live Entertainment	Sunday Brunch	Breakfast	Lunch	Dinner	High Chairs	Take Out	Valet Parking	Private Parties	Informal Dress	Casual Dress	Dressy	Reserv. Recom.	Reserv. Required	Reserv. Not Taken
North Sea Village	160	♦		♦	♦				♦					♦	♦	♦	♦	♦	♦		♦		♦		
Oliveto Cafe	286	♦	♦	♦				♦	♦	♦				♦	♦	♦			♦		♦		♦		
Oritalia	318	♦		♦				♦	♦	♦				♦		♦			♦		♦	♦	♦		
Pacific Grill (Pan Pacific)	116	♦		♦	♦			♦	♦	♦	♦	♦	♦	♦	♦		♦	♦			♦		♦		
Pacific Heights Bar & Grill	394	♦		♦	♦		♦		♦	♦		♦		♦		♦		♦			♦		♦		
Palio	288	♦		♦	♦	♦	♦	♦	♦	♦				♦	♦	♦	♦	♦	♦		♦		♦		
Pane e Vino	290	♦		♦				♦	♦					♦	♦		♦		♦		♦		♦		
Paragon	52	♦		♦					♦	♦	♦			♦	♦				♦		♦				♦
Pasha	360	♦		♦	♦	♦	♦		♦	♦	♦			♦		♦		♦	♦	♦	♦	♦	♦		
Piatti	292	♦	♦	♦					♦	♦				♦	♦	♦	♦		♦		♦			♦	
Piemonte Ovest	334			♦				♦	♦			♦		♦	♦	♦	♦		♦		♦		♦		
Postrio	118	♦		♦	♦		♦		♦	♦		♦	♦	♦	♦	♦		♦	♦		♦		♦		
Prego	294			♦	♦		♦		♦	♦				♦	♦	♦	♦		♦		♦		♦		
Remillard's	214	♦	♦	♦	♦		♦		♦	♦	♦	♦		♦	♦	♦			♦			♦	♦		
Rice Table, The	224			♦	♦				♦					♦	♦						♦		♦		
Ritz-Carlton Dining Room	216	♦		♦	♦	♦	♦	♦	♦	♦					♦			♦	♦			♦	♦		
Ritz-Carlton Restaurant	120	♦		♦	♦	♦	♦	♦	♦	♦	♦	♦	♦	♦	♦			♦	♦		♦		♦		
Rodin	218	♦	♦	♦		♦	♦	♦	♦						♦							♦	♦		
Rosmarino	336		♦	♦				♦	♦			♦		♦	♦		♦		♦		♦		♦		
Ruth's Chris Steak House	420	♦		♦	♦		♦		♦	♦				♦	♦	♦	♦	♦	♦		♦		♦		
Salud	354	♦		♦	♦		♦		♦	♦				♦	♦	♦	♦		♦		♦		♦		
Sam's Grill & Seafood	396	♦		♦	♦		♦		♦	♦				♦	♦	♦					♦		♦		
Sanppo	370								♦					♦	♦	♦	♦	♦	♦		♦				♦
Santa Fe Bar & Grill	410	♦		♦	♦		♦		♦	♦	♦			♦	♦	♦	♦		♦		♦		♦		
Scoma's	398	♦		♦	♦	♦	♦		♦	♦				♦	♦			♦	♦		♦				♦
Scott's Seafood	400	♦		♦	♦	♦			♦	♦		♦		♦	♦				♦		♦		♦		
Seltzer City Cafe	122	♦	♦	♦					♦					♦	♦	♦	♦		♦		♦		♦		
Sherman House, The	124		♦	♦	♦		♦		♦		♦	♦	♦	♦	♦			♦	♦			♦		♦	
Showley's At Miramonte	126	♦	♦	♦	♦	♦			♦					♦	♦	♦			♦		♦	♦			
Silks (Mandarin Hotel)	128	♦		♦	♦	♦	♦		♦	♦		♦	♦	♦	♦			♦	♦			♦	♦		
Sonoma Mission Inn	130	♦	♦	♦	♦	♦	♦		♦	♦	♦	♦		♦	♦		♦	♦			♦		♦		
South Park Cafe	220	♦		♦				♦	♦				♦	♦	♦		♦			♦			♦		
Spenger's	402	♦		♦	♦	♦	♦		♦	♦		♦	♦	♦	♦	♦		♦			♦		♦		
Spiedini	296	♦		♦	♦		♦		♦	♦				♦	♦	♦		♦			♦		♦		
Splendido	338	♦		♦	♦		♦		♦	♦	♦			♦	♦	♦	♦	♦	♦		♦		♦		
Spuntino	298	♦		♦	♦		♦		♦			♦	♦	♦	♦		♦		♦		♦				♦
Square One	340	♦	♦	♦	♦		♦		♦	♦				♦	♦		♦	♦	♦		♦	♦			
Stars	54	♦		♦	♦		♦		♦	♦	♦			♦	♦	♦		♦	♦		♦		♦		
Stars Cafe	56	♦		♦	♦		♦		♦	♦	♦			♦	♦	♦	♦		♦		♦				♦
Suppers	58	♦	♦	♦				♦	♦	♦					♦		♦		♦	♦	♦		♦		
Swan Oyster Depot	404	♦							♦			♦	♦		♦	♦	♦			♦					♦
Table 29	60	♦	♦	♦	♦	♦	♦	♦	♦	♦				♦	♦	♦		♦			♦			♦	
Tadich Grill	406	♦		♦				♦	♦	♦	♦			♦	♦		♦				♦				♦
Taiwan Restaurant	162	♦		♦	♦				♦					♦	♦	♦	♦				♦		♦		
Teatro	300	♦	♦	♦	♦			♦		♦	♦				♦				♦			♦	♦		

20

Features Guide

RESTAURANT	PG.	Wheelchair Access	100% Non-Smoking	Visa/Master Card	American Express	Discover	Diners Club	Checks Accepted	Beer & Wine	Full Bar	Live Entertainment	Sunday Brunch	Breakfast	Lunch	Dinner	High Chairs	Take Out	Valet Parking	Private Parties	Informal Dress	Casual Dress	Dressy	Reserv. Recom.	Reserv. Required	Reserv. Not Taken
Terra	342	♦	♦	♦				♦	♦						♦				♦				♦	♦	
Tommaso's	302	♦		♦					♦						♦		♦		♦		♦				♦
Tommy Toy's	164	♦		♦	♦	♦	♦		♦	♦				♦	♦			♦	♦				♦	♦	
Tommy's Joynt	66								♦	♦				♦	♦		♦				♦				♦
Tourelle	182	♦	♦	♦	♦			♦	♦	♦	♦	♦	♦	♦	♦			♦	♦		♦		♦		
Tra Vigne	304	♦		♦		♦	♦	♦	♦	♦		♦		♦	♦		♦	♦	♦		♦			♦	
Trader Vic's	230	♦		♦	♦		♦		♦	♦	♦				♦		♦		♦	♦	♦		♦	♦	
Trudys	132	♦		♦		♦		♦	♦	♦					♦		♦		♦		♦		♦	♦	
Tutto Bene	306	♦		♦	♦		♦		♦	♦	♦			♦	♦	♦	♦	♦	♦		♦		♦		
Vanessi's	308	♦		♦	♦		♦		♦	♦				♦	♦		♦		♦		♦		♦		
Venticello	310		♦	♦	♦				♦	♦					♦		♦		♦		♦		♦		
Victor's (St. Francis)	134	♦		♦	♦	♦	♦		♦	♦		♦		♦	♦		♦	♦	♦				♦	♦	
Vinoteca	312	♦		♦	♦	♦	♦		♦	♦		♦	♦	♦	♦	♦	♦		♦		♦		♦		
Vivande Porta Via	314	♦	♦	♦	♦			♦	♦	♦			♦		♦		♦		♦	♦	♦				♦
Washington Square	184	♦		♦	♦		♦		♦	♦	♦			♦	♦		♦		♦		♦		♦		
Waterfront, The	408	♦		♦	♦	♦	♦		♦	♦		♦		♦	♦		♦	♦	♦		♦		♦		
Wu Kong	166	♦		♦	♦		♦		♦	♦				♦	♦	♦	♦		♦		♦		♦		
Ya Ya Cuisine	358	♦		♦					♦					♦	♦				♦		♦				♦
Yank Sing	168	♦		♦	♦				♦			♦		♦		♦	♦		♦		♦		♦		
Yoshi's	372	♦		♦	♦	♦	♦		♦	♦	♦			♦	♦	♦	♦		♦		♦		♦		
Yuet Lee	170	♦							♦					♦	♦		♦		♦		♦		♦		
Zola's	344	♦	♦	♦	♦			♦	♦	♦	♦				♦				♦		♦		♦		

The Restaurants

The Helmand

══════ APPETIZERS ══════

AUSHAK, *Afghan ravioli filled with leeks, served on yogurt-mint and topped with ground beef sauce.*   **3.95**

MANTWO, *Home-made pastry shells filled with onions and beef, served on yogurt and topped with carrots, yellow split-peas and beef sauce.*   **3.95**

BOWLAWNI, *Pan-fried twin pastry shells filled with leeks and spiced potatoes, garnished with yogurt and mint.*   **3.95**

BANJAN BORAWNI, *Pan-fried eggplant seasoned with fresh tomatoes and spices, baked and served on yogurt garlic sauce.*   **3.95**

══════ SOUPS ══════

AUSH, *Home-made noodle soup served with beef sauce and mint yogurt.*   **2.95**

MASHAWA, *Beef, mung beans, chick-peas, black-eyed peas and yogurt soup.*   **2.95**

SHORWA, *Lamb and fresh vegetable soup.*   **2.95**

══════ SALADS ══════

SHORNAKHOD, *Potatoes and chick-peas on a bed of lettuce served with cilantro vinaigrette dressing.*   **2.95**

SALATA, *Afghan style mixed green salad served with vinaigrette or house dressing.*   **2.95**

430 Broadway • Chinatown • (415) 362-0641

ENTREES

KABULI, *Pallow (Afghan style rice) baked with chunks of Lamb Tenderloin, raisins and glazed julienne of carrots.* *9.95*

DWOPIAZA, *Marinated then grilled Tenderloin of Lamb, sauteed with yellow split-peas and tossed with onions lightly marinated in vinegar, served with pallow (Rice).* *10.95*

CHOWPAN, *Half a Rack of Lamb marinated, grilled and served on a bed of Afghan bread with sauteed eggplant and pallow.* *12.95*

SEEKH KABAB, *Char-broiled, marinated Lamb Tenderloin served with pallow.* *10.95*

AUSHAK, *Afghan ravioli filled with leeks, served on yogurt and topped with ground beef and mint.* *8.95*

MANTWO, *Home-made pastry shell filled with onions and beef, served on yogurt and topped with carrots, yellow split-peas and beef sauce.* *8.95*

VEGETARIAN SPECIAL, *A platter of baked pumpkin, pan-fried eggplant, sauteed spinich and okra sauteed in fresh tomatoes, served with pallow.* *10.95*

SABZY CHALLOW, *Spinach sauteed with chunks of lamb and Afghan seasonings, served with challow (Rice).* *8.95*

CHAPENDAZ, *Choice Tenderloin of Beef marinated, grilled and served on cilantro yogurt garlic sauce with sauteed lentil, wheat barley and challow.* *12.95*

KOURMA CHALLOW, *Lamb sauteed with Afghan seasonings and a variety of vegetables, served with challow.* *8.95*

THEEKA KABAB, *Char-broiled Beef Tenderloin marinated in yogurt, sun-dried baby grapes and herbs served with pallow.* *10.95*

KOUFTA CHALLOW, *Beef Meatballs with Afghan seasonings sauteed with sun-dried tomato, hot peppers and green peas in a fresh tomato sauce served with challow.* *7.95*

MOURGH KABAB, *Char-broiled, marinated Chicken Breast served with pallow.* *8.95*

MOURGH CHALLOW, *Chicken sauteed with spices and yellow split-peas, served with challow.* *7.95*

STARTERS

Grilled Asparagus and New Potatoes with Melted Brie
   and Smoked Bacon Vinaigrette 7.25
Ahi Tuna and Salmon Tartares with Creme Fraiche
   and Crisp Potatoes 7.00
Deviled Oysters with Tasso Cream and Fennel Salad   7.75
Duck Tostaditas with Achiote and Poblano Sauces . .   6.50
Artichoke and Escargot Strudel with
   Shiitake Mushroom Broth 7.25
Ravioli with Smoked Ham, Mascarpone and Basil . . .   6.75
Dungeness Crab Cakes with Lobster and Mustard Aiolis 8.25
Wild Mushroom Gratin with Herbed Sherry Cream
   and Walnut Crust 7.50

SOUP & SALAD

Spring Vegetable Soup with Grilled Asparagus 5.25
Seasonal Greens with Sundried Tomato Croutons   . .   5.25
Caesar Salad 6.25
Seasonal Greens with Maytag Blue Cheese, Roasted
   Beets and Spicy Pecans 6.25

---

1 Rincon Center • Financial District • (415) 495-2782

MAIN COURSES

Sauteed Prawns with Artichoke Crab Gratin, Spring Vegetables and Shellfish Broth	16.75
Grilled Breast of Chicken with Grilled Eggplant, Potato Gallette and Prosciutto Vinaigrette	15.50
Grilled Salmon with Lemon Fettucini, Asparagus, Lobster Oil and Asparagus Sauce	17.25
Potato and Wild Mushroom Torte with Warm Goat Cheese and Truffle Vinaigrette	15.50
Shellfish Jambalaya with Andouille Sausage and Texmati Rice	19.75
Grilled Filet Mignon with Bacon Onion Tartlet, Wild Mushrooms and Port Wine Sauce	19.50
Pan Roasted Breast of Duck with Sweetpotato Walnut Strudel, Braised Cabbage and Cranberry Juniper Sauce	17.50
Grilled Scallops with Black Bean Cake and Smoked Salmon Chipotle Sauce	17.25

DESSERTS

Deep Dish Fruit Pie a la Mode	5.50
Bourbon Chocolate Mousse with Minted Creme Fraiche	5.50
Butterscotch Creme Brulee with Pecan Cookies	5.50
Buttermilk Pound Cake with Lemon Sherbet and Berry Sauce	5.50
Malted Milk Chocolate Hot Fudge Sundae with White Chocolate Brownies	5.50
Trio of Sorbets with Fresh Fruit and Cookies	5.50

18% service added to parties of 8 or more
Please, no pipe or cigar smoking

ASK US ABOUT SUPPER CLUB
FRIDAY AND SATURDAY NIGHTS
ALSO
OUR PRIVATE PARTY FACILITIES

BREAKFAST STANDARDS

We cook our eggs: over-easy, over-medium, over-hard, sunny side up, poached, soft boiled, and scrambled. We scramble our eggs slowly to a soft, custardy consistency.

Two Eggs Any Style:
served with home fries and sour cream and choice of muffin, scone, light wheat, sourdough or light rye toast **$5.25**

Two Eggs Any Style
with thick sliced bacon, chicken-apple sausage, or grilled ham. Served with home fries and sour cream, muffin, scone, light wheat, sourdough or light rye toast **$6.75**

OMELETTES

Cooked in the French style (soft on the inside and firm on the outside)
Served with Home Fries and Toast or Muffin.

Fresh Herb **$5.75**

Grated Cheese **$6.50**

Herb and Cheese **$6.75**

Ham and Cheese **$7.25**

FRESH FRUIT & CEREAL

Freshly squeezed orange or grapefruit juice
    large **$3.00**
    small **$1.50**

Mimosa cocktail with orange juice and
    champagne **$3.00**

Fresh fruit plate with grapefruit sections,
    melon and seasonal fruits **$4.50**

Fruit cup **$3.25**

Fruit compote with poached seasonal fruits,
    garnished with yoghurt **$3.25**

Bran muffin with fresh fruit and yoghurt **$4.50**

Granola and fruit **$3.25**

Cereal and fruit **$2.50**

MORNING FAVORITES

Huevos Rancheros
fried eggs with salsa and melted cheese served on a thick flour tortilla with black beans and sour cream **$6.75**

Mexican Scramble
scrambled eggs with cheese and salsa served with black beans, homemade chorizo and a thick flour tortilla **$7.25**

Spicy Scrambled Eggs
scrambled eggs with salsa served with home fries and toast or tortilla **5.75**

Lox Scramble
with green onions served with home fries, bagel and cream cheese **$7.25**

Philadelphia
poached eggs served with our own scrapple, grilled tomatoes, and toast **$6.25**

Maryland
corned beef hash with poached eggs and choice of muffin, toast or cream scone **$6.75**

New York Plate
thinly sliced smoked salmon with cream cheese, toasted bagel, onions, tomatoes and cucumbers **$7.50**

California Plate
poached eggs on ham and toast with a lemon-herb butter sauce served with grilled tomatoes and home fries **$7.50**

Potato Pancakes
with homemade applesauce and sour cream **$5.75**

French Toast Deluxe
with fresh fruit and yoghurt. Served with real maple syrup **$6.25**

SANDWICHES

Served with homemade Potato Salad or Creamy Slaw
on Light Wheat, Light Rye, Sourdough or Baguette.

Bacon, Lettuce, Tomato and Homemade
   Mayonnaise **$6.25**

Turkey Club with Bacon **$7.25**

              Egg Salad.............. **$5.25**

              Chicken Salad **$6.75**

              Albacore Tuna Salad **$6.25**

              Roast Beef **$6.75**

              Roast Turkey **$6.75**

              Baked Ham **$6.25**

              Famous Meatloaf **$6.25**

GRILLED SANDWICHES

Served with homemade Potato Salad or Creamy Slaw
on Light Wheat, Light Rye, Sourdough or Baguette.

Sauteed Chicken Breast with pasilla
chilies and jack cheese on Baguette.
Served with black beans, salsa and
sour cream **$7.50**

Kosher NY Frank on baguette **$3.75**

Chili Dog with cheese and onions **$4.50**

Pan Fried Fresh Fish Sandwich **$6.75**

Grilled Cheese........................ **$4.75**

Grilled Cheese with Bacon **$6.75**

Tuna Melt with tomatoes and
cheddar cheese **$6.75**

Reuben Sandwich, corned beef, Russian
dressing, Swiss cheese and sauerkraut
on rye **$7.25**

House Smoked Turkey Breast with melted
jack cheese and mustardy mayonnaise
on baguette **$7.25**

Marinated Roasted Eggplant with roasted
red peppers and jack cheese on baguette.
Mixed green salad...................... **$6.75**

HOT LUNCH

Grilled Bockwurst
with potato pancakes and homemade
applesauce **$6.75**

Famous Meatloaf
with fried potatoes and mixed green salad **$7.25**

Pan Fried Fresh Fish with Lemon Butter
on spinach with potatoes and mixed
green salad......................... **$7.25**

Check our board or ask
your server about today's hot specials.

SOUP

Made fresh everyday with our own
rich chicken broth.

Cup ... **$1.75**   Bowl ... **$2.50**

Soup and Salad with Baguette and
   Butter **$5.25**

SALADS

Homemade Dressings: Russian, Blue Cheese,
Vinaigrette, Garlic-Yoghurt

Caesar Salad .... Lg. **$6.75** Sm. **$3.50**

Chicken Salad
on greens with marinated onions, tomatoes,
cucumber & hard boiled egg............. **$7.25**

Albacore Tuna Salad
on greens with marinated onions, tomatoes,
cucumber and hard boiled egg **$7.25**

Spinach Salad
with toasted pecans, feta cheese, black beans
and red onions .... Lg. **$6.75** Sm. **$3.50**

Mixed Green Salad **$3.25**

Potato Salad **$2.50**

Creamy Slaw
with boiled dressing.................... **$2.50**

CHILI

Full flavored and spicy.
Made with beef, beans,
chipotle chilis, garnished
with cheese and onions.

Cup ... **$2.50**
Bowl ... **$3.25**

Chili and Salad with Baguette and
   Butter **$5.75**

S A N D W I C H E S

SMOKED TURKEY, avocado, watercress , tomato chutney	6.95
GRILLED CHICKEN BREAST, roasted eggplant, onion jam	7.95
HAMBURGER or CHEESEBURGER, fully garnished	6.50
BARBECUED SLOPPY JOE with chips	6.25
GRILLED HAM AND SMOKED CHEDDAR with pesto	7.85
BEER SAUSAGE, grilled onions and tomato vinaigrette	7.25
FRIED SHRIMP CLUB with french fries	7.50

S A L A D S

MIXED GREENS with choice of dressing: 4.50
    California with smoked almonds
    Bleu cheese and currants
    House vinaigrette

WARM SPINACH, calamata olives, feta and apple smoked bacon	5.75
SHORELINE, chicory, arugula, endive, figs, pears and bleu cheese	5.50
CAESAR or BRUTUS (with coarse ground chili pepper)	6.95
SMOKED CHICKEN with apples, walnuts, bleu cheese and currants	8.50

ENTREES

FRESH FISH DAILY	A.Q.
SEAFOOD HASH on leek, mushroom and apple-smoked bacon ragout	11.50
PEPPER and LEMON CREOLE SHRIMP with garlic mashed potatoes	12.95
ROADHOUSE RISOTTO with asparagus, mushrooms and roasted potatoes	9.95
GRILLED SONOMA RABBIT with basil, garlic and spiced black beans	11.75
CHICKEN BREAST with tarragon mustard vinagrette and cheese grits	11.50
SMOKED PFTALUMA DUCK with winter fruit chutney	13.75
PORK CHOP with homemade ginger-apple sauce	11.50
BARBECUED BABY BACK RIBS with coleslaw and garlic mashed potatoes	10.95
SAUTEED CALF'S LIVER, homemade chili sauce, bacon and onions	9.75
GRILLED SKIRT STEAK, Tucson tavern marinade and 1937 sauce	12.95
BRAISED LAMB SHANK with shallots, mint and fennel	11.50
BEER SAUSAGES, sweet and sour cabbage, garlic mashed potatoes	9.95

DESSERTS

BAKED LEMON PUDDING with strawberry sauce	4.50
S'MORE PIE	4.25
CAPPUCCINO CHEESE CAKE	4.25
BUTTERSCOTCH BRULEE	4.50
PIE-O-RAMA	4.95
CHOCOLATE TOFFEE ICE CREAM SANDWICH	5.50
MILK SHAKES AND MALTEDS	3.00

CAMPTON PLACE
R e s t a u r a n t

Menu Changes Weekly

LUNCHEON

Shellfish Soup with Saffron 7.00
Spring Potato Soup with Braised Cipollinis 6.50
Grilled Gulf Shrimp Salad with Artichokes and White Beans 8.50
Warm Spinach Salad with Fried Calamari and Meyer Lemon Vinaigrette 6.50
Arugula Salad with Crispy Pine Nut Polenta, Blue Cheese and D'Anjou Pears 7.50
Asparagus with Roasted Morels, Aged Goat Cheese and Meyer Lemon Vinaigrette 8.00
Prosciutto with Warm Roucoulon Canneloni and Wild Mushrooms 7.00

* * *

Caesar Salad with Parmesan Crouton 6.00
Field Greens with Endive and Lemon Vinaigrette 5.50

* * *

Spicy Chicken Hash with Fried Quail Eggs 14.00
Vegetarian Club Sandwich with Goat Ricotta on Brioche 13.00
Grilled Quail with Mizuna Greens, Blood Oranges and Fried Garbanzo Beans 16.50
Salmon Brochette with Couscous Red Pepper Vinaigrette and Spicy Lobster Broth 17.00
Dungeness Crab Cakes with Maple Cabbage Slaw and Molasses Hushpuppy Pancakes 17.00
Grilled Nantucket Scallops with Warm Celery Root Salad and Apple Bacon Vinaigrette 16.50
Black Pepper Pappardelle with Wild Mushrooms, Asparagus and Pecorino Toscano 13.00
Seared Rare Tuna Napoleon with Kalamata Olives and Crispy Potatoes 15.50
Pan Roasted Chicken with Walnut Spatzle and Warm Frisee 16.00

340 Stockton St • Union Square • (415) 781-5155

DINNER

Shellfish Saffron Soup 7.00

Spring Potato Soup with Braised Cipollinis 6.50

Dungeness Crab Salad with Cucumber Aioli and Cilantro 8.00

Arugula Salad with Crispy Pine Nut Polenta, Blue Cheese and Butter Pears 7.50

Asparagus with Roasted Morels, Aged Goat Cheese and Meyer Lemon Vinaigrette 10.00

Prosciutto with Warm Roucoulon Canneloni and Wild Mushrooms 8.00

Wild Mushroom Risotto with Crispy Sweet Breads and Thyme Oil 12.00

* * *

Salad of Field Greens with Lemon Vinaigrette 6.00

Caesar Salad with Parmesan Crouton 7.50

* * *

Pan Roasted Chicken with Walnut Spatzle and Warm Frisee 25.00

Seared Rare Tuna Napoleon with Spinach and Kalamata Olives 22.00

Grilled Nantucket Scallops with Tomato Compote and Onion Puree 25.00

Grilled Quail with Herb Buttermilk Pancakes, Warm Escarole and Huckleberries 26.00

Roasted Lamb Rack with Sweet Potato Dumplings, Cipollini Onions and Haricots Vert 28.00

Grilled Salmon with Winter Vegetable Hash, Fried Parsnips and Horseradish Vinaigrette 26.00

Black Pepper Pappardelle with Asparagus, Roasted Garlic, and Pecorino Toscano 17.00

Grilled Veal Chop with Ancho Chili Mashed Potatoes and Chayote Squash 28.00

Grilled Swordfish with Caraway Potato Timbale and Savoy Cabbage 27.00

DESSERT

Classic Vanilla Creme Brulee 6.50

Campton Place Banana Sundae with Hot Fudge Sauce and Walnut Cake 6.50

Poached Black Pepper Pear with Gorgonzola, Lost Bread and Orange Honey 6.50

Strawberry Shortcake with Strawberry Ice Cream 6.50

Chocolate Truffle Tarte with Blood Oranges 6.50

Selection of Fresh Fruit Sorbets 5.50

Fruit and Cheese Plate 7.50

* * * * * *

Casa Madrona Hotel and Restaurant

"A 19th century reminder of a less hurried time."

Dinner Menu

Mesclun Salad 4.75 *
with balsamic vinaigrette and walnut parmesan crackers

Caesar Salad 6.75
with toasted hazelnuts

Spicy Grilled Prawn and Tomatillo Soup 7.50
a Casa Madrona specialty

Today's Homemade Soup 4.50

Warm Chenel Capriccio Cheese 9.00
wrapped in Napa cabbage and parma prosciutto

Seared Scallops 7.50
with caramelized imperial onion butter sauce

Lobster and Crab Cakes 9.50
with tamari butter and wasabi

Chilled Point Reyes Oysters 8.75 *
on the half shell with pepper vodka ice

---

801 Bridgeway St • Sausalito • (415) 331-5888

Giant Prawn Risotto 18.50
with saffron and spicy chorizo

Tuna, seared rare 16.00 *
with chilis, lime and orange vinaigrette

Angel Hair Pasta 12.75
with asparagus, toasted almonds
and goat cheese cream sauce

Marinated Salmon a la Mistral 17.50 *
with papaya, cucumber & mint puree, & spicy pineapple glaze

****

Roasted Petaluma Chicken 13.75 *
with 20 cloves of garlic and mountain bread

Braised Veal Shank 14.75
with wild mushrooms and soft polenta

Dry Aged New York Steak 19.50
with roasted shallots and mashed potatoes,
in a sherry dijon sauce

Roast Rack of Lamb 19.75
with artichoke hearts, olives and herbs
served with roasted new potatoes

* Recommended by Chef Kirke Byers as "Heart Healthy"

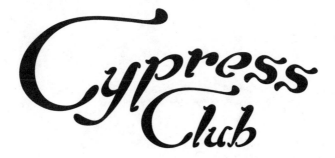

DAILY MENU

COLD

Celery heart salad with aioli, shredded egg and greens 6

Fennel cured salmon on a potato-rye cake with créme fraîche 7

WARM AND HOT

Sweet pea ravioli with scallops and vegetable broth 8

Hangtown fry with greens and a crepe 7

FISH AND SEAFOOD

Pan roasted sanddabs with roasted potatoes, fava beans and tarragon 14

Crispy crab cakes with citrus marinated vegetables 15

Grilled salmon with asparagus, bacon and herbal vinaigrette 16

Seared halibut with artichokes, roasted pepper and spring field greens 16

MEAT AND FOWL

Grilled duck breast with orange, rhubarb and port 15

Roasted lamb loin chop with spring peas, potato galette and mint pesto 15

Fire roasted chicken thighs with rosemary polenta, sweet peppers and ham 14

Charcoal fired pork loin with chayote-apple salad and blue corn naan 15

VEGETARIAN DISHES

Clay oven roasted vegetables with traditional naan bread 10

Roasted portobello mushroom sandwich with jack cheese and green bean salad . . . 12

Mushroom and fontal cheese tart with artichokes, walnuts and sherry vinegar 12

Seasonal Menu

COLD

Hearts of celery salad with thick aioli, greens and shredded egg 6
Leaves of romaine with caper vinaigrette and eggplant garlic croutons . . 6
Seasonal greens with blue cheese, currants and pine nuts 5
Smoked goose prosciutto with asparagus and tangerine 9

WARM AND HOT

Hangtown fry in a salad with pancetta and fried oysters 8
Grilled quail with soft polenta and pancetta vinaigrette 11
White bean soup with bresaola and parmesan toast 5
Crispy salmon and potato cake with marinated vegetables 8
Sweet pea raviolis with scallops and basil 8
Asparagus crostini with fontel and red pepper oil 8

FISH AND SEAFOOD

Pan seared sturgeon with red wine onions and savory lentils 20
Grilled Ahi with creamy potato and a crispy jumbo mushroom 21
Grilled swordfish with artichokes, bacon and black olive aioli 21
Whole roasted striped bass with preserved tomato and caperberries . . . 21

MEAT AND FOWL

Loin of lamb with eggplant purée, red pepper and garlic rapini 23
Medallion of venison with sweet cherries and morel mushrooms 24
Spit roasted rabbit with artichoke and spring vegetable ragout 19
Beef sirloin with roasted new potatoes and french green bean salad . . 24
Roasted pork chop with celery root purée and golden raisins 20
Rosemary chicken with lemon potatoes and arugula 20

Chef: Cory Schreiber   Sous Chef: Krista Anderson

Sunday Brunch; Dinner: Sun - Thurs 5:30 - 10, Fri - Sat 5:30 - 11 ●ⓁⒹ

LUNCHEON MENU

APPETIZERS

Pot Stickers from the Great Wall with Three Sauces 5.95
Griddled Corn Cake with Salsa Negra & Lime Sour Cream 5.50
Side Seared Ahi Sashimi with Rice Coins, Wasabi & Pickled Ginger 8.50
Vietnamese Shrimp & Crab Fresh Rolls With Hoisin Dipping Sauce 6.95
Soba! Chilled Buckwheat Noodles, Crisp Vegetables & Tossed Greens with Light Miso Dressing 6.95

SALADS

Inner City Caesar   small 4.95   regular 7.95
Garden Greens with Fresh Herbs & Champagne Vinaigrette 4.95
Romaine, Dried Tomatoes, Roquefort, Olives, Croutons & Mayfair Dressing 6.50

SANDWICHES

Barko Burger with Griddled Onions & Tri-Fries 7.50
Clubhouse with Roasted Turkey, Apple-Smoked Bacon & Tri-Fries 8.95
Crisped Soft Shell Crab & Tangy Slaw Served with Coastal Greens 9.75
Bangkok BBQ'd Pork Loin on Baguette with Crisp Vegetables & Chile-Chips 6.95
New Orleans Muffaletta with Mahler's Macaroni Salad 8.50
New York Pastrami on Rye with New Potato Salad 7.95
Ahi Tuna Melt on Freshly Baked Onion Focaccia 7.95

PASTA & MAIN COURSES

Chef's Daily Pasta or Risotto As Quoted
Lemon Tagliarini with Sea Scallops, Toasted Garlic & Cracked Pepper 11.00
Spaghettini with Prawns, Prosciutto, Arugula & Dried Tomatoes 12.95
Grilled Breast of Chicken on Fragrant Rice & Dressed Greens 10.95
Spicy Meatloaf & Gravy with Garlic Mashed Potatoes, Peas & Carrots 9.95
Pizza with Prosciutto, Wild Mushrooms, Tomato Sauce & a Blend of Cheeses 7.95
Niman Schell Beef Liver Sauteed with Red Onions; Mashed Potatoes & Green Beans 9.50
Fresh Salmon Croquettes with Creamed Corn, Mashed Potatoes & Green Beans 11.50
Grilled Ahi Tuna on Dressed Greens with Garden Vegetables & New Potatoes 10.95
Additional Specials & Fresh Seafood Change Daily • Ask About Our Fabulous Desserts!

---

100 Brannan St • SOMA • (415) 495-2021

DINNER MENU

APPETIZERS

Pot Stickers from the Great Wall with Three Sauces 5.95
Beer Batter Coco Prawns with Mango Mustard Marmalade 8.25
Potato Latkes & House Smoked Salmon, Chive Cream & Caviars 7.95
Side Seared Ahi Sashimi with Rice Coins, Wasabi & Pickled Ginger 8.50
Vietnamese Shrimp & Crab Fresh Rolls with Hoisin Dipping Sauce 6.95
Griddled Corn Cake, Salsa Negra & Lime Sour Cream 5.95
Tuscan Toast with Roasted Garlic & Aged Asiago 4.95

SALADS

Garden Greens with Fresh Herbs & Champagne Vinaigrette 4.95
Thai Fried Calamari Salad with Sweet, Hot Vinaigrette 8.50
Inner City Caesar—small 4.95   regular 7.95

PASTA

Chef's Daily Pasta or Risotto As Quoted
Classic Italian Puttanesca with Penne 7.00
Lemon Tagliarini, Grilled Sea Scallops, Toasted Garlic & Cracked Pepper 11.00

MAIN COURSES

Grilled Breast of Chicken with Wild Mushroom–Asparagus Ragout & Crisped Semolina Dumplings 12.95
Pan Roasted Duck Breast in its own Rich Stock with Crispy Polenta 15.95
Spicy Meatloaf & Gravy with Garlic Mashed Potatoes, Peas & Carrots 12.50
Smoked, Spiced Pork Chop, Sauteed Spinach, Succotash & Peach Chutney 14.95
Marinated Chicken Grilled Under a Press, Warm Vegetable Salad, Wild & Fragrant Rice 13.95
Bayou Jambalaya with Chicken, Shrimp, Andouille Sausage & Spicy Rice 17.50
Polenta Eggplant Strata with Parmigiano, Mozzarella & Roma Sauce 11.95
Garlic Prawns Wrapped in Prosciutto with Soft Polenta & Snap Peas 16.95
12 Ounce New York Steak, Roasted Potatoes & Crisp Vegetables 19.95
New Orleans Muffaletta with Mahler's Macaroni Salad 8.50
Barko Burger with Griddled Onions & Tri-Fries 8.50

Additional Specials & Fresh Seafood Change Daily • Enquire About Our Fabulous Desserts!

L'Avenue

Menu Changes Daily

APPETIZERS

FRESH MOREL MUSHROOMS – sauteed and served with a potato fritter
and natural sauce 8.75

SAUTEED FRESH SONOMA FOIE GRAS – served on toasted pane di
Noce with rhubarb-plum-port vinaigrette 10.75

CHAR RARE AHI TUNA CARPACCIO – served with green Thai curry
vinaigrette and crispy vegetable slaw 7.75

PINK SINGING SEA SCALLOPS, PRINCE EDWARD ISLAND
MUSSELS & MANILLA CLAMS – steamed in a spring onion sage and
fresh herbs 7.50

ROASTED PORTOBELLO MUSHROOMS – served on a freshly baked
foccacia with asparagus, herb salad, mozzarella cheese 7.75

SMOKED SALMON – with corn pancakes, golden American caviar,
creme fraiche and chives 8.75

MARYLAND CRAB CAKES – served with roasted tomato vinaigrette and
tartar sauce 8.75

APRIL SALAD – boneless quail stuffed with wild rice and sweet Texas
onion served on a foie gras crostini with a tangelo-rosemary
vinaigrette, pecans and mixed greens 7.75

SEARED SEA SCALLOPS – served with red endive salad, crispy taro root
and pink grapefruit vinaigrette 7.50

CRISPY HAMA HAMA OYSTER BLT – fried oysters layered with lettuce,
assorted tomatoes, apple wood smoked bacon, jalapeno mayonnaise
and toasted brioche 6.75

GORGONZOLA & ROASTED WALNUT SALAD – with mesclun greens
and croutons 7.00

HEARTS OF ROMAINE SALAD – with anchoiade, garlicy bread crumbs
and shaved Parmesan 6.75

ENTREES

OVEN ROASTED NATURAL CHICKEN – served with crispy polenta on
a bed of fresh peas, green beans, morel mushrooms, baby summer
squash and a natural sauce flavored with thyme and madeira ... 16.50

PAN ROASTED ESCOLAR – served with a potato-tomato terrine, fresh
morel mushrooms, a crayfish-leek sauce and steamed asparagus ... 16.75

GRILLED SALMON – served on a bed of artichoke puree with an arugula
salad, champagne, shallot and chervil sauce, and topped with crunchy
potatoes ... 16.75

PAN ROASTED VENISON FILET ... 19.75
OR **RANGE FED VEAL** – wrapped with sage, pan roasted and served
with potato napoleon, O'Hana Ranch vegetables and a claret sauce ... 17.75

OVEN ROASTED LAMB SIRLOIN – served on a bed of garlicy mashed
potatoes with portobello mushroom sauce, assorted spring vegetables
and roasted portobello mushrooms ... 18.25

PAN ROASTED DUCK BREAST – served medium rare with roasted
duck leg confit, with corn spoon bread, sauteed greens and angelena
plum sauce with port ... 16.75

OVEN ROASTED MAPLE CURED PORK LOIN – served on a bed of
half mashed baby yellow finn potatoes with chives, kale sauteed with
pancetta and pine nuts and natural sauce ... 16.75

DESSERTS

FROZEN GINGERBREAD WALL – layers of gingerbread with cinnamon,
vanilla and apple cake ice creams, served with caramel sauce ... 5.25

CHOCOLATE MOUSSE TORTE – with mixed nut crust served with
creme anglais and chocolate sauce ... 5.25

APPLE TARTE TATIN – served with cinnamon ice cream and caramel sauce ... 5.00

STRAWBERRY LEMON TRIFFLE – served with strawberry sauce ... 5.00

TROPICAL SUNSET GRANITA – strawberry papayas, mangos, guavas and
tangelo juices, served with macaroons ... 4.75

DESSERT

Espresso Chocolate Cheese Cake   5.75

Blueberry Buckle with Lemon Cream Sauce   5.50

Banana Cream Pie with Peanut Cookie Crust   5.50

Vanilla Bean Angel Food Cake with Blood Orange Sherbet
and Strawberry Compote   5.50

Lark Creek Butterscotch Pudding with Shortbread Cookies   4.75

Neapolitan Ice Cream Sandwich with Bittersweet Chocolate Sauce   5.75

Chocolate Devil's Food Cake with Vanilla Bean Chocolate
Chunk Ice Cream   5.50

Strawberry Rhubarb Turnover with Lemon Ice Cream   5.50

Platter of Homemade Cookies   4.75

Fresh Fruit Ice   4.50

234 Magnolia Ave • Larkspur • (415) 924-7766

DINNER

*Bradley's Caesar Salad 7.25

Split Pea Soup with Garlic Croutons 5.50

Pan Roasted Shad Roe with Crisp Caper and Lime Butter 10.00

Point Reyes and Fanny Bay Oysters with Malt Vinegar Dressing
and Homemade Cocktail Sauce 1.40 each

Field Lettuces with Red Wine Vinaigrette and Potted Cheese Toast 6.50

Garden Greens with Creamy Blue Cheese Dressing and Plump Sour Cherries 6.50

Fritto Misto of Prawns and Rockfish with Stewed Cranberry Beans 9.75

Homemade Ravioli with Shredded Ham Hocks, Swiss Chard and
Brown Sage Butter 7.25

Oven Baked Herbed Flatbread with House Cured Gravlax,
Scallion Creme Fraiche and Chives 11.50

Whole Roasted Sweet Onion with Air Dried Beef and
Lemon Parmesan Vinaigrette 6.50

Oak Roasted Morels with Creamy Polenta 12.50

Roasted and Chilled Artichoke with Tomato
Vinaigrette and Garlic Mayonnaise 7.50

★   ★   ★   ★

Pan Seared Scallops with Spring Vegetable
Salad and Tomato Vinaigrette 19.00

Grilled Beef Liver Steak with Oak Fired Onions and
Smoked Country Bacon 16.50

*Roasted Free Range Chicken with Lemon and Herbs,
Buttered Spinach and Mashed Potatoes with Chives 17.75

Grilled N.Y. Strip Steak with Creamy Hominy Casserole,
Field Greens and Lemon Vinaigrette 22.00

Braised Oxtails with Scalloped Turnips and Potatoes, Buttered Peas 16.50

Grilled Ahi Tuna with Roasted Potatoes, Buttered Asparagus
and Lemon Chervil Vinaigrette 19.50

*Steamed and Grilled Vegetable Platter with Herb Pesto 14.75

Grilled Double Cut Pork Chop with Braised Red Cabbage,
Root Vegetable Gratin and Roasted Garlic Aioli 16.75

Oak Oven Roasted Salmon with Fennel Braised Lentils,
Field Greens and Pancetta Vinaigrette 18.00

Grilled Rabbit with Wilted Bitter Greens
and Shoestring Sweet Potatoes 18.75

Mac Arthur Park

APPETIZERS

Onion Strings	3.95
Potato Skins with sour Cream and Chives	4.50
House Alder-Smoked Salmon with Brioche Toast and Cucumber Relish	6.95
Grilled Pasilla Peppers Filled with Jack and Goat Cheese, Orange-Jicama Salsa	5.75
Cajun Popcorn Shrimp Salad	6.95
Pan-Fried Crab Cakes with Citrus, Ginger and Mixed Greens	6.95

SOUPS

Today's Soup	3.95
Caramelized Onion Soup	4.75
Two Beer Chili with Jalapeño Corn Bread	4.50

SALADS

MacArthur Park Salad with Champagne-Herb Vinaigrette	4.25
With Maytag Blue Cheese Toasts	4.75
Caesar Salad with Garlic Croutons and Shaved Reggiano Cheese	6.75
Mixed Greens, Roasted Walnuts, Maytag Blue, Apples, Balsamic Vinaigrette	5.25
Oakwood-Smoked Breast of Chicken Tossed with Seasonal Greens	7.75
Cobb Salad	8.95
Mile High Seafood Salad with Prawns, Crab Meat, Avocado and Tomato	12.25

SANDWICHES

Grilled Freshly Ground Hamburger Cheeseburger	6.95
With a Cup of Two Beer Chili	7.95
Grilled Filet Mignon Steak Sandwich with Sliced Tomatoes and Basil Mayonnaise	9.75
Club (Oakwood-Smoked Chicken and Bacon)	6.95
Fresh Ahi Tuna, Grilled Rare with Wasabi Mayonnaise	8.50

607 Front St • Financial District • (415) 398-5700 • (Call for Additional Locations)

SIDE ORDERS

Fresh Vegetables 2.95
Cole Slaw 1.50
Baked Beans 1.95
Black Beans 1.95
French Fries 1.95
Garlic Mashed Potatoes 1.95
Bottle of MacArthur Park Barbecue Sauce (14.5 oz.) 2.95

BARBECUE

Baby Back Ribs
    Full Slab 14.75
    Half Slab 10.75
Ribs and Chicken 14.95
Half Chicken 8.95
Ribs, Chicken and Sausage 14.95

MOSTLY MESQUITE

Paillard of Chicken with Garlic Mashed Potatoes and
    Orange-Cranberry Relish 10.25
Homemade Sausages with Baked Beans and Spinach 8.75
Smoked Pork Chops with Shoestring Sweet Potatoes and Applesauce 11.75
Natural-Fed Chicken Grilled Under Bricks with Olive Oil and Fresh
    Herbs 12.95
Grilled Calf's Liver with Oakwood-Smoked Bacon and Caramelized
    Onions 9.75
Skirt Steak with Black Beans, Smoked Tomatoes and Leeks 12.75
Grilled Thick-Cut Lamb Chops with Tomato-Mint Relish and
    Roasted Garlic 16.75
Dry-Aged New York Steak with Onion Strings and Ancho
    Chile Butter (16 oz.) 18.95

◆ *Featured Dinner Menu Changes Daily* ◆

OPERA CAFE

APPETIZERS, BITES AND SNACKS
You could have an entire meal by eating through this section. It's called "noshing".

Chicken Soup with Matzoh Ball (Saturday & Sunday Only) .... Bowl **2.95**
Hot Potato Knish **2.95**
Soup of the Day .... Cup **2.50** Bowl **3.50**
Russian Cabbage Soup with Diced Brisket .... Cup **2.95** Bowl **3.95**
Guacamole and Crisp Chips with salsa **3.75**
Mixed Green Dinner Salad with tomato, cucumber, red onion and chopped egg **3.95**
Small Caesar Salad.. **3.95**
Fresh Chopped Chicken Livers with eggs, grilled onions and rye bread **4.75**
Pizelle Fromage - Thin crisp crust baked with fine cheese.......................... **4.75**
Pizelle Sonora **4.75**
    With tomato salsa, green onion, guacamole, ortega chili, sour cream & cheese
Hot Baked Giant Mushrooms with pesto, jack cheese and toasted baguette **4.95**
Smoked Chicken Quesadilla with guacamole and salsa .... ◄ **NEW!** **5.50**
Pnobscott Potato Skins "3 Big Ones" with cheddar, bacon, sour cream & scallions **5.75**
Crispy Duck with sweet sour glaze, almonds, scallions and cilantro **6.50**
Fresh Cheese Blintzes with Sour Cream & Jam (Saturday and Sunday Lunch Only) **6.50**
Not-So-Mini Reuben, corned beef, pastrami, turkey pastrami or turkey **6.95**
Nacho Max, "A plateful" crispy chips loaded with Mexican schtick **6.95**
Sparerib Appetizer **6.95**

SALADS

Chilled Half Melon with Fresh Berries and Frozen Yogurt .... ◄ **NEW!** **6.95**
Caesar Salad* **7.95**
    Romaine lettuce tossed with our homemade Caesar dressing*, fresh croutons
    & authentic Parmigiano-Reggiano cheese. Ask for anchovies.
    With Grilled Chicken Breast*.. **11.50**
Spinach Salad with crisp bacon, fresh mushrooms, chopped egg & warm mustard dressing **8.50**
    With Turkey.. **10.95**
    With Shrimp... **11.50**
Greek Salad with spinach, lettuce, tomatoes, anchovies, calamat olives, feta cheese, ... **8.95**
    pickled peppers, scallions and eggplant tossed with vinaigrette
Guy's Chinese Chicken Salad with Cantonese Chicken Breast **9.95**
Chicken Tostada **10.95**
    Grilled chicken on greens with guacamole, tomato, red onion, shredded cheese,
    black olives, cilantro, sour cream, salsa, refried beans and tortilla chips
Smoked Chicken on Spinach with Walnuts and Warm Mustard Dressing...................... **10.95**
Thai Duck Salad, soft rice noodles tossed with vegetables in ginger, ... ◄ **NEW!**   **11.95**
    vinaigrette, crisp greens, peanuts, scallions and cilantro

---

AWARD WINNING SANDWICHES
Served on Rye, Sliced Sourdough, Baguette, Onion Twist or Wheat (Croissant $.50 extra)
With Potato Salad, Cole Slaw and Pickle

Max-Sized: What we've always served. **Mid-Sized:** A smaller and less expensive version

	Mid	Max
Albacore Tuna, Lettuce and Tomato		7.95
Big Bacon Lettuce and Tomato on Toasted Sourdough		7.95
Chopped Chicken Liver, Eggs and Grilled Onions	6.95	7.95
Coca-Cola Glazed, Clove-Spiked Ham, Lettuce and Tomato	7.50	8.95
Smoked Chicken, Lettuce and Tomato		8.95
Potted Brisket of Beef	7.95	8.95
Kosher Style Corned Beef, Biggest and Best	7.95	9.50
Genuine New York Pastrami (We truck it in from the Bronx)	7.95	9.50
Turkey Pastrami, Peppered and Smoked	7.95	9.50
With lettuce and tomato. *"If you closed your eyes. . ."*		
Paprika Rare Roast Beef, Lettuce and Tomato	7.95	9.50
Roast Real Breast of Turkey, Lettuce and Tomato	8.50	10.50

◄ **NEW!**

Any sandwich with cheese $1.00 extra: Bavarian bleu, Swiss, jack, smoked gouda, dill havarti
Soup with Sandwich add $1.00

MAX'S COMBINATIONS

#1	Corned Beef and Pastrami on Rye	9.50
#2	Corned Beef, Pastrami, and Chopped Chicken Liver or Swiss Cheese on Rye	10.50
#3	Corned Beef, Pastrami and Turkey on Rye	10.50
#4	Roast Beef, Turkey, Jack Cheese and Avocado with Lettuce & Tomato on Rye	9.50

KING OF CLUBS
On toasted sourdough

#5	Bacon, Turkey and Jack Club with Lettuce & Tomato	8.95
#6	Tuna, Bacon and Jack with Lettuce and Tomato	8.95
#7	Vegetable Club on Toasted Sourdough	6.95
	Grilled eggplant, tomato, cucumber, cilantro, guacamole	
	N.Y. peppers, feta cheese and spinach with pesto mayonnaise	
#9	Warm Fresh Salmon Club	9.95
	Cucumber, avocado, tomato, spinach and pesto mayonnaise	

CROISSANT CLUBS
Served with a nice salad

Tuna Caper Salad with cucumber, tomato and spinach	7.50
Turkey and Bacon with dill havarti, cucumber, tomato and spinach	7.95
Gravlax with red onion, cucumber, tomato and spinach	7.95

VEGETARIANS
Not for Vegans

Vegetable Club on Toasted Sourdough	6.95
Grilled eggplant, tomato, cucumber, cilantro, guacamole, N.Y. peppers,	
feta cheese and spinach with pesto mayonnaise. Served with vegetarian salad.	
Salad Sampler, a selection of vegetarian salads from our salad buffet.	8.50
Stir Tossed Pasta with Lots of Vegetables and Pesto	8.95

mo's

Gourmet Hamburger

Best Burger	**$4.50**
(7 oz. patty, lettuce, tomato, red onion & Mo's mayo)	
Fries Add	1.00
Mo's Breast & Fries (hot)	6.25
(8 oz. breast of chicken, broiled with chili paste, thai curry etc.)	
Pita Chicken	6.25
Marinated, skewered, oriental spices, cilantro, onion, tomato & fries	
Chicken Parmigiana & Fries	6.50
(Our own Tomato Sauce & Cheese on Baguette)	
Polish Sausage	3.50
Fries Add	1.00
Chili Dog	4.75
(polish sausage & tongue rolling chili)	
B.L.T. & A with Fries	5.00
Grant Ave. Sandwich (Vegetarian)	5.00
(Avocado, sauteed mushrooms, Muenster cheese & fries)	
House Salad	3.00
Very Good Salad	5.00
(Hearts of Romaine, Tomato, Red Onion, Cheese & Avocado)	
Bowl of Homemade Chili & French Bread	3.25
Chili Cheese Fries	3.50

Add-Ons:

American Cheese	$.45
Swiss Cheese	.55
Sharp Cheddar	.55
Jack Cheese	.55
Muenster Cheese	1.00
Imported Blue	1.25
Apple Smoked Bacon	.95
Sauteed Onion	.60
Sauteed Mushrooms (Garlicky & Messy)	1.35
Avocado	1.00
Roasted Jalapeno	.50
Chili Beans	1.25
Fries	2.00
Nice T-Shirt	8.00

Desserts:

Old Fashioned Shakes (16 oz)	2.75
Root Beer Float	2.00

Customize your burger with Mo's tantalizing "add ons" and rediscover two of the things that make America great---a fine hamburger and your individual creativity.

Mo's burgers are made with the best quality center cut chuck. The meat is aged to meet our demanding high standards and is fresh ground daily. Our 7 oz., carefully hand-formed patties are then grilled to juicy perfection over volcanic rock on our custom-made grill.

Appetizers, Soups and Salads

Different Soup every day	$ 3.50
Grilled Pasilla pepper, tamale stuffing, tomatillo salsa	5.95
Warm Goat Cheese with roasted beets and mixed greens	4.85
Grilled Asparagus with sherry vinaigrette and tarragon aioli crouton	6.50
Home smoked Salmon with pasilla corn cakes and dill cream cheese	6.95
Grilled Chicken skewer with peppers, shiitakes and miso dressing	5.75
Mixed Greens and Herbs, seasoned pecans, sherry vinaigrette	4.90
Caesar Salad	6.55
Oriental Chicken Salad	8.50
Thai Lamb and Ginger Salad, curry vinaigrette	7.95

Sides and Condiments

Onion Rings	3.60
Roasted Garlic	2.75
Polenta with tomato and eggplant relish	2.95
Mashed Potatoes	1.95
Red! Beans with chopped red onion, sour cream and chives	3.50
Homemade Ketchup	.75
Mustards Grill T-Shirt	12.00
Mustards Grill Sweatshirt	19.00

Sandwiches

Hamburger or Cheeseburger	$ 6.95
Barbecued Chicken Breast with frenchfries and cole slaw	7.95
Grilled Ahi Tuna with basil mayonnaise and ginger	7.95
Salmon Club with remoulade	8.50

From the Woodburning Grill and Oven

Fresh Fish (see chalkboard)	A.Q.
Grilled Chicken Breast with roasted corn and tomatillo salsa (and spicy red beans)	10.95
Lemon and Garlic "mallet" Chicken with an array of summer vegetables	11.80
Smoked Long Island Duck with one hundred almond·onion sauce	14.90
Molasses BBQ Quail with cornbread (also greenbean & pepper salad with pecans)	14.95
Grilled Rabbit with wild mushrooms and tarragon·red wine sauce	15.95
Half slab Barbecued Baby Back Ribs with cornbread and slaw	10.95
Mongolian Pork Chop with braised sweet and sour cabbage	11.95
Calf's Liver with caramelized onions, bacon and homemade ketchup	9.90
Grilled Skirt Steak with thyme and garlic marinade (& red onion relish)	12.95
T. Bone Lamb Chops with artichoke & onion ragout	17.95

Desserts

Jack Daniel's Chocolate Cake with chocolate sauce	4.50
Lemon Meringue Pie with almond crust	4.25
Chocolate and Anise Brulee	3.95
Strawberry and Rhubarb Tart with vanilla cream	4.95
Crumble top Banana Cheesecake with caramel sauce	4.50
Caramel Hazelnut Apricot Tart with chocolate sauce and vanilla ice cream	4.75
Mocha Parfait with warm caramel sauce	4.50

Dinner: 7 Days a Week until 10   ●ⓁⒹ

APPETIZERS & SALADS

CRAB CAKES with roasted tomato-lemon
    horseradish sauce $7.75

SAUTEED CALAMARI VINAIGRETTE $5.75

FISH TACOS with fresh corn tortillas and
    a fiesta of accompaniments $7.50

FRIED CHICKEN WINGS with chipotle chili
    BBQ sauce $5.25

QUESADILLA with fresh salsa, guacamole and
    sour cream $6.95

PARAGON PIZZETTA changes daily $6.75

GRILLED GARLIC BREAD with tomato cruda $3.75

HOUSE GREEN SALAD balsamic vinaigrette $3.75

CAESAR SALAD with garlic croutons $4.95

ANTIPASTO SALAD with grilled vegetables,
    fontina and proscuitto $6.95

SMOKED CHICKEN SALAD with spinach,
    pancetta and sun-dried tomato vinaigrette $8.50

BURGERS & SANDWICHES
served with fries

HAMBURGER or CHEESEBURGER with fresh
    grilled onions $6.75

PARAGON BURGER with bacon, cheddar,
    and avocado $8.50

SEARED-RARE AHI SANDWICH with cilantro
    pesto and jalapeno mayonnaise $8.95

GRILLED EGGPLANT SANDWICH with spicy
    tomato sauce and fontina cheese $6.95

GRILLED CHICKEN SANDWICH with Italian
    foccasia with aioli and fresh basil $7.95

ENTREES

CRISPY PAN-SEARED SALMON with roasted red
    potatoes and shallot-saffron vinaigrette $9.95

ANGEL HAIR PASTA with sun-dried tomatoes,
    fresh basil and garlic $8.95

ROASTED HALF-CHICKEN with Long
    Branch potatoes and fresh vegetables $9.75

MAPLE CURED DOUBLE-CUT PORK CHOP
    Fresh yams and homemade applesauce $9.75

MARINATED SKIRT STEAK with tomato jalapeno
    salsa, garlic mashed potatoes and red chili
    onion rings $9.95

*YOUR SERVER WILL TELL YOU ABOUT SPECIAL ENTREES
AND OUR FRESHLY MADE DESSERTS*

BEVERAGES

FRESH GROUND COFFEE & DECAF	$1.25
HOT & ICED TEA	$1.25
SOFT DRINKS AND MINERAL WATER	$1.50
ESPRESSO	$1.50
CAPPUCCINO & LATTE	$1.50

Dinner: Mon - Fri 5:30 - 10:30, Sat - Sun 10 - 3

MENU CHANGES DAILY

◆ First Courses ◆

Tuna Tartare with Endive, Jeremiah's Provençale Sauce & Garlic Toasts — 10.00

Deep Fried Calamari with Moroccan Lemon Sauce — 9.25

Maine Crab Linguine with Sea Scallop, Marinated Tomatoes & Basil — 12.00

Star Route Farms Garden Salad with Orange Vinaigrette,
Toasted Pecans & Goat Cheese — 8.50

Warm Spinach Salad with Apple-Smoked Bacon, Frisée, Sherry Wine Vinaigrette
& Brioche Croutons — 9.00

Lamb Loin Paillard with Watercress, Fried Capers & Mint Vinaigrette — 9.50

Cream of Asparagus Soup with Herbed Crème Fraîche — 6.50

◆ Main Courses ◆

Sautéed Halibut with Mango-Chili Purée, Asparagus & Tomato-Mint Salsa — 20.00

Roast Salmon with Polenta, Red Pepper Sauce, Steamed Mussels
& Basil Pesto — 20.00

Grilled Swordfish with Basmati Rice, Artichokes, Cherry Tomatoes
& Lobster Remoulade — 19.50

Sautéed Quail with French Lentils, Swiss Chard, Truffle Aioli
& Tarragon — 20.00

Grilled Pork Tenderloin with Braised Red Cabbage, Mushroom Duxelles
& Whole Grain Mustard Sauce — 24.50

Roast Rack of Veal with Mashed Potatoes, Baby Vegetables
& Salsa Verde — 27.00

◆ Supper Menu ◆

Served from 10:30 p.m.

◆ ◆ ◆

House-Smoked Salmon with Horseradish Cream & Grilled Brioche - 10.50

Stars' Deluxe Antipasto Platter for Two with Parma Prosciutto, Roast Garlic, Eggplant, Artichokes, Olives, Green Onions, Shaved Parmesan Cheese, Pesto & Grilled Focaccia - 24.00

◆ ◆ ◆

Tuna Tartare with Endive, Jeremiah's Provençale Sauce & Garlic Toasts	10.00
Deep Fried Calamari with Moroccan Lemon Sauce	9.25
Maine Crab Linguine with Sea Scallop, Marinated Tomatoes & Basil	12.00
Star Route Farms Garden Salad with Orange Vinaigrette, Toasted Pecans & Goat Cheese	8.50
Warm Spinach Salad with Apple-Smoked Bacon, Frisée, Sherry Wine Vinaigrette & Brioche Croutons	9.00
Lamb Loin Paillard with Watercress, Fried Capers & Mint Vinaigrette	9.50
Cream of Asparagus Soup with Herbed Crème Fraîche	6.50

◆ ◆ ◆

◆ Dessert Menu ◆

Chocolate Chunk Soufflé served with dark rum custard sauce (please order 20 minutes in advance)	6.25
French Apple Tart served warm with double cream	5.50
Stars' Cream Puff with double espresso bean ice cream & warm caramel pecan sauce	5.75
Buttermilk Cheesecake served with Stars' spiced Bing cherries	5.75
Caramelized Brioche filled with vanilla ice cream, strawberries & raspberry sauce	5.75
Banana Cream Pie with crème fraîche & chocolate sauce	5.50
Assorted Cookie Plate	4.50

STARS CAFE

Menu Changes Daily

BEVERAGES

Coffee/Tea/Milk *1.50*
Espresso *2.00*
Cappuccino *2.00*
Double Espresso or
      Cappuccino *3.00*
Caffe Latte *2.00*
Cafe Mocha *2.00*
Hot Chocolate *2.00*
Orange or Grapefruit Juice
      Small *2.00*
      Large *2.75*
Tinman Organic Apple Juice .. *1.50*
Chardonnay Grape Juice *1.50*

BEERS

Domestic Beers
      Anchor Steam *2.50*
      Rolling Rock *2.50*
      Red Tail Ale *3.00*

Imported Beers
      Amstel Light *3.00*
      Becks *3.00*
      Buckler, Non-Alcoholic .. *3.00*
      Pilsner Urquell *3.00*
      Sapporo (22 oz.) *4.00*

555 Golden Gate • Civic Center • (415) 861-4344

APPETIZERS

Cafe Onion Rings 2.95
Roasted Red Peppers with Salsa Verde
    & Garlic Toasted Focaccia 5.50
Sizzling Prawns 7.00

SOUPS & SALADS

Grilled Roma Tomato Soup with Pesto 5.75
Mixed Green Salad with Citrus Vinaigrette 5.50
    with Creamy Blue Cheese Dressing 5.75
Butter Leaf Lettuce Salad with
    Creamy Olive Dressing & Toasted Walnuts 6.75
Marinated Goat Cheese with Fava Beans
    & Croutons 7.50
Caesar Salad with Garlic Croutons 8.00

MAIN COURSES

Mixed Seafood Light Fry & Chips 9.75
Celery Root Ravioli with Parmesan Cheese 10.00
Fettucine with Rabbit, Asparagus, Radicchio,
    Tomatoes & Mustard Cream 9.75
Half Roast Chicken with Cherry Tomato Gratin 11.50
Pan Fried Sand Dabs with Basmati Rice,
    Green Beans & Lemon-Caper Remoulade 11.50
Roast Pork Chop with Sweet Corn,
    Mashed Potato Cake & Barbecue Glaze 12.00

DESSERTS

French Apple Tart
    served warm with double cream 4.50
Stars' Cream Puff
    with double espresso bean ice cream
    & warm caramel pecan sauce 4.75
Buttermilk Cheesecake
    served with Stars' spiced Bing cherries 4.75
Caramelized Brioche
    filled with vanilla ice cream, Strawberries
    & raspberry sauce 4.75
Banana Cream Pie
    with crème fraîche & chocolate sauce 4.50
Assorted Cookie Plate 3.50

WINE LIST

Wines by the glass

Witter 1988 California Chardonnay	4.00
McDowell Valley 1989 White Zinfandel	4.00
DeLoach 1990 Russian River Valley Fumé Blanc	4.50
Quivira 1990 Dry Creek Valley Sauvignon Blanc	4.50
Stephen Zellerbach Vineyard 1988 Alexander Valley Cabernet Sauvignon	4.50
Bonny Doon 1990 Big House Red Table Wine	4.50
S. Anderson Tivoli Napa Valley Brut Noir	6.00

White Wines

Columbia 1989 Washington Johannisberg Riesling	12.00
Quivira 1990 Dry Creek Valley Sauvignon Blanc	18.00
Witter 1988 California Chardonnay	16.00
DeLoach 1990 Russian River Valley Fumé Blanc	20.00
Buena Vista 1989 Carneros Chardonnay	20.00
J. Lohr 1990 Monterey/Riverstone Chardonnay	20.00
Cuvaison 1989 Napa/Carneros Chardonnay	28.00
DeLoach 1989 Russian River Valley Chardonnay, O.F.S.	40.00

Red Wines

Bonny Doon 1990 Big House Red Table Wine	18.00
Ridge 1989 York Creek Zinfandel	20.00
De Loach 1989 Russian River Valley Pinot Noir	25.00
Markham 1989 Napa Valley Merlot	25.00
Kendall-Jackson 1988 Vintner's Reserve Merlot	30.00
Les Vieux Cepages 1987 McDowell Valley Syrah	30.00
Stephen Zellerbach Vineyard 1988 Alexander Valley Cabernet Sauvignon	18.00
Guenoc 1987 Lake County Cabernet Sauvignon	20.00

1800 Fillmore St • Pacific Heights • (415) 474-3773

MENU

Endive/Kumquat/Hazelnut Salad   6.75
Spinach/Pear/Gorgonzola Cheese Salad 6.75
Mixed Lettuces with Spiced Pecans and Grated Parmesan 6.50
Virginia Ham and Biscuits with Cream Gravy 7.50
Baked Semolina with Parmesan Cheese 8.00
Grilled Codfish Cakes with Tartar Sauce 9.00
Welsh Rarebit 8.00, with Smoked Bacon 10.00
Pasta of the Day 12.00
Bowl of Steamed Mussels 10.50
Bowl of Gumbo with Fried Cornbread 14.00
Barbequed Brisket with Cheese Hominy Grits 14.00
Grilled Fish with Vegetables 15.00
Grilled Chicken Breast with Root Vegetable Gratin 14.00
Braised Lamb Shank with White Beans, Eggplant and Tomatoes 14.00
Pot Roast with Mashed Potatoes and Vegetables 15.00
Crab Cakes with Roasted Red Pepper Sauce 16.00
Barbequed Brisket Sandwich with Southwestern Cole Slaw 10.00

Daily Selection of Desserts

1800 Fillmore Street, San Francisco, CA 94115 Tel. 474-3773
Tuesday - Saturday 5:00 P.M. - Midnight
Sunday 5:00 P.M. - 11:00 P.M.
Dinner 5:00 P.M. - 10:30 P.M.

MENU CHANGES REGULARLY

Table 29

TABLE 29.

Typical Daily Menus

FIRST

Forni-Brown Calistoga Mixed Greens - Tapenade Toasts	5.00
Butternut Squash Soup - Creme Fraiche	5.00
Warm Red Bliss, Purple and Yellow Finn Potato Salad - Wilted Frisee Onion-Garlic Compote	6.95
Laura Chenel's Fresh Goat Cheese Cake - Shaved Fennel - Rosemary Vinaigrette	7.50
Poached Gold And Purple Beet Salad - Baby Spinach - Tangerine Vinaigrette	7.50
Braised Canellini Beans - Poached Forni-Brown Baby Leeks	5.95
Wild Mushroom Salad - Shiitake and Oyster Mushrooms- Crouton, Bacon and Mixed Lettuces - Sherry Vinaigrette	7.95
Tuna Tartare - Spicy Vegetables and Radicchio Salad - Quail Egg - Croutons	7.95
Hog Island (Tomales Bay) and Fanny Bay (Olympic Peninsula) Oysters on the Halfshell - Champagne Vinegar Mignonette	7.50
Manila Clams steamed with Semillon, Herbs and Butter	8.95
Matsutake Mushroom Ragout - Artichoke Hearts and Cream	7.95

FISH

Ahi Tuna - Julienned Jicama Salad with Anaheim Chiles - Tomatillo Salsa	17.25
Maine Sea Scallops - Potatoes Rosti - Coleslaw of Fennel, Cabbage, Carrots and Radicchio	17.95
Thresher Shark - Kentucky Blue Lake Beans - Lemon Grass Vinaigrette	13.95
Spearfish - Cleveland Radishes and Turnips - Ginger Lime Butter	17.95

MEAT/POULTRY

Free Range Chicken from Maurer Farm - French Fries		15.25
Pork Tenderloin - Potato Cake - Garlic-Parsley Butter		17.50
Wolfe Ranch Quail, Grilled - Braised Carrots and Baby Artichokes		17.95
Rib Eye Steak - Goat-Cheese-Pepper-Potato Gratin - Roasted Shallot Cabernet Butter	(For Two)	27.50
Calves Liver - Frise Lettuce, Roasted Garlic and Marmalade of Red Onion and Currants		14.95

4110 St Helena Hwy • Napa Valley • (707) 224-3300

FIRST

Forni-Brown Gardens (Calistoga) Mixed Greens - Tapenade Toasts	5.00
Celery Root Soup - Parsnip Chips	5.00
New Potato Salad (Red Bliss, Purple, and Yellow Finn) Eggplant and Deep Fried Artichokes	7.95
Oysters on the Halfshell* Malpeque (Prince Edward Island) * and Kumamoto (Humboldt Bay) Champagne Vinegar Mignonette	7.95
Portobella, Shiitake and Oyster Mushroom Salad with Bacon and Croutons and Sherry Vinaigrette	7.95
Poached Gold and Purple Beet Salad - Arugula - Citrus Vinaigrette	6.50
Laura Chenel's Goat Cheese Cake, Shaved Fennel and Rosemary Vinaigrette	7.50
Matsutake and Chanterelle Mushroom Ragout - Toni's Bread Croutons - Beaujolais Sauce	9.95
Ahi Tuna Tartare Mixed with a Spicy Vegetable Mixture and Potato Chips	7.95
Chicken Thigh Salad with Whole Grain Mustard and Baby Spinach Leaves	6.95

FISH

Skate Salad, Sauteed Meuniere on Kentucky Blue Lake Beans and Radishes	9.95
Rex Sole Sauteed with Jicama and Anaheim Chili Julienne and Tomatillo Salsa	12.95
Maine Sea Scallops & Coleslaw (Fennel, Cabbage, Carrots and Radicchio)	12.95
Pink Shrimp Sauteed on Flat Noodles Sauced with Blood Orange Vinaigrette	9.95

MEAT/POULTRY

Grilled Free-Range Chicken from Maurer Farm on a Bed of Endive and Topped with Roasted Pepper Compote	9.95
Grilled Flank Steak on Herbed Focaccia and Grilled Red Onions - Roasted Garlic French Fries	11.75
Mesquite Grilled Calves Liver - Potato Cake - Red Onion Black Currant Compote	10.95
Wolfe Ranch Quail with Mashed Potatoes and Quail Sauce	8.50
Paine Farm Squab Marinated in Soy-Ginger on top of Braised Cannellini Beans and Baby Leeks	9.95

SMALL PLATES

Monsoon Steamed Buns (2) *stuffed with Mushrooms & Pork*	3.75
Vietnamese Spring Rolls *with Basil & Cucumber*	5.25
Chicken Sate (3) *with Peanut Coriander Sauce*	4.75
Wontons (8) *Pork, with Vinegar Ginger Sauce*	5.50
Shanghai Baby Sticky Ribs *with Sweet Black Vinegar Glaze*	6.25
Fresh Fish & Shrimp Stuffed Chilies *with Black Bean Sauce*	6.75
Lightly Fried Fresh Squid - *Thai Style*	6.75
Fresh Salt & Pepper Spot Prawns *with Lemon* (subject to availability)	7.75

SALADS

Hot & Sweet Napa Cabbage Pickle	2.75
Salad Greens *with Monsoon Dressing*	4.00
Salad Greens Thai Style *with Beef*	7.00
North Chinese Roast Eggplant *with Ginger*	5.50
Fresh Asparagus *with mustard-sesame seed dressing*	5.50
Monsoon Platter *Cha Siu; Hot and Sweet Cabbage; Sichuan Chicken Shreds; Asparagus; Eggplant; Mussels*	12.50

FRESH EGG & WHEAT FLOUR NOODLES

Thai Green Herb Sauce (*"Asian Pesto"*)	6.00
Shanghai - Style Vegetables *with Oyster Sauce*	8.50
Monsoon's Yellow Curry *with Beef & Chinese Chives*	9.00
Monsoon's Yellow Curry *with Fresh Gulf Shrimp*	10.50

MEAT/POULTRY

TEA SMOKED DUCK *with steamed Lotus Rolls & Special Sauce*	17.50
STIR-FRY CHICKEN *with Asparagus and Black Beans*	12.50
CLAYPOT OF BRAISED PORK SHOULDER *& White Radish*	13.00
REAL MU SHU PORK *with Beijing Pancakes*	12.75
MA PO DOUFU - *Sichuan Style Fresh Bean Curd with Pork*	12.50

SEAFOOD (subject to availability of fresh or live product)

GRILLED FRESH SEA SCALLOPS *with Ginger-Scallion Sauce*	16.50
GRILLED FRESH FISH FILET *with Ginger, Scallions & Black Beans*	17.50
FRESH WEST COAST SPOT PRAWNS *Salt & Pepper Style*	19.50
WHOLE STEAMED CATFISH *with Thai Cingor-Coconut Sauce*	AQ

VEGETABLES

DRY FRIED GREEN BEANS *with Sichuan Vegetable, Pork*	8.75
FRESH VEGETABLE OF THE DAY	6.50
GAILAN *(Chinese Broccoli)*	6.50
FRIED RICE OF THE DAY (Tuesday through Thursday)	5.75
THAI JASMIN RICE *served steamed in individual bowls*	1.00

MONSOON'S RECOMMENDED SPECIALTIES-
to be ordered in advance with your reservation (24 hour notice):

WHOLE HONEY ROAST SQUAB	17.50
WHOLE POACHED CHICKEN CANTONESE STYLE	19.50
WHOLE LIVE LOBSTER - *with Cantonese Egg & Ginger Sauce*	AQ
WHOLE DUNGENESS CRAB- *Cantonese or Salt & Pepper Style*	AQ
WHOLE LIVE SEK BON COD OR BOLINA COD STEAMED: *with Scallions, Ginger & Black Beans; Shanghai-Style with Mushrooms & Bamboo Shoots; or "Grand Old Man" (Seared Fresh Chilies, Ginger & Scallion Shreds with a Light Sauce)*	AQ
WHOLE SHANGHAI BRAISED DUCK*with Pearl Onions*	AQ
LION'S HEAD — *A Shanghai Caserole*	AQ
STEAMED FRESH BACON *with Black Fermented Mustard Greens*	AQ
WHOLE RED BRAISED PORK SHOULDER (for 6 or more) *with Hearts of Bok Choy*	AQ

Other dishes from Frog's Legs to Venison to Sea Cucumber can also be arranged for the asking.

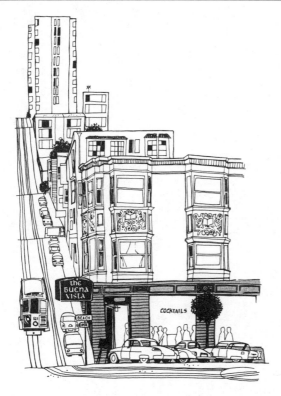

Irish Coffee

INTRODUCED TO THE U.S. AT THE BUENA VISTA BY STANTON DELAPLANE.

AKVAVIT	GIMLET	OLD FASHIONED
BLOODY MARY	GIN AND TONIC	PERNOD
BRANDY COFFEE	CHOCOLATE COFFEE	PIÑA COLADA
DUBONNET	IRISH CREAM COFFEE	PIMM'S CUP
GOLDEN FIZZ	FUZZY NAVEL	
NEW ORLEANS FIZZ	MARGARITA	TEQUILA SANGRITA
ROYAL FIZZ	MARTINI	LONG ISLAND ICE TEA

Imported Beers

AUSTRALIA	HOLLAND		IRELAND	CANADA	
Foster's	Heineken	Amstel Light	Guinness Stout	Molson Ale	Moosehead
ENGLAND	MEXICO		GERMANY	PHILIPPINES	
Bass Ale	Dos Equis XX & Corona		Beck's St. Pauli Girl	San Miquel	

Menu

Enjoy an IRISH COFFEE
New Orleans FIZZ

Chilled Aalborg AKVAVIT *with Beer Snit*
BLOODY MARY

Breakfast

Breakfast Specials served All Day with Fresh Hash Brown Potatoes and Toast.
(Sourdough Toast or English Muffin 75¢ Extra.)

HAM, BACON OR LINK SAUSAGE
  WITH 2 EGGS.............................6.25
COUNTRY SAUSAGE PATTIES
  WITH 2 EGGS.............................6.25
HAM AND CHEESE OMELET.................6.25
BACON AND CHEESE OMELET..............6.25
BAY SHRIMP OMELET......................6.50
PLAIN OR CHEESE OMELET.................5.75
CORNED BEEF HASH
  WITH POACHED EGGS 6.25
2 EGGS WITH HASH BROWN POTATOES
  AND TOAST 5.00
ORDER OF TOAST 1.25

STEAK AND EGGS...........................8.25
HAMBURGER PATTIE WITH 2 EGGS 6.25
EGGS BENEDICT 6.50
EGGS BUENA VISTA *(Same as Eggs Benedict*
  without hollandaise sauce).....................6.25
COUNTRY EGGS BENEDICT with
  Sausage Patties..............................6.50
JLK SPECIAL *(omelet with bacon bits,*
  onion, green pepper and mushrooms) 6.25
MEXICAN OMELET *(green chiles, Monterey Jack*
  cheese, green peppers and sour cream).........6.25
JIM RUFFULO BREAKFAST *(scrambled eggs,*
  bowl of chili and onion garnish)...............6.25
SOURDOUGH TOAST OR ENGLISH MUFFIN .1.65

SEE OUR WALL SIGNS FOR TODAY'S CHEF SPECIALS!
Chef's Specials & All Items Below Served From 11 AM

Seafoods

Ask about our **"FRESH FISH OF THE DAY"** Special
Served with Vegetable, Potato, Salad and Bread
PRAWNS *with French Fries, Vegetable, Salad*
  and Bread 9.75
EASTERN SCALLOPS *with French Fries, Vegetable*
  Salad and Bread...........................9.75

Salads

TUNA SALAD...............................6.25
CHICKEN SALAD...........................6.25
CHEF'S SALAD 6.25
SHRIMP LOUIE 7.25

Soups & Appetizers

SOUP OF THE DAY..........................2.75
CHILI....................................3.50
SHRIMP COCKTAIL.........................4.75
SEAFOOD CHOWDER.......................3.50

Entrees

Served with Green Salad and Sourdough Bread.
CHICKEN-FRIED STEAK *with Potato*
  and Vegetable 7.25
CLUB FRANKFURTERS *with Sauerkraut* 5.95
FRIED CHICKEN *with French Fries*
  and Vegetable 7.95
HAMBURGER STEAK *with French Fries*
  and Vegetable 7.95

Sandwiches

Served with Potatoes or Cole Slaw and Garnish.

GRILLED CHEESE 3.95
GRILLED HAM AND CHEESE 5.75
CHICKEN SALAD...........................4.95
HAMBURGER................................4.95
CHEESEBURGER 5.25
BV BURGER *(with Monterey Jack*
  cheese and bacon).........................5.60
CHEDDAR BURGER *(sautéed onions*
  cheddar cheese, bacon bits)..................5.60
TUNA.....................................4.75

HAM AND EGG 4.95
BACON, LETTUCE AND TOMATO.............4.95
TURKEY...................................4.95
CORNED BEEF ON RYE 4.95
PATTIMELT *(grilled hamburger,*
  American cheese on rye) 5.25
REUBEN GRILL *(grilled corned beef,*
  Monterey Jack cheese and sauerkraut on rye) 5.75
CLUB SANDWICH 5.75

CHEESECAKE ... 2.75   ASSORTED PIES ... 2.50   CAKE ... 2.50
Coffee, Tea, Sanka or Milk ... .95   Soft Drinks ... 1.25

·················· **DINNER PLATES** ··················
SERVED WITH MASHED POTATOES OR VEGETABLES, CHOICE OF
SALAD OR BEANS. BREAD ROLL AND BUTTER   5.25

ROUND OF BEEF
BARBECUED BEEF
CORNED BEEF
PASTRAMI
HAM OR TURKEY

············· **TOMMY'S BIG SANDWICH** ············
ON BREAD OR SOURDOUGH ROLL   3.49

ROUND OF BEEF
BARBECUED BEEF
CORNED BEEF
PASTRAMI
HAM OR TURKEY

············· **TOMMY'S JOYNT SPECIALS** ···········
3 DIFFERENT SPECIALS EVERY DAY
TYPICAL OFFERINGS

M O N D A Y
BRAISED OX TAILS WITH PASTA, BREAD AND BUTTER   4.45

T U E S D A Y
BREADED TURKEY CUTLETS PARMIGIANA WITH STEAMED RICE
MUSHROOMS AND ONION, BREAD AND BUTTER   3.95

W E D N E S D A Y
BROILED GROUND CHUCK STEAK SANDWICH ON SOUR ROLL
WITH SAUTEED ONION, MASH POTATOES AND MUSHROOM
SAUCE   4.25

1101 Geary Blvd • Civic Center • (415) 775-4216

THURSDAY
BRAISED LAMB SHANKS W/ VEGETABLES, BREAD, BUTTER   4.85

FRIDAY
BAKED CALAMARI WITH ITALIAN SAUCE, BREAD, BUTTER   4.45

SATURDAY
SWEET & SOUR SPARE RIBS WITH STEAMED RICE,
BREAD AND BUTTER   5.25

SUNDAY
BURGUNDY BEEF WITH RICE GOURMET, BREAD, BUTTER   5.95

············· OUR FAMOUS DISHES ·············

BUFFALO STEW   5.45
BUFFALO CHILI   4.45
BEANS~N~ BEER   1.50

············· OLD GERMAN RECIPE ·············

SAUSAGE SANDWICH   2.75
KIELBASA
KNACKWUST

BRATWURST PLATE   3.75

················ SALADS OF THE DAY ················

POTATOES   1.25 each
COLE SLAW
MIXED PICKLE BEANS
TOSSED GREENS

····················· DESSERT ·····················

APPLE STRUDEL   1.00
CARROT CAKE   1.15
CHEESE CAKE   1.25

Dinner: 7 Days a Week until 2am

MANDALAY
BURMESE & MANDARIN CUISINE

FOWL

SATAY CHICKEN (6 Skewers) 6.75
(barbecued chicken skewers served with Chef's special grounded peanuts,
coconut and pineapple dipping sauce)
MANDALAY CHICKEN 7.25
(Fried chicken slices sauteed with garlic and Chef's delicious hot sauce)
CURRIED CHICKEN 6.75
SHREDDED CHICKEN W/ GARLIC 6.75
(Shredded chicken prepared with black fungus and vegetables in hot sauce)
LEMON CHICKEN 7.25
(Our Chef's delicious lemon sauce over crispy white meat)
CRISPY CHICKEN 7.25 whole-14.00
(Lightly deep fried marinated steamed chicken served with our Chef's
delicious dipping sauce)
KUNG PAO CHICKEN 6.75
(Chicken cubes sauteed with vegetables and green pepper topped with peanuts)
SWEET AND SOUR CHICKEN 6.75
CHICKEN WITH SNOW PEA 6.75
RANGOON SMOKED TEA DUCK half 8.95

BEEF

MANDALAY BEEF 7.25
(Fried beef slices sauteed with garlic and Chef's delicious hot sauce)
CURRIED BEEF 6.95
SIZZLING BEEF 8.50
(Beef prepared with mushroom, bamboo shoot, green pepper and water chest
nuts served on hot iron plate)
SZECHUAN BEEF 6.95
MONGOLIAN BEEF 6.95
(Beef sauteed with green onion served on a bed of fried rice noodles)
GINGER BEEF 6.95
(Shredded beef sauteed with tender fresh ginger shreds)
BEEF WITH VEGETABLE 6.75

4348 California St • Richmond District • (415) 386-3895

SEAFOOD

MANDALAY SQUID 6.95
(Steamed squid served on bed of spinach, topped with fried onion slices and
our Chef's special hot and sour sauce)
CURRIED GREEN MUSSEL 7.25
SIZZLING THREE INGREDIENTS 8.95
(Scallop, prawns and squid prepared with vegetable served on hot iron plate)
FISH FILET 7.25
(Choice of : hot braised with yellow bean sauce or black bean sauce)
CURRIED FISH (Steaks) 6.95
MANDALAY PRAWNS 7.95
PEPPER SALTED PRAWNS 7.95
SWEET AND SOUR PRAWNS 7.95
SIZZLING PRAWNS 8.95
MU-SHU SHRIMP (with 4 Pancakes) 7.25

PORK

SATAY PORK (6 skewers) 6.75
(Barbecued pork on skewers served with Chef's special grounded peanuts,
coconut and pineapple dipping sauce)
CURRIED PORK 6.95
MANDALAY SMOKED PORK 6.95
(Sliced smoked pork prepared with bamboo shoot, green pepper, chinese
mushroom and cabbage)
SZECHUAN BEAN CURD PORK 6.25
SHREDDED PORK WITH GARLIC 6.75
MU-SHU PORK (with 4 Pancakes) 6.75

VEGETABLE

PICKLED CABBAGE 3.50
DRY PAN FRIED STRING 6.50
(Burmese style sauteed string beans with tasty spices)
EGGPLANT IN SZECHUAN SAUCE 6.25
HOT SAUCE BEAN CURD 5.95
SAUTEED SPINACH 5.25
CHINESE CABBAGE WITH MUSHROOM 6.25
MIXED VEGETABLE DELUX 5.25

NOODLES & RICE

ONH NO KAW SOI 5.75
COMBINATION CHOW MEIN 4.50
COMBINATION FRIED RICE 4.50
OWN TA MEIN 3.50
(Rice cooked with coconut milk)

Appetizers

Oysters in Hell	6.95	Creole Gumbo	
Jambalaya		small bowl / 4.95	large bowl / 6.95
with duck and chaurice sausage	5.50	Seafood chowder	
Fresh Oysters on the half shell	6.95	small bowl / 3.95	large bowl / 6.50
Shrimp in Shell	5.00	New Zealand Green Lip Mussels	
Shrimp Remoulade	5.50	*with dill mustard sauce*	7.95
Combination Plate	7.95	Elite House Salad	3.75
Oyster Shooter	1.50	Fresh Crawfish	4.50
Barbeque Garlic Bread	1.95	Deep Fried Calamari	5.95

Main Courses

Barbeque Baby Back Ribs	Half-order 8.50 Full order	13.50
Crab Cakes - Caper tartar sauce		12.95
Redfish Carolyn - Fresh Gulf crab & creole cream sauce		11.95
Boneless Breast of Chicken - Oyster & artichoke dressing		9.95
Roast Pork Loin - Sweet potatoes & cornbread dressing		10.50
Barbeque Shrimp - Hot pepper, butter sauce		12.95
Blackened Filet Mignon - Cajun butter		17.95
Baked Eggplant - Stuffed with Florida blue crab & Gulf shrimp		11.95
Blackened Red Snapper		10.95
Grilled Chaurice Sausage - Red beans & rice		9.95
Blackened Medallions of Pork - Apple ginger butter		12.95
Chef's Special Pasta of the Day		11.95
Braised Smoked Ham Shank - Red beans & rice		10.95

2049 Fillmore St • Pacific Heights • (415) 346-8668

SUNDAY BRUNCH

BUCK'S FIZZ	2.50	SAZERAC COCKTAIL	2.75
RAMOS FIZZ	2.50	PLANTATION MILK PUNCH	2.50
BLOODY MARY	2.50	FRESH SQUEEZED ORANGE JUICE	1.75

SEASONAL FRESH FRUIT
HOMEMADE CORNBREAD WITH CLOVER HONEY

GRILLED CHAURICE W/ SCRAMBLED EGGS -
SPICY LOUISIANA PORK SAUSAGE WITH SCRAMBLED EGGS

EGGS NEW ORLEANS -
POACHED EGGS WITH CRAB & HOLLANDAISE SAUCE

GRITS & GRILLADES -
VEAL IN A SPICY CREOLE SAUCE WITH HOT BUTTERED GRITS

EGGS SARDOU -
POACHED EGGS, CREAMED SPINACH, ARTICHOKES & HOLLANDAISE SAUCE

CHICKEN ROCHAMBEAU -
BREAST OF CHICKEN, HAM, MARCHAND DU VIN & BEARNAISE SAUCE

EGGS BENEDICT -
THE CLASSIC...INVENTED IN NEW ORLEANS

SPINACH OMELET -
CREAMED SPINACH IN A FLUFFY THREE EGG OMELETTE

OYSTER & BACON OMELET -
PLUMP OYSTERS, CRISP BACON & CREOLE CREAM SAUCE

EGGS HUSSARDE -
POACHED EGGS, HAM, MARCHAND DU VIN & BEARNAISE SAUCE

HUEVOS RANCHERO -
WITH BLACK BEANS & HOUSEMADE SALSA

SPINACH SALAD -
SLICED RED ONIONS, FRESH MUSHROOMS, FETA CHEESE, IN A VINEGRETTE

LOX & BAGELS -
SMOKED SALMON, TOMATO, RED ONION, CAPERS & CREAM CHEESE

ELITE CHEESEBURGER -
HOUSE MADE GROUND BEEF, TOMATO, LETTUCE, RED ONION, SPICY POTATOES

ELITE FILET HASH -
FILET MIGNON LIGHTLY SPICED AND SERVED WITH TWO POACHED EGGS

SMOKED SALMON & CREAM CHEESE OMELET -
FLUFFY THREE EGG OMELET WITH LIGHT CREAMY FILLING

COMPLETE BRUNCH *** $9.95

APPETIZERS

FRESH OYSTERS ON THE 1/2 SHELL	6.95
SHRIMP IN SHELL	5.00
SHRIMP REMOULADE	5.50
NEW ENGLAND GREEN LIP MUSSELS	7.95

UNLIMITED FRESH BREWED COFFEE   1.00   TEA   1.00

231

Light Entrees

Pasta of the Day

Fish of the Day

Grilled Fish of the Day
(Supplement 3.00)

Mushroom Omelet with Grilled Pancetta

Grilled Breast of Chicken with Braised Tomatoes

Chef's Special
(Supplement 3.00)

Smoked Duck Salad with Shrimp & Berries

Warm Spinach Salad with Bacon, Goat Cheese
& Scallops

11.50

Please no Pipe or Cigar Smoking in the Dining Room

DINNER

Smoked Salmon with New Potatoes 7.50

Asparagus & Truffle Terrine 6.50

Sautéed Sea Scallops with Passionfruit and Truffles 8.50

Foie Gras 231 16.50

Seared Salmon in Tomato Consommé 8.50

Crab with Turnips and Coriander 7.50

Warm Cabbage Salad 5.50

Duck Confit Salad 7.50

Lobster Salad 9.50

Warm Chicken Salad 8.00

Mixed Green Salad with Asiago & Nuts 5.50

Grilled Swordfish with Mango and Asparagus 19.50

Roasted Marinated Salmon with Black Chanterelles 20.50

Sweetbreads with Potato Tart and Carrot Sauce 17.50

Breast of Duck with Bittersweet Chocolate & Raspberry Vinegar 20.50

Roast Loin of Lamb in Filo with Fine Herbs 22.50

Filet of Beef Baked in Salt Crust 23.00

Honey Roasted Chicken with Grapefruit & Risotto 18.00

Pastry Chef's Selections of the Day

———

A T R I U M

F I R S T   C O U R S E

• Organic Baby Lettuces with Herb Roasted Pistachios and a Champagne
Lemon Vinaigrette   5.50   with Blue Cheese 6.25

Classic Caesar Salad   appetizer 6.50   entree 12.00

• Spinach Broccoli Salad with Carrot Strips, Radish Sprouts, Toasted Pine Nuts
and Balsamic Vinegar Dressing   appetizer 6.50   entree 11.50

Baked Escargots and Mushrooms with Fontina, Bread Crumbs and Thyme 6.75

Mediterranean Antipasto of Marinated Bufalo Mozzarella, Eggplant Pesto,
Roast Red Pepper and Marinated White Beans 6.25

Spring Asparagus with a Raspberry, Orange and Hazelnut Vinaigrette
and Goat Cheese Croutons 6.50

E N T R E E S

• Baked Dungeness Crabcakes with Cous Cous and a Sweet and Sour Melon Relish 16.75

Black Pepper Fettucine with Rock Prawns, Red Pepper and a Smoked Bacon,
Mushroom and Tomato Sauce 15.50

• Dungeness Crab Salad with Avocado, Romaine, Radicchio and Caesar Dressing 14.75

Grilled Hawaiian Swordfish with a Lemon Caper Butter 16.50

Grilled Norwegian Salmon with a Basil and Sweet Onion Soubise 16.50

• Baked Filet of Sole with a Roast Tomato Vinaigrette 15.50

• Grilled Breast of Chicken with a Zinfandel, Pomegranete and Black Peppercorn Sauce 13.50

Grilled Loin of Lamb with a Rosemary Roast Garlic Sauce 17.50

Grilled Black Angus Filet Mignon with a Brandy, Whole Grain Mustard
and Porcini Mushroom Sauce 18.75

L I G H T   E N T R E E S
* available with choice of any first course for **14.95**

Pizza with Artichoke Hearts, Pancetta, Olives, Asiago Cheese and Cabrian Tomato Sauce 9.75

• A Melange of Sauteed and Grilled Seasonal Vegetables over Basmati Rice 10.50

• Grilled Chicken Breast Salad with Roast New Potatoes, Sweet Peppers, Olives,
Feta Cheese and Romaine Lettuce 12.50

• Five Vegetable Egg Lasagne with a Spinach, Red Pepper and Basil Sauce 11.50

* Not valid in conjunction with dining membership cards.
• INDICATES A DISH LOW IN CHOLESTEROL AND SATURATED FATS.

A T R I U M

PLEASE SEE HOST ABOUT OUR PRIVATE PARTY FACILITIES
FOR CORPORATE PARTIES, WEDDINGS, BIRTHDAYS AND ALL OCCASIONS

Chef David Rosenthal

SPECIAL SELECTIONS

Appetizers

Ratatouille Lasagne with Smoked Whitefish
and Black Olive Pasta $14.00
Pan Fried Laura Chenel Goat Cheese with Carrot-Mint Salad $12.75
Terrine of Wild Pigeon with Sweetbreads and Fresh Morels $15.00

Main Course

Grilled Lamb Chops marinated in Homemade Yogurt
with Saffron Curry and Couscous $28.00
Veal Osso Buco with Peppery Rice Timbale and English Peas $23.00

Side Dishes

Couscous with Saffron Curry $3.00   Peppery Rice Timbale $3.00
Sweet Corn Cake with Roast Pepper-Corn Relish $3.75

Chef's Menu

Chilled Artichoke Hearts with Tomato Aioli
and Spring Vegetables
* * * * *

Watercress Soup with Blue Cheese Croutons
* * * * *

Sauteed Day Boat Scallops with Sweet Corn Cakes
and Lettuce filled with Shrimp and Pepper-Cilantro Relish
* * * * *

180 Rutherford Hill Rd • Rutherford • (707) 963-1211

DINNER MENU

Appetizers

Hamachi Sashimi and Ahi Tuna Tartare with Cucumber,
Soy Sauce and Wasabi $16.00
Sauteed Sonoma Duck Liver with Savory Apple Flan
and Port Wine-Black Pepper Essence $16.50
Risotto with Maine Lobster, Asparagus and Lemon-Thyme $17.00
Auberge Antipasto with Marinated Eggplant, Grilled Fennel,
Artichoke Heart, Aged Goat Cheese and Pickled Mushrooms $14.25

Soup and Salads

Caesar Salad $10.50
Chef's Preparation of Soup $7.00
Warm Salad of Pan Fried Snails with Wild Greens,
Garlic and Tomato $12.75
Wine Country Pie with Spinach, Sweet Peppers, Pepper Ham
and Fontinella Cheese $12.25

Main Courses

Grilled Free Range Chicken Breast with Parsley Pappardelle
and Morel Cream Sauce $23.00
Roast Rack of Lamb with Spring Garlic Gnocchi
and Sun Dried Tomatoes $29.00
Herb Crusted Beef Tenderloin with Goat Cheese Rellenos
and Ancho Chili Sauce $28.00
Sauteed Wild Lake Trout wrapped in Apple Smoked Bacon
with Baby Spinach, Feta Cheese and Warm Black Olive Vinaigrette $25.00
Grilled Pacific Salmon with Rosemary Baby Potatoes
and Roast Garlic Custard $26.00

Balboa Cafe

OPEN 7 DAYS A WEEK

BRUNCH

Eggs Benedict...7.50
Eggs Florentine...7.50
Corned Beef Hash with Poached Eggs...8.50
Scrambled Eggs, Country Sausage & Biscuits...9.75
Fritatta with Pancetta, Avocado, & Chiles..10.25

APPETIZERS

Marinated Red Lentil Salad with Minted Yogurt Sauce..........................7.00
Peasant Caviar with Artichoke Heart & Foccacia 7.50
Warm Cabbage Salad with Frisee, Walnuts & Cambozola......................6.75
Chile Rollatini with Cilantro Pesto..7.25
Caesar Salad...5.75
Seasonal Green Salad with Croutons & Tomatoes...................................4.75
     with Blue Cheese or Goat Cheese ....add 1.00

MAIN COURSES

BLT with Fries..6.75
Grilled Yucatan Sausage with Polenta and Tomato-Cilantro Sauce......10.75
Angel Hair Pasta with Zucchini, Sun-dried Tomatoes & Asiago 10.75
Marinated Skirt Steak with Lime Sour Cream & Fries 11.75
Herb-Peppered Beef Tenderloin with Red Wine-Shallot Sauce...............15.95
Poached Chicken Breast with Citron-Tarragon Sauce..............................10.75
Vegetable Cobb Salad..9.75
     with Chicken...10.75
Chicken Salad with Vegetables & Lemon-Tarragon Aioli.........................10.75
Tortilla-Floured Catfish with Corn-Tomato Sauce, & Fries.....................11.50
Spinach Linguine with Asparagus, Prosciutto, & Tomatoes....................11.25

CHICKEN & FISH DISHES SERVED LOW CALORIC ON REQUEST

BALBOA BURGERS

Balboa Burger - Half Pound Choice Chuck on a French Roll with Fries 7.50
     with Melted Jack or Swiss Cheese ....add .75
     with Sauteed Mushrooms...add .75
     with Cheddar & Pancetta..add .75
Bar Burger - Old Fashioned Round Burger...6.50

APPETIZERS

Lentil Soup with Tasso...4.50
Marinated Red Lentil Salad with Minted Yogurt Sauce.......................................7.00
Peasant Caviar with Artichoke Heart & Foccacia 7.50
Warm Cabbage Salad with Frisee, Walnuts & Cambozola..................................6.75
Chile Rollatini with Cilantro Pesto...7.25
Caesar Salad..5.75
Seasonal Green Salad with Croutons & Tomatoes...4.75
      with Blue Cheese or Goat Cheese ....add 1.00
Fried Gnocchi with Tomato-Basil Coulis..6.50

MAIN COURSES

BLT with Fries..6.75
Grilled Chicken Sandwich with Cole Slaw and Fries...8.75
Grilled Yucatan Sausage (Spicy)
      with Polenta and Tomato-Cilantro Sauce..10.75
Angel Hair Pasta with Zucchini, Sun-dried Tomatoes, & Asiago 10.75
Marinated Skirt Steak with Scallions, Lime Sour Cream, & Fries....................11.75
Herb-Peppered Beef Tenderloin with Red Wine-Shallot Sauce........................15.95
Poached Chicken Breast with Citron-Tarragon Sauce..10.75
Grilled Marinated Lamb Chops with Flageolets 14.75
Vegetable Cobb Salad..9.75
      with Chicken..10.75
Chicken Salad with Vegetables & Lemon-Tarragon Aioli................................10.75
Grilled Marinated Pork Chop with Kalamata-Olive Butter & Fries..................12.50
Tortilla Floured Catfish with Black Bean Sauce & Papaya Salsa......................12.75
Grilled Muscovy Duck Breast with Oyster Mushrooms & Brandy....................14.50
Saffron Fettuccine Primavera...11.00
CHICKEN & FISH DISHES SERVED LOW CALORIC ON REQUEST

BALBOA BURGERS

Balboa Burger - Half Pound Choice Chuck on a French Roll with Fries 7.50
      with Melted Jack or Swiss Cheese ....add .75
      with Sauteed Mushrooms...add .75
      with Cheddar & Pancetta..add .75
Bar Burger - Old Fashioned Round Burger...6.50

L U N C H E O N
MENU CHANGES DAILY

E N T R E E S

ROASTED CHICKEN SALAD WITH POTATOES, BALSAMIC VINAIGRETTE AND HERB MAYONNAISE
11.95

GRILLED ATLANTIC SALMON WITH WILD MUSHROOM RAGOUT, ROAST GARLIC AND HOLLANDAISE
14.50

SEARED HAWAIIAN SWORDFISH WITH GRILLED VEGETABLES AND ORANGE VINAIGRETTE
14.95

FISH 'N' CHIPS: CRISP FRIED ROCK COD WITH POMMES FRITES AND MALT VINEGAR
11.75

GRILLED HALF CHICKEN WITH BLACK BEAN SALAD AND MANGO SAUCE
14.50

LINGUINI WITH MANILA CLAMS, GULF PRAWNS AND WHITE WINE
12.25

GRILLED MARINATED SKIRT STEAK WITH GARLIC HASH BROWNS AND COLE SLAW
12.50

GRILLED REUBEN SANDWICH WITH HOUSEMADE CHIPS
8.95

GRILLED PORK CHOP WITH MASHED POTATOES AND SNAP PEAS
13.95

CLUB BURGER WITH APPLEWOOD SMOKED BACON AND POMMES FRITES
8.95

CHICKEN HASH A LA BIX
9.95

DINNER

STARTERS

HOUSESMOKED FISH CHOWDER WITH SPINACH
5.00

POINT REYES PACIFIC OYSTERS ON THE HALF SHELL WITH MIGNONETTE
7.95

HEARTS OF ROMAINE WITH BLUE CHEESE OR VINAIGRETTE DRESSING
4.95

MIXED BABY GREENS WITH BALSAMIC VINAIGRETTE AND GARLIC CROUTONS
5.25

GRILLED SPRING ASPARAGUS WITH TARRAGON AIOLI AND CRISPY ONION RINGS
7.50

FRIED OYSTER CAESAR SALAD
7.95

GRILLED DAYBOAT SCALLOPS WITH SWEET ONION GRITS, RADICCHIO AND BACON VINAIGRETTE
8.95

DUNGENESS CRAB CAKE WITH COUSCOUS SALAD, BABY GREENS AND CILANTRO OIL
9.00

SEARED SONOMA FOIE GRAS WITH ARTICHOKE AND SHERRY
9.75

CRISP POTATO AND LEEK PANCAKE WITH SMOKED SALMON AND CAVIAR
9.50

STEAK TARTARE
8.95

ENTREES

GRILLED YELLOWTAIL JACK WITH SWEET CORN, BLACK BEAN SALAD AND MANGO SALSA
18.25

PEPPER SEARED ATLANTIC SALMON WITH ZUCCHINI, MUSHROOMS AND RED WINE BUTTER
18.95

GRIDDLED LOCAL SAND DABS WITH GREEN BEANS AND TARTAR SAUCE
16.50

LINGUINI WITH GULF PRAWNS, WHITE WINE AND MANILA CLAMS
17.50

CHICKEN CUTLET WITH GARLIC MASHED POTATOES AND CAPER BROWN BUTTER
16.95

BREAST OF DUCK WITH CONFIT CABBAGE SALAD AND GREEN PEPPERCORN VERMOUTH SAUCE
17.95

GRILLED PORK CHOP WITH SNAP PEAS AND MASHED POTATOES
17.50

GRILLED FILET MIGNON WITH BEARNAISE AND POMMES FRITES
22.50

ROAST RACK OF LAMB WITH HERB ROASTED VEGETABLES AND PERSILLADE
23.75

CLUB BURGER WITH APPLEWOOD SMOKED BACON AND POMMES FRITES
9.95

CHICKEN HASH A LA BIX
11.95

SAVOY
Poissons et **Fruits de Mer**

BRASSERIE
San Francisco

BRASSERIE SAVOY SHELLFISH PLATTERS
Platters of Oysters, Mussels, Shrimp and Other Fresh Seafoods

Small	Medium	Extravaganza
16.50	30.00	60.00

FRESHLY STEAMED, CHILLED SHELLFISH SELECTIONS

Oysters served with Mignonette Sauce .... Market Price

Gulf Shrimp .... 1.50 ea.

1/2 Dozen Pink Pacific Scallops 3.50

1/2 Dozen Mussels 3.50

1/2 Cracked Dungeness, Served Warm or Chilled 9.50

1/2 Lobster, Served Warm or Chilled 11.75

APPETIZERS

Brasserie Savoy Salad.. 4.50

Creamy Clam Chowder.. 5.00

Savoy Caesar Salad with Country Flat Bread... 6.50

Arrugula and Fried Calamari Salad.. 6.50

Warm Salad Greens with Smokehouse Bacon and Cheese Fondue 6.50

Smoked Salmon with Mascarpone.. 7.25

BRASSERIE FARE "A LA SAVOY"

Steamed Mussels with Spicy Sausage and Smoked Chicken.................................... 13.50

Cassoulet: An Oven Crock with Lamb, Duck, Sausage and White Beans.......................... 12.50

Roasted Chicken Served with Basil Mashed Potates in a Natural Sauce......................... 11.50

Fish and Chips.. 12.50

Salmon with Roasted Potatoes, Broccoli, and Organic
Black and White Cannelini Beans in a Vinaigrette Sauce.. 14.50

Quail with Garlic Sausage, Smoked Bacon and Choucroute 14.50

Grilled Tuna Served with an Artichoke in a Sundried Tomato Sauce.............................. 15.50

Bouillabaisse: Mixed Seafood served in a Saffron Shellfish Broth................................ 16.50

Casserole of Shrimp and Scallops with Potato Gnocchi.. 16.00

Brasserie Savoy 16-Oz. Porterhouse Steak, choice of Frites or Onion Rings................... 18.50

SIDE DISHES

Savoy Frites......................... 3.50	Fried Cornmeal Dusted Onion Rings.......... 3.50
Seasonal Vegetables........................ 4.25	Beer Battered Fried Green Beans............... 4.75

STARTER DRINKS

Dubonnet on the Rocks (Red or White) 3.50
Emilio Lustau Dry Fino Sherry 3.50
Kir or Kir Rouge 5.00
Champagne Cocktails – Cassis, Raspberry, or Peach 6.50

STARTERS

Soup of the Day 3.95
Freshly made Potato Chips with Warm Oregon Blue Cheese 3.95
Provençal Pizza with Onions and Roasted Peppers 3.50
Steamed Prince Edward Island Mussels, Ginger and a Zinfandel Broth 6.95
Chilled Assorted Seafood Plate with a Curry Mayonnaise 7.95
Grilled Local Smoked Sausage with a Spicy Romesco Sauce 6.25
Five-Spice Duck with Cucumbers and Mushrooms 7.25

SALADS

Forni-Brown Organic Greens with a Wine Country Vinaigrette 4.75
with Crumbled Oregon Blue Cheese 5.50
Classic Caesar Salad with Parmesan Cheese and Garlic Croutons 6.50/10.00
Radicchio and Arugula with Sun-Dried Tomatoes, Asiago Cheese, and Balsamic Vinaigrette 6.00
Provençal Salad of Wild Greens and Herbs with Warm Marinated Goat Cheese 6.25

SANDWICHES

Grilled Brava Burger – "Best in the Valley" 7.75
Grilled Chicken Breast Sandwich with Iacopi's Pancetta and Gruyere Cheese 8.25
Grilled BBQ Pork Tenderloin with
a Roasted Shallot Spread 8.00

All served with our Homemade Fennel Coleslaw

3010 St Helena Hwy • St Helena • (707) 963-9300

RISOTTO AND PASTA

Fresh Pasta – Daily Selection 8.95/11.95
Risotto – Daily Selection 9.50/12.50
Penne Pasta with chopped Tomatoes, Balsamic Vinegar, and Basil – No Butter or Oil 10.75

MAIN COURSES

Fresh Fish prepared specially daily – Price Varies
Bouillabaisse – Fresh Poached Fish, Shellfish, and Vegetables in a Saffron Broth 15.25
Grilled Pork Tenderloin with Pickled Grapes, "Sweet and Sour" style 13.75
Cassoulet from Puy – French Lentils, Pork Tenderloin, Chicken, and Turkey Sausage 12.75
Grilled Filet of Beef with Parsnip Mashed Potatoes 15.75
Coq au Vin – Half Chicken Roasted with Mushrooms and Red Wine 12.75
Grilled Chicken Thighs with Green Peppercorns and Glazed Carrots 12.00
Roasted Breast of Muscovy Duck served with Buttered Leeks and Crispy Onions 15.50

DESSERTS

Apple Raisin Strudel in Filo Pastry with Tahitian Vanilla Bean Cream 5.25
Michler's Chocolate Chip Crème Brulée 5.75
Warm Chocolate Souffle Cake served with Cappuccino Ice Cream 5.25
Hazelnut Chocolate Ice Cream with a Salad of Citrus Fruit 5.75
Brava Terrace T-Shirt 12.95

Espresso "Illy" 2.00   Cappuccino 2.75   Decaffeinated Cappuccino 2.75

BEVERAGES

Mineral Water	small	1.75
	large	4.75
Sodas		1.25
Sport Ice Tea		1.50
Coffee/Tea		1.25

DESSERT WINES BY THE GLASS

1989 Markham, Muscat Blanc 2.50
1989 Joseph Phelps, Delice du Semillon 3.50
1991 Freemark Abbey, Edelwein Gold 7.50

PORTS

Vintage Late Bottled Selections 7.50
20 Year Aged Tawny 6.75
Quady Starboard 7.00
Quady 1986, Frank's Vineyard 4.75
N.V. Port Selections 4.75
Fonseca Bin 27 4.50

SHERRIES

Emilio Lustau, Light Fino 3.00
Emilio Lustau, Amontillado 3.00
Lustau, Almacenista 4.75
Lustau, East India Solera 4.75

MADEIRA

Blandy's 5 year 4.25
Blandy's 10 year 8.50

708 Bush Street
San Francisco, Ca. 94108
391·8480

GOURMET TASTING MENU

Saute of Foie Gras with Fresh Mango and Ginger Sauce

- served with -

Vouvray Champalou, 1990 (French Chenin Blanc)

*   *   *   *   *

Shrimp and Shiitake Cake with a Cool Lime Mayonaisse

- then -

Seared Rare Ahi with Housemade Noodles and Red Onion Jam

- served with -

Navarro Gewürztraminer, 1990 (½ bottle)

*   *   *   *   *

- Grapefruit and Cinnamon Granité -

- then -

Roast Rack of Lamb with a Guava and Pistachio Crust

- then -

Roquefort and Grapefruit *Salad*

- served with -

Etude Pinot Noir, 1989 (½ Bottle)

Dessert of Choice or Glass of Port Wine

*   *   *   *   *

$70.00 per Person for Two

APPETIZERS

Lomi-Lomi Salmon Napolean with Aquavit and Caviar

Basil Raviolis of Goat Cheese and Macadamia Nuts

Shrimp and Shiitake Cakes with a Cool Lime Mayonaisse

Sauteed Foie Gras with Mango and Ginger Sauce*

SALADS

Baby Spring Lettuces with a Passionfruit Dressing

Baked Roquefort and Grapefruit Salad

Warm Goat Cheese on Young Spinach with Balsamic Honey

Freshly Prepared Soup of the Day

MAIN COURSE

Duck Confit and Warm Wild Mushroom Salad with Fresh Mango

Yellow Fin Tuna on House Noodles with Red Onion Jam

Roasted Duck Breast with Thai Herbs and Caramelized Pear

Noisettes of Veal with Coconut Milk, Lime and Basil

Rack of Lamb with a Guava and Pistachio Crust*

CHOOSE ONE EACH OF APPETIZER, SALAD, MAIN COURSE AND DESSERT
- Thirty-Five Dollars -

* Add Two Dollars

Pastoral

LUNCH - MENU CHANGES MONTHLY

Entrée Salads

DUCK SALAD WITH BELGIAN ENDIVE, RADICCHIO, WALNUTS, SNOW PEAS, RED ONIONS,
PEARS AND BALSAMIC VINAIGRETTE _____ 8.75
CAESAR SALAD: ROMAINE LETTUCE TOSSED WITH GARLIC CROUTONS,
SUN-DRIED TOMATOES, ANCHOVY AND CAESAR DRESSING _____ 7.95
KOREAN CHICKEN SALAD WITH JULIENNED VEGETABLES, POTATOES, APPLES,
HAZELNUTS AND SOY-RICE VINAIGRETTE _____ 8.25
GRILLED TUNA SALAD NIÇOISE WITH GREEN BEANS, GRILLED YELLOW SQUASH,
CAULIFLOWERS, RICE SALAD, RED ONIONS, AND ANCHOVIES _____ 8.95

Sandwiches

SMOKED TROUT SANDWICH WITH DILL, CREAM CHEESE, CUCUMBERS,
WATERCRESS AND MARINATED RED ONIONS _____ 7.25
MOZZARELLA AND GRILLED EGGPLANT SANDWICH WITH BASIL, GRILLED ONIONS,
SUN-DRIED TOMATOES AND AÏOLI _____ 6.75

Pasta

FETTUCINE DELLA CASA WITH BACON, TOMATOES, PINE NUTS, FETA,
PARMESAN AND CREAM _____ 8.50
CAPELLINI WITH HOUSE-CURED SALMON, SORREL, CRÈME FRAÎCHE, ASPARAGUS
AND CAVIAR _____ 9.50
VEGETABLE RAVIOLI WITH RED PEPPER SAUCE, GOAT CHEESE, BASIL,
ROASTED GARLIC AND GRILLED ZUCCHINI _____ 8.75

Entrées

FISH OF THE DAY
BAKED CHICKEN BREAST STUFFED GOAT CHEESE AND MINT; WITH
RED POTATOES AND VEGETABLES _____ 10.75
GRILLED CHICKEN-BASIL SAUSAGES WITH POLENTA, SAUTÉED SPINACH AND
RED ONION RELISH AND MUSTARD _____ 9.25
GRILLED CHINESE EGGPLANT WITH ALMOND COUSCOUS, CURRIED ONIONS AND FENNEL,
AND SAUTEED VEGETABLES _____ 8.75

DINNER - MENU CHANGES MONTHLY

Appetizers

SOUP OF THE DAY _____ 3.95
MIXED GREEN SALAD WITH CROUTONS _____ 4.50
MIXED GREEN SALAD WITH BLUE CHEESE _____ 5.25
CAESAR SALAD _____ 5.75
SPINACH SALAD WITH GOAT CHEESE, ALMONDS, PLUMS, RED ONIONS,
   AND BEET VINAIGRETTE _____ 5.75
PROSCIUTTO AND GRILLED ASPARAGUS WITH EXTRA VIRGIN OLIVE OIL _____ 6.95
SAUTEED CRABCAKES WITH AÏOLI, GREEN BEANS AND FRISEE SALAD TOSSED WITH
   TOMATOES, BASIL, RED ONIONS, OLIVES AND CAPERS _____ 7.50
PASTORAL SALAD (FOR TWO) WITH AVOCADO, MUSHROOMS, BRAISED LEEKS
   GRILLED RED ONIONS, ARTICHOKE HEARTS AND TAPENADE CROUTONS _____ 9.50

Pasta

FETTUCINE DELLA CASA WITH BACON, FETA, TOMATOES, PINE NUTS, PARMESAN
   AND CREAM _____ 9.50
CAPELLINI WITH HOUSE-CURED SALMON, SORREL, CRÈME FRAÎCHE, ASPARAGUS
   AND CAVIAR _____ 10.50
VEGETABLE RAVIOLI WITH RED PEPPER SAUCE, GOAT CHEESE, BASIL,
   ROASTED GARLIC AND GRILLED ZUCCHINI _____ 9.75

Entrées

FISH OF THE DAY
SAUTÉED FILÉT MIGNON WITH BLUE CHEESE SAUCE, ROASTED POTATOES,
   AND VEGETABLES _____ 17.50
GRILLED LAMB LEG WITH BRAISED RED CABBAGE, GRILLED POTATOES, GREEN BEANS,
   ARTICHOKES AND MUSTARD-THYME SAUCE _____ 14.50
BAKED CHICKEN BREAST STUFFED WITH GOAT CHEESE AND MINT; WITH
   WILD RICE FLAN AND VEGETABLES _____ 13.75
GRILLED CHINESE EGGPLANT WITH ALMOND COUSCOUS, CURRIED ONIONS AND FENNEL
   AND SAUTEED VEGETABLES _____ 12.50

a la carte

GRILLED VEGETABLES _____ 4.00   SAUTÉED SPINACH _____ 4.00
STEAMED RICE _____ 1.25   BUTTERED PASTA _____ 4.00

ESPRIT

Salads

Bruschetta	An Appetizer of Grilled Bread with Basil, Tomato, Garlic and Olive Oil	$2.75
Green Salad	Romaine with Parmesan Cheese and a Garlic-Balsalmic Vinaigrette	$3.00
Warren Webber	Mixed Baby Lettuce Salad with Baked Goat Cheese on Garlic Crouton	$5.75
Caesar Salad	Romaine, Anchovies, Garlic, Parmesan Cheese and Toasted Croutons	$6.25
Caffe Cobb Salad	Grilled Chicken Breast, Blue Cheese, Bacon, Avocado, Chopped Egg, Tomato and Garden Lettuces with a Garlic-Balsamic Vinaigrette	$7.75

Grilled Items

Caffe Burger	Grilled Niman Schell Hamburger on a Soft Roll with Lettuce, Tomato, Red Onion, Kosher Dill and Mayonnaise	$6.00
Fontina Burger	Caffe Burger with Fontina Cheese	$6.50
Blue Burger	Caffe Burger with Blue Cheese (Sauteed Onions or Mushrooms $1.00 extra)	$6.75
Muffuletta Burger	Caffe Burger with Garlic, Olives, Giardiniere, Relish	$6.75
Grilled Salmon Sandwich	with Housemade Mayonnaise and Mixed Greens on Grilled French Bread with a Cucumber and Carrot Salad	$8.75

Pizza

		9"	13"
Margherita Pizza	Mozzarella with Garlic, Basil and Tomato	$7.25	$13.50
Pesto Pizza	Pesto with Mozzarella and Parmesan	$8.75	$16.50
Verdure Pizza	Sauteed Onions, Mushrooms, Grilled Eggplant, Tomatoes, and Herbs	$9.25	$17.50
Sausage Pizza	Italian Hot and Fennel Sausage, Mozzarella and Fontina	$9.00	$17.00
Mushroom Pizza	Porcini and Seasonal Mushrooms, Mozzarella	$9.00	$17.00

235 16th St • China Basin • (415) 777-5558

s o d a   f o u n t a i n

Milk Shake or Malt	Vanilla, Chocolate, Strawberry Espresso	**$3.75** **$4.25**	
Ice Cream Soda	Vanilla, Chocolate or Strawberry	**$3.00**	
Italian Soda	Soda with flavored syrups of Mandarino, Apricot, Raspberry, Passion Fruit or Cranberry	**$1.95**	
		Single	Double
Ice Cream Cone	Vanilla, Strawberry or Chocolate	**$1.50**	**$2.25**
Hot Fudge Sundae		**$4.50**	
Caffe Turtle	Vanilla Ice Cream, Hot Fudge, Hot Caramel, Pecans and Whipped Cream	**$4.50**	
Root Beer Float	Root Beer with Vanilla Ice Cream	**$3.00**	
Fountain	Coke, Diet Coke, Root Beer or 7-up	**$1.50**	
Flavored Cokes	with Cherry, Vanilla or Lemon	**$1.75**	
Milk	Regular or Lowfat	**$1.50**	

Egg Cream	**$1.95**	**Fresh Squeezed Lemonade**	**$1.75**
Iced Black Currant Tea	**$1.50**		
		Lemonade Spritzer	**$1.75**
Fresh Squeezed Orange Juice	**$1.75**		

c a f f e   e s p r e s s o

All coffee drinks, regular or decaf, are made with Spinelli Coffee

Coffee	Viennese Blend	**$1.00**
Twining's Tea	Earl Grey, English Breakfast, Black Currant, Peppermint, Cammomile or Rosehips	**$1.00**

		Single	Double
Caffe Latte	**$2.25**	**Espresso**	**$1.00**	**$1.50**
Caffe Mocha	**$2.50**	**Cappucinno**	**$2.00**	
Caffe Vanilla	**$2.50**	**Hot Chocolate**	**$2.50**	

b a r

Beer		**House Wine**	glass	1/2 litre
Rolling Rock	$2.00	Red	$2.50	$6.00
Anchor Steam	$2.25	White	$2.50	$6.00
Sierra Nevada Pale Ale	$2.25		15oz	30oz
Becks Light	$2.50	**Pellegrino Mineral Water**	$2.00	$3.50

CHATEAU SOUVERAIN®

LUNCH MENU

APPETIZERS

VEGETABLE BISQUE
with pesto and creme fraiche   5.00

GRILLED CREAMY BUCKWHEAT POLENTA
with a ragout of tomatoes, leeks, and dry jack cheese   4.50

DEEP FRIED CALAMARI
with cilantro aioli   6.00

GRILLED AND MARINATED PRAWNS
with a sweet red pepper vinaigrette   7.50

SMOKED SALMON WITH AMERICAN CAVIAR
buckwheat blinis and creme fraiche   8.00

ENTREES

GUMBO WITH CHICKEN, SEAFOOD AND ANDOUILLE SAUSAGE
and garlic croutons   9.50

SALAD OF DUCK CONFIT
with sweet roasted peppers, walnuts, blue Castello and apples   9.50

VEGETARIAN PASTA WITH GRILLED SHIITAKE MUSHROOMS
fresh tomatoes, garlic, basil and olive oil   9.50

SMOKED CHICKEN RAVIOLI
with a creamy parmesan dill sauce   10.50

GRILLED MARINATED FLANK STEAK
with a cabernet mint sauce   13.50

GRILLED CHICKEN BREAST ON WILTED SPINACH AND ARUGULA
with mango, and jicama chips   9.50

GRILLED SALMON
with a scallion and a roasted red pepper sauce   15.00

400 Souverain Rd • Geyserville • (707) 433-3141

DINNER SELECTIONS

APPETIZERS

LEEK, SMOKED CHICKEN AND GOAT CHEESE TART   8.50

LINGUINI PASTA WITH ROCK PRAWNS
roasted peppers, capers and arugula   9.50

AHI TARTARE WITH AVOCADO AND BASIL TOAST
and Sonoma greens   8.50

INDONESIAN SHRIMP WITH CILANTRO, GARLIC
marinated cucumber salad   8.50

RAVIOLI WITH FENNEL, PROSCIUTTO AND SWISS CHARD   10.50

SPINACH SALAD WITH SAUTEED PEARS
blue castello and walnuts   7.50

SALAD OF SONOMA GREENS   6.00

ENTREES

GRATIN OF DUNGENESS CRAB
with blood orange buerre blanc
Sonoma dry jack cheese and brioche crust   26.00

SAUTEED SALMON WITH A SMOKED TOMATO BUTTER
sundried tomato salsa   25.00

GRILLED BLACK ANGUS TENDERLOIN
in a cabernet garlic sauce
with roasted red pepper bernaise and rosemary pesto   26.00

SCALLOP AND SMOKED SALMON BOUDIN
fresh dill and lemon buerre blanc sauce   26.00

HERB-CRUSTED CAMPBELL RANCH SPRING LAMB RACK
with caramelized garlic and shallots in a roasted garlic sauce
red lentil puree   30.00

RED TAIL VENISON ON CELERY ROOT PUREE
with a mint juniper zinfandel sauce   27.00

DESSERT MENU

TIRAMISU
creme anglaise

VELVET HAMMER ICE CREAM
with anise cookies

CHOCOLATE MOUSSE CAKE
with mocha creme anglaise

TANGERINE PECAN TORTE

Christopher's Café

LUNCH

CAESAR SALAD fresh romaine with garlic croutons & fresh grated parmesan
                                                    salad for one $6.95
                                                    salad for two $7.95

GARDEN HOUSE SALAD   fresh mixed greens w/garlic croutons, $4.50
                     cherry tomatoes and balsamic vinaigrette
                     with gorgonzola OR goat cheese $4.95

SALMON SHRIMP AND CRABCAKE SALAD On a bed of arugula and endive $7.50
       Tossed in a roasted tomato·vinaigrette with caper mayonaise

BOSC PEAR AND PROSCUITTO SANDWICH served warm and open faced $6.50
                     Served with shoestrings and mixed greens

CRAB SANDWICH   handpicked dungeness crabmeat with melted Jack cheese $7.75
                 and sauteed onions, aioli - served open faced with a
                 mixed green salad

SAUTE
PASTA- EGG TAGLAIRINI WITH PACIFIC SHUCKED OYSTERS,mirepoix,lemon zest $7.50
                     sweet butter and cream

CHICKEN AND ANDOUILLE SAUSAGE RAGOUT with mushrooms, cepes, tomato $7.25
                     concasse, fresh herbs, white wine and parmesan cheese

GRILLS

BROCHETTE OF SALMON AND MAKO SHARK   with a fresh herb lemon zest $7.75
                     aioli- Served on a bed of mixed greens with
                     lentil salad

BLACKENED ROCK COD with basil butter-served with grilled goat $6.50
                    cheese polenta and salsa fresca

BROCHETTE OF PORK LOIN AND SMOKED CHICKEN   center cut pork loin and $7.50
                     and tender breast of chicken marinated with cinnamon
                     juniper, allspice, bay leaves and house smoked with
                     applewood-served with fresh chutney, country white
                     bean stew and vegetables

PILLARD OF CHICKEN with basil almond pesto $6.95
                   Served with new potatoes and vegetables

HAMBURGER   ground chuck on a soft roll with tomato, sweet onion,
             cornichons, housemade mayonaise & shoestring potatoes $6.50

                     with tillamook cheddar OR roast chili (add .50)

---

690 Van Ness Ave • Civic Center • (415) 346-8870

94

DINNER

GRILLED SWEET CORN SOUP with red bell pepper puree $4.00

CAESAR SALAD   fresh romaine lettuce with garlic croutons and fresh $8.95
                grated parmesan

GARDEN HOUSE SALAD fresh mixed greens with garlic croutons, kalamata $3.95
                            with gorgonzola or goat cheese $4.95

ANTIPASTA PLATE   with grilled fennel, eggplant, roasted tomatoes, $5.50
                   asparagus, proscuitto, mushrooms and kalamata olives

FRIED OYSTERS   with cocktail sauce $5.50

MANGO AND AVOCADO SALAD $4.75

SAUTE

PASTA   Spinach Tagliarini with julienned breast of chicken, $12.95
           mushrooms, cepes, tomato concassee, basil and parmesan

SAUTEED CHINESE LAMB   leg of lamb sauteed with jalapeno, ginger, red
                        bell peppers, hoisen sauce, served with spicy green
                        rice and pineapple jicama salsa $12.95

ROASTED BREAST OF LONG ISLAND DUCK   served with baked polenta, $14.25
                      asparagus and mango chutney

PANFRIED SAND DABS served with tartar sauce, new potatoes & vegetable $13.25

GRILLS

"BLACKENED" ROCK COD   served with lime zest butter, corn stew and $12.50
                        vegetables

GRILLED SWORDFISH   with olive butter, lentils and asparagus $14.95

BROCHETTE OF LAMB   cubed leg of lamb marinated with red wine, sweet $14.95
            onions, tarragon and garlic, grilled and served with fresh
            herb aioli, tomato-eggplant gratin and polenta

SMOKED POUSSIN   with fresh herb aioli, country white beans and $13.50
                  mixed green salad

GRILLED MARINATED PORK CHOPS   with barbeque sauce, black beans and $12.95
                     asparagus

HAMBURGER   ground chuck on a soft roll with tomato, lettuce,
             sweet onion, cornichons & shoestring potatoes $7.00
                          with cheddar OR roast chili   (add .50)

15% gratuity will be included for parties of six or more persons.
$10.00 corkage fee.

MENU CHANGES DAILY

Domaine Chandon

Menu Changes Daily

Luncheon

Appetizers

SPRING ONION SOUP with Chives and Creme Fraiche 5.50

CARAMELIZED GRANET ONION AND LEEK PIE with a Feta Vinaigrette 6.75

HOME SMOKED RED TROUT FILET Marinated in Onions on a Bed of Frisée with Warm Potato Slices 7.95

CRISPY POTATO CAKE with PHILIPPE'S SMOKED SALMON and Horseradish Cream 8.75

GRILLED WOLFE FARM QUAIL with Watercress, Belgian Endive, Polenta Croutons and a
Warm Pancetta Vinaigrette 8.95

Fish

ROASTED RED HOT CHILIPEPPER FILET with Black Beans and a Red Anaheim Ragout 12.50

MUSSELS STEAMED IN PINOT MEUNIER, Bay, Thyme, Garlic and Grilled Olive Bread 13.50

GRILLED SALMON with a Sweet Pepper-Grilled Corn Vinaigrette, Yellow Finn Potatoes and Frisée 15.00

TUNA PEPPERSTEAK with Potato Purée and Leek Coulis 16.00

Poultry-Meat

PORK AND SUNDRIED TOMATO SAUSAGES with Celery Root-Potato Cakes and Roasted Red Onions 10.00

ROASTED CHICKEN BREAST with Deep Fried Sage Polenta and a Green Olive-Artichoke Ragout 13.50

ROAST PAINE FARM SQUAB with a Celery Root Purée, English Pea Coulis and Grilled Sunburst Squash 14.50

ROASTED LEG OF LAMB with a Yukon Gold Potato-Goat Cheese Gratin and Black Olive Jus 14.95

Desserts
each at 6.00

TUSCAN CREAM CAKE with Sabayon and Fresh Fruit

CREME BRULEE SCENTED WITH LAVENDER FLOWERS and a Merlot Poached Pear

COFFEE AND CREAM ICE CREAM SANDWICH with a Crunchy Peanut Butter Layer and Hot Fudge

SUMMER POLENTA PUDDING soaked in a Blackberry Coulis with Mascarpone Cream

WARM CHOCOLATE FEUILLETTE with Strawberry Ice Cream and Chocolate Sauce

ALMOND CANNOLIS with Cheesecake Ice Cream and Sundried Apricot Coulis

CHOCOLATE SORBET AND MEYER LEMON ICED CREAM with Biscotti Cookies

1 California Dr • Yountville • (707) 944-2892

DINNER

☆☆ APPETIZERS ☆☆

ASPARAGUS SOUP with Chervil and Creme Fraiche	$6.00
CREAM OF TOMATO SOUP in Puff Pastry	$6.00
HOME-SMOKED SALMON with a Crispy Potato Cake and Horseradish Cream	$8.75
HOME SMOKED RED TROUT FILET Marinated in Onions on a Bed of Frisée with Warm Potato Slices	$7.95
GARDEN GREENS with Herbs	$6.00
ROASTED BEET SALAD with Arugula, Baby Radicchio, Crumbled Feta Cheese and Tapenade Toast	$7.50
GRILLED WOLFE FARM QUAIL with Soft Polenta, Pancetta, and Green Olives	$8.95

☆☆ FISH ☆☆

TUNA PEPPERSTEAK with Potato Purée and Leek Coulis	$24.00
MESQUITE GRILLED ATLANTIC SALMON Asparagus, Grilled Yucon Gold Potatoes and a Sweet Pea Coulis	$24.00

☆☆ MEAT & POULTRY ☆☆

ROASTED PORK TENDERLOIN with Wilted Brussel Sprouts, Apple-Smoked Bacon and a Sweet Garlic Jus	$23.00
GRILLED VEAL CHOP with a Dijon Jus and Roasted Sunchokes	$26.00
ROAST RACK OF LAMB with a Potato-Goat Cheese Gratin and a Roast Garlic-Tarragon Jus	$27.00
ROASTED SQUAB with Celery Root-Potato Cake and Braised Escarole	$26.00
WILD SCOTTISH PHEASANT with Apple-Sweetpotato "Hashbrowns", Morels and Blackberries	$28.00
SWEETBREAD "MILLEFEUILLE" with a Shallot-Truffle Juice Butter	$24.00

BREADS

Jalapeno Corn Stix	$1.25
Cheddar Cheese Bun	1.50
Dutch Crunch Dinner Rolls (2)	1.05
Buttery Leek and Basil Loaf	2.90
All of the above	5.95

BOWLS

Different Soup every day	3.50
Manila Clam Chowder	6.95
Red Curry Mussel Stew	6.80
Sirloin and Black Bean Chili	4.95
Veal Osso Bucco with roasted winter vegetables	12.95

SMALL PLATES

Various fresh chilled Shellfish always available	A.Q.
Onion Rings with homemade ketchup	3.50
Sauteed Asian style Prawns with pickled ginger	5.45
Crabcakes with sherry-cayenne mayonnaise	7.75
Smoked Salmon with horseradish cream and bitter greens	6.95
Garlic Custard with mushrooms, seasoned walnuts and chives	5.60
Grilled Japanese Eggplant, roasted pepper vinaigrette	4.95
Stuffed fresh Pasilla Pepper, grilled, with avocado salsa	6.25
Quesadilla with hazelnuts and tomatillo salsa	6.50
Buffalo Chicken Wings, Stilton bleu cheese dip	4.95
Grilled sesame Chicken with shiitake mushrooms, carrots and chinese mustard	5.25
Marinated Pork Loin satay with mango chutney	5.60

SANDWICHES

Reddened Snapper with guacamole	7.25
Marinated Eggplant, grilled, with Fontina cheese	6.50
Cobb (smoked turkey, avocado, bacon, Stilton cheese, tomato)	7.95
Roast Leg of Lamb, watercress, tomato apricot chutney	7.50
Diner Chili Dog	5.95
Hamburger or Cheese hamburger	7.75

SALADS

Unintimidating Mixed Greens with vinaigrette................ 4.80
     or bleu cheese dressing............................... 4.95
Caesar.. 6.50
Several Salads on a Plate: smoked salmon, goat cheese with
     sweet peppers, beets & lentils with Stilton bleu,
     artichoke heart & fennel, curried carrots with pecans.. 8.95
Chinese Chicken with crispy seasoned peanuts............... 8.50

LARGE PLATES

Fresh Fish Daily.. A.Q.
"Chicken on a Bisquit" with Virginia Ham and cream gravy.... 9.50
Grilled Chicken Breast with dijon, chervil and ginger 11.95
Pork Chop with ginger apple sauce and glazed carrots........10.95
Calf's Liver with apple smoked bacon and red onions........ 9.90
Grilled Rabbit with ancho chile succotash..................12.50
Barbecue Beef Short Ribs with mashed potatoes..............12.95
Grilled Skirt Steak with wild west sauce...................12.95
Veal Osso Bucco with roasted winter vegetables (see BOWLS)

SIDES AND CONDIMENTS

Cole Slaw.. 2.50
Vegetable... 2.50
Polenta with tomatoes, garlic and asiago.................. 2.50
French Fries.. 3.25
Mashed Potatoes... 2.50
Avocado Salsa... 2.50
Mint and cilantro Tomatillo Salsa......................... 1.95
House cured sweet dill Pickles............................ 1.95
One of our nice T Shirts..................................12.50
Crew neck Sweatshirt (also nice)..........................25.00
World Famous "DON'T WORRY" Wristwatch.....................29.95
Official Team Fog City Diner Cap..........................13.50
Exclusive Fog City Diner Sportfishing Cap.................13.50
Way cool Baseball Jacket (Embroidered wool and leather)...225.00

DESSERTS

Chocolate Pecan Brownie ala mode with chocolate sauce....... 5.50
Dutch Apple Pie... 4.50
Dutch Apple Pie ala mode.................................. 5.25
Pear Apricot Currant Bread Pudding with vanilla caramel..... 4.50
Chocolate Orange Creme Brulee............................. 4.25
Ten Dollar Banana Split.......................TODAY ONLY... 6.25
Root Beer Float (Black Cow)............................... 2.95
Milk Shakes and Malteds................................... 3.00
Bailey's Egg Cream (I.D. required)........................ 3.50

No pipes, cigars or those silly clove cigarettes.
Yes, everything is available "To Go" (tell your friends).

LUNCHEON MENU

APPETIZERS

Vegetable Soup with Indian Curry 5.00

Caesar Salad with Anchovies, Sourdough Croutons and Grilled Shrimp 7.50

Salad of Tender Lettuces and Bitter Greens 5.75

Warm Wedges of Flatbread with Sour Cream, House~Smoked Sturgeon and Salmon 9.00

SALADS AND SANDWICHES

Smoked Duck Salad with Greens, Citrus and a Tart Dried~Cherry Vinaigrette 10.50

Maytag Blue Cheese and Artichoke Salad with Lettuces and Greens 7.75

Buttermilk Fried Chicken Salad with Roasted Corn and Ozark Ham
in a Honey Salad Dressing 9.75

Prawn Salad with Tarragon~Apple Vinaigrette 13.25

Roasted Red Onion and Wild Mushroom Salad with Mountain Gorgonzola
and a Leek Vinaigrette 9.50

Home~Ground Grilled Hamburger with Homemade Everything 9.75

Stanford Clubhouse with Sonoma Chicken 12.25

Grilled Chicken Breast with Roasted Eggplant
and Coriander~Chili Mayonnaise on a Baguette 10.50

ENTREES

Grilled Vegetables with Tomato Jam 9.50

Crabcakes with Warm New Potato Salad 15.00

Grilled Salmon with a Horseradish Crust and Watercress Sauce 16.50

Scallop and Prawn Risotto 15.50

Baked Chicken with Sourdough Pudding and a Smoked Tomato Sauce 14.00

Grilled Medallions of Marinated Pork Loin with Grilled Apple
and Green Peppercorn Sauce 12.00

DINNER MENU

FIRST COURSE

House~Smoked Salmon and Sour Cream on a Warm Potato Pancake
with Manchurian Osetra Caviar 10.00

Mushroom, Ozark Ham and Mascarpone Ravioli
with a Sherry Vinegar~Shallot Sauce 8.50

Shellfish Risotto with Scallops and Prawns 11.00

Grilled Shiitake Mushrooms Marinated in Olive Oil and Balsamic Vinegar 8.00

Prosciutto di Parma with D'Anjou Pears and Herbed Flatbread 9.50

Chilled Artichoke with a Caper~Saffron Dip 7.50

Grilled Foie Gras with Late Harvest Riesling Sauce 14.50

SOUP AND SALAD

Caramelized Onion and Thyme Broth with Spring Vegetables 7.00

Organic Lettuces and Greens
with Extra Virgin Olive Oil~Aged Sherry Vinaigrette 7.00

Jumbo Asparagus with a Fine Herbes Vinaigrette and Prawn Rémoulade 9.50

MAIN COURSE

Grilled Vegetables with Wild Rice Cakes and Tomato Jam 16.50

Salmon wrapped in Rice Paper with a Red Pepper~Citrus Coulis 24.00

Roast Saddle of Venison with Golden Delicious Apples
in a Currant~Green Peppercorn Sauce 27.00

Grilled Rocky Chicken Breast with a Potato~Black Pepper Gratin
in a Roasted Garlic~Whole Grain Mustard Sauce 21.00

Smoked and Grilled Sturgeon on a Bed of Cabbage, Bacon and Onions 26.00

Cider~Cured Pork Roast with a Plum Tomato Relish, Thyme Roasted Potatoes
and a Cider Vinegar Sauce 21.50

Oak~Roasted Rack of Lamb with a Corn and Pozole Custard
in a Red Wine~Roasted Red Pepper Sauce 28.50

Grilled Squab with a Ragout of Caramelized Vegetables in Zinfandel Sauce 26.00

Sautéed Veal Medallions with Black Olive Orzo and a Preserved Lemon~Caper Sauce 25.00

Niman Schell Rib Eye with Aged Jack Cheese Potatoes
and an Anchor Steam Beer Sauce 24.50

Whenever possible we use naturally~raised meat, game, poultry, seafood and certified organic produce.

Sunday Brunch; Dinner: 7 Days a Week 5:30 - 11   Ⓑ Ⓛ Ⓓ

FOURTH STREET GRILL

Appetizers & Salads

Black Bean Soup garnished with queso seco	$3.00
Guacamole & tortilla chips	$5.25
Black Pepper Oysters: Fresh oysters poached with black pepper and lime juice, served chilled	$8.50
Deep Fried Calamari: Monterey calamari in a cayenne-beer batter, served with Fourth Street Grill chile sauce	$5.75
Queso Frito: Melted Humboldt County jack cheese, coated with Sonoran spices served with tortilla chips.	$4.50
Mixed Baby Greens with house dressing	$5.50
Spinach, Bacon & Mushroom Salad tossed with mustard dressing, garnished with sieved egg and cracked black pepper	$7.50
Spinach and Feta Salad with red onion, Calamata olives and fresh mint . .	$8.75
Fourth Street Grill César Salad	$8.75
Oaxacan Chicken Salad: made with all-natural chicken, Oaxacan black beans, Fourth Street Grill chile sauce, queso seco, guacamole & tortilla chips on a bed of romaine.	$8.95
Taquitos del Dia: Crisp fried corn tortillas with seasonal filling, Fourth Street Grill chile sauce, guacamole & salsa on a bed of romaine	$5.75
Botano Plate: Two Taquitos de Dia, Calamari, Black Pepper Oysters, salsa fresca, Oaxacan black beans, guacamole, tortilla chips, queso seco & Fourth Street Grill chile sauce	$9.75

1820 Fourth St • Berkeley • (510) 849-0526

Hardwood Grill

Yucatàn Sausages: A house specialty made with pork, chicken chiles, garlic
  & wine, served with black beans and shoestring potatoes $12.50

New Mexico Red Sausages: Fourth Street Grill housemade sausages made
  with pork, beef, New Mexico red chiles, garlic & ale.
  Served with black beans & shoestring potatoes $11.50

Pork Baby Back Ribs with Fourth Street Grill BBQ sauce.
  Served with black beans & shoestring potatoes $12.75

Spit Roasted Chicken: Half of an all-natural chicken marinated with chiles,
  oregano, lemon & olive oil.
  Served with black beans, rice and salsa cruda $10.75

Steak Sandwich: Niman-Schell New York Steak (6 oz.) served on baguette
  with roasted tomato au jus and shoestring potoatoes $12.50

Fourth Street Grill Hamburger, made with freshly ground Niman-Schell
  Chuck. Served with shoestring potatoes $8.50
  With: Chiles or Cheese .... add 75¢   Bacon or Guacamole $1.50

Sauté

Niman-Schell Baby Beef Liver: Sautéed liver with caramelized onions and
  bacon. Served with rice and vegetable $8.25

Grilled Cheese Sandwich made with Humboldt County jack cheese, fire
  roasted chiles, red onion & cilantro on Semifreddi's bread.
  Served with market salad & cup of soup $7.50

BLT made with smoked bacon, tomatoes & romaine on toasted
  Semifreddi's bread, served with market salad $7.75

Sample of Specials Featured Daily

Fresh Washington State Dungeness Crab Florentine: Sautéed with bermuda
  onions and chiles and tossed with roasted purple garlic, yellow tomatoes
  and fresh tomato and herb fettucinis, served on a bed of spinach, topped
  with artichoke mayonnaise and garnished with parmesan cheese $14.00

Baked Penne Pasta: Sautéed spring vegetables baked with a chile-lemon
  cream and topped with bread crumbs and fresh, local made mozzarella . $12.00

Dinner: Tues - Thurs until 9, Fri - Sat until 10, Sun 4 - 9   ●ⓁⒹ

Four Seasons Clift Hotel
SAN FRANCISCO

F R E N C H   R O O M

STARTERS

* Oriental Lobster-Dumpling Soup with Scallions, Shiitake	7.50
Sweetbread Medallions, White Corn and Mushroom Ragoût, Herb Jus	9.50
Terrine of Foie Gras, Grilled Brioche and Brandied Cherries	15.50
French Room Caesar Salad, Sourdough Croutons, Grated Reggiano Parmesan	6.75
Baby Spinach Salad, Pancetta Vinaigrette, Warm Goat's Cheese Croutons	7.50
* Marinated Sea Scallop and Fennel on a Rosemary Brochette	10.50
Smoked Atlantic Salmon, Grappa-Cured Graved-Lax, Spiced Creme Fraiche	11.50
* Fusilli, Eggplant "Caponata"	9.50

Geary and Taylor St • Union Square • (415) 775-4700

Smokey Prawn Chowder, Bintji Potatoes, Baby Leeks   7.50

Capellini, Tomato Cream, Prosciutto, Mushrooms and Peas   9.50

ENTRÉES

Prime Rib of Beef, Yorkshire Pudding, Horseradish Cream   27.50

Medallions of Maine Lobster, Bacon Fried Rice, Chive Butter   32.50

Loin of Lamb on a Bed of Spinach, Roasted Garlic Jus   32.00

Crisp House Smoked Duckling, Soy-Mango Glaze, Scallion Pancakes   28.00

* Free Range Chicken, Grilled Fennel, Oven Roasted Tomato, Garlic 25.00

Broiled Filet Mignon or New York Strip Steak, Confit of Mushrooms,
  Foie Gras Potatoes   31.50

Pacific Salmon with Black-Eyed Pea Salad and Crayfish Gravy   28.00

Grilled Swordfish Steak, Crabmeat Fritters, Tomato Remoulade   31.00

* Ragoût of Seafood, Orrechiette, Red Wine Sauce   28.00

French Room Vegetable Sampling Plate   20.00

* These Selections are Nutritionally Balanced, Lower in Calories,
Cholesterol, Sodium & Fat

Sunday Brunch; Dinner: 7 Days a Week 6 - 10:30   ●●Ⓓ

LUNCH

Soup du Jour	Cup: 1.85	Bowl: 3.00

Smoked and Fresh Salmon Terrine	5.00
Mussel Salad with Apples, Potatoes, Aioli and Carry	4.75
Endive Salad with warm Goat Cheese	4.75
Mixed Green Salad	3.25

Frisee Salad with warm Bacon Dressing and Croutons	6.50
Chicken Sandwich with Avocado and Cheese	7.00
Roquefort Ravioli with Basil and Pinenuts	6.50
Basque Tuna Burger with Salad	7.00
Beef Carpaccio with Lemon, Olive Oil and Ardi–Gasna	7.00

Steamed Mussels, Shallots and Fresh Herbs Vinaigrette	7.00
Duck Confit with Potatoes, Garlic and Parsley	8.50
Basque Sausage with Peppers and Onion Confit	7.00
Steamed Salmon with Crunchy Fennel and Citrus Vinaigrette	10.00
Red Wine Drunken Pork Shoulder with Braised Cabbage and Pears	10.00
New York Minute Steak with Fries	11.75

DINNER

Soup of the Day	Cup: 1.85	Bowl: 3.00

Avocado Salad with Oranges, Basil and Basque Cheese	5.00
Mashed Potatoes and Duck Confit Patti	5.00
Escargot Turnover, Garlic, Parsley and Greens	5.50
Lentil Salad with Mustard Vinaigrette and Smoked Duck	6.00
Artichoke and Sea Scallops Ragout with Balsamic Vinaigrette	6.00
Smoked and Fresh Salmon Rillettes	7.00
Mixed Green Salad	3.25

Beef Carpaccio with Capers, Lemon, Olive Oil and "Ardi-Gasna"	8.50
Frisee Salad with warm Bacon Dressing and Croutons	6.50
Roquefort Ravioli with Basil and Nuts	8.00
Steamed Mussels, Shallots and Fresh Herbs Vinaigrette	8.00
Split Basque Sausage with Peppers and Onions confit	7.50

Steamed Salmon with Crunchy Fennel and Citrus Vinaigrette	10.75
Tuna Steak with Onion Marmalade	11.00
Breast of Chicken "Pane" with Braised Endive	10.00
Red Wine Drunken Pork Shoulder with Braised Cabbage and Pears	10.00
Braised Sweetbread with White Beans Puree and Baby Leeks	12.75
Marinated Roast Rack of Lamb with Natural Juices	14.75
New York Steak "Black Angus" with Red Butter	12.75/18.00

French Fries	1.75
Steamed Spinach	2.00
Potatoes Gratin	2.00
Seasonal Vegetables	2.00

Daily Special	A/Q

MADRONA MANOR

Welcome to the restaurant at Madrona Manor!
I'm pleased to offer you a choice of two price fixed menus.
These menus represent the finest and freshest
ingredients as well as expressing our talents.
Menu items are also available ala carte for the price indicated.
I have also selected wine to compliment each course or
feel free to choose a wine from our Award Winning Wine List.
Bon Appetit!
Todd Muir

THE MADRONA MANOR PRIX FIXE MENU
$40.00

Complimentary Hors d'hoeuvres

PACIFIC SALMON CAKES
made with capers, tarragon and other herbs,
served with a tomato, tarragon and
saffron sauce
8.00

Pedroncelli Chardonnay
'89 Sonoma County
4.50

ARTICHOKE AND BEET SALAD
with olive oil, herbs, and orange served with
greens from the garden
and pecarino cheese
7.50

FILET OF BEEF
marinated and grilled served with roquefort butter, asparagus,
grilled polenta and a cabernet wine sauce
24.00

Hafner Cabernet Sauvignon
'86 Alexander Valley
6.50

STRAWBERRY COCONUT NAPOLEON
puff pastry layered with fresh strawberries and
coconut pastry cream served with raspberry sauce
7.00

Chateau De Baun
'88 Symphony
4.25

THE GOURMET PRIX FIXE MENU
$50.00

SALMON PATE
with smoked sea bass and served with a
sorrel tomato and olive oil sauce
9.00

Dehlinger Chardonnay
'89 Russian River
4.50

BABY CARROT SOUP
from the garden made with chicken stock
served with roquefort custard royal
5.50

PURPLE ASPARAGUS BUNDLES
with parma proscuitto, brunoise of vegetables
and white truffle oil
7.00

Murphy Goode
Pinot Blanc
'90 Alexander Valley
4.50

LAMB LOIN
stuffed with a chicken basil farce
served with lamb reduction, golden beet timbale,
swiss chard from the garden and potato wedges
25.00

Domaine Michel
Cabernet Sauvignon
'87 Sonoma County
7.50

AMARENA CHERRIE ICE CREAM
baked in a phyllo purse with creme anglaise
7.00

Chateau De Baun
'88 Symphony
4.25

coffee/mignardises

(wine, tax and service not included)

APPETIZERS ~ SALADS

CHARLOTTE'S FAVORITE
Masons Signature, Famous Thin-Cut Fresh French Fries
Three Dollars And Fifty Cents

MASONS SYMPHONY
Medallion of Fresh Lobster on an Artichoke Heart, California Foie Gras on a
Bed of Green Beans, and Baby Lettuce Topped with Petaluma Duck
Twelve Dollars And Fifty Cents

CARPACCIO OF PETALUMA SMOKED DUCK
On a Bed of Green Napa Cabbage, Golden Delicious Apple, Walnuts,
and Mission Figs With a Hazelnut Dressing
Nine Dollars And Fifty Cents

MASONS CAESAR SALAD
The Classic American Salad, Prepared Tableside, For Two
Seven Dollars Per Person

FRESH TRENETTE WITH BASIL PESTO
Multi-Colored Fresh Pasta, Lightly Tossed with Basil, Sweet Garlic, and Tomato Fondue
Seven Dollars

SMOKED SALMON PANCAKE
Thin Slices of California Smoked Salmon and Golden New Potato Pancake
Topped With Domestic Black Caviar Served with Chive Sauce
Nine Dollars And Fifty Cents

WARM SALAD OF PETIT GRIS ESCARGOT
Special Choice Greens of the Season Topped with Wild Mushrooms and
Baby Snails, Enhanced with Sweet Garlic and Italian Parsley
Nine Dollars

OAXACA TAMALES
Assortment of Authentic Corn "Masa" Stuffed with Chicken and Beef,
Wrapped in Corn Husk Served with Tomato Cilantro Salsa
Seven Dollars

OYSTERS ON THE HALF SHELL
The Freshest Variety of Oysters Available, Served on the Half Shell
With a Champagne Mignonette or Chef Claude's Spicy Cocktail Sauce
Nine Dollars And Fifty Cents

BABY SONOMA FIELD GREEN
The Finest Greens of the Season with Montrachet Goat Cheese Tossed in a Light Balsamic Dressing
Six Dollars

950 Mason St • Nob Hill • (415) 392-0113

ENTREES

KIAWE GRILLED SALMON
Grilled Fresh Pacific, on a Bed of Field Greens, Wilted with a Warm Tomato Coulis Vinaigrette
Nineteen Dollars And Fifty Cents

REX SOLE
The Finest Pacific Sole, Sauteed and Served With Chives, Lemon and Butter
Sixteen Dollars And Fifty Cents

PRAWNS WITH GINGER
Sauteed Butterflied Tiger Prawns with Ginger Essence,
Served on a Bed of Multi Colored Stracci Fresh Pasta and Tomato Basil Sauce
Nineteen Dollars And Fifty Cents

CHICKEN A L'ALGERIENNE
Half Boneless Petaluma Free Range Chicken, Marinated with Fresh Herbs and Lemon,
Served with Couscous and Lightly Spiced Vegetables
Seventeen Dollars And Fifty Cents

SAUTEED CALF'S LIVER
Pan Seared Fresh Calf's Liver with Sweet Maui Onion and
Served with a Reduced Sauce of Sherry /Wine Vinegar
Eighteen dollars And Fifty Cents

DRY AGED NEW YORK STEAK OR FILET MIGNON
Kiawe Broiled to Your Liking, Served with an Array of
Fresh Garden Vegetables and Bearnaise Sauce
Nineteen Dollars And Fifty Cents

FILET MIGNON GREEN PEPPERCORNS
Thin Cut of Filet mignon, Sauteed and Flamed with Cognac, Served with a Green Peppercorn Sauce
Nineteen Dollars And Fifty Cents

ROASTED SQUAB
Thin Slices of Boneless Squab Served with Fresh Spinach Leaves,
Caramelized Baby Onion, and a Light Juniperberry Sauce
Nineteen Dollars And Fifty Cents

CALIFORNIA RACK OF LAMB
The Finest Sonoma Lamb Rack, Roasted With Fresh Herbs and Garlic Persillade,
Accented with Essence of Thyme au Jus
Twenty-Three Dollars And Fifty Cents

VEAL SWEETBREAD
Crisply Sauteed Sweetbread, Served with a Light Creamy Tarragon Sauce and a Basmati Rice Pilaf
Nineteen Dollars And Fifty Cents

VEAL ESCALOPES FORESTIERE
Tender Slices of Domestic Veal Loin, Sauteed with Wild Mushrooms and Tarragon Chardonnay
Sauce
Nineteen Dollars And Fifty Cents

MASONS STEAK TARTARE
Freshly Hand Chopped Raw Filet Mignon Served with Charlotte's Favorite,
Prepared to Your Taste, Tableside
Nineteen Dollars And Fifty Cents

Dinner: Mon - Sat 5:30 - 10

Wine Train Menu - Dining Car

Our Chef Recommends . . .

Domaine Chandon Brut
$25.00

Spring Mountain Sauvignon Blanc 1987
$19.00

* * * * *

Rutherford Hill Chardonnay 1988
$22.00

Star Hill Pinot Noir 1988
$31.00

Mt. Veeder Cabernet Sauvignon 1986
$35.00

1275 McKinstry • Napa Valley • (707) 253-2111

Prix Fix Dinner:

CHEF'S SEAFOOD ASSORTMENT
Prawns, Scallops, Smoked Salmon and Caviar
* * * *
SEASONAL YOUNG LETTUCES
Tossed with Hazelnut and Sherry Vinaigrette
Wedge of Cambozola Cheese
* * * *
HARLEQUIN SORBET
Raspberry, Kiwi and Papaya

Your Choice of:
FILET OF PACIFIC SALMON
Poached in Court Bouillon with Lobster Sauce
or
MIXED GRILL
Rack of Lamb, Filet Mignon and Quail
With Pancetta, Rosemary, Sauce Chasseur
or
CERTIFIED BLACK ANGUS FILET MIGNON
Marinated in Red Wine and Fresh Herbs
Served Roasted with a Cabernet and Roquefort Sauce
* * * *

Desserts
CHOCOLATE DECADENCE
or
WINE TRAIN DAILY SPECIAL
* * * *

Coffee, Tea and Decaf

No Gratuities Required
$45.00
(PLUS 12% SERVICE CHARGE)
MENUS CHANGE SEASONALLY

LUNCH

APPETIZERS

Yellow Corn and Black Truffle Soup
$5.00

Vegetable, White Bean and Basil Soup "Pistou"
$5.00

Small Salad Greens with Walnut Oil and Lemon Juice
$5.00

Hearts of Romaine Tossed with Aged Parmesan and Garlic Anchovy Croutons
$6.50

Warm Potato Salad with Salmon Tartar
$8.00

Dungeness Crab Cakes with Tartar Sauce
$7.50

Grilled Chicken Salad with a Chili Dressing and Mango Chutney
$7.00

SANDWICHES AND MAIN COURSES

A Niçoise Style Salad with grilled Tuna
$12.00

Dungeness Crab Salad Sandwich on Sourdough
$10.00

Ahi Tuna Salad Sandwich with Capers and Cornichon on Toasted Country Bread
$9.00

Bratwurst grilled with Red Onion Relish and Dijon Mustard on a Toasted Baguette
$9.50

Penne Pasta with Braised Lamb Shoulder and Thyme
$11.00

Halibut with Hazelnuts and Lemon Concasée
$12.00

Grilled Salmon with Herb Dressing and Salad
$12.00

Chicken sautéed with Peppers, Olives, Saffron and Cous-Cous
$13.00

Grilled Rib Eye Steak with Herb Butter and Red Wine
$14.50

Chopped Sirloin Burger with Rosa's Homemade Relish
$9.00

DINNER

Menu Changes Daily

APPETIZERS

Vegetable, White Bean and Basil Soup "Pistou"
$5.00

Small Salad Greens with Walnut Oil and Lemon
$5.00

Hearts of Romaine with Aged Parmesan and Garlic Anchovy Croutons
$6.50

Smoked Salmon and Salmon Tartare
with a Caraway Cabbage Salad and Toasted Brioche
$10.00

Warm Asparagus and Vinaigrette with Sherry Vinegar and Virgin Olive Oil
$7.50

Sautéed Sea Scallops served with Potatoes Provencal
$7.50

Fresh Escargot with Hazelnuts, Roquefort and a Garlic Potato Purée
$9.00

A Country Salad with Breast of Squab, Foie Gras and Walnut Oil
$11.00

Fresh Duck Foie Gras with an Artichoke, Pearl Onion and Sorrel Ragout
$12.50

MAIN COURSES

Sea Bass roasted with Morels and Green Asparagus Tips
$17.00

Salmon served "Ala Nage" with Coriander and Tarragon
$17.00

Chicken sautéed with Peppers, Olives, Saffron and Cous-Cous
$15.00

Grilled Muscovy Duck Breast with Prunes, Onions and Duck Liver
$18.00

Milk fed Veal Chop roasted with Port Vinegar and braised Savoy Cabbage
$19.00

Roast Saddle of Lamb with Candied Garlic Cloves, and Thyme
$18.00

Ranch Raised Venison Medallions with Caramelized Pears
and Sweet Potatoes
$22.00

Black Angus Filet Mignon with Carrot Vichy, Red Wine and Basil
$21.00

THE PAN PACIFIC HOTEL

LUNCH

Soup of the Day 5.75

Chicken and Coconut Soup 5.50

♦ *Ravioli of Eggplant, Morels and Herbs 6.50*

Balinese Beef Satay with Thai Basil and Roasted Peanut Sauce 6.00

Crab Cakes with Creme Fraiche and Tobiko Caviar 7.25
As an Entree 12.50

♦ ♦ ♦ ♦

Caesar Salad with Shaved Reggiano Cheese 6.50

Warm Scallop Salad with Baby Spinach, Meyer Lemon and Chili Vinaigrette 7.25

♦ *Baby Greens Tossed in Lemon Vinaigrette 6.25*

♦ ♦ ♦ ♦

♦ *Grilled Mahi Mahi on Acme Sourdough and Oriental Slaw 12.00*

♦ *Grilled Salmon with Black Bean Butter Sauce, Somen Noodles 14.50*

Roasted Artichoke, Shiitake Mushrooms, Zucchinis, served on Bulgar Pilaf
with Tomato Fondue 11.50

Rock Shrimp Sandwich on Grilled Sourdough Corn Rye, Cucumber and Soja Beansprouts 11.50

Grilled Breast of Free Range Chicken with Kumquat and Mango Relish 12.75

♦ *Pacific Chicken Salad on Field Greens, Rice Wine Vinaigrette 11.75*

Classic American Burger, Grilled Onions and Kettle Chips 9.75

Grilled Tuna Nicoise on mixed Baby Greens with Olives,
Potatoes, Lemon Thyme Vinaigrette 16.00

♦ *These dishes are prepared with a reduced salt and fat content*
in compliance with The American Heart Association guidelines.

Please inquire with the Manager for special arrangements.

---

500 Post St • Union Square • (415) 771-8600

DINNER

♦ *Grilled Quail Marinated with Five Spice,*
Blood Orange Vinaigrette served on Sonoma Greens 8.50

Crab Cakes with American Sturgeon Caviar 8.50
As an Entree 20.50

♦ *Baby Octopus with Chili and Ginger Dressing 8.75*

Sea Scallops Tossed in a Spicy Mint Sauce
served in a Rice Paper Basket 8.50

Chicken and Coconut Soup 5.50

Soup of the Day 5.50

♦ ♦ ♦ ♦

Caesar Salad with Shaved Reggiano Cheese 7.25

Apple and Cress Endive Salad with Spiced Pecans, Smoked Gouda
Warm Bacon Dressing 7.00

Napa Valley Garden Greens Tossed in a Lemon Vinaigrette 6.25

Grilled Tenderloin of Beef, Stir-Fried Shiitake
Mushrooms, Balsamic Vinegar Essence Sauce 22.00

♦ *Seared Ahi Tuna in a Citrus Vinaigrette with Artichokes 22.00*

Roasted Breast of Pheasant, served with Kumquat and Mustard Seed Chutney 19.50

Tiger Prawns and Scallops on Somen Noodles with Mild Chili and Black Bean Sauce 22.50
As an Appetizer 11.00

Roasted Breast of Duck, Gravenstein Apples, Currants and Curry Sauce 17.50

♦ *Provimi Veal Chop, Meyer Lemon and Szechuan Pepper Corns 24.00*

Pan Roasted Salmon, Wrapped in Rice Paper with a Macadamia
Nut Crust, Lemon Grass and Lobster Sauce 20.50

Rack of Lamb, brushed with Spicy Hunan Sauce 26.00

♦ *Trio of Grilled Fish of the Day on a Lentil and*
Thai Basil Risotto 21.50
As an Appetizer 9.50

♦ *These dishes are prepared with a reduced salt and fat content*
in compliance with The American Heart Association guidelines.

Please join us for lunch &
receive a complimentary
beverage and dessert.

Sunday Brunch; Dinner: 7 Days 5:30 - 10:30   Ⓑ Ⓛ Ⓓ

MENU CHANGES DAILY
CHEFS
Anne and David Gingrass

LUNCH

ANNE'S FAVORITE LUNCH SANDWICHES

Grilled chopped steak with onion rings, fried vegetables, and homemade ketchup 9.00

Grilled yellowfin tuna on olive bread with Maui onions and french lentil salad 12.00

Club sandwich with smoked prawns, arugula and grilled bacon on six grain toast 14.00

Home smoked pastrami on pumpernickel with herbed mustard and pickled cabbage 10.00

PASTAS

Grilled gulf shrimp with angel hair, arugula basil pesto and caramelized onion vinaigrette 12.00

Duck and roasted leek raviolis with caramelized onions and balsamic black pepper sauce 10.00

Asian vegetable raviolis with bok choy and mushroom sake sauce 10.00

Chicken and leek sausage with herb linguine, potatoes and mustard orange sauce 10.00

Nantucket clam-filled dumplings with angel hair pasta and spicy parsley sauce 11.50

MAIN COURSES

Roasted Chinese duck with mango vinaigrette and baby spinach salad 15.00

Grilled paillard of salmon with potato watercress salad and celery root remoulade 16.00

Grilled farm raised chicken with baby beets, asparagus and pecan vinaigrette 14.00

Mandarin style Wolfe ranch quail with spicy cinnamon pineapple sauce and baby greens 14.00

Sauteed scallops with black olive, basil, and olive oil vinaigrette on baby greens 14.00

Barbecued szechuan steak with five spicy greens and sweet potato chips 13.50

Grilled veal paillard with apple sweet onion vinaigrette and wild mushroom polenta 15.50

Sonoma lamb chops on herbed potato puree with olive roasted garlic sauce 15.00

DINNER

APPETIZERS

Sweet pea and watercress soup with creme fraiche 6.50

Giant blini with smoked salmon, sour cream and salmon caviar 13.50

Black pepper and pistachio sausage with warm bok choy salad 9.50

David's homemade charcuterie plate with marinated artichoke salad 9.50

Sauteed gulf prawns on a shrimp pancake with pickled vegetable salad and lemongrass sauce 13.50

Marinated tuna with sticky rice salad and horseradish soy vinaigrette 11.50

PASTA COURSES

Louisiana crayfish risotto with fried leeks and roasted red peppers 13.00

Smoked lamb and sun dried tomato raviolis with cumin curry sauce and marinated eggplant 11.00

Black pepper fettucine with caramelized onions and stilton cheese sauce 11.00

Grilled quail with spinach and soft egg ravioli 11.50

Grilled sea scallops with saffron angel hair pasta, fresh basil and sun dried tomato sauce 12.50

MAIN COURSES

Tuna steak grilled rare with uni butter and crispy mixed vegetables 19.50

Roasted Sonoma lamb with garlic potato and nicoise olive sauce 22.00

Chinese style duck with spicy mango sauce on arugula leaves and onions 21.50

Barbecued baby lamb chops with mint vinaigrette and potato sticks 25.00

Grilled squab with black pepper noodle cakes and spicy mushroom sauce 19.50

Roasted salmon with an almond black pepper crust on warm spinach salad 22.50

Crisply sauteed sweetbreads with warm radiccio salad and mustard fruits 19.50

Grilled farm raised chicken stuffed with spinach and pinenuts on creamy parmesan polenta 19.00

Roast rack of veal with caramelized onion butter and arugula salad 25.00

Mandarin style Wolfe ranch quail with blood oranges and baby greens 19.50

THE RITZ-CARLTON
SAN FRANCISCO

The Restaurant

APPETIZERS

Seasonal Oysters on the Half Shell,
Tarragon Cocktail Sauce 9.50

Eggplant and Roasted Pepper Terrine,
Anchovy Olive Essence 7.50

Smoked Salmon with Crisp Potatoes,
Horseradish Cream 12.00

Parma Ham with Shaved Fennel, Parmigiano-Reggiano,
Anchovy Toast 9.00

Warm Caramelized Onion, Goat Cheese and Mushroom Tart,
Seasonal Greens and Walnuts 9.00

Raddichio and Belgian Endive Salad,
Oregon Blue Cheese, Pears and Pecans 7.50

Grilled Marinated Quail, Pear Ginger Chutney,
Goat Cheese Croutons, Seasonal Greens 10.50

Seasonal Greens with Garlic Croutons,
Your Choice of Tarragon Goat Cheese Cream,
Shallot Thyme Vinaigrette or Honey Mustard Dressing 6.50

Three Onion Soup 6.00

Soup of the Day 5.75

600 Stockton St • Nob Hill • (415) 296-7465

120

CHEF STEPHEN MARSHALL'S
SEASONAL DINNER

Leek and Watercress Soup

Salad of Warm Mushrooms and Sundried Tomatoes

Cornmeal Crusted Veal Sweetbreads,
Peppers and Balsamic Vinegar

Trio of Mirror Tortes

$35.00

ENTREES

Warm Scallop and Shrimp Salad with Spinach,
Avocado, Ginger and Sesame Seeds   15.00

Nicoise Salad, Grilled Ahi Tuna, Classic Garnishes,
Three Tapanade Croutons   14.50

Pan Steamed Shellfish with Coconut Milk,
Red Curry and Cilantro on Couscous   15.00

Warm Duck Confit Salad with Lentils,
Spinach and Cranberry Onion Compote   13.50

Vegetable Plate with Cracked Wheat Salad,
Lemon Herb Gremolata   12.50

Fresh Pasta of the Day   15.00

Grilled or Pan Steamed Salmon Medallions
with Orange and Ginger   16.00

Seared Rare Ahi Tuna with Rosemary,
Coriander and Black Peppercorns   19.00

Grilled Soy Glazed Beef Filet,
Eggplant Marmalade, Tarragon Essence   21.00

Grilled Chicken Breast with Mustard, Basil and Pistachios   14.50

Pan Fried Herbed Lamb Loin with Fennel Compote,
Artichokes and Sundried Tomatoes   18.50

Grilled Veal Chop with Wild Mushrooms,
Hazelnuts and Polenta   22.00

Welcome to the Seltzer City Cafe, Our One-of-a-kind Creation.

A SELECTION OF ENTREES:

SELTZER CITY ALFRADA $7.77
A CLASSIC DISH COMBINING CREAM, ROMANO, PARMESAN CHEESE, TOASTED PINENUTS, SHALLOTS, GARLIC, FRESH HERBS AND FRESHLY CRACKED BLACK PEPPER SERVED OVER FRESH PASTA.

LEMON CAPER CHICKEN $7.77
FRESH BREAST OF CHICKEN GRILLED TO PERFECTION AND SERVED WITH A LIGHT LEMON CAPER SAUCE, ACCOMPANIED BY FRESH VEGETABLES AND STEAMED RICE.

QUESADILLA $6.66
FLOUR TORTILLAS FILLED WITH CALIFORNIA JACK CHEESE, TOPPED WITH OUR VERY OWN VEGETARIAN, BLACK BEAN CHILI AND SERVED WITH FRESH SALSA.
(WITH SOUR CREAM ADD $.75; WITH POACHED CHICKEN BREAST ADD $1.50).

LOX, EGGS, AND ONIONS $5.55
FRESH EGGS AND ALASKAN SMOKED SALMON ARE SCRAMBLED WITH PURPLE ONIONS AND SERVED WITH A SELECTION OF FRESH SEASONAL FRUIT AND CREAM CHEESE BAGEL.

WEST TEXAS RIBEYE $8.88
A 7 OUNCE RIBEYE GRILLED WITH A SECRET FAMILY RECIPE SERVED WITH FRESH VEGETABLES, MASHED POTATOES AND CREAM GRAVY.

MATZO BREI WITH RASPBERRY OR PASSION FRUIT SYRUP $6.66
A TRADITIONAL DISH COMBINING EGG, MATZO, AND SELTZER IN A PANCAKE STYLE, WITH NATURAL SYRUP.

SESAME NOODLE SALAD $7.77
A VERY POPULAR CREATION OF FRADA'S MADE WITH FRESH EGG NOODLES SERVED UNDER SKINLESS AND BONELESS BREAST OF CHICKEN AND OUR VERY SPECIAL SESAME PEANUT DRESSING. OUR SESAME DRESSING HAS BECOME SO POPULAR WE HAVE IT BOTTLED FOR PURCHASE ...ASK YOUR SERVER!

SOUPS AND SALADS:

OUR SOUPS AND SALADS COMBINE THE FRESHEST INGREDIENTS AND INCLUDE OUR UNIQUE SPINACH-BASIL BAGUETTE BREAD. TWO HOMEMADE SOUPS ARE OFFERED DAILY. OUR SALADS OFFER SELECTED SEASONAL GREENS GENTLY TOSSED WITH OUR HOUSE VINAIGRETTE OR OUR HOMEMADE LIGHT POPPYSEED DRESSING.

SOUP DU JOUR - CUP	$2.75	BOWL	$3.75
HOUSE SALAD - SMALL	$3.77	LARGE	$5.55
	SOUP & SALAD	$5.75	

A SELECTION OF SANDWICHES:

ADD $2.00 TO INCLUDE HOUSE SALAD OR FRESH POTATO SALAD OR SOUP DU JOUR.

CHICKEN SALAD SANDWICH $4.95
OUR CHEF'S SPECIAL RECIPE, MADE DAILY IN OUR OWN KITCHEN COMBINING POACHED CHICKEN, CELERY, PURPLE ONION, TOASTED PECAN, APPLE CARROTS, STOPLIGHT BELL PEPPERS, MAYONNAISE AND FRESH HERBS SERVED ON TOMATO BASIL BREAD.

ALBACORE TUNA SALAD SANDWICH $4.95
THE HIGHEST GRADE DOLPHIN-SAFE TUNA COMBINED WITH A DELICIOUS MAYONNAISE DRESSING SERVED WITH LETTUCE, TOMATO, AND PICKLE ON TOMATO BASIL BREAD.

VEGGIE BURGER $4.88
A DELICIOUS ALL VEGETABLE PATTY GRILLED ON AN ONION ROLL WITH LETTUCE, TOMATO, SWEET ONION AND PICKLE. ADD $.75 FOR SAUTEED MUSHROOMS, $1.00 FOR BLACK BEAN CHILI, OR $.75 FOR YOUR CHOICE OF JACK, CHEDDAR OR SWISS CHEESE.

SELTZER CITY BURGER $4.95
GRILLED EXTRA LEAN GROUND BEEF ON AN ONION ROLL WITH LETTUCE, TOMATOES, SWEET RED ONION AND A PICKLE. ADD $.75 FOR SAUTEED MUSHROOMS, $1.00 FOR BLACK BEAN CHILI, OR $.75 FOR YOUR CHOICE OF JACK, CHEDDAR OR SWISS CHEESE.

BAGEL, LOX AND CREAM CHEESE $5.55
SLICED ALASKAN SMOKED SALMON SERVED ON AN ONION BAGEL WITH CREAM CHEESE, SWEET RED ONION, TOMATOES, LETTUCE & CAPERS.

SIDE: DISHES TO COMPLEMENT YOUR MEAL:

FRADA'S FABULOUS KNISHES $2.50
TAKE HOME 6 FOR $12.00 OR A BAKER'S DOZEN FOR $21.00 (SAVE $11.50)

POTATO: THE ORIGINAL LIGHTLY PEPPERED FILLING OF POTATO AND ONION IN OUR SPECIAL PASTRY SHELL. TO THIS TRADITIONAL BASE, WE ADD FRESH INGREDIENTS TO MAKE THE OTHER POPULAR COMBINATIONS INCLUDING:

BROCCOLI-CHEESE KNISH: FILLED WITH CHUNKS OF BROCCOLI AND GRATED CHEDDAR CHEESE
KASHA KNISH: SAVORY BUCKWHEAT GROATS, A UNIQUE ETHNIC SPECIALTY
SWISS CHARD, GARLIC & MUSHROOM KNISH: FOR GARLIC LOVERS!

FRESH POTATO SALAD $2.25
VEGETARIAN BLACK BEAN CHILI $2.95
MASHED POTATOES & CREAM GRAVY $2.77

SEASON FRESH FRUIT $3.95
BAGEL CREAM CHEESE & TOMATO $1.77
SAUTEED MUSHROOM $2.55

THE SHERMAN HOUSE

N.V. Mumm RE
Brut Prestige
$8 gl.

Lobster in Filo with Spring Peas and Tarragon Cream

* * *

Artichoke and Smoked Salmon Soufflé

* * *

1990 Acacia Carneros
Pinot Noir
$6 gl.

Roast Duck with a Savory Apple Thyme Galette
and Kumquat Marmalade

* * *

1990 Muscat de
Beaumes de Venise
$7 gl.

Warm Rhubarb Crumble Tart with Strawberry Ice Cream

* * *

Coffee

55.00

2160 Green St • Pacific Heights • (415) 563-3600

APERITIFS & WATERS

Kir Royal 9.50

Virgin Mary 5.00

Dubonnet Red 5.00

Perrier, Evian Water (large) 7.00

N.V. Roederer Estate Brut *glass* 8.00

1988 Guenoc Estate Chardonnay *glass* 6.00

1987 Domaine Michel Cabernet Sauvignon *glass* 6.00

A LA CARTE

Lobster Minestrone with Sea Shell Pasta au Pistou 8.00

Risotto of Duck Confit with Warm Plum Salad and Caramel Vinegar Sauce 8.50

Squab Salad with Early Asparagus and Black Truffle Vinaigrette 9.00

* * *

Rack of Lamb Pastorale with Spring Vegetables
and Natural Juices Enhanced with Roasted Garlic 28.00

Seared Salmon with Potatoes and Artichokes Parisiennes,
a Little Watercress Salad and Meyer Lemon Vinaigrette 26.00

Striped Sea Bass Baked on a Bed of Sweet Onions with
Creamy White Beans and Sage 25.00

Sunday Brunch; Dinner: Sun - Thurs 5:30 - 9:30, Fri - Sat 5:30 - 10 Ⓑ Ⓛ Ⓓ

SHOWLEY'S
AT MIRAMONTE

Spring Dinner Menu
Changing Daily

Starters:

Vineyard sampler of our own veal pistachio pate, duck rillettes and marinated goat cheese -- 7.00

Petrossian smoked salmon with capers, sliced red onions and apple chutney -- 8.00

Bitter greens tossed with lardons, garlic slivers served with marinated chevre and garlic toast points -- 6.00

Mixed greens tossed from Forni-Browns organic garden with mustard vinaigrette and parmesan -- 5.00

Caesar salad with baby romaine, croutons and parmesan --6.50

Steamed whole scallops in the shells with shallots, garlic, saffron, fennel, cream and chardonnay --8.00

Grilled Japanese eggplant served on a bed of caramelized onions with balsamic vinegar, capers & pesto -- 6.50

Risotto with tiger shrimp, sweet bell peppers, saffron, and wild mushrooms -- 7.00

Santa Fe lasagna with New Mexican chilies, chevre, flour tortillas. cilantro pesto and aged jack cheese -- 7.00

Four onion soup with creme fraiche and pesto -- 5.00

Main Course Selections:

Sauteed Eastern monkfish with leeks, garlic, wild mushrooms, and pink peppercorns -- 15.00

Grilled farmed raised white sturgeon served with a caper aioli sauce -- 16.00

Sauteed veal sweetbreads with mushrooms, shallots and whole grain mustard sauce -- 16.50

Grilled New York steak served with mushrooms madeira sauce and garlic mashed potatoes -- 19.00

Curried leg of lamb with poppadums, rice sticks and apple ginger chutney -- 15.00

Grilled range lamb loin served with a merlot-rosemary sauce -- 18.00

Grilled pork tenderloin served with an ollalieberry-cabernet sauce -- 15.00

Seared duck breast marinated in balsamic vinegar with green peppercorn sauce and apple chutney -- 19.00

Roast chicken halves partially boned and stuffed under the skin with sundried tomatoes, shallots, mushrooms, and parmesan served with a garlic sauce -- 13.00

Grilled chicken breast, boned and served with a lemon mustard cream sauce -- 14.00

Fresh fettucine with grapevine-smoked chicken and sauteed garden vegetables -- 14.00

Penne pasta tossed with fresh ricotta, tomatoes, black pepper and parmesan -- 11.00

Dinner: Tues - Sun 6:00 - 9

Luncheon

Grilled Prawns with Basmati Rice Salad and Spicy Asian Pesto 9.50
Chicken and Sun Dried Tomato Spring Rolls 7.00
Hearts of Romaine with Croutons and Sesame Dressing 7.25
Sesame Chicken and Asparagus Salad 8.00
Seasonal Farm Greens with House Vinaigrette 6.50

Prawn Dumpling Soup 5.75
Tomato Lemongrass Soup 5.50
Our Daily Soup 5.50

Scallops and Prawns in Black Bean Sauce with Fried Rice 16.75
Steamed Salmon in Chinese Cabbage with Citrus Sauce 16.50
Marinated Grilled Poussin with Shoestring Potatoes 17.75
Peking Duck Salad with Noodles 15.00
Lobster Ravioli with Scallion Butter Sauce 18.00
Asian Spiced Lamb with Potato Cucumber Purée and Asparagus 17.50
Light Lunch A.Q.
Daily Special

Dinner

Grilled Prawns with Greens and Spicy Asian Pesto 10.00
Chicken and Sun Dried Tomato Spring Rolls 8.50
Smoked Salmon with Crispy New Potatoes, Créme Fraîche and Caviar 9.25
Hearts of Romaine with Croutons and Sesame Dressing 8.75
Seasonal Farm Greens with House Vinaigrette 7.50

Prawn Dumpling Soup 6.50
Tomato Lemongrass Soup 5.50

Asian Marinated Lamb with Potato Cucumber Purée and Roasted Eggplant 25.00
Grilled Ahi Tuna with Lemon Cilantro Butter 24.00
Lobster Ravioli with Scallion Butter Sauce 26.00
Grilled Veal Chop with Shiitake Mushrooms and Black Bean Sauce 27.00
Steamed Salmon in Chinese Cabbage with Citrus Sauce 22.00
Gingered Seafood Stew 25.00
Peking Style Orange Duck (for two) 45.00

Ken Hom
Consulting Chef

Michele Sampson
Executive Chef

Voted 9th Best Hotel in the World by
Institutional Investor Magazine 1991-92

SONOMA MISSION INN®& SPA

LUNCH
AT THE GRILLE

MAIN PLATES

Poached salmon
vegetable roulades, roasted tomato vinaigrette ... 13.50

Grilled Sonoma turkey paillard
citrus fruit, field greens, toasted walnut dressing ... 12.50

Dungeness crabcakes
warm vegetable slaw, roasted garlic tartare sauce ... 15.50

Seared ahi tuna
oriental vegetables, lotus-root chips ... 14.50

Grilled chicken breast
lemon chutney, minted tabouleh ... 12.50

Pan-seared sea bass with a coriander-cumin crust
saffron coulis, sweet onion confit ... 13.25

Marinated flank steak
blue cheese, tobacco onions ... 14.00

Tomato linguine
porcini mushrooms, green onions, steamed mussels, clams ... 12.75

18140 Sonoma Hwy • Sonoma • (707) 938-9000

DINNER
AT THE GRILLE

SALADS

Caesar salad
shaved parmesan, croûtons ... 7.50

Spinach salad
smoked onions, marinated mushrooms,
warm blue cheese dressing ... 7.50

Mixed Sonoma greens
shallot vinaigrette ... 6.75

MAIN PLATES

Sautéed salmon
niçoise vegetables, basil pesto ... 19.50

Grilled swordfish
tomato linguine, asiago cheese sauce,
black olive tapenade ... 21.00

Rosemary-crusted sea bass
carrot coulis, haricots verts, potato gnocchi ... 18.50

Filet of beef
crispy twice baked potato, baby mustard greens,
fresh tomato crudité ... 25.50

Roast chicken breast
stuffed with wild mushrooms on potato purée,
fennel, saffron tomato sauce ... 18.50

Rack of lamb
leek and potato gratin, grilled vegetables ... 28.50

Roast pheasant
rhubarb sour-cherry sauce, wild rice soufflé ... 22.00

T R U D Y S
R E S T A U R A N T

APPETIZERS

CAESAR SALAD WITH AGED ASIAGO 4.50 / 7.50

TOSSED SALAD WITH KONA KAI GREENS,
SIMPLY DRESSED 4.95

PEAR, GORGONZOLA, PINE NUTS, ENDIVE & RADICCHIO
IN A HAZELNUT VINAIGRETTE 7.95

VIETNAMESE SHRIMP & CRAB CAKES ON MINTED GREENS
WITH NUOC CHAM 6.50

POTATO LATKES WITH HOUSE SMOKED SALMON,
CREME FRAICHE & CAVIAR 7.50

GRIDDLED PASILLA CORN CAKE WITH SALSA NEGRA
& LIME SOUR CREAM 5.50

TUSCAN TOAST WITH AN ANCHOVY BASIL BUTTER
& ROASTED GARLIC 5.95

POT STICKERS FROM THE GREAT WALL WITH THREE
DIPPING SAUCES 5.95

BEER BATTERED COCO PRAWNS WITH MANGO MUSTARD
MARMALADE 8.75

PASTAS, ET CETERA

A CLASSIC ITALIAN PUTTANESCA WITH SPAGHETTINI 7.50

HICKORY GRILLED CHICKEN RISOTTO WITH A TOUCH OF
ROSEMARY OIL 9.50

PRAWNS, ARTICHOKES, DRIED TOMATOES, OLIVES & ROAST
GARLIC ON FRESH PASTA 15.50

MAIN COURSES

ROTISSERIED HALF CHICKEN, GARLIC MASHED POTATOES
& MIXED VEGETABLES 12.95

PAELLA: LOBSTER, CHICKEN, SHELL FISH & SAUSAGE
IN SAFFRON / TOMATO BROTH 17.95

SAUTEED CALVES LIVER SMOTHERED IN ONIONS WITH
SCALLOPED POTATOES 11.95

STEAK SUZANNE: GRILLED BLACK ANGUS FILET MIGNON
WITH WOODLAND MUSHROOM SAUCE, SCALLOPED
POTATOES, PEAS & CARROTS 18.50

SMOKED & GRILLED 12 OZ. PORK CHOP WITH GREEN
APPLE MARMALADE, SWEET POTATO LATKES & SUGAR
SNAP PEAS 14.50

TURKEY SCALLOPINI WITH CRANBERRY BUTTER SAUCE,
SAGE BREAD, MASHED POTATOES & MIXED VEGETABLES
13.50

FRESH SEAFOOD CHANGES DAILY
• SAMPLE DAILY SPECIALS •

FAIRY'S FEAST: A SELECTION OF AMATORY MORSELS
INCLUDING LOVE APPLE, MARINATED ARTICHOKES,
CUBAN SUPERMAN OLIVES, RAW OYSTERS, GRILLED
ASPARAGUS AND SPICY STEAMED SPOT PRAWNS ON A
BED OF DRESSED SPINACH 10.95

FARM RAISED AND RAN AWAY SALMON GRILLED WITH
GINGER LIME VINAIGRETTE, GRILLED PENCIL ASPARAGUS
AND SESAME SOBA NOODLES 14.95

CARNAL SMOKED AND JEZEBEL ROASTED SPICED GOAT
SLICED THIN WITH WOODLAND MUSHROOMS,
OVEN ROASTED POTATOES AND BEANS FROM
THE BLUE LAKE 13.95

Appetizers

Choice of Norwegian or Scottish Smoked Salmon . . . . $ 13.50
   Hand-carved table-side

Butterfly of Domestic & Imported Caviars . . . . $ 52.00
   With traditional garnish

Santa Cruz Abalone . . . . $ 12.50
   Shredded with Chervil and Tomatoes in a Saffron Broth

Chef Joël's Duck Paté of Sonoma Foie Gras . . . . $ 16.00

Shrimp Noodles on Spinach Leaves . . . . $ 9.50
   Fresh Sea Urchin Roe, Roasted Shallots & Pimento Sauce

Fillet of Baby Salmon . . . . $ 11.50
   Braised with Golden Caviar and Dry Vermouth

Soups & Salads

Consommé of Duck . . . . $ 7.50
   With Cheese Profiteroles

Chilled Mousseline of
   Leek & Sorel . . . . $ 7.50

Maine Lobster Bisque . . . . $ 8.25

Celery Victor's . . . . $ 9.50
   Chilled, Braised Celery Heart, Bay Shrimps,
   Tomatoes, Vinaigrette Dressing

Main Courses

Fillet of Pacific Salmon .... $ 26.00
Tarragon Sauce

Napoleon of California Smoked Sturgeon .... $ 26.00
With Indian Garlic Papad, Cardamon and Pinot Noir Sauce

Symphony of Scallops, Sea Bass & Salmon .... $ 25.00
Wrapped in Roasted Seaweed and Coulis of Parsley

Gratin of Scampi with Shiitake Mushrooms .... $ 28.00
And Peruvian Purple Potatoes

Sauteéd Maine Lobster in Sweet Basil Sauce .... $ 34.00
On North Beach Pasta

Vegetarian Plate .... $ 19.00
Artichoke Bottom filled with a Medley of Celery, Cucumber, Cauliflower,
Mushrooms, Spring Onion, Lightly Cooked and Marinated in Tomatoes
and Saffron

Sauteéd Breast of Range-Fed Chicken .... $ 19.50
With Crayfish, Mango, Papaya and Exotic Fruit Curry Sauce

Breast of Muscovy Duck Stuffed with Chinese Mushrooms .. $26.00
Medjool Date and Anis on Crispy Noodles

Roasted Tenderloin of Pork Glazed with Vermont Maple Syrup $ 22.00
Caraway Sauce and Candied Shallots

Veal Medallions with Stuffed Morel & Pistachios .... $ 32.00
Roasted Oregon Hazelnut Sauce

Lightly Smoked Rack of Lamb .... $ 29.00
Four Beans Ragout, Sweet Garlic Sauce

Filet of Beef with Gratin of Mustard & Fine Herbs .... $ 28.00

Desserts

Stilton Blue Cheese .... $ 7.50

Selection of Victor's Pastries From The Cart .... $ 6.50

Choice of Victor's Hot Soufflés .... $ 9.50
Please allow 15 minutes for preparation.

Frosted Nougatine & Fresh Fruit Salad .... $ 7.50

Gratin of Spring Berries .... $ 7.50
With Grand Marnier Sabayon

BEEF

STIR-FRIED BEEF ผาช่เตาธาฐ์ **$6.00**
With ginger chips and green onions (country style)

STIR-FRIED BEEF ผาช่เตาธาผู๋ต **$6.00**
With four varieties of seasonal mushrooms, in an oyster sauce.

PORK

SAUTEED PORK ผาช่เผ็กธาผู๋ตธิธ เต่าช่ผ๋าณธาช่ธี่ **$6.00**
With mushrooms and cashew nuts in oyster sauce.

SLICES OF PORK AND FRESH SHRIMP เตช่ตุตผาช่เผ็ก **$6.00**
Served over baked eggplant with a light garlic seasoning. (Country style)

SLICED AND SAUTEED PORK ธาชี่ผู๋วผาช่เผ็ก **$7.00**
With bean thread noodles, wild black mushrooms and banana blossoms.

POULTRY

BREAST OF CHICKEN AND SHRIMP เตช่ตุต **$6.00**
Served over baked eggplant, with a hint of garlic. (Country style)

STIR-FRIED BONELESS CHICKEN ผาช่มาธ่ธาฐ์ **$6.00**
With fresh ginger and green onions. (country style)

SEAFOOD AND SHELLFISH

WHOLE FISH **$8.00**
Marinated in spices, and wok-fried. (Country style - exquisite!)

SAUTEED SHRIMP **$8.00**
With winter melon in an oyster sauce. (As served in the Buddhist Patriarch's Palace.)

SHRIMP OR PRAWN CURRY **$8.00**
In a heavy coconut sauce. (Please specify mild, medium, hot or very hot.)

DEEP-FRIED POMPANO FISH **$9.00**
Served with tomatoes, cucumbers, onions, and sweet and sour sauce.

HOUSE SPECIALTIES

A-MOK FISH MOUSSE **$9.00**
Made with coconut milk and spices, steamed in a banana leaf. (A tropical ecstasy!)

CHICKEN AND MUSHROOMS **$9.00**
Galanga and lime' leaves with coconut milk and spices, baked in a banana leaf.

STUFFED CHICKEN LEGS (ANGKOR PALACE) .. **$9.00**
Baked to crispy perfection.

BARBECUED JUMBO RIVER PRAWNS **$10.00**
*Served in the shell with white lotus blossom sauce of coconut milk,
powdered ginger, roasted peanuts and green onion.*

SAUTEED FROG LEGS **$10.00**
Cambodian style & finger licking good!

TWO SQUABS **$12.00**
Deep-fried and crispy with lemon mint and garlic sauce.

SIZZLING MIXED SEAFOOD CURRY PLATTER . **$12.00**
A Rhapsody of flavors (please specify mild, medium, hot, or very hot sauce.)

THE ANGKOR PALACE ROYAL FIRE POT . **$20.00**
Beef, squid, prawns, clams, octopus, fish slices and vegetables. This noble dish, **$30.00**
which was once served only at the king's table, is now offered to our **$40.00**
discrimating guests. Cooked at your table by our staff.

LUNCH MENU

ENTREES

"JERKED" CHICKEN *A Jamaican Bar-B-Q* seasoned w/ ginger, chiles, garlic scallions, and allspice. Served with fried coo-coo and sauteed vegetables 9.95

"ANGRY" PORK TENDERLOIN w/ black beans, rice, salsa cruda & warm flour tortillas 11.95

SEAFOOD SPECIAL . . . . priced daily

DIEGO'S DAILY PASTA SPECIAL *Delve into his twisted mind!* . . . . priced daily

ROCK SHRIMP QUESADILLA w/ black beans and salsa cruda 9.00

PEARL'S PATTY a yuca turnover w/ chicken, beef, pork, olives & raisins on spicy tomato sauce 6.95

DINNER MENU

SOUPS, SALADS & LITTLE THINGS

*ASSORTED HOMEMADE BREADS 2.75

*JAM HOUSE MIXED GREEN SALAD w/ a roasted tomato vinaigrette 5.00

*HEARTS OF PALM & JICAMA SALAD w/ papaya & a green onion-coconut dressing 6.50

*TROPICAL ROMAINE SALAD w/ spicy corn bread croutons, goat parmesan and a coconut-garlic dressing 6.50

*BLACK-EYED PEA FRITTERS w/ ajilimojili sauce 4.50

*DEEP FRIED CATFISH "FINGERS" w/ Trinidadian pepper & cilantro sauces 7.50

*SOUP O DE DAY 4.50

*OYSTER HOT SHOT! served in a shot glass w/ chile-ginger salsa 1.50

TAPAS

*AHI TUNA CARPACCIO w/ sesame-ginger-soy vinaigrette and deep fried onion strings . .
. . . . 9.00

*MARINATED SEAFOOD PLATE a nightly assortment the freshest available seafood
served w/ an array of salsas, vinaigrettes and marinades 10.00

*ROCKSHRIMP QUESADILLA w/ roasted chiles, corn, mushrooms, green onions & jack
cheese 10.00

*PORK SPARE RIBS w/ spicy chipotle chile-orange-honey glaze and emerald noodles 7.75

*HOUSE CURED SALMON w/ olive-pecan tapenade, lemon-parsley toasts and warm goat
cheese 8.00

*SEARED SCALLOPS WITH POTATO CRUST and a citrus-ginger beurre blanc . . 9.75

*PEARL'S PATTY- a yucca dough turnover w/ beef, chicken, pork, almonds, olives &
raisins 8.00

*CHEF DELICIOUS' JERKED CHICKEN OR PORK 8.00

MAIN COURSES

*PENNE PASTA GRATIN w/ prawns, roasted peppers, corn, garlic & tomato-chipotle chile
sauce 12.50

*GRILLED CHICKEN BREAST "ALA BAYOU" w/ red beans, grilled eggplant,
andouille sausage, tasso ham, mushrooms, garlic and a spicy creole hollandaise sauce . . 14.00

*SAUTEED DUCK BREAST w/ cornbread stuffing, sweet potato puree, braised red cab-
bage and ginger-mango demi glace 14.50

*BLACKENED RIB EYE STEAK w/ corn-chayote succatash, garlic-potato gratin & ancho
chile butter 17.50

*ANGRY PORK *(HE'S BACK AND MADDER THAN EVER)* w/ spicy black beans, coconut
rice, salsa cruda and warm flour tortillas 14.50

*GRILLED RARE AHI TUNA w/ sesame cabbage, shiitakes & ginger-star anise butter
sauce 16.00

*GRILLED MAHIMAHI w/ a "tandoori" glaze (cumin-lemon-garlic curry paste), papaya
salsa, tomato chutney, banana-cucumber raita & eggplant relish and almond couscous . . 15.00

CHEF JOEY ALTMAN   SOUS CHEF DIEGO SALINAS

APPETIZERS

ONION CAKE

蔥油餅

1.75

•

DUMPLINGS

紅油煮餃

3.50

•

EGG ROLLS

春卷

3.75

•

DEEP FRIED DUMPLINGS

炸水餃

3.95

•

FRIED DUMPLINGS
WITH SWEET AND SOUR SAUCE

甜酸餃

4.25

•

MO SI VEGETABLES

米穗菜

7.95

•

SIZZLING RICE SHRIMP

鍋巴蝦仁

10.25

•

217 Columbus Ave • North Beach • (415) 788-7527 • (Call for Additional Locations)

ENTRÉES

à la carte
OLD COUNTRY HOT AND SPICY DISHES
·
fish

THREE DELICACIES
燴三鮮
11.50
·
BRANDY'S DINNER
何家湖南菜
11.50
·
OLD COUNTRY SCALLOPS
湖南干貝
10.25
·
HUNANESE WHOLE FISH
湖南全魚

small 12.50   medium 13.75   large 14.95
·
BRAISED ROCK COD FILLETS
紅燒魚塊
7.50
·
BRAISED FISH BALLS WITH VEGETABLES
紅燒魚丸
7.50
·

SMOKED PRODUCTS

brandy ho's
hunan smoked products

Our smoked products, including ham and bacon, are smoked and prepared here on the premises. We burn real old fashioned hardwood in the smoking process to obtain the distinct strong taste so popular in Hunan Province of Old China. (Note: Much stronger smoked flavor then domestic meats.)
·
OUR OWN SMOKED HAM

7.95
·
OUR OWN SMOKED CHICKEN

7.95
·

CHINA MOON CAFE

MENU CHANGES EVERY THREE WEEKS

Nibbles:

Mandarin Breadtwists $2.75 (small bundle) $4.75 (large bundle)
Szechwan-Style Cold Stringbeans with Minced Dried Shrimp $2.25

Appetizers:

House Salad of Baby Lettuces, Crunchy Red Cabbage & Fresh Waterchestnuts
in a Ginger Vinaigrette $4.75

Meatball Soup! Tiny Pork Meatballs, Glass Noodles & Spinach in a Roasted
Garlic & Chicken Broth $4.75

Crispy Springrolls Stuffed with Minced Beef, Fresh Chiles & Glass Noodles
with a Peanut-Lime Dipping Sauce $5.50

Individual Pizzeta Topped with Red Onion Confit, Sweet Chinese Eggplant Coins,
Wok-Seared Shiitake Mushrooms & Fresh Coriander Pesto $7.75

Cold-Tossed Salad of Plum Wine-Marinated Chicken Ribbons, Baby Greens,
Gingered Red Cabbage Slaw & Toasted Almonds in a Sweet Mustard
Sauce $7.75

Peking Antipasto: Cold Wok-Seared Spicy Shellfish with Lemony Cold
Dragon Noodles, Orange-Pickled Carrots & a Salad of Baby Greens $9.50

---

639 Post St • Union Square • (415) 775-4789

Gingery Carrot Soup with Toasted Almonds $4.75
  Crispy Springrolls Stuffed with Curried Vegetables, Fresh Chiles, Glass
  Noodles & Crushed Peanuts $5.50

Deep-Fried Corn & Pork Won-Ton with a Green Chili Dipping Sauce, Corn & Fresh Water
  Chestnut Relish $6.50

Cold-Tossed Salad of Fresh Maine Crabmeat, Baby Lettuces, Chinese
  Chives, Fresh water Chestnuts & Crispy Rice Sticks in a Lemon-Ginger
  Vinaigrette $7.75

Entrées:

Pot-Browned Noodle Pillow Topped with Spicy Pork Ribbons, Ruby Chard,
  Wild Mushrooms & Fresh Asparagus in a Light & Spicy Hoisin-Orange
  Sauce $17.75

Stir-Fried Broad Chinese Egg Noodles with Chunks of Fresh Bass, Fresh
  Water Chestnuts, Baby Bok Choy, Carrot Batons & Purple Basil in a
  Spicy Fresh Lemon Sauce $16.75

Mick Mandarins! Crispy Nuggets of Chicken Breast in a Tart & Tangy Strange-
  Flavor Sauce with Sautéed Chinese Greens & Almond Fried Rice $17.50

Sandpot Casserole of Fresh Clams & Prince Edward Island Mussels with Wok-Seared
  Andouille Sausage Coins, Napa Cabbage & Asparagus Nuggets in a Zesty Hot
  & Sour Sauce with Scallion Fried Rice $16.50

Pot-Browned Noodle Pillow Topped with Spicy Chicken, Ruby Chard, Spring Peppers,
  Zucchini & Crispy Cashews in Hot Bean Sauce $17.25

Steamed King Salmon on a Bed of Daikon Wheels with Ginger-Black Bean Vinaigrette,
  Pan-Fried Corn Fritters & Scallion Fried Rice $18.50

Sandpot Casserole of Pork Sparerib Nuggets, New Potatoes, Oven-Dried Plum
  Tomatoes & Sweet Chinese Eggplant in a lightly Spicy Tomato-Soy Sauce with
  Scallion Fried Rice $16.75

Barbara Tropp * Chef/Owner

China Moon Cafe uses only fresh ingredients & no MSG.
Autographed copies of <u>The Modern Art of Chinese Cooking</u> and
<u>The China Moon Cookbook</u> are available at the host stand.

GREAT EASTERN RESTAURANT

A
$11.50 per person

EGG ROLL
BARBECUED SPARERIBS
WON TON SOUP
CASHEWNUT CHICKEN
SWEET & SOUR PORK
GREAT EASTERN FRIED RICE
3 - 4 PERSONS ADD:
BEEF WITH OYSTER SAUCE
5 OR MORE PERSONS ADD:
KUNG BOW PRAWN
TEA & FORTUNE COOKIE

B
$13.50 per person

FRIED SHRIMP BALL
BARBECUED SPARERIBS
HOT & SOUR SOUP
CASHEWNUT CHICKEN
PRAWNS IN LOBSTER SAUCE
GREAT EASTERN FRIED RICE
3 - 4 PERSONS ADD:
MONGOLIAN BEEF
5 OR MORE PERSONS ADD:
PEKING SPARERIB
TEA & FORTUNE COOKIE

SEAFOOD

HONEY GLAZED WALNUT & SAUTE PRAWNS	9.75
SPICED SALT BAKED PRAWNS	9.75
BOILED FRESH PRAWNS	9.25
PRAWNS WITH CASHEWNUT	7.75
PRAWNS IN LOBSTER SAUCE	7.75
KUNG BOW PRAWNS	7.75
SWEET & SOUR PRAWNS	7.75
SAUTE PRAWNS & SCALLOPS	12.00
OYSTER WITH GINGER & SCALLION	7.50
BOILED GEODUCK CLAMS	11.00
SLICE FISH WITH TENDER GREEN	8.50

FOWL

CRISPY FRIED CHICKEN (HALF)	8.00
STEAMED CHICKEN WITH SCALLION (HALF)	8.00
CASHEW NUT CHICKEN	7.00
ALMOND CHICKEN	7.00
KUNG BOW CHICKEN	7.50
CHICKEN WITH LEMON SAUCE	7.50
SWEET & SOUR CHICKEN	7.00
STEAMED SQUAB WITH SMOKED HAM & MUSHROOM	13.00
PEKING DUCK	23.00

PORK

MOO SHU PORK	6.50
PEKING SPARERIBS	6.75
SPICED SALT BAKED SPARERIBS	6.75
DOUBLE COOKED PORK	6.50
SWEET & SOUR PORK	6.50
STEAMED PORK HASH WITH SALT DUCK EGG	5.75
STEAMED PORK HASH WITH SHREDDED SCALLOP	6.75

BEEF

BEEF WITH SAR CHAR SAUCE	7.00
MONGOLIAN BEEF	7.00
KUNG BOW BEEF	7.00
STEAK CUBES WITH GREEN PEAS & ONION IN SWEET SAUCE	7.50
STEAK CUBES WITH TENDER GREEN	7.50
BEEF WITH OYSTER SAUCE	7.00
SCALLION & GINGER BEEF	7.00
BEEF WITH SNOW PEAS	7.50
BEEF WITH CHINESE BROCCOLI	7.50

CLAY POT

ROAST PORK WITH OYSTER CLAY	8.00
FRIED STUFFED BEAN CAKE, BLACK MUSHROOM CLAY POT	6.75
DUCK FEET WITH SEACUCUMBER CLAY POT	7.00
BROILED LAMB WITH FRIED BEAN CURN CLAY POT	7.75
TURNIP & BEEF STEW CLAY POT	6.75
CHICKEN WITH SALT FISH BEAN CAKE CLAY POT	7.00
SIZZLING CHICKEN CLAY POT	6.75
FRESH CRAB WITH BEAN THREAD CLAY POT	Market Price

CHOW MEIN

GREAT EASTERN COMBINATION CHOW MEIN	5.75
CHICKEN CHOW MEIN	5.25
BEEF CHOW MEIN	5.25
BARBECUED PORK CHOW MEIN	5.25
PRAWNS CHOW MEIN	5.75
SOY SAUCE CHOW MEIN	5.25
BEEF CHOW MEIN WITH TOMATO	5.25
BEEF CHOW FUN WITH BLACK BEAN SAUCE	5.25
SCRAMBLED EGG WITH PRAWN CHOW FUN	6.00
FRIED RICE NOODLES SINGAPORE STYLE	5.25
FRIED RICE NOODLES WITH SHREDDED DUCK MEAT	7.00
FRIED RICE NOODLES WITH DUCK MEAT & SNOW CABBAGE	7.00
FRIED NOODLES WITH CRAB MEAT	7.50

Harbor Village Restaurant

Appetizers

Minced Squab in Lettuce Cups	14.00
Chilled Seafood Assortment Platter	13.50
Barbecue Assortment Platter	12.00
Marinated Octopus with jelly fish salad	12.00
Cured Boneless Pork Shank with jelly fish salad	12.00
Spicy Shredded Chicken Salad	12.00
Jelly Fish Salad with sliced beef	9.00
Fried Sesame Prawns	9.00
Barbecued Tenderloin of Pork	8.00
Crispy Spring Rolls	8.00

Soup

Double-Boiled Fish Maw with Shiitake mushrooms	14.00
Soup of Sundried Scallops and bamboo forest mushroom	12.00
Madam Sung's Hot and Sour Fish Chowder	12.00
Empress Seafood Soup with Scallops, shrimp and egg	12.00
Beef Soup with cilantro and egg	8.00
Fresh Tomato and Beef Soup	8.00
Won-Ton Soup	8.00
Chicken and Sweet Corn Soup	8.00
Hot and Sour Soup, Mandarin style	8.00

Shark-Fin

Emperor's Braised Shark-Fin	21.00
Superior Shark-Fin Soup with crab roe	21.00
Imperial Scrambled Eggs with Shark-Fin and Crab Meat	18.00
Prince's Shark-Fin Soup with shredded chicken	10.00

Abalone

Sliced Abalone braised with fried fish maw	26.00
Fresh Abalone braised with goose webs	24.00
Abalone with stewed sea cucumbers	24.00
Whole Superior Abalone braised in essence of oyster (Advanced Order)	Market

Seafood

Stir-Fried Prawns with ham	16.00
Sizzling Prawns with spicy Szechuan sauce	14.00
Fresh Prawns in Garlic Sauce	14.00
Stir-Fried Sea Conch and Scallops with fresh vegetables	16.00
Fresh Sea Scallops stir-fried Mandarin style	12.00
Filet of Flounder stir fried with fresh vegetables	11.50
Sizzling Jumbo Oysters in mild black pepper sauce	9.50

Poultry

Crackling Peking Duck, carved table side	30.00
Sliced Boneless Chicken steamed with ham and broccoli	15.00
Boneless Squab stir fried with Virginia ham	13.50
Barbecue Chef's Succulent Roast Chicken	12.00
Clay Pot of Chicken with taro and cured meats	12.00

Meats

Sizzling Beef in a mild black pepper sauce	13.00
Mongolian Beef with ginger and scallion	9.50
Beef in Oyster Sauce with flour crisp	9.50
Tenderloin of Pork stir fried in pepper salt	9.50
Clay Pot of Spare Ribs in a chun kong honey sauce	9.00
Classical Sweet & Sour Pork with pineapple	8.00

Vegetables

Clay Pot of Vegetarian Stew with glass noodles and dried shrimp	9.50
Garden Vegetables with a crab meat topping	9.50
Seasonal Chinese Greens in soy sauce	8.00

Rice and Noodles

Fook-Chow Fried Rice with duck and vegetable topping	14.00
Ying-Yang Fried Rice with dual sauces of chicken and seafood topping	12.00
Pineapple Boat Fried Rice	10.00
Fried Rice with salted fish and chicken	9.00
Pan Fried Noodles with seafood	9.00
Sizzling Noodles with beef	8.00
Chicken Chow Mein, Hong Kong style	7.00

Desserts

Double Boiled Siamese Bird's Nest with sweet coconut cream	30.00
Fried Water Chestnut Jelly Rolls	4.80
Mango Pudding with mixed fresh fruits	3.00
Almond Tofu with mixed fresh fruits	2.20
Puree of Honeydew Melon with tapioca	2.20

Menu includes list of fish fresh from our tanks. Dim Sum menu also available.

^{Hong Kong} *East Ocean* Seafood Restaurant

APPETIZERS

EAST OCEAN APPETIZERS (SERVES 5 PEOPLE)	20.00
POT STICKER (6 PIECES)	6.00
CHICKEN SALAD (PER PERSON)	3.00
MU-SHU PORK	8.00
DEEP FRIED SCALLOP AND FRESH PEAR (5 PIECES)	7.50
WOK-CHARRED CALAMARI	8.00
DEEP FRIED MINCED SHRIMP ROLL (6 PIECES)	6.00
DEEP FRIED MIX TOFU ROLL	8.00
WOK-CHARRED CHICKEN WINGS	6.00
MINCED SEAFOOD IN LETTUCE CUP (5 PIECES)	10.00

SOUP

SEAFOOD BISQUE	10.00
WAR WON-TON SOUP	10.00

SEAFOOD

STEAMED WHOLE LOBSTER WITH MINCED GARLIC	SEASONAL
PRAWNS WITH HONEY GLAZED WALNUTS	12.00
PAN FRIED JUMBO PRAWNS IN SIZZLING WOK	15.00
DAI CHIN SEAFOOD IN CLAY POT	15.00
SMOKED COD FISH	18.00
WOK-CHARRED JUMBO PRAWNS	15.00

BEEF

MEDALLIONS OF BEEF EAST OCEAN STYLE	12.00
PAN FRIED BABY RIBS WITH BARBECUE SAUCE	11.00

PORK
MANDARIN RIBS   11.00

POULTRY
PEKING DUCK (WHOLE)   25.00
MARINATED CHICKEN WITH BLACK BEAN SAUCE   10.00
LEMON CHICKEN   10.00

VEGETABLES
BUDDHA'S DELIGHT   12.00
DEEP FRIED TOFU   8.00

RICE AND NOODLE
PAN FRIED SEAFOOD NOODLES   12.00
   SERVED IN A SIZZLING WOK
TOSS-FRIED PRAWNS CHOW FUN WITH   9.00
   BLACK BEAN SAUCE
YING SANG STYLE FRIED RICE   12.00

DESSERT (PER PERSON)
DRY FRUIT WITH ICE CREAM   2.50
STUFFED SWEET SESAME BALLS (5 PIECES)   5.00

COMBINATION DINNER

APPETIZER
HAND-TOSSED CHICKEN SALAD

ENTREE
PEKING DUCK (TABLE SIDE SERVICE)
SHREDDED BEEF WITH TENDER GREEENS
BLACK COD FISH WITH SPICY SAUCE
STEAMED WHOLE LOBSTER WITH MINCED GARLIC
SERVED WITH STEAMED RICE

DESSERT
ICE CREAM

DELICIOUS DIM SUM LUNCHEONS SERVED DAILY

Flower Lounge Restaurant

SEAFOOD

Smoked Black Cod Fish 15.00
Marinated in a unique sauce and thoroughly smoked, very tender and juicy.

Wok-Charred Black Cod Fish 15.00
No. 1 Top quality from Vancouver, deep fried, lightly salted with Chinese five spices.

Wok-Charred Geoduck 15.00
Sauteed sliced geoduck with Chinese five Spices.

Geoduck with Bean Sprout 15.00
Sauteed sliced geoduck with bean sprout & young chive.

Steamed Fresh Oysters 7.50

Dai Chin Seafood in Clay Pot 12.00
Sauteed seafood, braised tofu in hot chili sauce. Served in clay pot.

Steamed Catfish with Black Bean Sauce (whole) . . . *Seasonal*

Pan Fried Fillet of Sole (whole) . . . . *Seasonal*
Pan fried fillet and deep fried the bone with tender green vegetable in oyster sauce.

Fresh Abalone with Vegetable 20.00
Sliced of preserved abalone with tender green vegetable in oyster sauce.

Fresh Maine Lobster Two Styles (Choice Any Two) . . *Seasonal*
A - Steamed with Garlic Sauce   B - Pan Fried with Ginger & Scallions
C - Wok-Charred   D - Hot & Spicy Sauce

Pan Fried Fresh Scallop and Shrimp with Chef's Sauce . . 12.00
Fresh marinated scallops and shrimp with black pepper and honey sauce.

Wok-Charred Jumbo Prawns 12.00
Deep fried jumbo prawns with shell, lightly salted with Chinese five spice.

Prawns & Scallop in Szechuan Style 12.00
Fresh marinated scallops & prawns in hot & spicy sauce.

Jumbo Prawn with Honey Glazed Walnuts 12.00
Deep fried prawn served with special sauce and walnut on the other side.

Shrimp in Szechuan Style 11.00
Fresh marinated prawns sauteed in hot & spicy sauce.

5322 Geary Blvd • Richmond District • (415) 668-8998

Fresh Scallop with Nuts 11.00
Sauteed scallop with fried dried scallop and pine nut.

Crab with Green Onion & Ginger . . . . Seasonal
Pan fried fresh whole crab with green onion & ginger.

Wok-Charred Crab . . . . Seasonal
Fresh whole crab deep fried with light salt & five spice.

Steamed Crab in Special Wine Sauce . . . . Seasonal
Steamed fresh whole crab sauteed in special wine sauce.

POULTRY

Peking Duck (whole) 20.00
Whole duck air-dried & barbecued until deep brown and crispy.
Carved & served tableside with plum sauce, green onion, fresh cucumber
and steamed special buns. A classic preparation from China's Capital.

Roasted Chicken (half) 9.00
The color red is a Chinese symbol of good fortune. Here the chicken is
marinated and roasted.

Chicken in Spicy Sauce with Tender Greens 9.00
Marinated boneless chicken sauteed in spicy sauce with tender mixed greens.

Chicken with Cashew Nut 9.00
Diced chicken sauteed with cashew nuts.

Kung Po Chicken 9.00
Diced chicken pan fried in a spicy Szechuan sauce.

MEAT

Wok-Charred Baby Ribs 10.00
Tender marinated baby ribs deep fried, with light salt and Chinese five spices.

Kung Po Beef 10.00
Fillet of beef cubes sauteed in a spicy Szechuan sauce.

Medallion Beef Korean Style 10.00
Fillet of flank steak, tender marinated and cooked Korean style.

Beef with Fresh Mushrooms in Oyster Sauce 9.00
Paper thin beef sauteed with oyster sauce and mushrooms.

Baked Ribs 10.00
Baked pork ribs with House Special Sauce in clay pot.

Mandarin Ribs 9.00
Tender marinated pork ribs, light batter, deep fried Mandarin style.

Sweet & Sour Pork 9.00
Tender marinated pork, light batter, deep fried and glazed with sweet and
sour sauce made with rice vinegar, pineapple and bell pepper.
Served in a pineapple boat.

HOUSE OF NANKING

Appetizers

Vegetable Buns	3.25
Pot Stickers	3.00
Fried Squids	4.25
Fried Eggplant	3.50
Onion Cake	1.75

Sald

Bon Bon Chicken	4.25
Shrimps Salad	4.95
Vegetable Salad	3.50

Soup

Sizzling Rice Soup	3.75
Hot & Sour Soup	3.75
Nanking Fish Soup	3.75
Won Ton Soup	3.75

Mu-Shui
(*Served with 4 Chinese Pancakes*)

Mu-Shui Vegetable	5.00
Mu-Shui Beef	5.75
Mu-Shui Chicken	5.50
Mu-Shui Pork	5.25
Mu-Shui Shrimps	6.95

919 Kearny St • Financial District • (415) 421-1429

Chow Mein

Beef Chow Mein.	3.30
Pork Chow Mein.	3.30
Chicken Chow Mein	3.30

Fried Rice

Beef Fried Rice.	3.30
Pork Fried Rice.	3.30
Chicken Fried Rice.	3.30
Shrimps Fried Rice.	3.95
Sub Cum Fried Rice	3.95

Entrees

Mongolian Beef.	5.25
Nanking Beef	5.25
Hunan Beef.	5.25
Dry Braised Beef	5.25
Broccoli Beef.	5.25
Chicken Fillet with Tsing-Tao Beer Sauce	4.95
Kung Pao Chicken	4.95
Cashew Chicken	4.95
Nanking Chicken	4.95
Hot & Sour Chicken.	4.95
Peking Duck.	A.Q.
Nanking Stuffed Mushrooms	5.25
Twice Cooked Pork.	4.95
Pork with Black Bean sauce	4.95
Ma-Po Bean Curd	4.95
Nanking Pork	4.95
Prawns with Tsing-Tao Beer Sauce	6.95
Kung Pao Squid.	5.50
Kung Pao Prawns	6.95
Hunan Prawns	6.95
Nanking Prawns.	7.95
Sizzling Rice Prawns	6.95
Twin Prawns w/Double Happiness Sauce	7.50
Nanking Scallops	7.95
Chow San Shen.	6.95
Hunan Chili Fish (whole)	9.00
Dry Braised String Beans	4.50
Eggplant Szechuan Style	4.50
Sizzling Rice Assorted Vegetable.	4.95
Two Kind Vegetables	4.95
Family Bean Curd	4.50

湖 南 備 湘 村

HUNAN VILLAGE RESTAURANT

POULTRY

CHICKEN WITH SNOW PEAS 7.50

BLACK BEAN SAUCE CHICKEN 6.25

SPICED FRIED CHICKEN (in a garlic sauce) 6.25

CASHEW CHICKEN 6.25

SWEET AND SOUR CHICKEN 6.25

KUNG PAO CHICKEN 5.95

HOT PEPPER CHICKEN 5.95

TUNG AN CHICKEN 5.95

GENERAL TSOU'S CHICKEN 5.95

CURRY CHICKEN 5.95

BEAN SAUCE CHICKEN 5.95

HUNAN VELVET CHICKEN 5.95

SMOKED TEA DUCK (half). 9.50

CRISPY DUCK (half) 9.50

PEKING DUCK (roasted whole duck served with crepes) 25.00

BEEF

BEEF WITH SNOW PEAS 7.50

BEEF WITH OYSTER SAUCE 7.50

MONGOLIAN BEEF 7.50

DRY-SAUTEED BEEF 6.75

HUNAN BEEF 6.75

KUNG PAO BEEF 6.75

BEEF WITH GREEN BELL PEPPERS 6.75

BROCCOLI BEEF 6.75

VEGETABLE BEEF 6.75

BEEF WITH CELERY 6.75

SCALLION BEEF. 6.75

MONGOLIAN LAMB 8.95

SCALLION LAMB 8.50

839 Kearny St • Chinatown • (415) 956-7868

SEAFOOD

DRY BRAISED PRAWNS 10.50

HOT BRAISED PRAWNS (with shells) 10.50

HUNAN SPECIAL TWIN PRAWNS 8.95

PRAWNS WITH SNOW PEAS 8.95

MU SHU PRAWNS (served with four crepes) 7.95

CASHEW PRAWNS 7.95

SIZZLING RICE PRAWNS 7.50

SHRIMP A LA HUNAN 7.50

PRAWNS IN LOBSTER SAUCE 7.50

KUNG PAO PRAWNS (deep fried) 7.50

HUNAN HOT PRAWNS (sauteed) 7.50

PORK

MU SHU PORK (with four crepes) 6.50

SWEET AND SOUR PORK 6.50

SWEET AND SOUR RIBS (served on a bed of lettuce) 6.50

HUNAN SMOKED PORK 6.50

PORK WITH DRIED BEAN CURD 6.50

HUNAN TWICE COOKED PORK 5.95

HUNAN HOT SAUCE PORK 5.95

BEAN SAUCE PORK 5.95

DRY-BRAISED STRING BEANS WITH SMOKED PORK 7.50

VEGETABLES

HUNAN SPECIAL BEAN CURD POT 7.50
(with shrimp, beef, squid, and mushrooms)

DRY-BRAISED STRING BEANS 5.50

HUNAN HOT SAUCE EGGPLANT 5.50

BLACK MUSHROOM WITH TENDER GREENS 5.50

HUNAN BEAN CURD (sauteed) 4.95

the mandarin

Why the name "The Mandarin"

Since the mid-19th Century, European and American traders, diplomats, missionaries, soldiers and tourist began to appear in great numbers along the China coast. They soon noticed that there was a small elite group in the empire with their own distinctive costume, language, and above all, an exquisite style of living. The early Western visitors referred to them with the romanized term "MANDARIN." "Man" was short for "Manchus," the rulers of China at that time, and "Da-rin" literally means "Big Shot." an honorific salutation for all government officials.

This imperial officialdom or Mandarin class consisted mainly of the educated literati whose love for literature, art, philosophy and stylish living equaled, if not surpassed, their zeal for state affairs. It goes without saying that their exquisite style of living included the culinary arts. While European aristocrats took pride in their armors and stables, in Chinese high society a good household chef was far more treasured and envied by all. The fame of some of these chefs even overshadowed that of their masters. Society sought after their secret recipes as eagerly as they did paintings and calligraphy. Since no Mandarin could resist epicurean lures, to titillate the palate was a sure way to win friendship and favor.

In the West, the term "Mandarin" has been liberally extended to mean anything exquisite, stylish or exotic from China, such as "Mandarin jacket," "Mandarin duck," "Mandarin orange" and "Mandarin," once the court language and now the national spoken tongue of China. In short, MANDARIN has become a synonym for what is best of China, and we are proud to name our restaurant THE MANDARIN.

Noodles & Rice

Curry Mi-Fun   12.00
Chinese vermicelli with shredded meat and onions stir-cooked with curry

Dan Dan Mein with Spicy Meat Sauce   12.00

Seafood Chow Mein   12.00

Mixea Vegetables Chow Mein   12.00

Mandarin Double-Fried Noodles   12.00

Ham Fried Rice   2.00 *per person*

Steamed Rice   1.00 *per person*

Yangchow Fried Rice   9.50

Shrimp Fried Rice   9.50

Beef Fried Rice   9.50

Meats

Mongolian Beef   15.00

Mongolian Lamb   15.00

Ming's Beef   15.00

Ginger Beef   15.00

Oyster Sauce Beef   15.00

Peking Sweet and Sour Pork   15.00

Sweet and Sour Spareribs   15.00

Tangerine Beef   15.00

Crispy Beef   15.00

Spring Crepes   16.00
Pancake wrap filled with pork and fresh vegetables

Beef with Snow Peas   15.00

Beef with Bell Pepper   15.00

900 Northpoint St • Ghirardelli Square • (415) 673-8812

Mandarin Specialties

(ONE DAY ADVANCE NOTICE REQUIRED)

□ *Peking Duck* □
(WHOLE DUCK SERVES 4 OR MORE)

Ours alone. And yours to relish. Prepared with prideful care
from our very own recipe originating from Peking itself! Served
with Chinese pao-ping, scallions and plum sauce

35.00

□ *Beggar's Chicken* ⊔
(WHOLE CHICKEN SERVES 4 OR MORE)

The Mandarin takes great pleasure in being the first and only
Chinese restaurant in America, we believe, to serve this chicken
which is unusual in name. And in fact, unusual in presentation.
A fowl finely flavored, encased in clay, and baked

35.00

□ *Shark's Fin Soup* □
(SERVES 4)

availability

□ *Stuffed Cucumber Soup* □
(SERVES 4)

16.00

□ *Mandarin Cold Platter Hors d'Oeuvre* □

□ *Mongolian Fire Pot* □
Also known as Genghis Khan's Fire Pot
(SERVES 4 OR MORE)

A charcoal-burning chafing pot containing highly flavored
chicken broth with thinly sliced meats — chicken, beef,
fish, shrimp, vegetables, oyster, bean curd and rice noodle

38.00 PER PERSON

新亞洲大酒樓
new asia

APPETIZERS

BARBECUED PORK	4.50
SPRING EGG ROLL (3)	4.50
FRIED WONTON (10)	4.00
FRIED PRAWNS (6)	5.50
BARBECUED SPARERIBS (8)	5.00
PRAWN DUMPLINGS (8)	8.00

POULTRY

ALMOND CHICKEN	6.00
CASHEW CHICKEN	6.50
MUSHROOM CHICKEN	6.75
CHICKEN SALAD	8.50
CRISPY CHICKEN	7.50
KUNG PO CHICKEN	6.50

SEAFOOD

PRAWNS IN LOBSTER SAUCE	7.00
PRAWNS IN BLACK BEAN SAUCE	7.50
CRYSTAL PRAWNS	9.00
PRAWNS IN CURRY SAUCE	7.50
PRAWNS WITH PINEAPPLE	7.25
SALT AND PEPPER PRAWNS IN SHELL	8.25
PRAWNS WITH WALNUTS IN WHITE WINE SAUCE	8.50
PAN FRIED PRAWNS IN SHELL	8.00
FRIED ROCK COD IN SWEET & SOUR SAUCE	6.50
BRAISED ROCK COD IN BROWN SAUCE	6.50

SPICED ROCK COD IN BLACK BEAN SAUCE	6.75
STIR FRIED CUBES OF ROCK COD	6.75
CRISPY FRIED OYSTERS	6.50
FRESH OYSTER SAUTEED WITH GINGER	7.00
CLAMS IN BLACK BEAN SAUCE	7.50
CLAMS IN HOT & SOUR SAUCE	8.50
LOBSTER WITH SNOW PEAS	14.50
LOBSTER WITH BEAN SAUCE	14.00
NEW ASIA LOBSTER	15.00
BRAISED ABALONE AND MUSHROOM	14.00

VEGETABLES

SNOW PEAS & WATER CHESTNUTS	5.50
MIXED VEGETABLES	5.50
STIR FRIED TENDER GREEN	5.00
MUSHROOM IN OYSTER SAUCE	7.00
VEGETABLES DELIGHT	5.50
BEAN CURD & MUSHROOM SAUTEED	6.00
BRAISED DICED MUSHROOM AND WALNUTS	6.25

DUCK, SQUAB

CRISPY ROASTED SQUAB	15.00
SQUAB MACAO	9.00
SAUTEED SQUAB WITH MUSHROOM	10.00
SAUTEED SQUAB WITH LEMON	11.00
ALMOND PRESSED DUCK	6.25
HONG KONG ROASTED DUCK	5.25
GINGER PINEAPPLE DUCK	7.25
PEKING DUCK	26.00

BEEF

BEEF IN OYSTER SAUCE	7.00
NEW ASIA STEAK CUBES	8.50
BEEF CUBES WITH TENDER GREENS	7.50
STIR FRIED BEEF IN HOT BEAN SAUCE	7.50

PORK

SWEET & SOUR PORK	6.00
STEAMED SPARERIBS IN BEAN SAUCE	6.50
MANDARIN PORK RIBS	7.50
CATHAY PORK CHOP	7.50

772 Pacific Ave • Chinatown • (415) 391-6666

RICE

BARBECUED PORK FRIED RICE	3.00
BEEF FRIED RICE	3.50
SHRIMP FRIED RICE	4.00
YANG CHOW FRIED RICE	4.25
NEW ASIA FRIED RICE	6.00

CHOW MEIN

BARBECUED PORK CHOW MEIN	4.50
MIXED VEGETABLES CHOW MEIN	4.50
TOMATO BEEF CHOW MEIN	4.75
TOSSED CHICKEN CHOW MEIN	5.00
ALMOND CHICKEN CHOW MEIN	5.00

COMPLETE CHINESE DINNERS

THE MANDARIN
minimum service for two

POT STICKERS
HOT AND SOUR SOUP
BEAN SAUCE CHICKEN
ASSORTED VEGETABLES
DICED PORK WITH CASHEW
FRIED RICE
FORTUNE COOKIES
TEA

For three persons add:
DRY BRAISED PRAWNS

For four persons add:
MONGOLIAN BEEF

For five persons add:
SAUTEED CRAB MEAT OVER BROCCOLI

For six persons add:
HOT SPICED SCALLOPS

$10.50 per person

THE NEW ASIA
minimum service for two

SPRING ROLL
SOUP DU JOUR
CASHEW CHICKEN
SWEET AND SOUR PORK
MIXED VEGETABLES
FRIED RICE
FORTUNE COOKIES
TEA

For three persons add:
BEEF UNDER SNOW

For four persons add:
PRAWNS IN LOBSTER SAUCE

For five persons add:
BRAISED ROCK COD IN BEAN SAUCE

For six persons add:
STIR FRIED SCALLOPS WITH BROCCOLI

$9.50 per person

THE SEAFOOD GOURMET
minimum service for two

FRIED PRAWNS
COMBINATION SEAFOOD SOUP
CASHEW PRAWNS
DEEP FRIED ROCK COD IN SWEET AND SOUR SAUCE
SAUTEED CRAB MEAT WITH MUSHROOM
SHRIMP FRIED RICE
FORTUNE COOKIES
TEA

For three persons add:
STIR FRIED SCALLOPS WITH BROCCOLI

For four persons add:
NEW ASIA LOBSTER

For five persons add:
DEEP FRIED OYSTER IN HOT SAUCE

For six persons add:
BRAISED ABALONE AND MUSHROOM IN OYSTER SAUCE

$12.00 per person

Dinner: 7 Days a Week 5 - 9:30   Ⓑ Ⓛ Ⓓ

NORTH SEA VILLAGE

豬·牛肉類
豚と牛肉料理

PORK & BEEF

四川牛肉（辣）　　四川ビーフ（辛味）
1. SZECHUAN BEEF (Hot)　　　　　　　7.50

木須肉　　　ムシュポーク（豚と野菜炒め）
2. MU SHU PORK　　　　　　　　　7.50

蜜桃牛柳絲　　牛肉の細切りとクルミのあんかけ
3. SHREDDED BEEF WITH GLAZED WALNUTS　7.50

香煎牛仔骨　　牛のあばら肉（リブ）にんにくソース添え
4. SHORT RIBS WITH GARLIC SAUCE　　8.75

鐵板黑椒牛柳（辣）　みじん切り牛肉とブラックペッパー・ソース（辛味）
5. SHREDDED BEEF W/BLACK PEPPER SAUCE (Hot)　7.50

魚翅類　　SHARK'S FINS
每位
(PER PERSON)

紅燒鶏絲翅　　ふかひれと鶏肉のあんかけ
10. STEWED SHARK'S FIN WITH CHICKEN MEAT　9.50

蟹肉魚生翅　　ふかのひれとかに肉のあんかけ
11. STEWED SHARK'S FIN WITH CRAB MEAT　12.00

紅燒大鮑翅　　ふかひれとかきのソース入りスープ
12. BRAISED SUPERIOR SHARK'S FIN WITH BROWN SAUCE　20.00

300 Turney St • Sausalito • (415) 331-3300

海鮮類
魚介料理   SEAFOOD

翡翠鸚螺片   巻貝と野菜炒め
1. SAUTEED SLICED CONCH WITH TENDER GREENS   9.50

桂林炸蝦丸
2. FRIED SHRIMP BALLS WITH MINCED WATER CHESTNUT   8.50

韮王象拔蚌   ス子具とニラ炒め
3. SAUTEED GEODUCK WITH TENDER GREENS   12.00

豉汁帶子蒸豆腐   蒸しホタテと豆腐、黒豆ソース添え
4. STEAMED SCALLOPS AND TOFU W/BLACK BEAN SAUCE 9.50

碧緑紅燒海参   煮込みナマコ・軟かい青物添え
5. BRAISED SEA CUCUMBER WITH TENDER GREENS   12.00

蠔皇鮮鮑片   あわびと牡蛎（かき）ソースかけ
6. SAUTEED ABALONE WITH OYSTER SAUCE   24.00

上湯焗龍蝦   イセエビとしょうが・たまねぎ炒め
7. BRAISED LOBSTER WITH GINGER AND SCALLION   Seasonal

煲仔菜
鍋料理   CLAY POT

東江豆腐煲   豆腐と四季の野菜のスープ
1. SEASONAL VEGETABLE WITH TOFU   9.50

沙爹牛肉煲   マレーシア・サテー風 牛肉とバーミセリ(麺)
2. MALAYSIAN SATAY BEEF WITH VERMICELLI   7.25

一品海鮮粉絲煲   魚介類の盛り合わせとバーミセリ(麺)
3. COMBINATION SEAFOOD WITH VERMICELLI   9.50

海鮮八珍豆腐煲   珍味八種魚介類の鍋もの
4. EIGHT PRECIOUS CLAY POT   8.00

薑葱生蠔煲   カキフライしょうが・ニラ添え
5. PAN FRIED OYSTERS WITH GINGER & SCALLIONS   7.95

Taiwan Restaurant
Distinctive Chinese Cuisine

Taiwan Specialties

Boneless Duck Web (Cold)...............7.95
Taiwan Pickled Cabbage with Pork
    Tripe Soup...........................4.50
Petals of Pork Soup.........................4.50
Fish Ball Soup.................................4.75
Sing Chu Meat Ball Soup................4.75
Squids in Broth with Chinese
    Cabbage............................ 4.50
Squid with Celery........................... 4.75
Taiwan Pickle Cabbage with
    Shredded Pork Tripe............4.50
Taiwan Country Favorite..................4.95
Crispy Prawns..................................6.95
Pork in Red Wine Sauce..................5.95
Fresh Red Snapper Fillet in Red
    Wine Sauce..........................6.50
Fresh Red Snapper Fillet in White
    Wine Sauce..........................6.50
Wok-Fried Oysters with Black
    Soybean..............................5.95
Taiwan Country Favorite Spareribs.5.95
Taiwan Crispy Fried Oysters............5.95
Pork Chop on Soup Noodles...........3.75
Pork Chop on Steamed Rice...........3.75
Sweet Rice en Crock.......................2.25
White Turnip Cakes.........................2.75
Fried Rice Noodles with Shredded
    Pork.....................................3.95
Wood Ears with Shredded Pork.......4.95
Taiwan Special Deep Fried Bean
    Curd..................................... 4.50
Wok-Fried Seafood Vermicelli.........4.75
Special Seafood Rice......................4.75
Sweet Rice with Pork Mushrooms
    Steamed in Bamboo Leaf....2.50

Seafood

Shrimp a la Shanghai......................6.95
Shrimp with Snow Peas..................6.95
Spiced Prawns.................................6.95
Szechwan Prawns (Catsup Sauce)....6.95
Happy Family (Mixed Seafood)...........6.95
Sweet and Sour Shrimp...................6.95
Curry Shrimp...................................6.95
Broccoli Prawn................................6.95
Deep Fried Crispy Calamari............5.25
Crab Mandarin..........................Seasonal
Braised Sliced Fresh Red Snapper
    Fillet....................................6.50
Sweet and Sour Sliced Fresh Red
    Snapper Fillet......................6.50
Sweet and Sour Fish-Whole.......Seasonal

Pork

Sweet and Sour Pork.......................5.95
Sweet and Sour Spareribs.............. 5.95
Fish Flavored Pork-Szechwan.........5.75
Twice-Cooked Pork-Szechwan........5.75
Mustard Green with Shredded Pork.5.75

Mui Shi Specials

Mu Shi Pork-include 4 crepes...............5.95
Mu Shi Chicken-include 4 crepes.........5.95
Mu Shi Beef-include 4 crepes...............5.95
Mu Shi Shrimp-include 4 crepe.............6.95

Sizzling Iron Platter

Sizzling Beef Platter........................5.95
Sizzling Platter of Bamboo Shoots
    with Black Mushrooms.........5.95

Fowl

Lemon Chicken	5.95
Bean Sauce Chicken	5.25
Cashew or Almond Chicken	5.50
Curry Chicken	5.25
General Tsuo's Chicken	5.95
Sweet and Sour Chicken	5.95
Garlic Chicken	5.25
Broccoli Chicken	5.25
Velvet Chicken	5.95
Fish Flavored Chicken	5.95
Deep Fried Chicken Wings	4.25
Spicy Chicken Wings	4.75
Crispy Chicken	6.00
	12.00
Crispy Duck	8.00
	16.00
Smoke Tea Duck	8.00
	16.00
Combination Fresh Vegetables with Chicken	5.95

Beef & Lamb

Mandarin Beef of Lamb	5.95
Mongolian Beef of Lamb	5.95
Beef with Oyster Sauce	5.75
Beef a la Shangtung	5.95
Curry Beef	5.75
Tripe with Hot Sauce	5.75
Mandarin Braised Beef Ligament	5.95
Bean Curd Beef	5.75
Broccoli Beef	5.75
Combination Fresh Vegetables with Beef	5.95

Rice & Noodles

Kuo Teh (6)	3.05
Steamed Dumplings (6)	3.05
Vegetarian Steamed Dumplings (6)	3.05
Peking Special Chow Mein of Fried Rice	4.50
Braised Beef Lighament Noodles	4.50
Sesame Paste and Meat Sauce Noodles	3.95
Boiled Leeks Shrimp Pork Dumplings	4.05
Japanese Seafood Noodles	4.95
Beef Chow or Beef Fried Rice	3.75

Bean and Meat Sauce Noodles	3.75
Szechwan Hot Sauce Noodles with Meat Sauce	3.75
Soup Noodles with Braised Beef Own Gravy	3.75
Noodles with Szechwan Pickles	3.75
Petals of Pork Noodles or Rice Noodles	3.95
Beef or Pork or Chicken Chow Fun	3.95
Shrimp Chow Fun	4.50
Rice Cakes Soup	3.95
Steamed Buns (4)	2.75
Steamed Rice	0.60
Brown Rice	0.75

To Fu

Spicy Hot To Fu	4.50
Mandarin Braised To Fu	4.50
Curry To Fu	4.50
Mustard Green To Fu	4.50
Mushrooms To Fu	5.25
Taiwan Special Deep Fried To Fu	4.50

Vegetarian Specials

Basil with Egg Plant	4.50
Red-Cooked Egg Plant	4.50
Fish Flavored Egg Plant	4.50
Dry Braised Green Beans	4.50
Wok-Fried Bean Sprouts	3.95
Wok-Fried Spinach with Garlic	4.50
Wok-Fried Bok Choy Hearts	4.50
Chinese Cabbage with Dried Shrimp (Boiled)	4.50
Mustard Greens with Flat Bean Curd	4.95
Vegetarian Sweet and Sour Pork	4.25
Vegetarian Cashew Chicken	4.25
Combination Vegetables Deluxe	4.95
Snow Peas with Mushrooms and Waterchestnuts	4.95
Mushi Vegetables-include 4 crepes	4.95
Combination Vegetables Soup	4.25
Hot and Sour Soup	4.25
Combination Vegetables Chow Mein	3.75
Vegetables Fried Rice	3.75
Bean Sauce Noodles	3.75

Dinner: Sun - Thurs until 10, Fri - Sat until 12   ●ⓁⒹ

PRIX FIXE DINNER

$38.00 Per Person
Minimum Service for 2 Persons
(All Items Included)

APPETIZER
LOBSTER POT STICKERS WITH CHILI SAUCE

SOUP
SEAFOOD BISQUE CHINOISE WITH YOUNG CHIVES

ENTREES
WOK-CHARRED PRAWNS WITH CHINESE FIVE SPICE
& FRESH MUSHROOMS

PEKING DUCK WITH LOTUS BUNS

DEEP FRIED TENDERLOIN OF PORK WITH CHINESE FRUIT
IN CASSIA NECTAR

FOUR FLAVORS FRIED RICE

DESSERT
PEACH MOUSSE ON STRAWBERRY COMPOTE

APPETIZERS

PAN FRIED FRESH FOIE GRAS WITH SLICED FRESH PEAR &
WATERCRESS IN SWEET PICKLED GINGER SAUCE
(MINIMUM SERVICE FOR TWO)   14.95

BAKED FRESH NEW ZEALAND MUSSELS IN GARLIC
& BLACK BEAN SAUCE   8.95

LOBSTER POT STICKERS WITH CHILI SAUCE (4)   8.95

CHICKEN SALAD WITH SPICY PLUM DRESSING   8.95

ENTREES

FILET OF CHICKEN SAUTEED WITH FRESH MUSHROOMS, SNOW PEAS & PECANS	14.95
PAN FRIED BREAST OF CHICKEN WITH LEMON GRASS	15.95
FILET OF CHICKEN SAUTEED WITH SWEET BASIL & EGGPLANT	16.95
BREAST OF DUCKLING SMOKED WITH CAMPHORWOOD & TEA LEAVES SERVED WITH PLUM WINE SAUCE	18.95
BRAISED STUFFED QUAIL COUNTRY STYLE (2)	18.95
MONGOLIAN B.B.Q. LAMB WITH HOISIN SAUCE & FRESH MINT ON A BED OF MARINATED SPINACH	16.95
VEAL FILET WITH SZECHWAN SAUCE	17.95
DEEP FRIED TENDERLOIN OF PORK WITH CHINESE FRUITS IN CASSIA NECTAR	14.95
PAN FRIED MEDALLION OF BEEF WITH GARLIC & WINE	16.95
FRESH OYSTERS SAUTEED WITH FRESH GINGER ROOTS & GREEN ONIONS	15.95
WOK CHARRED PRAWNS WITH CHINESE FIVE SPICE & FRESH MUSHROOMS ON A BED OF MARINATED SPINACH	16.95
VANILLA PRAWNS & RAISINS WITH FRESH MELON	16.95
GARUPA FILETS IN BLACK BEAN & GINGER SAUCE	15.95
PAN FRIED SEA SCALLOPS WITH SLICED FRESH PEAR IN SWEET GINGER SAUCE	16.95
STEAMED NORWEGIAN SALMON FILLETS WITH SCALLIONS, GINGER & BEAN SAUCE	17.95
SAUTEED FRESH CLAMS WITH SPICY THAI CURRY SAUCE	15.95
SIGNATURE DISH: FRESH MAINE LOBSTER WITH YOUR CHOICE OF GARLIC CHIVES OR PEPPERCORN SAUCE	MARKET PRICE

Dinner: 7 Days a Week 6 - 10   ●ⓁⒹ

——CHICKEN——

"Beggar's" Chicken 富 貴 鷄 ··············· One Day notice in advance
Whole chicken seasoned simply with soy sauce, salt, and ginger, coated with clay and baked
according to an ancient North China legend. The clay crust, which is broken open at the table, seals in
all the chicken's natural juices and flavor. Advance notice required.

Deep-Fried Spiced Chicken 炸 八 塊 ···························7.95
Chicken pieces marinated with five-spice seasoning and deep-fried. The Colonel never had it so good!

Sweet And Sour Chicken 咕 嚕 鷄 ···························6.95
Chunks of boneless chicken deep fried and glazed with red Shanghai-style sweet-and-sour sauce made
with vinegar, ginger, and onions.

Kung Pao Chicken 宮 保 鷄 丁 ····························6.95
Finely diced boneless chicken sauteed with bits of spicy red   Named for a fourteenth-century
Imperial minister, a famous gourmet of his era.

Diced Chicken With Bean Paste 醬 爆 鷄 丁 ··················6.95
Diced boneless chicken sauteed Shanghai style with red Chinese bean paste.
Rich-flavored and exotic, but not spicy.

——F I S H——

Fish Filet With Sweet And Sour Sauce 醋 溜 魚 塊 ···········8.95
Deep-fried fish filet dressed with a tangy, amber-colored sauce of dark soy.
A Shanghai specialty.

Braised King-Fish 紅 燒 黃 魚 ····························8.95
King fish salt-marinated and braised with scallions, dark soy sauce, and white pepper.

King-Fish Fritters 麵 拖 黃 魚 ····························8.95
Slices of king fish filet coated with a golden crust, deep-fried.
A Shanghai version of fish and chips.

Fish Filet In Wine Sauce 糟 溜 魚 塊 ·······················8.95
Slices of tender white fish, steamed, and dressed with a creamy Shaoxing rice wine sauce.

PRAWNS & CRAB

Shrimp and prawns, a favorite throughout coastal Shanghai, are a specialty of Wu Kong.

Crystal Shrimp 清 炒 蝦 仁 **13.95**
Tender small shrimp imported from China and used only for this dish, are sauteed with delicate Shanghai seasonings. Wu Kong's signature dish, and a true classic.

Braised Shrimp With Chili Sauce 干 燒 蝦 仁 **10.95**
Medium-sized shrimp braised Northern style with a moderately spicy chili-soy sauce.

Kung Pao Shrimp 宮 保 蝦 仁 **10.95**
Fresh shrimp sauteed with bits of spicy red peppers. Named for a fourteeth-century Imperial minister, a famous gourmet of his era.

DUCK

Braised Duck w/Green Onions 京 蔥 扒 鴨 .... (Half)13.00 (Whole)25.00
Pieces of juicy duck, first steamed, then braised in dark soy sauce with ginger and scallions. A classic Shanghai preparation.

Aromatic Crispy Duck 香 酥 鴨 ......(Half)13.00 (Whole)25.00
Whole duck, first steamed, then marinated with aromatic Chinese five-spice powder, then baked until crisp and goldon. Spicy, but not hot.

CHEF SPECIALTIES

Sauteed Eels 炒 蟮 糊 **7.95**
Sliced imported eels quickly stir-fried Shanghai-style with dark soy sauce and white pepper.

Sauteed Eels w/Green Pepper & Bamboo Shoots
生 炒 蟮 片 **9.95**
Sliced eels stir-fried as above with green pepper chunks and bamboo shoots.

Tofu Shreds With Shrimp 蝦 仁 乾 絲 **6.95**
Fine threads of firm tofu served with fresh shrimp. A Nanking specialty.

Shredded Pork With Cabbage 肉 絲 爛 糊 **5.95**
Thin strips of pork braised slowly in cream sauce, country style, with Chinese cabbage.

Eight Treasures In Pepper Sauce 八 寶 辣 醬 **6.95**
Diced chicken, pork, shrimp, bamboo shoots, and seasonal ingredients braised in spicy pepper paste. A Shanghai favorite.

Dried Scallops With Egg 桂 花 干 貝 **6.95**
Flavorful dried scallops served with fluffy eggs omelet style.

Shrimp Omelet 蝦 仁 炒 蛋 **6.95**
A delicately flavored Shanghai omelet with fresh shrimp.

Minced Pork Omelet 元 寶 蛋 餃 **8.95**
A folded omelet stuffed with minced pork, symbolizing "gold nugget" in Shanghai.

Crab's Challenge 賽 螃 蟹 **7.50**
Minced fish blended with egg white and dry scallops and sauteed. Presented to look almost like crab, this is a popular Beijing banquet dish. A Northern delicacy and a specialty of the house.

Yank Sing

Deem sum (or dim sum) is the generic name for hundreds of bite-sized delicacies first created for the Imperial Court of the Sung Dynasty nearly 1,000 years ago. The idea behind deem sum was to harmonize flavors so that dozens of tastes could be enjoyed at the same meal. As the Emperor fled from the Mongols, the concept was spread to each Chinese province on the way to Canton. By 1900, Canton was known as the best place in China to have deem sum, which literally means "to touch the heart".

Yank Sing was founded in 1958. The name "Yank Sing" means "City of the Ram" and is a synonym for Guangzhou, the capital of the Guangdong Province in China.

How Deem Sum Works

We have over 100 varieties of deem sum (with some 60 varieties served daily), but no formal menu. Servers go through the restaurant with carts. To order, simply ask the food servers to give you whatever that you see on the cart that you like. You can sample shrimp, scallop, duck, chicken, beef, pork and vegetable dishes in one sitting. If you want a specific item, but do not see it on the carts, please ask a food server for help.

Each time you select an item from the cart, the server will stamp your guest check. At the conclusion of your meal, the waiter will total up your bill by adding up the stamps.

We have a few rice and noodle entrees (listed on the table tent), but our specialty is deem sum.

> Typical complete meal price including beverage is between $9.00 and $14.00

427 Battery St • Financial District • (415) 781-1111 • (Call for Additional Locations)

Steamed Items

Shrimp Gow
A delicious mixture of shrimp and bamboo shoots in translucent pastry bonnets.

Barbecued Pork Buns
Light, fluffy, snow white buns filled with barbecued pork.

Scallop Siu Mye
A combination of scallops, straw mushrooms, shrimp paste and cilantro in a light wrapping.

Snow Pea Leaves Dumplings
Delicious dumplings stuffed with dried scallops, chicken and snow pea leaves.

Basil Seafood Dumplings
Delectable dumplings stuffed with shrimp, crab meat, basil and chives.

Pan-Fried Items

Pot Stickers
Golden, crispy dumplings with savory pork and vegetable filling.

Pan-Fried Chicken Buns
Crispy buns filled with chicken, mushrooms and bamboo shoots.

Stuffed Green Peppers
Fresh, tasty fish paste on fresh squares of green peppers.

Desserts

Egg Custard Tarts
Sweet and light custard in flaky pastry shells.

Mango Pudding
Refreshing mixture of mango and gelatin.

Baked Items

Chive Pastry Shells
Flaky pastry shells filled with shrimp, chicken and chives.

Curry Meat Turnovers
Mild curry pork filling in flaky triangular shells.

Barbecued Items

Peking Duck by the Slice
Fresh sliced duck (made on the premises), served with seashell buns and a sweet Hoisin sauce.

Barbecued Spare Ribs
Tender, meaty spareribs marinated in a tangy sauce.

Deep-Fried Items

Spring Rolls
Shredded barbecued pork and vegetables in crispy, skins.

Phoenix Shrimp
Fresh, whole shrimp wrapped in delicate shrimp paste with cilantro and covered with golden batter.

Silver-Wrapped Chicken
Aromatic chicken, marinated in Yank Sing's own special sauces, and deep-fried in foil.

Crab Claws
Delectable snowcrab claws stuffed with shrimp and crab meat, fried in a golden batter.

Scallion Prawns
Prawns wrapped with bacon and scallions.

Seaweed Chicken Rolls
Boneless chicken rolled in sesame seeds and seaweed.

More than 100 varieties of Deem Sum are available.
This listing is only a small sample.

YUET LEE

海鮮類　SEAFOOD

波士頓龍蝦 (時價) BOSTON LOBSTER	Season
白灼鮮中蝦 QUICKLY BOILED MEDIUM PRAWNS	10.00
椒鹽焗中蝦 PEPPER AND SALT ROAST PRAWNS IN SHELL	12.50
干煎鮮中蝦 PAN FRIED PRAWNS IN SHELL *(Special Sweet and Sour Sauce)*	12.50
卷葱大肉蟹 (時價) CRAB SAUTEED WITH GINGER AND GREEN ONION	Season
豉椒大肉蟹 (時價) SAUTEED CRAB W/PEPPER AND BLACK BEAN SAUCE	Season
清蒸大肉蟹 (時價) STEAMED FRESH CRAB	Season
咖喱大肉蟹 (時價) FRESH CRAB IN CURRY SAUCE	Season
豉椒炒大蜆 SAUTEED CLAMS WITH PEPPER AND BLACK BEAN SAUCE	8.00
豉汁蒸原壳生蠔 STEAMED FRESH OYSTER WITH BLACK BEAN SAUCE *(half dozen)*	8.00
椒鹽焗鮮鱿 PEPPER AND SALT ROAST FRESH SQUIDS	9.00
油泡鴛鴦鱿 SAUTEED FRESH & DRIED SQUIDS	6.00
清炒明蝦球 SAUTEED PRAWN	10.00
宮保明蝦球 KUNG PAO PRAWN	8.00
菜遠明蝦球 PRAWNS WITH CHINESE GREENS	8.00
腰果明蝦球 PRAWNS WITH CASHEW NUT	8.00
滑蛋明蝦球 SCRAMBLED EGG WITH SHRIMP	8.00
菜遠崇魚片 SLICES OF STEELHEAD FISH WITH CHINESE GREEN	8.00
崇魚二味 SAUTEED STEELHEAD FILET WITH GREENS AND A CHOICE OF SOUP OR STEAMED BEAN CAKE	19.00
清蒸龍利 (時價) STEAMED FONDERE	Season
清蒸鮮石斑 (時價) STEAMED ROCK COD	Season
清蒸鮮崇魚 (時價) STEAMED STEELHEAD	Season

牛肉類　BEEF

白灼牛柏葉 BOILED BEEF TRIPE	5.75
豉椒牛柏葉 BEEF TRIPE WITH PEPPER AND BLACK BEAN SAUCE	5.75
滑蛋牛肉 BEEF WITH SCRAMBLED EGG	5.75
豉椒牛肉 BEEF WITH PEPPER AND BLACK BEAN SAUCE	5.75
沙爹牛肉 SATAY BEEF	5.75
腰果牛肉 BEEF WITH CASHEWS	5.75
薑葱牛肉 BEEF WITH GINGER AND GREEN ONION	5.75
菜遠牛肉 BEEF WITH CHINESE GREEN	5.75
蘭遠牛肉 SAUTEED BEEF WITH CHINESE BROCCOLI	5.75

1300 Stockton St • Chinatown • (415) 982-6020 • (Call for Additional Locations)

猪肉類 PORK

京都鮮肉排　PEKING SPARERIBS *(Sweet and Sour)* 7.00
紅梅咕嚕肉　PORK WITH SWEET AND SOUR PLUM SAUCE 5.00
豉椒肉片　SAUTEED SLICED PORK WITH BLACK BEAN SAUCE 5.50
菜遠肉片　SAUTEED SLICED PORK WITH CHINESE GREENS 5.50
沙爹肉片　SAUTEED SLICED PORK WITH SATAY SAUCE 5.50
薑蔥鮮腰肝　SAUTEED PORK LIVER & KIDNEY WITH GINGER AND GREEN ONION 7.50
韮芽炒腰花　SAUTEED PORK KIDNEY WITH BEAN SPROUTS AND CHIVES 6.50
西芹炒腰花　SAUTEED PORK KIDNEY WITH CELERY 6.50
酢炸豬大腸　DEEP-FRIED PORK INTESTINE 6.00
腰果肉丁　SAUTEED SLICED PORK WITH CASHEW NUT 5.50
咸蛋蒸肉餅　STEAMED MINCED PORK WITH SALTED EGG 5.50
咸魚蒸肉餅　STEAM MINCED PORK WITH SALTED FISH 5.50
豉椒炆肉排　BRAISED SPARERIBS WITH PEPPER AND BLACK BEAN SAUCE 5.50
蜜汁叉燒　BARBECUED PORK 4.50

雞 類 CHICKEN

香燒肥乳鴿　ROAST SQUAB 10.00
菜胆肥雞(一隻)　BOILED CHICKEN WITH GREEN (whole) 16.00
　(半隻)　(half) 8.00
卷蔥肥雞(一隻)　BOILED CHICKEN WITH GINGER AND GREEN ONION (whole) 16.00
　(半隻)　(half) 8.00
白切雞(一隻)　FRESH BOILED CHICKEN (whole) 16.00
　(半隻)　(half) 8.00
　(一碟)　(plate) 4.50
腰果雞丁　CASHEW NUT CHICKEN 5.75
蠔油雞球　BONELESS CHICKEN CUBES WITH OYSTER SAUCE 5.75
鮑魚雞球　BONELESS CHICKEN CUBES WITH ABALONE 7.75
豆豉雞球　CHICKEN WITH BLACK BEAN SAUCE 5.75
蠔油炆雞　BRAISED CHICKEN WITH OYSTER SAUCE 5.00
鮑魚炆雞　BRAISED CHICKEN WITH ABALONE 6.75
豆豉炆雞　BRAISED CHICKEN WITH BLACK BEAN SAUCE 5.00

煲仔菜 CLAY POT

咸魚鷄粒豆腐煲　SALTED FISH WITH DICED CHICKEN AND BEAN CAKE 7.00
鳥豆塘虱　BRAISED CAT FISH WITH BLACK BEAN AND ROAST PORK 6.50
鮑魚鴨掌　ABALONE WITH DUCK FEET 6.50
薑蔥豬肝　PORK LIVER WITH GINGER AND GREEN ONION 5.00
八珍豆腐　MIXED MEAT WITH BEAN CAKE 6.00
大馬站　ROAST PORK, BEAN CAKE AND SHRIMP SAUCE 5.00
柱侯牛腩　BEEF STEW WITH SPECIAL SAUCE 5.00
五香牛什　AROMATIC BEEF *(combination of Tripe and Intestines)* 5.00

1770 ~ 1827

APPETIZERS

Smoked Salmon with Potato Pancakes	$6.50
Prawns in Garlic Butter Sauce	$6.50
Herring in Sour Cream and Apples	$5.50
Escargot in Garlic and Herb Butter	$5.50

SOUPS

Soup of the Day	$2.00
Gulasch Soup	$3.00

SALADS

Mixed Green Salad with House Dressing	$3.00
Tomato Salad Vinaigrette	$3.00
Cucumber Salad with Sour Cream Dressing	$3.00

SIDE ORDERS

Potato Pancakes	$3.50
Red Cabbage	$3.00
Sauerkraut	$3.00
Homemade Spaetzle	$3.00

DESSERTS

Cake of the Day	$3.50
Apple Strudel with Vanilla Sauce	$3.50
Beethoven Special	$3.50
Gelato Ice Cream or Gelato Sherbert	$2.50

DINNER

*Includes Soup of the Day or Mixed Green Salad
with House Dressing, Vegetable and Garnie*

Fresh Fish of the Day, *Two Fresh Vegetables
and Potatoes* AQ

Schweinebraten - *Roasted Pork Loin with Onion,
Garlic and Carraway with Potato Pancakes* $13.50

Sauerbraten - *Marinated Brisket of Beef in Sweet
and Sour Ginger Sauce with Potato Pancakes* $14.50

Rindsrouladen - *Stuffed Rolled Beef in
Burgundy Sauce with Potato Pancakes* $14.50

Bratwurst - *Veal Sausage, Bavarian Sauerkraut
and Potatoes* $10.50

Vegetable Plate - *Two Fresh Vegetables, Sauteed
Mushrooms, Potato Pancakes and Red Cabbage* $12.00

Bauernschmaus - *Bavarian Sauerkraut,
Kassler Rippchen, Bratwurst and Schweinebraten* $14.50

Roasted Half Chicken *with Herbs and Mushrooms* $12.50

Prawns *in Garlic Butter Sauce, Two Fresh Vegetables
and Potatoes* $14.90

Wienerschnitzel - *Breaded Milk Fed Veal Cutlet* $14.90

Paprikaschnitzel - *Milk Fed Veal Cutlet in
Paprika Sauce and Mushrooms* $14.90

Zwiebel Roastbraten - *Aged New York Steak with
Browned Onions* $15.50

Rack of Lamb - *Roasted with Herbs* $15.90

a la carte - $2.00 less per item

*The Beethoven Restaurant is available for private luncheons.
We also cater any occasion.*

STARTERS AND LIGHTER FARE

Chilled Oysters on the Half Shell
with Lemon Pepper Mignonette
10.50

Smoked Duck Quesadilla
with Green Chile, Tetilla Cheese, Pumpkin Seeds
8.50

Manila Clams
Steamed in Chardonnay, Garlic and Herbs, with Vegetable Julienne
and Garlic Toast
7.50

Pepper Crusted Ahi Tuna
Pan-Seared with Crisp Potato Pancake and
Mango-Corriander Vinaigrette
8.50

Black Pepper Fettuccine
Tossed in Virgin Olive Oil with Spicy Lamb Sausage,
Wild Mushrooms, Tomato and Chevre
appetizer 7.50   entree 13.50

Grilled Whole Artichoke
with Warm Marinated Goat Cheese, Finished with Hazelnut Crust
and Hazelnut Vinaigrette
8.50

Lobster and Crab Enchiladas
Rolled in Corn Crepes,
served on Spicy Red and Yellow Tomato Coulis
13.95

Pan-Fried Dungeness Crab Cakes
served over Greens with Mustard Caper Vinaigrette
appetizer 7.50   entree 14.50

Grilled Salad Nicoise
Served Warm with Fresh Ahi Tuna, Traditional Garnishes
and Lemon-Dill Vinaigrette
12.95

1075 California St • Nob Hill • (415) 771-1140

Mixed Spring Greens with Vinaigrette
5.95

Caesar Salad
Baby Hearts of Romaine with Reggiano Parmesan
6.95

ENTREES

Sesame Chicken Salad
with Crisp Vegetables, Toasted Cashews and Lemon-Ginger Dressing
10.95

Junior Club Sandwich
with Roasted Turkey Breast, Cheddar and Apple-Smoked Bacon,
served with Gaufrette Potatoes
9.50

Crab Louis
Freshly Picked Dungeness Crab Meat, Avocado, French Beans,
Greens and Louis Dressing
14.50

Chuckburger
with Cheddar, Lettuce and Tomato on Poppyseed Roll,
served with French Fries
9.50

Chicken Pot Pie
Poached Chicken and Vegetables in a Sherry Laced Cream
with Puff Pastry
9.50

Dungeness Crab Cakes
Pan-Fried, served with French Fries and Mustard Seed Remoulade
13.50

Grilled Salad Nicoise
served Warm with Fresh Ahi Tuna, Traditional Garnishes
and Lemon-Dill Vinaigrette
12.95

Grilled Norwegian Salmon
Served over Spinach and Nasturtium Salad with
Toasted Almond Vinaigrette and Onion Crisps
13.95

Lobster and Crab Enchiladas
in Corn Crepes with Black Beans and Spicy Tomato Coulis
13.95

Peppered Filet of Beef
served on a Crisp Rosti Potato
with Morel-Cognac Cream
14.50

Veal Piccata
Milk Fed Loin Sauteed with Lemon, Capers and Parsley
13.95

CR

Carnelian Room

Menu Changes Seasonally

APPETIZERS

Oysters on the Half Shell
Horseradish Cream   8.

Smoked Scottish Salmon
with Tassajara Rye Crustini   10.

Chilled Roasted Prawns with Tomatoes and Basil
Extra Virgin Olive Oil   11.

Beluga Caviar with Blini and Crème Fraîche
Iced Stolichnaya Vodka   60.

Smoked Duck Breast with Papaya Confit   9.

Steak Tartare prepared Tableside   10.

•

Dungeness Crab Cakes
with Jalapeño Coulis   11.

Risotto Vialone with Pears and Gorgonzola   8.

Spinach Ravioli with Prawns, Diced Tomatoes and Pesto   11.

SOUPS

Onion Soup Grantinée
with Gruyère Cheese   6.

San Francisco Crab and Seafood Chowder   7.

Lobster Bisque with Cognac   8.

SALADS

Belgian Endive Salad with Apples and Pecans   8.

French Bean Salad with Sauteed Foie Gras de Canard   15.

Caesar Salad for Two
with Reggiano Parmesan   14.

Sonoma Mixed Field Greens
with Laura Chenel Goat Cheese   7.

ENTREES

Roasted Northwest Salmon
with Caramelized Shallots   24.

Sauteed Petrale Sole Fillet
with Parsley and Almonds   23.

Pacific Baby Abalone
Lemon Beurre Blanc   36.

Live Maine Lobster
Baby Vegetables and Tarragon   36.

Linguine with Rock Shrimp and Shiitake Mushrooms
Basil Broth   19.

Grilled Ahi Tuna
Vodka and Caviar Sauce   26.

•

Sauteed Free Range Chicken Breast
with Morel Mushrooms   19.

Twice Roasted Half Petaluma Duckling
with Soy and Brown Sugar   21.

Individual Rack of Lamb with Eggplant Purée
Mediterranean Herbs   29.

Filet Mignon with Wild Mushroom Gratinée
Truffle Sauce   28.

THE GARDEN COURT

Appetizers

♥ *Grilled Prawns with warm Potato Salad
and Spicy Mango Coriander Oil*
$9.95

*Morel Mushroom Purses
with Sonoma Foie Gras and Morel Brandy Cream*
$10.50

*Cinnamon Seabass Gravlax and Caviar Napoleon
with Carrot, Beet and Dill Creme Fraiche Quenelles*
$7.50

*Smoked Salmon and Trout Terrine
with Artichoke Tomato Relish, Wheat Crouton and Horseradish Aioli*
$7.75

♥ *Duo of Tomato with Teleme Cheese,
Proscuitto Vinaigrette and Kalamata Olives*
$6.75

Soups

*Lobster Bisque
Mirepoix of Fennel, Cucumber and Lobster Roe*
$6.75

♥ *Duck Broth of Beet and Celeriac garnished
with Duck Confit, Cabbage and Sour Cream*
$5.75

---

2 New Montgomery • Financial District • (415) 392-8600

Salads

♥ *Spring Field Greens with Sweet Potato,*
Spicy Cream Cheese Sandwich and Radiccio Vinaigrette
$5.50

Hearts of Baby Romaine with Pimento and Crisp Lardons served
with a Roasted Garlic and Cracked Black Pepper Dressing
$6.00

Entrees

♥ *Herb Layered Steamed Salmon*
Halibut Fillet with Vegetable Spaghetti and Pomegranate Syrup
$21.00

♥ *Crispy Skillet Sea Scallops in Lemon Artichoke Broth*
served with Saffron Risotto Timbale
$19.75

♥ *Grilled Pacific Swordfish*
on Squid-Broccoli Rabe Salad and Anchovie Caper Mayonnaise
$20.50

♥ *Grilled Tuna Medallions*
with Ginger Linguini, Daikon-Cucumber Relish and Pineapple Coconut Syrup
$20.95

♥ *Yogurt Honey Marinated Free Range Chicken*
with Lentil Broth and Rhubarb Onion Chutney
$17.75

Broiled Black Angus Sirloin
with Pinot Noir Butter, Double Baked Stuffed Purple Potatoes and Baby Leek Pudding
$22.50

Pan Seared Domestic Lamb Chops
with Basmati Rice Wrapped Grape Leaves and Eggplant Tomato Jam
$23.50

Sauteed Venison Medallions
with Warm Compote of Brussels Sprout, Chestnut, Rutabagas and Mini Berry Tartlet
$25.50

Meadowood
Napa Valley

THE RESTAURANT

LUNCH

Starters

Fresh Fish Soup   4.75
Arugula, Frisee and Radicchio with Virgin Olive Oil   5.00
Baked Brie Croûton with Forest Mushrooms, Pancetta and Paprika   5.75
Halibut Gnocchi with Baked Tomatoes and Gruyère   5.50
Miyagi Oysters with Champagne Sauce and Caviar   6.25

Main Course Salads

Warm Mushroom Salad   11.50
Warm Eggplant Salad with Garlic Toast and Bell Pepper Sauce   10.75
Two Cabbage Salad with Duck Confit   11.00

Entrees

Daily Special   A.Q.
Crab Cake with Fried Zucchini and Basil Oil   12.75
Smoked Salmon on a Corn Cake with Sour Cream and Herbs   12.50
Eggplant and Tomato Gratin with Melted Mozzarella and Fried Sage   11.75
Pan Fried Atlantic Salmon with Crispy Potatoes, Asparagus, and Soy Juice   13.50
Grilled Sea Scallops, Salmon and Prawns with Miso and Saffron Pasta   14.50
Veal Piccata and Fettucine with Capers and Sun Dried Tomatoes   13.50
Grilled Breast of Chicken with Polenta and Ratatouille   11.50
Veal and Risotto Croquettes on Herbed Tomatoes   10.50

900 Meadowood Lane • St Helena • (707) 963-3646

APPETIZERS

MEDITERRANEAN FISH SOUP with Rouille, Croûtons, and Grated Cheese	5.50
ARUGULA, RADICCHIO, and FRISEE LETTUCES with Walnut Vinaigrette	6.00
SAUTED DUNGENESS CRAB CAKE and CRISPY JULIENNE of LEEK on Lobster Pesto Sauce	8.00
WARM MIYAGI OYSTERS on the HALF SHELL with Champagne Sauce and Two Caviar	8.00
HOMEMADE FOIE GRAS on Artichoke Salad and Sourdough Toast	11.50
DRY HERB MARINATED SALMON with American Caviar	8.00
PLAT de TAPAS with Shrimp, Mushrooms, Calmari and Stuffed Mussels	8.50

ENTREES

PAELLA CATALAN (20 Minutes for Preparation) with Lamb Sausage, Chicken, Mussels, Clams, Monkfish, Shrimps and Calamari	24.00
ROASTED ATLANTIC SALMON with Crispy Skin, Salsify and White Truffle Vinaigrette	22.50
GRILLED SEA SCALLOPS with Mashed Potatoes, Spinach, Caviar, and Garlic Basil Sauce	20.50
BAKED FARM HEN BREAST with Spanish Olive Oil, Garlic, Ruby Crescent Potatoes, Fresh Herbs and Wild Mushrooms	18.50
GRILLED PRIME NEW YORK STEAK with Cabernet Caramelized Shallot Sauce and Fresh Thyme Potatoes	24.50
ROASTED VENISON with Chestnut Puree, Mushrooms, Confit of Shallots and Huckleberry Sauce	24.00
GRILLED and ROASTED CALIFORNIA RACK of LAMB with Sautéd Vegetables and Garlic-Mustard Juice	25.00
BAKED SWEETBREADS PERPIGNAN with Tomatoes, Garlic, White Wine, Flageolet White Beans, and Peppers	19.50
STEAMED HALIBUT with Clams, Aïoli Broth and Poached Potatoes	21.50
GRILLED VEAL CHOP with Morel-Tarragon Juice and Artichoke Ragout	24.00

Sunday Brunch; Dinner: 7 Days a Week 5:30 - 10 ●ⓁⒹ

T⁰URELLE CAFE & BAR

— LIGHT DISHES AND APPETIZERS —

PIZZETTA with onion, goat cheese and bacon
(*NAVARRO GEWURZTRAMINER*)   4.00

PIZZETTA with sweet peppers, oregano and feta cheese   4.75

BUTTERNUT SQUASH RAVIOLI with brown butter and sage   5.25

TIMBALE OF POLENTA with wild mushrooms and mascarpone cheese   4.00

STEAMED MUSSELS with leeks, tarragon and dijon mustard
(*ST. SUPERY SAUVIGNON BLANC*)   7.00

SMOKED AHI with horseradish creme fraiche   6.50

SEARED VENISON CARPACCIO with shiitake mushrooms and parmesan
(*CONDE DE VALDEMAR RIOJA*)   7.25

DUCK LIVER PATE with mixed greens and cornichon   4.25

— SALADS —

WARM GOAT CHEESE served on baby greens with walnuts and crostini   6.75

MIXED WILD GREENS with glazed walnuts and danish blue cheese   6.25

HEARTS OF ROMAINE tossed with creamy parmesan dressing and
toasted croutons   5.75

GRILLED PRAWN SALAD with mixed greens, sweet pepper, eggplant
and orange-cumin vinaigrette ♥   13.75

— FROM THE OAK FIRED PIZZA OVEN—

FRESH MOZZARELLA PIZZA with sundried tomatoes, basil and
artichoke hearts   10.50

COPPA AND MARINATED TOMATO PIZZA with port salut cheese   12.75

CALZONE with spinach, artichokes, sundried tomatoes and smoked
mozzarella   12.00

*(WITH ANY PIZZA OUR CHEF RECOMMENDS A HALF BOTTLE OF
FONTODI CHIANTI CLASSICO, RESERVA)*

3565 Mount Diablo Blvd • Lafayette • (510) 284-3565

— PASTA —

SPAGHETTI PUTANESCA with anchovies, capers, olives, garlic and
tomatoes ♥   11.00

TAGLIERINI with mushrooms, sausage, and smoked tomato   13.00

PENNE BOLOGNESE with parmesan cheese and parsley   10.75

— ENTREES —

*TOURELLE'S COUNTRY EUROPEAN CUISINE FEATURES SELECTIONS
FROM OUR SMOKER, GRILL AND OAK FIRED PIZZA OVEN.*

GRILLED HOUSE MADE GARLIC SAUSAGE with herb polenta   12.00

SAUTEED CHICKEN BREAST with artichoke, roasted tomato and
olive ragout   15.00

GRILLED HOUSE SMOKED PORK CHOP with sundried
cranberry-tomato relish (RIOJA, CONDE DE VALDEMAR)   15.00

SAUTEED SCALLOPINI OF VEAL with marsala, proscuitto, lemon
and sage (ACACIA, PINOT NOIR)   19.50

DUCK COOKED TWO WAYS: sauteed breast and braised leg with
coriander, olives and orange   17.50

GRILLED LOIN OF LAMB with a roasted garlic-eggplant sauce
(STAG'S LEAP CABERNET SAUVIGNON)   17.00

ROASTED QUAIL with raisin-pistachio stuffing and braised
mustard greens   19.50

GRILLED MEDALLIONS OF FILET MIGNON with horseradish-basil
creme fraiche (TOURELLE MERLOT)   18.00

— SAMPLE OF DAILY SPECIAL SELECTIONS —

SAUTEED HALIBUT with spiced tomato and cilantro puree   17.00

GRILLED SALMON with scallop-brandy sauce
(JOSEPH PHELPS CHARDONNAY)   17.50

GRILLED AHI with orange, basil and cracked pepper ♥
(ST. SUPREY, SAUVIGNON BLANC)   18.00

♥ *Items prepared are lower in calories, fat and cholesterol.*

Our Chef has paired specific glasses of wine with a few of our specialties.

Sunday Brunch; Dinner: Sun - Thurs 5:30 - 10:30, Fri - Sat 5 - 11   ● Ⓛ Ⓓ

MEET ME AT THE SQUARE

LUNCH AND DINNER MENUS CHANGE DAILY

Today's Specials

Seafood Ravioli Filled with Shrimp, Scallops & Crab in a Light Marinara Sauce	12.95
Angel Hair Pasta with Breast of Chicken, Mushrooms, Red & Green Bell Peppers & Garlic Cream	10.95
Fresh Filet of Halibut Grilled with Sauce Romesco, Served on a Bed of Spinach	14.50
Grilled Sirloin of Lamb en Brochette, Served with Rice Madras & Major Grey's Chutney	15.95
Appetizer Special: Fresh Virginia Oysters on the Half Shell	6.95

Starters

Toasted Meat Ravioli with Spicy Tomato Sauce	4.95
Calamari Fritti	5.95
Artichoke Stuffed with Shrimp	5.95
Herb Marinated Goat Cheese & Roasted Peppers	4.95
Scottish Smoked Salmon with Capers & Onion	8.95
Tortellini alla Panna	4.95
Fried Zucchini	3.50
Smoked Trout, Cucumber Salad & Horseradish Cream	5.95
Marinated Herring Filet	4.95
Fresh Asparagus with Warm Vinaigrette Dressing	4.95

Today's Soup

Manhattan Clam Chowder	3.95

Salads

Fresh Seasonal Mixed Green Salad	4.95
with Roquefort or Goat Cheese	5.95
Caesar Salad	5.95
Bay Shrimp Louie	10.95
Fisherman's Salad of Calamari, Bay Shrimp & Scallops Vinaigrette	10.95

Washington Square Bar & Grill

1707 Powell St • North Beach • (415) 982-8123

Pastas

Penne Arrabbiata: Spicy Tomato	9.25
Ravioli, with Tomato or Cream Sauce	10.95
Fettuccine Alfredo	9.75
Spaghettini al Pesto	9.75
Angel Hair with Tomato, Basil & Garlic	9.75

Meat

The WSB&G Hamburger with Fries	7.50
The WSB&G Hamburger, Jack Cheese	7.95
Veal Scaloppine, Piccata	16.95
Veal Scaloppine, Marsala	16.95
Veal Parmigiana	14.95
Filet Mignon with Sauteed Mushrooms	16.95
New York Steak with Maitre d' Butter	18.95

Seafood

Calamari Saute with Mushrooms, Marsala or Arrabbiata Sauce	12.50
Fresh Sauteed Scallops, Champagne Beurre Blanc	14.50
Petrale Dore, Lemon Velvet Sauce with Capers	14.95
Prawns della Casa, Aldo	16.50
Prawns Provencale	16.50

Poultry

Chicken Piccata or Marsala	10.95
Chicken Parmigiana	11.95

Side Orders

Sauteed Mushrooms	3.95
Garlic Bread	2.50
Sauteed Onions	2.95

WSB&G's Desserts

Housemade Cheesecake w/Fresh Strawberries	4.50
Creme Caramel	3.95
Raspberry Gelato	3.95
Chocolate Mousse Cake	4.95
Coffee Dutch Almond Gelato	3.95
French Vanilla Ice Cream with Hot Fudge	3.95 / 4.50
Coeur a la Creme, Raspberry Puree	4.50
Baba au Rhum	3.95
Fresh Strawberries with Cointreau	3.95
Tarte Tatin	3.95

MANY ITEMS ON THE MENU
EACH DAY ARE PREPARED
WITH LOW FAT,
AND ARE LOW IN CALORIES

Washington Square Bar&Grill

Dinner: Mon - Sat 5:30 - 11, Sun 4 - 10:30 ●ⓁⒹ

*A LEGEND OF
ELEGANT SIMPLICITY*

LA GRANDE CUISINE SIMPLE

******

SWORDFISH STEAK
With Potato Pancake and Vodka Sour Cream Sauce. $19.00

ROASTED RABBIT
With Puree of Potato and Salt Cod. $22.00

SAUTED VEAL IN A LEMON CAPER BROTH
With Potatoes "Under the Sun". $25.00

ROAST RACK OF LAMB AND SPARE RIBS
With French Baked Potato and Roulade Provencale. $26.00

DESSERT

CREPES AND BANANA FONDANT
WITH BITTER CHOCOLATE ICE CREAM, AND ORANGE GLAZE. $8.00

APPLE PIZZA BAKED UPSIDE DOWN. $9.00

**CREME AMARETTO IN A CRUNCHY FILLO CUP,
AND NOUGATINE ARCH.** $10.00

**CHOCOLATE MOUSSE "TROMPE L'OEIL",
WITH RED FRUIT COULIS.** $9.00

**WARM ALMOND CAKE WITH MANGO SLICES
AND MINT CARAMEL ICE CREAM.** $10.00

1630 Powell St • North Beach • (415) 397-4339

LE MENU ROYAL

(Choice of One Assiette Per Course)

PREMIERE ASSIETTE

CHILLED SNOW WHITE'S SOUP WITH CAVIAR
Creme de Choux-fleur Froide et Caviar

WOVEN PASTA AND SHELLFISH
Les Pates Tressees et Crevettes Hawaiennes

DEUXIEME ASSIETTE

SAUTEED FRESH FOIE GRAS AND PEAR STAIRCASE
Le Foie Gras de Canard au Vinaigre de Framboise

CRISPY QUAIL IN A NEST OF SUGAR PEAS
La Caille Fritte Farcie d'Endives

TROISIEME ASSIETTE

GRAPE ICE ON A CANDIED GRAPE LEAF
Le Granite de Raisin sur Feuille d'Adam Cristalizee

LEMON GRASS INFUSION
Consomme a l'Herbe Citronnee

QUATRIEME ASSIETTE

MAINE LOBSTER IN A SIMPLE FASHION
Le Homard au Beurre et Sushi Croquant

FILET OF BEEF WITH A PASTRY CAP
Le Boeuf en Croute, Essence de Truffes Fraiches

CINQUIEME ASSIETTE

CHEESES AND SALAD
Les Fromages et la Petite Salade

SIXIEME ASSIETTE

GRAND MARNIER SOUFFLE BAKED IN AN ORANGE SHELL
Le Souffle Orange en Orange

$70.00 Per Person

Dinner: Tues - Sun 5:30 - 10 ●●Ⓓ

Bistro Clovis

BAR A VIN

Menu Changes Seasonally

Appetizers;

* Onion Soup "Les Halles" 3.60

* Duck Pate with Cherries &
    Pistachios served with
    onion marmalade 4.90

* Terrine of smoked Salmon,
    smoked Sturgeon and smoked
    Whitefish 6.80

* Salmon Mousse with Cucumber
    Salad 6.20

* Coquille St. Jacques 5.50

* "Androuet" Cheese selection 6.30

1596 Market St • Civic Center • (415) 864-0231

Entrees;

* Baked Goat Cheese with Garden Lettuce . . 6.50

* Sonoma Lamb Salad 7.50

* Veal Sweetbreads with Red
   Butter Vinegar 14.00

* Smoked Salmon and Mushroom Crepes 9.60

* Rabbit with Rosemary and Peppercorns . . 10.50

* Chicken with Goat Cheese and Herbs . . . 9.50

* Fish Cassoulet 12.00

* Beef Bourguignon 9.50

* Baked Endive and Ham in Mornay sauce . . 9.00

* Vegetarian Plate 7.50

Desserts;

* Chocolat Cream Grand Marnier 4.50

* Poached Pear with Cassis Cream 3.70

* Tarte des Demoiselles Tatin
   with creme fraiche 5.70

* Souffle Glace Nougatine 3.90

FRENCH ONION SOUP
4.75
MUSSELS WITH SAFFRON FUME
5.25
CRISP SWEETBREADS WITH LEMONS, LEEKS AND CAPERS
5.95
HOUSE CURED SALMON WITH DILL MASCARPONE CREAM
6.95
COUNTRY PATE WITH ONION JAM AND TOMATO-CURRANT CHUTNEY
4.75
GRILLED ASPARAGUS ON BLACK PEPPER BRIOCHE
5.50

LEEKS WITH RED BEET VINAIGRETTE
4.75
MIXED GREENS WITH DIJON VINAIGRETTE
4.50
ARUGULA, ENDIVE, SWEET CORN AND PARMESAN
5.75
WARM CHICORY FRISEE WITH APPLE SMOKED BACON AND GOAT CHEESE
6.25

155 Steuart St • Financial District • (415) 495-6500

SEARED SCALLOPS WITH EGGPLANT, TOMATO AND GARLIC RAGOUT
11.95
SALMON PAILLARD WITH COARSE GRAIN MUSTARD CREAM AND TOMATOES
12.95
TIGER PRAWNS AND WHITE BEANS, LEMON, PARSLEY, MUSTARD AND AIOLI
9.95

SPIT ROASTED MINT AND GARLIC HALF CHICKEN
10.75
ROASTED CHICKEN BREAST "COQ AU VIN" STYLE
11.50
SPIT ROASTED DUCK WITH PICKLED FIG CHUTNEY
13.50
GRILLED SONOMA RABBIT WITH SOUR CHERRY GAME SAUCE
12.95
PORK CHOP WITH TOMATO-SCALLION VINAIGRETTE
11.95
GRILLED ENTRECOTE AND POMMES FRITES
19.95
BRAISED LAMB SHANK WITH MOROCCAN COUS-COUS
12.50
GRILLED VEAL CHOP WITH HERBS DE PROVENCE
18.95

SEASONED ONION RINGS
3.95
POMMES FRITES
3.95
POTATOES 3RD ARRONDISSEMENT
5.50

HOUSEMADE SORBETS
4.95
HYSTERICAL COOKIE PLATTER
4.95
MARINATED SUMMER FRUIT AND BUTTERMILK BISQUIT
5.25
CHERRY AND APRICOT BRIOCHE PUDDING
5.95
CHOCOLATE TRUFFLE CAKE WITH MANGO SAUCE
5.50

Sunday Brunch; Dinner: Sun - Thurs until 10, Fri - Sat until 11

Restaurant - Banquet Room - Catering
152 Kearny Street, San Francisco ❖ 434-3688/3689

APPETIZERS

Onion Soup Gratinee 5.50   Escargots de Bourgogne 6.75
Spicy Bay Shrimps Gazpacho 5.75   Vegetable Soup of the Day 4.25
Seasonal Baby Mixed Green Vinaigrette 4.25 or Roquefort Cheese 5.00
Chambord Home Cured Prosciutto with Cantaloupe 6.50
Avocado Tomato Salad Orange Vinaigrette 6.50
Smoked Salmon or Gravlax, Romaine Lettuce Mimosa 7.25
Oyster on Half Shell Sauce Mignoletto 8.50

SALADS

BBQ Chicken Salad in Sesame Oil Dressing 11.95
Garden Vegetables plates nicoise with Tuna 11.95
Pan Fried Jumbo Sea Scallops Salad with Radishes 7.25   Large 13.95
Caesar Salad with Bay Shrimps and Avocado 11.95
Asslette Charcutierc Cold Meat Selection 12.95

SEAFOOD

Pan Fried Petrale Sole Filet with Capers Lemon Butter 14.25
Poached Salmon Steak, Fresh and Sun Dried Tomato Relish 15.95
Pan Fried Snapper Filet, topped with Bell Pepper and Preserved Lemon 12.25
Monk Fish Stew Flavored with "Reunion Island Spices" 15.25
Classical Trout Filet in Almonds Butter 11.75
Home made Crab Ravioli 13.25
Linguini with Clams and Mussels 12.25

ENTREE

Mixed Grilled Lamb Chops and Merguez 16.95
Filet - Mignon with Five - Peppercorn Sauce 16.50
Stuffed Chicken Breast with Wild Mushrooms and Prosciutto 12.25
Veal Scaloppini, Piccata or Mustard Sauce 17.25
Skirt Steak a L'echalotte 13.95
Beef Bourguignon 11.95
Duck Breast Mango Sauce 14.95

DESSERTS

Chocolat Tart 4.50   Wild Turkey Chocolat - Pudding 4.50
Dark and White Chocolat Mousse 4.50   Cream Caramel 4.50
Poached Pears in Red Wine and Cinnamon 4.50
Fresh Fruits with Sorbet 4.50   Ice Cream 3.75
Cheese - Cake of the Day 4.50

COFFEE - TEA

Columbian Dark Roast Café 2.00   Tea 2.00   Mint Tea 2.00
Espresso 2.25   Cappucino 2.75   Fresh Brewed Decaffeininated Coffee 2.00

*Open for Breakfast, Lunch, and Dinner 7 am. to 9:30 p.m. Monday thru Saturday
Sunday; Breakfast Only. We accept Visa, Mastercard, American Express*

CAFÉ

JACQUELINE

SEASONAL MENU

CAFÉ

American Coffee 2... Espresso 2.50

Cappuccino 2.50... Doppio 2.50

Filtre 5.00... Café Latté 2.50

Thé 2.50

SOUP

Onion au gratin 7.50

Soup du jour 4.50

SALAD

Butter Lettuce 4.00

Cucumber 4.50

Watercress 4.50

Tomato herbe 4.50

Spinach Bacon Pine Nut 7.50

1454 Grant Ave • North Beach • (415) 981-5565

ENTRÉE SOUFFLÉ

(Serves Two)

Gruyére 18

Combined with Mushroom 19... Garlic 19

Broccoli 19... Spinach 19

Cauliflower 19... Leek 19

Rôquefort 21... Tomato Cilantro 19

Prosciutto Mushroom 22

(Additional Combination Soufflés Available & Daily Specialties)

Soufflé Specials of the Day

White Corn, Ginger, Garlic,

Asparagus, Shiitake Mushrooms,

Seafood (Shrimp& Scallop)

DESSERT SOUFFLÉS

(Serves Two / Four)

Fresh Fruit Soufflé (In Season)

Chocolate 19... Grand Marnier 21... White Chocolate 22

Mousse au chocolat Grand Marnier

Bon Appétit!

LUNCH - Menu Changes Monthly

MENU

___ Lentil Soup with Crisp Bacon and Fresh Herbs $6.00
___ Minestrone of Prawns, Mussels, and Scallops finished with a Basil Pistou $7.50
___ Mixed Young Greens tossed with Fresh Herbs and Hazelnut Vinaigrette $5.00
___ Caesar Salad, with Romaine Lettuce, Croutons and Fresh Grated Parmesan Cheese $7.00
___ Grilled Citrus Chicken Salad on Organic Greens $12.50
___ Oriental-Style Salad with Soy Beans, Fresh Coriander, Carrots and a Sesame Oil Vinaigrette
served with Market Fish $13.50
___ Potato Gnocchi and Clams served with Marinara Sauce $12.00
___ Bolognese-Stuffed Cannelloni with Sauce of Artichokes, Onions and Garlic $13.50
___ Crisp Calamari, Sauce Américaine served with Fresh Green Vegetables $13.50
___ Tart of Tomato Confit, Smoked Ham and Gruyere topped with Fresh Greens $13.00
___ Roasted Pear with Cracked Black Pepper and Champagne Gastrique
served with Roquefort Cheese $11.00
___ Omelette with Mushrooms and Fresh Herbs, with a Green Salad and Homemade Chips $12.50
___ Beef or Chicken Sandwich, Tapenade, Aioli, Fresh Tomatoes and Greens $15.00/$13.50
___ Dungeness Crab and Asparagus Cake with Tomato Gelée $13.00
___ Crispy skin Salmon, Spicy Sauce, Corn-Potato Pancakes with Cucumber Relish $15.00
___ Pan-Roasted Fillet of Petrale drizzled with Lemon and Olive Oil
served with Steamed Farm Vegetables $14.50
___ Breast of Chicken served with its Own Juices, Matchstick Potatoes and Young Greens $14.00
___ Creamy Risotto of Pork with Carrots, Onions, Bacon, Capers, and Crispy Basil $15.00

THREE COURSE PRIX FIXE LUNCH - $15.00
Your Choice of Soup or Salad, Entree, Homemade Sorbet - Menu changes daily

---

847 Montgomery St • Financial District • (415) 397-5969

DINNER - Menu Changes Seasonally

HORS D'OEUVRES

Terrine of Roasted Eggplant and Red Pepper Fresh Herb Marinade 11.00

Venison Loin Salad with Ragout of Mushrooms, Spiced Apples, and Walnut Vinaigrette 13.00

Dungeness Crab and Asparagus Cake with Tomato Gelee 13.00

Braised Young Fennel, Greek-Style, Served with Tomato, Nicoise Olives and Basil Croquette 12.00

Curly Cabbage stuffed with Smoked Salmon, perfumed with Dill, Lemon Sauce 14.00

Fresh Oysters on the Half Shell with Champagne Vinegar and Shallots 11.00

Duck Foie Gras Sauteed, served with Confit of Sweet Potato in White Port and a Sage "Surprise" 14.00

Roasted Pear with cracked Black Pepper, Champagne Gastrique and Roquefort 11.00

Talmouse of Prosciutto and Parmesan with Celery Root Green Onion Salad and Virgin Olive Oil 12.00

Shrimp, Scallops and Calamari in Consomme with Lemon, Fresh Herbs and light Caviar Cream 14.00

Sea Scallops in Pastry Shell A La Duglere 12.00

LA SALADE

Young Greens with Hazelnut Dressing and Fresh Herbs 6.50

ENTREES

Crispy Skin Roasted Salmon with Wild Mushrooms and a Potato Tarragon Coulis 25.00

Striped Bass Fillet, sautéed and served with Spicy Citrus Sauce and Braised Fennel 27.00

Maine Lobster sautéed, with Artichokes in a Thyme Flower Juice with Fresh Herbs 31.00

Swordfish Tournedos Pan Roasted, wrapped with Bacon, Parsley Juice and Crisp Potatoes 26.00

Chicken Breast stuffed with Gorgonzola, and Eggplant Cannelloni with Fresh Tomato Sauce 25.00

Grilled Tournedos of Beef with a Classic Red Wine Sauce, Shallot Confit and Blinis of Potatoes 26.00

Pan Roasted Veal Chop with a Chive Sauce and Potatoes Dauphine 29.00

Roast Rack of Lamb served with a Garlic, Caper Puree and Thyme Sauce (for two) 26.00

Roast Duck with a Confit of Turnips in Port Wine, a Griblette of the Legs 27.00

Braised Oxtail with Onions, Natural Juices, Young Carrots and Potatoes Soufflés 24.00

LEGUMES

Potato Soufflés $5.50

Alain Rondelli ✿ Chef de Cuisine

Dinner: Mon - Sat 6 - 9:30

FLEUR DE LYS
R E S T A U R A N T

STARTERS

LOBSTER AND COCONUT MILK SOUP
FLAVORED WITH LEMON GRASS AND GINGER $11.50

*

CHILLED CUCUMBER SOUP,
VODKA SORBET AND AMERICAN STURGEON CAVIAR $ 9.50

* *

SYMPHONY OF FLEUR DE LYS APPETIZERS $16.00

*

NEW YORK STATE FOIE GRAS,
AND BLACK PEPPER AND FRESH HERB GELEE $22.00

*

SEA URCHIN MOUSSELINE
PRESENTED ON SEA SCALLOP, ASPARAGUS SAUCE $14.50

*

MAINE LOBSTER AND MACARONI "AU GRATIN" $21.50

*

FRESH NORWEGIAN SALMON
BAKED IN A TENDER CORN PANCAKE,
TOPPED WITH GOLDEN CAVIAR, WATERCRESS SAUCE $16.00

*

BELUGA CAVIAR
ACCOMPANIED BY CELERY ROOT BLINIS $48.00

* *

MARYLAND CRAB CAKES,
ON BABY LETTUCES AND GREOJA SAUCE $13.75

*

ROASTED EGGPLANT AND PURE GOAT MILK CHEESE
ON BABY SPINACH $10.00

*

777 Sutter St • Union Square • (415) 673-7779

MAIN COURSES

HERB CRUSTED SALMON "AU JUS"
ON WILTED RADICCIO WITH CRACKED PEPPER POLENTA $28.50

*

BROILED SEA BASS,
IN A GOLDEN POTATO CRUST
ACCENTED WITH A RHUBARB COULIS $27.50

*

PAN FRIED STURGEON
WITH MASHED POTATOES, ROASTED
PEPPERS ON BLACK OLIVE ESSENCE $29.00

*

SEARED AHI TUNA,
ON LIGHTLY CREAMED SPINACH,
SESAME OIL VINAIGRETTE $27.50

*

MUSCOVY DUCK BREAST,
THINLY SLICED, SERVED WITH
SAUTEED APPLES AND GREEN PEPPER CORN $26.50

*

BONELESS SQUAB,
PRESENTED WITH AN ARRAY
OF VEGETABLES, CAPERS AND PORT WINE SAUCE $28.50

*

MARINATED LOIN OF VENISON
GLAZED WITH MUSTARD SABAYON,
SAUCE "POIVRADE" $29.50

*

VEAL CHOP
COVERED WITH ONION "PERSILLADE"
ZUCCHINI, EGGPLANT AND TOMATO PIE $28.50

*

GRILLED FILET MIGNON
SERVED WITH RATATOUILLE AND
ROASTED GARLIC $28.50

*

OVEN ROASTED LAMB LOIN
PARSNIP FLAN AND MUSTARD SEED SAGE SAUCE $30.00

*

PORK TENDERLOIN
CILANTRO FLAVORED ON BLACK BEANS
AND SMOKED BACON, FRESH CORN RELISH $25.50

* * *

THE FRENCH LAUNDRY

Five-Course Prix-Fixe Menu

Changes Daily
$46.00

~ *APPETIZERS* ~

Artichoke with Garlic Mayonnaise
A Sauté of Scallops with Bacon and Mustard
Carpaccio of Tuna with Red Onion
on Red Cabbage
Smoked Chicken with a Tomato Ginger Salsa
Curried Chicken Mousse with Apricot Chutney
Crisp Duck with Apricot Chutney
Rock Shrimp in Chili Butter

~ DINNER ~

Red Pepper Soup with Cumin Cream
Braised Rabbit
Green Salad and Cheeses
Panzanella
Grilled Lamb
Cold Avocado Soup
Duckling with a Curry Glaze

~ DESSERTS ~

Raspberries in a Chocolate Meringue
Pears Helene
Coffee Walnut Sponge Cake
Chocolate Chinchilla
Apple Clafouti
Poached Figs with Ginger Ice Cream
Apple and Huckleberry Clafouti

SOUP OF THE DAY   4.50

LOBSTER BISQUE   6.50

FROG LEGS SOUP "PAUL BOCUSE"   7.00

ONION SOUP GRATINEE   5.50

MIXED BABY LETTUCE   5.00

HEART OF ROMAINE WITH ROQUEFORT   6.50

ENDIVES AND WATERCRESS   6.50

SEVRUGA CAVIAR   28.00

SAUTEED PRAWNS   8.50
with a Thai spice sauce

SMOKED SALMON   8.50
served with capers and toast

SEAFOOD SAUSAGE   7.00
served with a lobster sauce

MOUSSELINE OF SCALLOPS   7.25
with LOBSTER and MORELS
served with a champagne sauce

---

465 Davis Court • Financial District • (415) 981-7824

FEUILLETE OF LOBSTER AND SPINACH   10.50
served with a sauterne and paprika sauce

ESCARGOTS DE BOURGOGNE   7.00
sauteed with garlic butter

GRILLED TUNA   16.00
served with a fresh basil oil

ROULADES OF PETRALE SOLE FILETS   16.00
*served with tagliarini and
glazed with a sauvignon blanc sauce*

ROAST SALMON   18.00
topped with arómates

BAKED SEABASS   16.00
served over diced vegetables and a citrus butter

SPECIALTY BOUILLABAISSE
$24.00

L'Olivier is a member of the
"Charte de la Bouillabaisse" from France.

BREAST OF MUSCOVIE DUCK   18.00
served with an orange-vinegar sauce

STUFFED BREAST OF CHICKEN   15.50
with shitake mushrooms and red bell peppers

CALIFORNIA SQUAB   22.00
served with an apple-vinegar sauce

SAUTEED SCALOPPINI OF VEAL   18.00
served with a whole grain mustard sauce

RABBIT CASSEROLE WITH LEEKS   17.00
served in its own juice

RACK OF LAMB   19.50
with thyme and honey

TOURNEDOS OF FILET MIGNON   20.00
served with a shallot and cabernet sauvignon sauce

Roland & Jamie
Passot

RESTAURANT

2316 Polk St., San Francisco, Ca 94109   (415) 776-5577

Appetizers

Tartar Of Salmon Served On A Corn And Potato Pancake
In A Horseradish Cream Sauce 9.50

Ravioli Of Foie Gras Wrapped In
Cabbage Leaves With A Truffle Vinaigrette 15.00

A Simple "Green" Salad 6.50

Salad "Pressee" With Layered Smoked Salmon,
Crab And Asparagus 13.50

Ragout Of Aspargus, Baby Vegetables,
Wild MushroomsWith Basil 12.50

Imperial Chinese Beluga Caviar (1 Ounce)
Served On A Corn And Potato Pancake** 38.50

Cold Gallantine Of Sonoma Foie Gras
With A Sauterne Aspic And Country Bread* 18.50

Vegetable Consomme With a Leek Flan 7.00

Parsley And Garlic Soup With A Ragout Of Snails
And Shiitake Mushrooms 7.50

Entrees

Roast Atlantic Salmon on bed of Pureed Onions
with Merlot Wine Sauce 22.50

Sliced Breast Of Barbarie Duck
With A Wild Blueberry Sauce 22.50

Roti Of Quail And Squab Wrapped In Crispy Potato
Strings In A Natural Juice With Truffles* 26.00

Roast Loin Of Rabbit Stuffed With Garlic And Spinach
In Thyme And Rosemary Juice 18.50

Beef Tenderloin With A Beaujolais Sauce
Served With A Bone Marrow Flan And Confit Of Shallots 25.00

Roast Rack Of Lamb And Loin Stuffed
With Couscous And Cranberries In A Tarragon Sauce 24.50

Potato Spiral of Sweetbread and shiitake Mushrooms "Ragout"
with a Port Sauce and a Parsley Coulis 24.50

- - - - - - - - - - -

"Discovery Menu"

Please choose from our a la carte menu
a five course menu consisting of an
appetizer, soup, sorbet, entree and dessert.

$ 45.00 per person

* 5.00 addition if chosen on the discovery menu
** 20.00 addition if chosen on the discovery menu

- - - - - - - - - -

Please no cigars or pipes.
We accept Mastercard, Visa, American Express and Diners Cards.
For parties of 7 or more, 15 % service will be added.

Le Castel

Les Salades

Coeur Romaine au Roquefort	5.50
Heart of Romaine with Blue Cheese Dressing	
Salade Maison	5.50
House Specialty	

Hors d'Oeuvres

Coquilles St. Jacques Provencale	$ 6.75
Sauteed Scallop with Basil Garlic Tomato Sauce	
Pâté Maison	5.75
House Specialty Paté	
Toast á la Moélle	5.25
Bone Marrow on Toast	
L'escargot de Bourgogne	7.00
Burgundy Snail in the Shell	
Cervelle de Veau au Beurre Noir	5.50
Veal Brain, Herbs Butter and Vinegar	

Les Entreés

Les Nouilles aux Fruits de Mer Mixed Seafood Pasta with Basil, Mussel Sauce	$ 14.75
Le Confit de Canard Alsacien en Choucrôute Crispy Duck Breast Alsacian Style	15.75
Le Poisson Grillé du Jour avec la Sauce du Chef Grilled Fresh Fish with Chef's Special Sauce	16.00
Les Ris de Veau en Crôute Mousseline Estragon Sweet bread in the crust, Tarragon Sauce	15.00
Le Filet Mignon Grillé, Coeur d'Artichaud, Sauce Béarnaise Grilled Beef Filet with Artichoke and Bearnaise Sauce	18.50
L'Homard Frais aux Pâtes á Sauce Nantua Fresh Maine Lobster with Pasta and Nantua Sauce	23.50
L'Escalope de Veau à la Moutarde Ancienne, et Champignons Sauvages Veal Scalopini with Wild Mushrooms in Old Fashioned Mustard Sauce	19.00

Les Desserts

$5.50

Creme Brûlée	*Crêpes Suzette*
Selection de Patisseries	*Fresh Fruits of the Season*

Les Boissons Chaudes

Café Maison	*Café Decafeiné*	*Thé*	$2.00
Café Expresso			2.50
Cappuccino			3.00

Le Central

SALADS

Butter lettuce 4.75
Belgian Endives, Roquefort Cheese 7.95
Greek Salad 5.45
Tomato w/ Onion, Tuna or Anchovies,
    Egg, Olives 5.95
Grilled Egg Plant and Tomato w/Fresh Herbs....5.25
Fresh Leeks Vinaigrette (in season).......................4.95
Fresh Celery Root Remoulade (in season) 5.95
Marinated Goat Cheese w/ Tomatoes 5.95
Roasted Fresh Beets w/ Mixed Spring 7.95

SALAD NICOISE
(Lettuce, Green Beans, Potatoes, Bell Pepper,
Tomatoes, Anchovies, Tuna, Egg)............................**12.95**

APPETISERS

Norwegian Smoked Salmon 8.95
Filet of Smoked Trout, Potato Salad
      Horseradish sauce 8.95
Escargots de Bourgogne 6.75
Paté de Campagne *(Country Style)* 4.95

CRAB CAKE BEURRE BLANC **5.95**

INDIVIDUAL ONION TARTE **4.95**

SAUCISSON CHAUD **5.95**

(Warm Garlic Sausage, Potato Vinaigrette)

PATES – PASTA

Fresh Ravioli of the Day 11.95
Special pasta of the Day .... A.Q.
Cannelloni 12.25

POISSONS – FISH

Grilled or Poached Filet of Salmon 15.75
   Beurre Nantais
Grilled Jumbo Prawns, Saffron Risotto 16.95
Cold Salmon, Sauce Verte 15.25
Sea Scallops Sauté Provençale 14.95

VIANDES – MEATS – POULTRY

Steak Tartare 18.95
Steak Pommes Frites (French Fries) with Sauteed Onions 17.95
Filet Mignon au Poivre (Pepper Sauce) 19.95
Rack of Lamb Persillé (for one person) 19.95
Roast Chicken Pommes Frites 12.25
Cold Roast Chicken Mayonnaise 12.25
Grilled Paillard of Chicken w/ Pasta 12.95

BOUDIN NOIR (Blood Sausage) 11.75
   Pommes Frites, Apple
CHOUCROUTE GARNIE a l'ALSACIENNE 12.95
CASSOULET "LE CENTRAL" 11.95

Restaurant Le Trou

~ Les Apéritifs ~

Prosecco Venegazzu Méthode Champenoise   5.50

Kir Royale   6.50

Pineau des Charentes   4.75

Lillet Blonde   4.00

~ Les Entrées ~

Asparagus Soup
with Crème Fraîche   4.75

Onion, Pancetta and Goat Cheese Tart   5.00

Beet Custard
with Creamed Leeks, Walnuts, and Pickled Carrot   5.00

Salad of Baby Greens   4.25

Mussel Salad
with Fennel, Roasted Peppers, and Baby Arugula   5.50

~ _Les Principaux_ ~

Beef Culotte
with Sauce Provengale   14.50

Rabbit Ragoût
with Mushrooms, Shallots and Greens with a Rice Timbale   14.00

Dry Marinated Breast of Duck
served with Black Currant Sauce with Wild Rice   15.50

Lamb Loin Chops and Crépinettes with Garlic Sauce
served with French Lentils, Eggplant, and Baby Spinach   16.00

Our Seafood Selection varies daily
based on the freshest available product   AQ

~ _Les Desserts_ ~

Créme Brûlée   4.25

Lemon Curd Tart with Mango   5.00

Chocolate Pate with Créme Anglaise   5.25

Tarte Tatin with Créme Fraîche   5.00

Muscat de Lunel, Orange Muscat   5.75

Dinner: Tues - Thurs 5:30 - 9, Fri - Sat 5:30 - 10   ●●Ⓓ

Menu Changes Daily

M E N U   D U   J O U R

boudin of fresh lobster, shrimp and scallops with two sauces
or
grilled salmon, ox tail jus and potatoes mousseline
or
grilled scallops with a saffron sauce, squash flan
or
fresh foie gras sautéed with truffles and spinach $ 5.00
or
steamed young lobster with caramelized carrot galette $ 5.00

grilled Maine lobster with beurre blanc and shrimp quenelles $ 5.00
or
grilled swordfish in a court bouillon of vegetables and thyme
or
roasted veal chop with truffles and seasonal mushrooms
or
sautéed medallions of fallow deer with caramelized apples and zinfandel sauce
or
fresh breast of guinea fowl filled with foie gras and spinach, port truffle sauce

mixed baby lettuce with cambozola cheese

chocolate cake layered with chocolate mousse, white chocolate ice cream
and lemon sorbet
or
sautéed apples and figs with apple sorbet
and goat milk-honey ice cream
or
poached pear in red wine with candied ginger ice cream

prix fixe at $68.00

648 Bush St • Union Square • (415) 989-7154

CARTE DE LA SAISON

petit filet cru d'agneau garni aux pointes d'asperges 11.50
lean raw lamb marinated in herbal vinaigrette with asparagus

huîtres chaudes, beurre vermouth au caviar osetra 13.00
oysters poached, sauce vermouth garnished with osetra caviar

salade de cailles tiède aux artichauts et aux pignes 15.00
warm quail salad with artichokes and pine nuts

saumon savage au jus de queue de boeuf, aux pomme de terre mousseline 14.00
grilled salmon, ox tail jus and potatoes mousseline

potage du chef 13.50

filet de thon grillé au caviar noir et thym 30.00
grilled tuna in a court bouillon of vegetables and thyme

suprême de faisan rôti aux morilles et avec son riz sauvage risotto 32.00
roasted breast of pheasant with morels and wild rice risotto

escalopes de veau sautées forestières 32.00
sautéed veal medallions with garnish of wild mushrooms

sauté de ris de veau aux écrevisses de Sacramento 31.00
sweet breads sautéed served with crayfish sauce

noisettes d'agneau grillées au poivre vert, sauce civet 34.50
grilled filet of lamb with green peppercorns, sauce zinfandel

mignon de boeuf avec la mousse de foie gras, coulis de truffes 33.75
filet mignon with foie gras mousse and black truffles

salade mélangée 9.50

fromage
cheese

soufflé glacé de la saison 9.50   *les sorbet de fruits frais 9.50*
frozen soufflé   fresh fruit sorbets

mousses aux chocolats blanc et noir 9.50
white and dark chocolate mousse with raspberry sauce

*l'assiette de délices et gourmandises 13.00 **

LES HORS D'OEUVRE

Crevettes et Pates Cheveux d'Ange   9.
Prawns with angelhair pasta

Escargots en Pots aux Croutons   8.
Burgundy snails with croutons

Gratin de Homard en Chemise   14.
Fresh Maine Lobster wrapped in a crepe, nantua sauce

Cervelle de Veau au Beurre Noir   6.
Sauteed calf brains with capers and balsamic vinegar

LES SOUPES

Consomme a l'essence de Canard et Shiitake   5.
Duck consomme with shiitake mushrooms

Soupe du Jour   6.

LES SALADES

Salade d'Epinards aux Aiguilette de Canard Fume'   8.
Salad of spinach leaves with smoked duck breast

Melon et Saumon Fume' en Fleur au Caviar   9.
Cantaloupe melon and smoked salmon with caviar (American sturgeon caviar)

---

125 E. Sir Francis Drake Blvd • Larkspur • (415) 461-3700

LES ENTREES

Saumon Poche Sauce Ciboulette   18.
Fresh poached salmon in a chive sauce

Confit de Canard au Chou Rouge   17.
Confit of duck breast on a bed of red cabbage

Ris de Veau Bordelaise aux Endives braisees   19.
Veal sweetbreads with braised endive

Poulet Grand Mere   17.
*Roast chicken with parisian potatoes, mushrooms, julienne of
smoked duck and baby vegetables*

Roulade de Porc Duxelle de Champignons a l'emince'   17.
de Canard Fume'
Tenderloin of pork with a puree of mushrooms and julienne of smoked duck

Coquilles Saint-Jacques Poelees Emile   20.
Sea scallops sauteed and crowned with a ragout of seafood

Selle de Chevreuil Grand Veneur   24.
Roasted saddle of venison with chestnut puree and carmelized pears

Filet de Beouf au Poivre Vert et Calvados   24.
Filet of beef with green peppercorns and calvados sauce

Carre d'Agneau Roti, Sauce Bearnaise   26.
Marinated Rack of Lamb with Bearnaise Sauce

LES DESSERTS

Choix de Patisseries   6.

Les Fruits de Saison   7.
Berries of the season

Souffle Individuel   8.
Souffle for one (Please order with entree)

Cafe 1.50   The 1.50   Espresso 2.00

THE RITZ-CARLTON
SAN FRANCISCO

DINING ROOM

Appetizers

Quail on Crisp Potato Nest, Spring Greens
Three Asparagus Salad, Dungeness Crab,
Chive Vinaigrette
Smoked Sea Scallops, Horseradish Cream,
Cucumber and Mache
Cured Salmon with Fennel, Lemon and
Extra Virgin Olive Oil
Seared Foie Gras, Pickled Beets, Haricot
Vert and Wilted Greens
Lobster and Scallop Soup with Saffron

Fish and Seafood

Sturgeon Roasted in Fennel Oil,
Fennel and Sweetpeas
Salmon with Ginger, White Port and Lime
Grilled Fillet of Halibut with Artichoke,
Red Pepper and Basil
Roast Lobster with Spring Vegetables,
Two Sauces

Meat

Veal and Sweetbread Medallions,
Morel Mushrooms and Asparagus
Duck Breast with Rhubarb Raspberry
Compote
Fillet of Beef, Carmelized Shallots,
Potato Artichoke Gratin
Lamb Loin with Crisp Potato Crust,
Wild Mushroom and Leek Ragout

---

600 Stockton St • Nob Hill • (415) 296-7465

Chef Gary Danko Proudly Presents his Recommendations

Degustion Menu

Tuna Tartar Napoleon
Iron Horse Brut Rose 1988

Grilled Scallops Wrapped in Cucumber Caviar, Saffron Sauce
Chateau LaVille Haut-Brion 1983

Seared Squab Breast Foie Gras and Squab Confit Ravioli
Mercury 'Clos Des Myglands' Joseph Faiverly 1989

A Selection of Androuet Cheeses Presented Tableside

Lemon and Strawberry Millefeuille
Renaissance Late Harvest Sauvignon Blanc 1983

Menu $ 55
Wines $ 35   Menu Changes Weekly

Dinner: Tues - Sat 6 - 10:30

Rodin

FIRST COURSE

- ❖ Stuffed Pasta in Gratin

- ❖ Oysters Rockefeller en Croute with Golden Caviar

- ❖ Calamari Stuffed with Salmon, served with Pasta

- ❖ Sliced Roast Duck with Papaya, Orange Pernod Sauce

SECOND COURSE

- ❖ Spring Rack of Lamb Marinated (served medium rare) in a Red Wine Herb Sauce (2.00)

- ❖ Medallion of Salmon with Timbale of Scallops and Saffron Sauce

- ❖ Breast of Pheasant with wild Rice, New Zealand Black Currant Sauce

- ❖ Sauteed Loin of Venison with Cognac and Port wine, served with wild Mushrooms (2.00)

- ❖ Filet Mignon en Croute, Tarragon Demi-Glaze

1779 Lombard St • Marina • (415) 563-8566

THIRD COURSE

❖ Baby Leaves with Mustard Vinaigrette

FOURTH COURSE

❖ Grand Marnier Soufflé

❖ Raspberry Soufflé with Chambord Sauce (4.00)

❖ Baked Alaska

❖ Apple Tart with Nougatine Ice Cream

❖ Raspberry Charlotte

❖ Poached Pear with Chestnut Mousse

—————————— PRIX FIXE MENU $39.00 ——————————

À LA CARTE

First	$9.00
Second	$22.50
Third	$8.00
Fourth	$7.50

SOUTH PARK CAFE

APPETIZERS

Blinis   5.00
Russian Pancakes with Crème Aigre, Golden Caviar & Smoked Salmon
Chicken Foie Gras with Honey Onion Confit & Celery Vinaigrette   4.50
Duck Rillettes   4.50
Baked Goat Cheese with Frisée   4.00
Sautéed Sweetbread Salad with Leeks & Walnut Vinaigrette   6.50
Smoked Trout Salad with Roasted Potatoes & Caper Vinaigrette   5.75
Salad of Mixed Baby Lettuce with Balsamic Vinaigrette   3.50
Soupe du Jour   3.00

MAIN COURSES

'Nage' of Petit Gris Snails and Vegetables in Parsley Broth   8.95
Boudin Noir with Sautéed Apples   9.95
Steamed Mussels with Cream   9.95
Leg of Duck Confit with Lentil Vinaigrette   9.95
Sautéed Grain-Fed Chicken à la Normande   10.95
Bourride   11.95
Fish Stew with Rouille
Gigot d'Agneau with Roasted Garlic Sauce   10.95
Roast Leg of Lamb
Braised Young Rabbit à l'Ancienne with Tarragon   11.95
Roast Duck Breast with Honey Red Wine Sauce   11.95
Pork Tenderloin with Green Peppercorn Sauce   11.95
New York Strip Steak with Sauce Choron   12.95
Grilled Salmon with Two-Color Beurre Blanc   13.95

108 S Park Ave • SOMA • (415) 495-7275

APPETIZERS

Steamed Artichoke with Mustard Vinaigrette   4.50
Baked Goat Cheese with Chicory   4.00
Smoked Tuna Tartare on Garlic Croutons   4.00
Soupe du Jour   Cup   1.75   Bowl   3.00

SALADS

Green Salad with Balsamic Vinaigrette   3.00
Salade D'Avignon   6.00
Baby Lettuce, Endive, Beets, Raisins, Walnuts and Apples with Curry Vinaigrette
Salade Frisée   5.50
Chicory with Sautéed Chicken Livers and Bacon Vinaigrette
Grilled Chicken Salad with Roasted Peppers   7.00
Seafood Salad with Julienne of Vegetables and Citrus Vinaigrette 7.95
Grilled Flank Steak Salad with Roquefort Vinaigrette   7.25
Duck Confit Salad   7.25
Chicory and Baby Lettuce with Duck Confit and Marinated White Beans

SANDWICHES

French Ham on Baguette   4.75
Camembert on Baguette   4.75
Croque Monsieur   5.25   Croque Madame   5.75
Prosciutto with Marinated Eggplant and Fresh Mozzarella   6.25
Grilled Lamb with Caramelized Onions, Tomato and Pepper Goat Cheese   7.00

French Fries   1.50

MAIN COURSES

Steamed Mussels with Cream and White Wine   7.00
Vegetable Tarte   7.25
Grilled Sausage with Warm Lentil Vinaigrette   7.25
Boudin Noir with Sautéed Apples and French Fries   7.00
Grilled Chicken with Roasted Pepper Butter and French Fries   7.25
New York Strip Steak with Sauce Choron   7.95
Grilled Salmon with Orange Basil Beurre Blanc   8.95
Roast Pork Loin with Herbs and Green Peppercorn Aioli   8.95

DESSERTS

Lemon Tart   3.00
Crème Brulée   3.50
Fresh Fruit Tart   3.50
Marquise au Chocolat   3.95
Chocolate Mousse Cake with Pistachio Crème Anglaise
Sorbet   3.25

shuruat (appetizers)

LAMB SAMOSA (2)	4.50
Crisp patties stuffed with spiced minced lamb	
VEGETABLE SAMOSA (2)	3.75
Crisp patties stuffed with spiced potatoes & green peas	
VEGETABLE PAKORA	3.75
Mixed vegetable fritters	

roti (freshly baked bread)

NAN	2.25
Leavened bread	
ONION KULCHA	2.75
Nan stuffed with onions	
KEEMA NAN	4.50
Leavened bread stuffed with mildly spiced ground lamb	
PARATHA	2.50
Buttered and layered whole wheat bread	
GARLIC NAN	3.75
Nan stuffed with garlic	
CHAPPATI	2.00
Basic Indian bread made from whole wheat	

tandoori
(specialities from the mesquite clay pit)

TANDOORI CHICKEN	Full	17.95
Chicken marinated in yogurt and roasted	Half	9.50
CHICKEN TIKKA KABAB		13.50
Boneless chicken cubes, marinated in spices and roasted		
BOOTI KABAB		14.95
Cubes of lamb, marinated in spices and roasted		
SEEKH KABAB		14.95
Minced lamb mixed with onions, herbs and spices and roasted		

bahar-e-murgh (exquisite chicken curries)

CHICKEN TIKKA MASALA   13.95
Charcoal broiled chicken in a moderately spiced sauce

CHICKEN MAKHANWALA   13.95
Shredded Tandoori chicken in a sauce of butter, tomatoes & spices

KARAHI CHICKEN   13.95
Boneless chicken stir fried in bell peppers, onions & tomatoes

CHICKEN SAGWALA   12.95
Chicken cooked with spiced creamed spinach

bahar-e-sabaz (aromatic vegetarian specialities)

MATTAR PANEER   9.95
Cubed farmer's cheese and green peas in a spiced gravy

BENGAN BARTHA   9.95
Eggplant baked in clay oven and cooked in onions, tomatoes & spices

CHANNA MASALA   9.00
Garbanzo beans in a special blend of spices

SAG ALOO   9.95
Creamed spinach and potatoes, mildly spiced

BHINDI MASALA (Seasonal)   9.95
Spiced okra

DAL MAKHANI   9.00
Creamed lentils, delicately spiced

gosht laziz (fragrant tender lamb curries)

ROGAN JOSH   15.50
Lamb cubes cooked in a blend of tomatoes & spices

SAG GOSHT   15.50
Lamb cooked with spiced creamed spinach

GOSHT VINDALOO   15.50
Lamb in a hot spicy sauce with potatoes

samunder se (seafood delicacies)

PRAWN BHUNA   16.00
Prawns in a spicy gravy

FISH MASALA   16.00
Fish cubes cooked in a spicy sauce

biriyani (savory rice dishes)

VEGETABLE BIRIYANI   11.95
Saffron flavored basmati rice with vegetables & nuts

PILLAU   4.75
Saffron flavored basmati rice with garnish of peas

CHICKEN BIRIYANI   14.95
Saffron flavored basmati rice with spiced chicken

The Rice Table

When Dutch, Portuguese, and English traders first came to the Indonesian Islands, they found that throughout the Islands and most especially on Java, there were hundreds of different food dishes, most enjoyed by even the poorest village people. Through Dutch control of the Indonesian "Spice Islands," Holland became one of the wealthiest nations on Earth. It supplied the World's most valuable "riches" to a European continent eager to add flavor to its food. Spain vied for the "Spice Islands," but found America instead, while looking for the shortest route to Indonesia. During their three-hundred years of domination, the Dutch gathered together the food dishes that were most appealing to them and served them in huge colonial feasts they called "rijstafel" or rice table.

Because Indonesians had been cooking with almost every spice known to man for thousands of years before Europeans became familiar with even pepper and nutmeg, many complex spicing methods and exotic flavors evolved that are still beyond the frontiers of some western palates. However, at the Rice Table, we have chosen tastes and textures we feel are both representative of Indonesian cuisine and enjoyable to the average diner. We sincerely hope that your dining pleasure will reflect our pride in Indonesian food.

Though many Indonesian dishes are liberally spiced with different kinds of chili peppers, the hot sambals that are served separately with your dinner should be used, with caution, to hotten the food to your taste. All dishes are meant to be eaten with rice and are spiced accordingly.

The Rice Table Staff

1617 Fourth St • San Rafael • (415) 456-1808

The Rice Table Dinner

15.95
per person

The House Specialty. If ordered for two or more, includes all of the dishes listed below on this page as well as Sumpia (appetizer), Acar (pickled vegetables), and Serundeng (roasted coconut).

The Rice Table "Special"

18.95
per person
2 person minimum

The Rice Table Dinner with two more dishes, of our choice, added.

Sate

13.75

Marinated pork or chicken on bamboo skewers. Barbecued over real charcoal.

Udang Goreng

14.25

Shrimp fried in butter and asam (tamarind) fruit.

Keri Ayam

12.25

Mild chicken curry... Indonesian style.

Semur

12.75

Pieces of beef cooked in butter, soy sauce, and cloves.

Bihun Goreng

11.95

Fried rice-noodles.

Nasi Goreng

12.75

Indonesian fried rice.

Jamur Goreng

11.95

Mushrooms stir-fried with tamarind and tofu.

Sate Manis

12.75

Pieces of pork cooked in sweet & sour sauce.

Keri Domba

13.75

Indian style lamb curry.

Ayam Pangang

13.75

Barbecued half chicken smothered in a chili and soy sauce.

Dinner: Thurs - Sat 5:30 - 10, Sun 5 - 9

● ● Ⓓ

« *SALADS* »

SONOMA WILD BABY FIELD MIX
CARROT CONFETTI, RED AND YELLOW TOMATOES
THREE VINEGAR VINAIGRETTE
$4.00

ORGANIC BABY SPINACH AND FRESH CORN
WALNUTS AND CAMBOZOLA TOASTPOINTS
MUSTARD VINAIGRETTE
$5.00

CLASSIC CAESAR WITH ROMAINE HEARTS
$6.50

THAI CALAMARI
JICAMA, RED ONION AND CARROT CONFETTI
SESAME RICE WINE VINAIGRETTE
$7.50

« *APPETIZERS* »

HALF DOZEN DAILY FRESH OYSTERS
$8.50

CORNMEAL BREADED OYSTERS
CHIVE AIOLI AND DIJON BUERRE BLANC
POTATO, RED ONION AND SMOKEY BACON
$8.00

COLD OVEN ROASTED SHRIMP
WITH RED PEPPER ROUILLE
$8.00

SMOKED NORWEGIAN SALMON
ONION POTATO CAKE AND SALMON CAVIAR
$11.00

555 2nd St • SOMA • (415) 543-2282

BLACK TIGER PRAWNS AND CILANTRO WONTONS
SPICY GINGER BALSAMIC AND CARROT CONFETTI
$6.00

WILD MUSHROOM LASAGNETTE
VEGETARIAN
$7.50

RABBIT PATE WITH BROWN WALNUT BREAD
MUSTARD VINAIGRETTE AND RED ONION CHUTNEY
$7.50

EGGPLANT PESTO WITH PARMESAN FOCACCIA
$5.50

« *ENTREES* »

LUMACHE RIGATE PASTA
CABERNET INFUSED TOMATO AND OVEN ROASTED EGGPLANT
EXTRA VIRGIN OLIVE OIL AND MODENA BALSAMIC
AGED PARMESAN GRANA PADANO
$8.00

GRILLED SWORDFISH AND TIGER PRAWNS
ROASTED RED PEPPER ROUILLE AND YELLOW PEPPER COULIS
BLACK TURTLE BEANS
$10.00

SAGE MARINATED LAMB CHOPS
PEAR-POTATO CURRY SAMOSA AND CILANTRO CREME FRAICHE
ASPARAGUS
$14.00

PAILLARD OF PACIFIC SALMON
BABY SPINACH, RED ONIONS AND FRESH CORN
MUSTARD AND CHIVE AIOLI AND LOTUS CHIPS
$12.00

LOBSTER RAVIOLI IN SEABROTH
FRESH TOMATO, ARTICHOKES AND TOBIKO
$15.00

ROASTED PETALUMA ORGANIC CHICKEN
ONION, CARROT, CELERY AND CORN
MILD CARAMELIZED GARLIC SAUCE
SWEET POTATO RISSOTO
$14.00

SEARED AHI TUNA
RED AND YELLOW PEPPERS COULIS
ANGEL HAIR PASTA WITH SCALLION PESTO
BABY BOK CHOY
$16.00

Dinner: Mon - Fri 5 - 10:30, Sat 6 - 10:30   ●ⓁⒹ

Jack's Restaurant

Menu Changes Daily

APPETIZERS

Imported Escargot (Snails) (6) Bourguignonne 7.00
Pâté Maison 3.75
Imported Sardines 2.75
Imported Pâté de Foie Gras Truffé 18.50

Smoked Salmon 8.75
Celery en Branche 1.75; Parisiénne 2.25
Jumbo Ripe Olives 2.25

SOUPS

Mock Turtle with Sherry 3.50
Cold Jellied Consommé 2.75
Leek and Potato Soup 2.50

Onion Gratinée 3.50
Cream of Mushroom 3.00
Consommé en Tasse 3.50

SALADS

Romaine 4.25
Lettuce 3.50
Avocado, Half 4.50; with Shrimp 8.25
Fresh String Beans 5.50
Hearts of Palm, French Dressing 4.25
Celery Victor with Anchovies 4.00

Sliced Tomato 3.50
Sliced Avocado Salad 4.25
Shrimp Salad 9.25
Mixed Green 3.75
Belgian Endive, French Dressing 5.75
Fresh Artichoke Heart Salad 8.50

OYSTERS and SHELLFISH

Eastern Oysters (6) on Half Shell 8.25
Steamed Clams, Plain or Bordelaise 10.75

Cracked Crab 11.75
Olympia Oysters, Cocktail Sauce 8.25

EGGS and OMELETTES

Omelette with Fresh Mushrooms 7.50
Smoked Salmon with Scrambled Eggs á la Jack's 7.75

Eggs Meyerbeer 7.00

PASTAS and SAUTEES

Ravioli Milanaise or Spaghetti a l' Italienne 8.50   Chicken Livers Sauté with Fresh Mushrooms 8.25

DAILY SPECIALS

Leek and Potato Soup 2.50
London Broil with String Beans 8.75

Omelette with Bacon 7.50
Cold leg of lamb with Green Salad 8.25

FISH

Filet of Sole, Tartar Sauce 8.75
Fresh Filet of Petrale, Doré or Meunière 12.50

Sandabs, Meunière 8.75
Broiled Swordfish with Boiled Potaoes 15.50

615 Sacramento St • Financial District • (415) 421-7355

ROASTED and GRILLED MEATS

Double French Lamb Chops 16.25
Rump Steak 13.75
New York Cut, Single Sirloin 16.75
Chateaubriand with Fresh Vegetables (for 2) 38.00
Broiled Pork Chops 12.25

Sirloin Steak Minute 12.75
Lamb (for 2) with Potatoes Boulangère 38.00
Broiled Veal Chops 18.25
Broiled Sweetbreads á la Maitre d'Hotel 12.50
Broiled Salisbury Steak with Mushroom Sauce 8.75

FOWL

Roast Turkey, Dressing, Cranberry Sauce 9.75
Chicken en Casserole, Vegetables (for 2) 18.50
Broiled or Roast Squab 14.75; en Casserole, Vegetables 16.25
Chicken Sauté à Sec with Fresh Mushrooms, Artichokes à la Jack's 11.75
Roast Tame Duckling, Bigarade Sauce, Apple and Raisin Dressing 14.50

POTATOES

Hash Brown or Lyonnaise 3.25; au Gratin 3.25

Julienne or Long Branch 3.25

VEGETABLES

Zucchini, Tomatoes Sauté 2.50
French Fried Egg Plant 3.75
Wild Rice Polonaise 3.75
Artichoke: Hot or Cold with Mustard Sauce 3.50

Fresh String Beans 3.75
Creamed Fresh Spinach 2.75

SPECIAL SAUCES and GARNISHES

Mushrooms Sauté 3.50   Hollandaise 3.50   Poivrade 3.50

CHEESE

Danish Blue 2.75

Danish Port Salut 2.75

DESSERTS

Chocolate Mousse 3.25
Café Diable (for 2) 7.50
Roman Punch 4.25
Ice Cream 2.00; with Chocolate Sauce 2.50
Banana Fritters with Vanilla Sauce 3.00

Sliced Bananas in Cream 1.75
Crepes Suzette (for 2) 8.75
Zabaglione (for 2) 5.50
Cheese Cake 3.00
Fried Cream with Rum 3.25
Fresh Raspberries 4.50

DINNER

$18.25 per person (served from 5 to 9 p.m. only)

SOUPS	Leek and Potato Soup	Consommé en Tasse
SALAD	Tossed Mixed Greens	Sliced Tomatoes
ROAST	Broiled Rump Steak	Broiled Chicken (1/2)
VEGETABLES	Zucchini Tomato Sauté	Creamed Spinach
DESSERTS	Ice Cream	French Pancakes
	Sherbet	Cheese Cake

Dinner: Mon - Fri until 9:30, Sat - Sun 5 - 9:30

●ⓁⒹ

AT THE BEGINNING

COSMO TIDBITS   10.50
*An assortment of the Trader's finger foods: Crab Rangoon, Crispy Prawns,
Smoke-Oven Spareribs and Barbecued Pork.*

CRISPY PRAWNS   11.75
Accompanied by hot mustard and Vic's Chinese table sauce.

SMOKE OVEN SPARERIBS   9.25
Pork ribs smoked slowly over oakwood.

TRADER VIC'S EGG ROLL   6.25

CHO CHO   6.50
Thin strips of beef marinated in teriyaki sauce, grilled and served over a flaming hibachi.

BBQ PORK   4.50
Marinated, smoked in the Chinese oven and thinly sliced.

ENTREES FROM
THE CHINESE SMOKE OVENS

*Trader Vic's is proud to continue a 1,000 years old Chinese tradition: no open flame, only convection
heat and smoke from an oakwood fire gently roast and smoke the following fresh seafood and meats.*

FILET OF BEEF   23.00
With garlic mayonnaise.

CHINATOWN DUCK   18.75
One Half Duck marinated in Five Spices, served with chutney.

NEW YORK CUT STEAK   23.00
Trader Vic's mustard.

INDONESIAN LAMB ROAST   27.00
*Rack of lamb marinated, smoked, and accompanied by
chutney and peanut sauce. Served with green papaya salad
and stir fried vegetables. A Trader Vic's specialty.*

OAKWOOD CHICKEN   14.75
With savory seasonings.

PETALUMA SQUAB   24.00
With asian spices and cumberland sauce.

FRESH SEA BASS   20.50
With caper sauce.

FRESH PACIFIC SALMON   20.50
With caper sauce.

TRADER VIC'S CURRY

You can choose from two preparations of curry:
The traditional Trader Vic's Calcutta Curry, spicy and richly sauced; or
Island Curry, a lighter style prepared with traditional curry spices and fresh fruit juices.

CALCUTTA LAMB CURRY   16.50   ISLAND LAMB CURRY   16.50

CALCUTTA PRAWN CURRY   20.00   ISLAND PRAWN CURRY   20.00

CALCUTTA CHICKEN CURRY   15.50   ISLAND CHICKEN CURRY   15.50

EXOTIC ENTREES

STEAMED PACIFIC CATCH   20.50
Fresh Pacific fish steamed with Thai lemon grass and steeped in the Trader's
soy-sesame sauce. Served with Chinese noodles.

MAUNA KEA MAHI MAHI   18.75
Hawaiian mahi mahi sauteed and cloaked with a silky sauce perfumed with vanilla pods.
Elegant, exotic, and one of our chef's best dishes.

TAHITIAN SWORDFISH DALI DALI   20.25
Fresh swordfish steaks, lively seasoned with coriander seeds and peppercorns,
and served with fresh papaya.

PRAWNS TRADER VIC   20.00
Jumbo prawns prepared with lemon grass and spicy tomato sauce.

PACIFIC COAST ABALONE   32.50
Abalone caught off the Monterey coast and prepared in a classic
California style – lightly coated and sauteed.

POACHED SALMON   21.00
With fennel and salmon caviar.

FRESH MAINE LOBSTER   34.75
A one and one-half pound fresh lobster, steamed or barbecued, served with herbed vinaigrette.

MEDALLION OF VEAL MOREL   26.25
Tender loin of veal, prepared with morel mushrooms and a light sherry-cream sauce.

PAPER THIN FILET OF BEEF   25.00
Flaming Hong Kong sauce.

NEW YORK BONE MARROW STEAK   25.00
Served with french fried onions.

C A L I F O R N I A
CULINARY ACADEMY

The Academy Grill

LUNCH

APPETIZERS
San Francisco Bay Shrimp Cocktail . . . 4.75
Crisp Onion Strings . . . 2.95
Southwestern Won Tons . . . 3.95
Buffalo Chicken Wings . . . 4.25

SALADS AND SOUPS
New England Clam Chowder . . . 2.25 cup / 3.50 bowl
Soup of the Day . . . 1.95 cup / 2.50 bowl
Caesar Salad . . . 5.95
Cobb Salad . . . 6.25
Chinese Chicken Salad . . . 6.50
Seasonal Green Salad . . . 3.95

GRILL
Oriental Breast of Chicken . . . $ 6.95
Fresh Market Fish . . . market price
CCA BURGER
Freshly Ground Beef from our Butchery Class,
Seasoned and Grilled to Order
with your choice of 2 toppings . . . $ 5.50
Gilled Onions, Smoked Bacon, Sauteed Mushrooms,
Cheddar Cheese, Swiss Cheese

SANDWICHES
Roasted Daily our Deli Selections
Academy's Cured Corned Beef, Pastrami, Roasted Turkey,
Roast Beef on Sour Dough, Rye of Kaiser Roll . . . $ 4.95
The Academy Club . . . $ 5.95

625 Polk St • Civic Center • (415) 771-3536

SPECIALTIES
Chef's Pot Pie . . . 6.95
Omelettes
Mushroom, Cheese, Smoked Bacon . . . 6.50

BLUE PLATES
Mon - Meatloaf with Hot and Sweet Mustard Sauce
Tues - Old-Fashioned Chicken and Dumplings
Wed - Fettuccine with Pesto Cream
Thur - Cider Glazed Pork Loin
Fri - Seafood Jambalaya
served with soup or salad and dessert . . . 7.95

DINNER

FAMILY STYLE
10.95
Academy Salad, Soup, Dessert and your choice of Entree
Eggplant Parmesan
Chicken Scallopini Marsala
Italian Sausage and Peppers
Olive Oil and Rosemary Grilled Fish of the Day

APPETIZERS
Fresh Mozzarella with Plum Tomatoes and Basil . . . 4.25
Academy Salad . . . 2.95
Minestrone Soup . . . 2.95
Pasta of the Day . . . 3.25
Garlic Bread . . . 1.95

ENTREES A LA CARTE
Eggplant Parmesan . . . 7.25
Chicken Scallopini Marsala . . . 7.95
Italian Sausage and Peppers . . . 6.95
Olive Oil and Rosemary Grilled Fish of the Day . . . 8.95
Osso Bucco . . . 8.95
Chicken Cacciatori . . . 7.95
Pasta of the Day . . . 6.95
Rosemary and Thyme New York Steak . . . 12.95

DESSERTS
Amaretto Cake . . . 2.50 Ricotta Tart . . . 2.50
Biscotti with Espresso Mousse . . . 2.50

Dinner: 7 Days a Week 6 - 8:45

ACQUERELLO

...*Antipasti*...

Gamberi al Brandy con Porri Fritti *9⁵⁰*
PRAWNS SAUTEED IN BRANDY, SERVED WITH FRIED LEEKS

Insalata di Spinaci e Belga con Gorgonzola e Pere *7⁰⁰*
TENDER SPINACH AND BELGIAN ENDIVE SALAD WITH GORGONZOLA AND PEARS

Carpaccio di Branzino con Pomodori e Basilico *8⁵⁰*
CARPACCIO OF SEABASS WITH EXTRA VIRGIN OLIVE OIL, TOMATOES AND BASIL

Bresaola della Valtellina e Sedano Tartufato *8⁵⁰*
AIR-CURED BEEF WITH SLIVERED CELERY AND BLACK TRUFFLES

...*Primi Piatti*...

Zuppa d'Aragosta *8⁵⁰*
RICH LOBSTER SOUP WITH AROMATIC VEGETABLES

Tortelloni di Asparagi, Salsa Vellutata al Tartufo Nero *11⁰⁰*
ASPARAGUS TORTELLONI WITH BLACK TRUFFLES AND PARMESAN

Rigatoni con Pesto alla Trapanese *8⁵⁰*
PASTA WITH PESTO OF TOMATO, BASIL AND ALMONDS - TRAPANI STYLE

Tagliolini alle Vongole Profumate con Aglio Arrostito *9⁰⁰*
HOMEMADE TAGLIOLINI WITH CLAMS AND ROASTED GARLIC

Gnocchetti alle Erbe in Guazzetto di Pomodoro *8⁵⁰*
POTATO HERB GNOCCHI IN A FRESH TOMATO SAUCE

1722 Sacramento St • Nob Hill • (415) 567-5432

...*Secondi Piatti*...

Filetto di Manzo alla "Zalaffi" 18⁵⁰
ROLLED FILET OF BEEF WITH PROSCIUTTO, PARMESAN AND ROSEMARY

Nocette d'Agnello con Aceto Balsamico e Menta 19⁵⁰
SEARED LAMB LOIN WITH BALSAMIC VINEGAR AND MINT

Petto d'Anatra con Marsala, Uvetta e Pinoli 18⁰⁰
TENDER DUCK BREAST WITH MARSALA, RAISINS AND PINENUTS

Animelle di Vitello al Madeira e Funghi 18⁰⁰
SCALOPPINE OF VEAL SWEETBREAD WITH MADEIRA AND CRIMINI MUSHROOM

Medaglioni di Maiale in Crosta d'Erbe di Giardino 17⁵⁰
ROAST PORK LOIN IN ROSEMARY AND THYME CRUST

Salmone in Crosta di Origano al Salmoriglio 18⁵⁰
OREGANO CRUSTED SALMON WITH SALMORIGLIO SAUCE

Trancio di Tonno alla Siciliana 19⁰⁰
FRESH TUNA WITH ROASTED PEPPERS AND BLACK OLIVES

While we prefer payment by cash or check,
we accept Mastercard, Visa, Diner's Club or Discover Card
✦
Smoking allowed in the Bar Area only
✦

Private parties and Catering available. Inquire.
✦✦✦

ANTIPASTI & INSALATE

CHIFELETTI della CASA - pan-fried potato gnocchi ... 4.00

CAPUZI GARBI - sauerkraut braised with onions, apples & prosciutto ... 4.00

FRITTURA di POLENTA - fried polenta with Fontina cheese ... 4.25

CAPONATA - marinated eggplant, olives, tomatoes, capers, pine-nuts ... 4.50

INSALATINA NOSTRANA - mixed seasonal greens vinaigrette ... 4.25

INSALATA BOHEMIA - thinly sliced cabbage with paprika vinaigrette ... 4.00

INSALATINA de PATATINE - new red potatoes and onions in a light mustard vinaigrette ... 4.00

CALAMARI POLESANI - zesty marinated baby squid ... 4.50

BRODI & MINESTRE

GNOCHETTI in BRODO - semolina, cheese & egg dumplings in broth ... 4.25

MINESTRINA - assorted vegetables **or** pastina in a light broth ... 4.00

IOTA UNGARESE - hearty minestrone with sauerkraut, potatoes & beans ... 4.50

PRIMI PIATTI

CRAFI ALBONESI - our ravioli filled with 3 cheeses, raisins & pine nuts
served with a sirloin sauce ... 11.50

MANICOTTI della CASA - crepes filled with chicken, veal & ricotta
served with bechamel & Napoletana sauce ... 11.25

PAPPARDELLE con GAMBERETTI - pasta with crayfish saute in a light tomato sauce ... 13.50

LINGUINE alla PESCATORA - pasta with seafood: marinara or white sauce ... 10.50

FETTUCCINE al SALMONE - salmon & vodka fume sauce with julienne of bell peppers ... 13.50

LINGUINE al PESTO - in a light cream basil sauce with pine-nuts ... 11.25

PAPPARDELLE ISTRIANE - served with roasted sweet red peppers & olives ... 12.00

••• all pasta made in house •••

SECONDI PIATTI

POLENTA e BRODETTO - grilled polenta with snapper & calamari saute
flavored with balsamic vinegar & tomato sauce ... 11.75

CALAMARI FRITTI - pan-fried squid (we use fresh oil for each serving) ... 11.25

GAMBERONI alla TRIESTINA - prawns saute in a brandy sauce ... 15.25

PESCE del GIORNO - selected fresh fish ... A/Q

AGNELLO ai FERRI - broiled leg of lamb marinated in fresh herbs ... 13.75

FILETTO di AGNELLO - lamb fillets with a glaze of pomegranate ... 15.25

SPIEDINI di AGNELLO - lamb brochettes in a rosemary oil marinade ... 14.25

SCALOPPINE di VITELLO - veal saute with mushrooms or capers ... 14.25

VITELLO al CARSO - medallions of veal with grapes & grappa saute ... 16.50

COTOLETTA ALBONESE - N.Y. cutlet stuffed with prosciutto & cheese
coated with herbed breadcrumbs & pan fried ... 14.75

FILETTO di MAIALE - pork tenderloins braised in milk & rosemary ... 13.75

MOUSSAKA - layered lamb, eggplant, cheese & tomato in the Eastern Adriatic Style ... 12.00

CONIGLIO ISTRIANO - rabbit marinated in juniper, braised & served with polenta ... 13.25

POLLASTRO al FORNO - range chicken roasted with rosemary & basted with Sherry ... 12.25

Dinner Menu

Appetizers

BRUSCHETTA $4.95
sourdough bread, virgin olive oil, garlic, tomato, herbs

BRESAOLA CON MACHE $7.95
air cured beef tenderloin with Mache, goat cheese and citron dressing

ANTIPASTO MISTO $7.95
eggplant caponada, coppa, radicchio, prosciutto, mozzarella, roasted garlic

CARPACCIO ALLA NOSTRA MANIERA $7.50
thin-sliced aged beef, capers, Parmesan, olive oil, lemon

CALAMARI FRITTI $5.50
fried squid

OSTRICHE STAGIONE $7.50
seasonal fresh oysters on a half shell

Salads

INSALATA DI GAMBERONI $7.50
chilled prawns with caleriac tossed in aioli, basil and sundried tomatoes

INSALATE DI CESARE per person $6.50
classic Caesar salad made at the table (for two minimum)

INSALATE DEL GIARDINO $4.95
radicchio, arugula, baby spring mix, balsamic dressing, crumbled gorgonzola

INSALATE DI CONTADINO $5.75
spinach, cucumbers, tomato, onions, Greek feta cheese, Calamata olives,
oreganato dressing

INSALATE DI RADICCHIO E SPINACI $8.50
imported radicchio, spinach with pancetta balsamic Vinaigrette (warm)

Soup

ZUPPA DEL GIORNO
soup of the day

ZUPPA DI MINESTRONE $3.75
vegetable soup

65 Moraga Way • Orinda • (510) 253-1322

Pasta

PAPARDELLE GRANELLO DI PEPE DEL BUONGUSTAIO $12.95
green peppercorn pasta ribbons with grilled chicken, eggplant, radicchio (low cholesterol)

PANSOTTI ALLA CREMA DI NOCI $11.00
spinach pasta stuffed with ricotta cheese, walnut cream sauce

AGNOLOTTI ALLA CREMA $9.95
discs of pasta stuffed with chicken, prosciutto, cream cheese sauce

GNOCCHI BOLOGNESE $9.95
freshly-made potato dumplings with classic mushroom meat sauce

CAPELLINI CON POMODORO E BASILICO $9.00
angel hair pasta with fresh basil, tomato (low cholesterol)

CANNELLONI ALLA ROSSINI $12.50
delicate, thin crepes stuffed with veal, spinach, ricotta, herbs

RIGATONI QUATTRO FORMAGGI $11.00
pasta with mozzarella, fontina, gorgonzola, parmesan

TRE COLORE TAGLIARINI AL VONGOLE $13.95
three color Tagliarini with clams, swiss chard, lemon zest, toasted bread crumbs

PASTA CON PESCE DEL GIORNO A.Q.
pasta with fresh fish of the day

Pizza

PIZZA DEL GIORNO   price varies

Main Course

POLLO DIAVOLA $12.95
half roasted chicken marinated in garlic, hot pepper, fresh mint

COSTOLETTINI D'AGNELLO $17.95
grilled lamb chops with eggplant relish

VITELLO ALLA ALEXANDER $15.95
thin pounded free range veal, green olives, lemon wine sauce

SALTIMBOCCA ROMANA $16.95
thin pounded veal with prosciutto, cheese, sage leaves, white wine

BRACIOLA DI VITELLO $19.50
18 oz. broiled free-range veal chop

ANIMELLE ALLA FINANZIERA $15.50
sweetbreads with artichokes panecetta, cipollini onions

PIATTO DEL BOSCAIOLO ALLA GRIGLIA $16.95
lamb chop, venison sausage, quail and creamy horseradish sauce

CONTROFILETTO AL SCALOGNO $18.50
certified Angus New York strip steak with roasted shallots and brandy sauce

GAMBERONI PESCATORA $14.50
prawns saute, shallots, lemon, wine

FRESH FISH SPECIALS DAILY   A.Q.

PRIX FIXE MENU

INSALATE TRICOLORE
Seasonal Baby Greens, Tomato, Radish and Onion
or
MINESTRA ALLA FLORENTINA
A Fine Italian Vegetable Soup with Pasta

***

Choice of:

TORTELLINI ALLA BOSCAIOLA 12.95
Cheese Tortellini with Peas, Prosciutto and Porcini Mushrooms
or
PICCATA AL POMPELMO 13.95
Veal Piccata with Grapefruit
and Pink Peppercorn
or
TRIO DI PESCE ALLA GRIGLIA 14.95
Grilled Swordfish, Salmon and Prawns

***

Choice of:

TORTA AL RUM
Italian Rum Cake
or
TIRAMISU
or
GELATI MISTI

Coffee, Decaffeinated Coffee or Tea

---

950 Mason St • Nob Hill • (415) 772-5199

SECONDI PIATTI

	$	Lire
Ossobuco Alla Milanese	18.50	*22,200*
Veal Shanks Braised in Tomato Sauce, Served with Riscotto		
Saltimbocca Alla Romana	19.95	*23,940*
Sautéed Veal with Sage and Prosciutto		
Involtini Di Vitello "Bella Voce"	19.95	*23,940*
Veal Roll Stuffed with Mozzarella, Eggplant and Prosciutto		
Piccata Al Marsala	19.95	*23,940*
Thin Slices of Veal with Wild Mushrooms and Marsala Sauce		
Pollo Grigliato Al Dragoncello	15.50	*18,616*
Marinated Broiled Chicken with Tarragon		
Suprema Di Pollo Alla Parmigiana	15.50	*18,616*
Chicken Breast Parmigiana		
Spiedini Di Carne	18.95	*22,740*
Grilled Beef, Veal, Quail and Sausage		
Costelette D'Agnello Con Salsa Di Peperoni Rossi	19.95	*23,940*
Grilled Lamb Chops, Red Pepper Sauce		
Bistecca di Bue Ai Ferri Con Arugula	18.95	*22,740*
Sliced New York Steak with Arugula		
Pesce Spada Alla Griglia	18.50	*22,200*
Grilled Swordfish with Sautéed Spinach		
Salmone Al Basilico	18.50	*22,200*
Broiled Salmon Filet in Basil Sauce		
Scampi Imperiali	19.95	*23,940*
Scamp in Cognac Sauce, Served with Black Pasta		

Half Order Pastas are Available as an Appetizer.

Menu Degustazione

Dining at The Blue Fox is an Italian gastronomical experience.
Our portions are designed for this three course feast followed by a sumptuous dessert.
For your enjoyment you may select any
Antipasto, Primo Piatto, Secondo Piatto and Dolce at a complete price of $55.00
(This specially priced menu is not available in connection with any promotion)

Antipasti

"Scampi alla Livornese" Prawns Sautéed in Lemon, Parsley & Butter $11.00 *
Code di Gamberoni alla Livornese

Salmon Carpaccio with Endive, Mascarpone & Leeks $13.00
Salmone con Endivia, Mascarpone e Porri

Prosciutto from Parma with Pear & Tangerine Chutney $12.50
Prosciutto di Parma con una Tritta di Pera al Mandarine

Beef & Veal Carpaccio with Parmigiano Cheese & Wild Mushroom Salad $13.50 *
I Due Carpacci con Parmigiano e Insalatina di Funghi Selvatici

Caesar Salad with Toasted Hazelnut Bread Croutons $8.50
Insalata al Modo di Cesare

Assorted Organic Green Salad $9.00
Insalatina Verde

~~ ~~ ~~ ~~

Primi Piatti

Tortellini with Cream & Parmigiano Cheese $11.00*
Tortellini in Panna

Risotto with Wild Mushrooms $15.50*
Risotto con Funghi Selvatici

Linguini with Clams, White Wine & Parsley $12.50
Linguini alle Vongole

Lobster Agnolotti with Lobster Sauce $13.50
Agnolotti d'Aragosta, Salsa d'Aragosta

Gnocchi with Gorgonzola Cheese $11.50*
Gnocchi alla Salsa di Gorgonzola

Cannellini Bean Soup with Prosciutto $8.50
Zuppa di Cannellini ai Prosciutto

Tortellini in Chicken Broth $8.00*
Tortellini in Brodo

659 Merchant St • Financial District • (415) 981-1177

Secondi Piatti

Grilled Salmon with Champagne Saffron Sauce $25.50
Salmone alla Griglia, Salsa di Spumante e Zafferano

Sautéed Halibut with Artichokes, Capers & Sundried Tomatoes $26.50*
Rombo in Padella con Carciofi, Caperi e Pomodori Secchi

Roasted Breast of Sonoma Chicken with Prosciutto & Fontina Cheese $22.50*
Petto di Pollo alla Valdostana

Veal Scallopine with Capers, Lemon & Parsley $23.50*
Piccata di Vitella

Sautéed Veal Chop, Butter & Sage $27.50
Costoletta di Vitello In Padella, Salvia e Burro

Roasted Rack of Lamb, Balsamic Vinegar Sauce $27.50*
Carre d'Agnello, Salsa di Agro Dolce

Fillet of Beef with Green Peppercorn & Grappa Sauce $27.50*
Filetto di Bue alla Salsa Pepe Verde e Grappa

Roasted Breast of Muscovy Duck with Tangerine Sauce $27.50
Petto d'Anitra con Salsa di Mandarine

Sautéed Loin of Venison, Oyster Mushrooms with Juniper Berry Sauce $28.00
Filetto di Cervo al Forno con Salsa di Ginebra

~~ ~~ ~~ ~~

The Blue Fox Classic Menu
*(This specially priced menu is not available in connection with
any promotion or after 7:00 pm on Fridays & Saturdays)*

$39.50

Choice of:
"Scampi alla Livornese" Prawns Sautéed in Lemon, Parsley & Butter

"Tortellini in Panna" Tortellini with Cream & Parmigiano Cheese

Choice of:
Grilled Salmon with Champagne Saffron Sauce

Roasted Breast of Sonoma Chicken with Prosciutto & Fontina Cheese*

"Piccata di Vitella" Veal Scallopine with Capers, Lemon & Parsley*

Fillet of Beef with Green Peppercorn & Grappa Sauce*

Choice of:
Tiramisù, Espresso Mascarpone Delight

"Gelati Misti" Assorted Homemade Ice Cream

~~~

*For parties of six or more a 15% gratuity may be added to the check.
A separate dessert menu will be presented after you enjoy your entrées.*

IL CUORE DELLA CUCINA ITALIANA

MENU CHANGES REGULARLY

PASTA

We make our pasta by hand here on the premises daily.
To give you the freshest ingredients possible we cook
the pasta and sauces to order. Please allow extra time.

TORTELLINI ALLA PAESANA 10.50

Homemade Tortellini in a Butter and Cream Sauce with
Peas, Prosciutto, Mushrooms and Parmesan Cheese

ROTONDI DI SPIGOLA 10.75

Homemade Ravioli Stuffed with Sea Bass, Ricotta
Cheese and Spinach in a Tomato and Cream Sauce

RAVIOLI AL POMODORO E BASILICO 9.75

Homemade Ravioli Stuffed with Ricotta Cheese and
Spinach in a Tomato and Fresh Basil Sauce

FETTUCCINE DI MARE 12.75

Homemade Flat Egg Noodles in a Light Red Sauce
Topped with Assorted Fresh Seafood

CAPELLINI ALLE CAPESANTE 10.50

Homemade Angel Hair Pasta Topped with Fresh
Scallops, Fresh Tomato and Garlic

TAGLIERINI TRAMONTANA 9.75

Homemade Thin Flat Noodles, Diced Tiger Prawns, Fresh
Spinach and Fresh Tomato in a Light Cream Sauce

2223 Union St • Marina • (415) 929-0407

PENNE ALLA NORCINA   9.75
Small Tube Pasta with Sausage,
Mushrooms and Prosciutto in a Light
Cream Sauce with Romano Cheese

FUSILLI ALLA CAPODIMONTE   9.75
Corkscrew Pasta in Tomato Sauce with Sauteed
Eggplant and Fresh Mozzarella Cheese

FETTUCCINE SAPORI   10.50
Homemade Flat Spinach Noodles with Smoked
Chicken, Smoked Prosciutto and Shitaki Mushrooms
in a Cream Sauce

SECONDI PIATTI

GRIGLIATA DI SALSICCE   12.00
Grilled Italian Sausages Served with Grilled Polenta
and Spicy Broccoli

POLLO ALL'ERBE   10.75
A Half Grilled Chicken Marinated with Fresh Italian Herbs,
Served with Vegetables and Roasted Potatoes

SALTIMBOCCA ALLA ROMANO   13.75
Veal Rolls Filled with Prosciutto, Sage and Fontina
Cheese in a Roman Wine Sauce

SCALOPPINE AL BURRO E LIMONE   13.75
Veal in a Butter, Lemon and Caper Sauce, Served
with Vegetables and Roasted Potatoes

FILETTO AL RADICCHIO   17.75
Grilled Beef Filet Topped with Radicchio in a Balsamic
Vinegar Sauce Served with Roasted Potatoes

LOMBATA DI VITELLO   17.75
14 oz. Grilled Veal Chop Served with Vegetables and
Roasted Potatoes

FRITTO DI CALAMARI E GAMBERI   11.75
Fried Calamari and Shrimp Served with a Rughetta
and Tomato Salad

SPIEDINI DI VEGETALI   13.75
Two Skewers of Grilled Fresh Garden Vegetables Marinated
in a Garlic Balsamic Vinegrette, Served over Grilled Polenta

ANTIPASTI E INSALATE
Hors d'Oeuvres & Salads

Antipasto Misto la Buca   7.50
Smoked Salmon, Speck, Calamari, Olives, Dry Tomatoes in Olive Oil

Speck All'olio e Limone e Olive Nere   5.25
Smoked Prosciutto served with Virgin Olive Oil, Lemon, & Black Olives

Bruschetta   1.50
Toasted Garlic Bread with Olive Oil

Salmone Affumicato al Coriandolo e Scalogno alla Crema Acida   6.25
Smoked Salmon, Coriander, Shallots & Homemade Sour Cream

Fagioli Borlotti Alla Toscana   3.25
Borlotti Beans, Virgin Olive Oil, Garlic & Sage

Insalata di Calamari   5.95

Insalata Calda di Pollo e Mandorle   5.50
Warm Chicken Salad with Almonds & Balsamic Vinegar

MINESTRE E PASTE ASCIUTTE
BUCA GIOVANNI makes all their own pasta & soup on the premises!

Minestrone alla Lucchese   3.10

Capellini alla Salsa Del Giorno   9.95
Angel Hair Pasta with Sauce of the Day

Fettuccine Alfredo   8.25

Fettuccine al Prosciutto E Asparagi   9.25

Linguine al Funghi Porcini   14.50
Linguine with Fresh Italian Porcini Mushrooms

800 Greenwich St • North Beach • (415) 776-7766

LE CARNI, LA SELVAGGINA, IL PESCE
A Variety of Meats, Birds, Fish & Seafood
As your Waiter for the Fresh Fish of the Day

Filetto Di Manzo   15.95
Broiled Beef Filet

Medaglioni di Filetto alle Erbe Fini E Funghi Pleuroti   16.50
Beef Filet Sauteed with Fine Herbs & Oyster Mushrooms

Petti di Pollo al Cartoccio All'aceto Balsamico   13.45
Boneless Breast of Chicken, Mushrooms & Prosciutto in Parchment Paper, Balsamic Vinegar

Petti Di Pollo Con Asparagi E Prosciutto   14.25
Breast of Chicken, Prosciutto & Asparagus

Pollo Alle Olive E Aceto Balsamico   12.95
Chicken Sauteed with Black Olives, Rosemary, Garlic, Balsamic Vinegar

Medaglioni Di Capriolo Mandorle E Carciofini   16.95
Medallions of Venison with Almonds & Artichokes

Medaglioni Di Cervo Con Funghi Porcini   18.95
Venison Medallions with Porcini Mushrooms

Agnello Ripieno di Mortella, Erbette e Porcini Fasciato in Foglie Di Vite, Arrosto Toscano   16.50
Lamb Stuffed with Mortadella, Herbs, Porcini Mushrooms Wrapped in Grape Leaves

Bistecchine di Agnello a Scottadito All'Aceto Balsamico   16.50
Lamb Chops Sauteed with Herbs, Garlic & Wine or Olives, Oregano, & Capers

Coniglio Alla Brianzola Con Bacche di Ginepro Aglio, Grappa, Noci   15.20
Rabbit with Juniper Berries, Garlic, Grappa, Wine & Walnuts

Coniglio Alla Grappa, Prosciutto, Ruta & Funghi Pleuroti   15.20
Rabbit with Grappa, Prosciutto, Rue & Oyster Mushrooms

Coniglio Arrosto Al Forno Toscana Rosmarino E Patatine   15.20
Roast Rabbit with Rosemary & Roasted Potatoes

Coniglio Saltato Agrodolce "Roma Antica"   15.25
Rabbit Saute with Honey, Vinegar, Leeks, Almonds & Rue

Rabbit Saute with Porcini Mushrooms, Garlic, Sage & Wine   17.50

"Cucina Del Mercato"

Menu Changes Daily

ASSORTED ITALIAN APPETIZERS
Sm. 6.00   Lg. 11.00

GRILLED EGGPLANT
with Balsamic Vinegar and Gorgonzola
5.50

SOFT POLENTA
with Wild Mushroom Sauce
5.00

ORGANIC MIXED GREEN SALAD
3.50

SOUP OF THE DAY   A.Q.

GNOCCHI
with Gorgonzola Sauce
8.50

RAVIOLI (CHEESE & SPINACH)
Wild Mushroom Sauce
8.95

PENNE
with Spicy Tomato Sauce & Basil
7.25

EGG LINGUINI
with Tomato, Pesto, and Fried Sage
8.50

59 Columbus Ave • North Beach • (415) 956-9737

FETTUCCINI
with Pink Trout, Thyme, and Mascarpone
9.25

PASTA OF THE DAY   A.Q.

SEAFOOD SPECIAL OF THE DAY   A.Q.

CALAMARI STEAK
with Green Olive Sauce
10.25

GIANT PRAWNS GRILLED
with Mixed Green Salad
13.95

PORK MEDALLIONS
with Fennel Seed Sauce
12.95

LAMB SHANK BRAISED
with Rosemary over Polenta
13.95

OXTAIL & PORK SAUSAGE BRAISED
in Tomato Sauce
11.25

CHICKEN BREAST SAUTE
with Fresh Garlic Puree
10.50

SWEETBREADS OF VEAL
with Wild Mushroom Sauce
13.50

MEAT SPECIAL OF THE DAY   A.Q.

FRESH PASTA all'uovo & semolina

FETTUCCINE

FETTUCCINE ai QUATTRO FORMAGGI 9.95
4 cheeses: provolone, fontina, parmesan, romano and heavy cream

FETTUCCINE ALFREDO 9.25
heavy cream, butter & parmesan cheese

FETTUCCINE al POMODORO 7.95
filet of fresh tomato and basil

FETTUCCINE alla BOLOGNESE 9.25
ground beef, mushrooms, fresh tomatoes & herbs

LINGUINE

LINGUINE alla CARBONARA 9.75
parmesan cheese, egg yolk & pancetta

LINGUINE FRUITTI de MARE (SEAFOOD) 11.95
clams, shrimp, calamari, tomatoes, wine and herbs

LINGUINE alla PESCATORE 11.95
fresh tomato, prawns, basil, shallots, dry white wine, sweet butter & garlic

CANNELLONI

CANNELLONI ROMANO 12.75
filled with a special meat stuffing rolled in white pasta in our special sauce
 or made with pesto

CANNELLONI FRUTTA di MARE 12.75
filled with a special seafood stuffing-crab, shrimp & clams, parmesan cheese
and a bechamel

PENNETTE

PASTA PRIMAVERA 9.75
pennette made with cauliflower, broccoli, zucchini, carrots, olive oil & garlic

PENNETTE con RICCOTTA 9.75
made with fresh tomato sauce blended together with riccotta cheese served
over pen shaped pasta

PIZZA / CALZONE

ROASTED EGGPLANT PIZZA 9.25
roasted eggplant and virgin olive oil

MARGHERITA 7.75
mozzarella, virgin olive oil, basil

al PESTO 7.95
pizza made with basil, parsley and garlic   Vegetarian pesto . . . 8.95

GARLIC & CLAMS 8.25
Mozzarella, olive oil, fresh garlic with baby clams

QUATTRO STAGIONI 8 75
ham, baby artichokes, mushrooms, whole olives

CAPRICCIOSA 8.95
mozzarella, artichokes, olives, sun-dried tomatoes

CALABRESE 8.95
southern style Italian sausage, olives, sweet red onion, virgin olive oil

LA SICILIANA 9.95
capers, sliced tomatoes, anchovies, mozzarella and parmesan cheese

alla SERGIO 8.95
mushrooms, sausage, pepperoni, salami, bell peppers, onion, virgin oil

CREATE YOUR OWN PIZZA (limit 4 items) 9.25

PIZZA VIA VENETO 9.75
mozzarella, gorgonzola cheese, radicchio and walnuts

CALZONE alla PUGLIESE 9.95
made with sun-dried tomatoes, artichokes, gorgonzola cheese, prosciutto,
ricotta cheese and capers

SEAFOOD CALZONE 10.25
made with prawns, shrimp, clams, marinated calamari, ricotta cheese

VEGETARIAN CALZONE 8.95
made with dices tomatoes, basil, bell peppers, mushrooms, capers, smoked
mozzarella and whole olives

CALZONE OR PIZZA ai QUATTRO FORMAGGI 9.95
smoked mozzarella, gorgonzola, ricotta and teleme   with prosciutto . . 10.95

FOCACCETTA alla BARESE 7.50
mini focaccia with melted mozzarella, prosciutto cotto (ham), or mortadella
served with a side salad

Calzone *Baked in our Wood Fired Brick Oven*

20 ▶ *Chicken* with pancetta*, spinach, mozzarella, onions, mushrooms, parmesan cream sauce.   **10.75**

22 ▶ *BBQ Chicken* with BBQ sauce, mozzarella, cilantro, roasted garlic, onions, oregano.   **9.95**

23 ▶ *Marinated Eggplant* with ricotta, mozzarella, fresh tomato, roasted garlic.   **9.50**

Fresh Pasta *Made Daily on the Premises*

Fettucini with...

30 ▶ *Fresh Basil Pomodoro* — a light sauce of fresh tomato and basil.   **8.95**

31 ▶ *Calzone's Alfredo* — parmesan cream sauce, mushrooms, wine and fresh spinach.   **9.75**

32 ▶ *Bolognese* — a rich, hearty tomato sauce made with Niman-Schell beef, pancetta*, pork and sausage.   **10.25**

33 ▶ *Asparagus* —chicken, toasted pine nuts, sun-dried tomatoes, parsley, garlic, fresh basil, extra virgin olive oil, parmesan, toasted bread crumbs.   **10.95**

34 ▶ *Sautéed Wild Mushrooms* — smoked duck sausage, red onions and fresh herbs.   **12.95**

Fresh Linguine with...

40 ▶ *Sausage* — cannellini beans, broccoli di rabe, Swiss chard, extra virgin olive oil, garlic, crushed red pepper, fresh herbs, parmesan.   **10.75**

43 ▶ *Sautéed Chicken Livers* — mushrooms, onions, sweet marsala cream sauce.   **9.75**

45 ▶ *Fresh Clams* — white or red sauce, yellow squash, red onions.   **12.75**

Fresh Angel Hair with...

46 ▶ Prawns — pancetta*, radicchio, spinach, roasted red bell peppers
sautéed in extra virgin olive oil and mustard vinaigrette.   12.95

47 ▶ Prawns — pancetta*, fresh corn, cilantro, red bell pepper
pomodoro, avocado; sprinkled with jalapeño jack cheese.   13.95

48 ▶ Garlic Brie Cream Sauce — toasted pine nuts and asparagus.   10.75

49 ▶ Fresh Sea Scallops — fresh fennel, anisette and roasted
red bell pepper purée.   14.50

Fresh Pasta Specialties

50 ▶ Calzetti — a buckwheat pasta served with broccoli, fennel, pancetta*,
mushrooms, yellow squash, potatoes, seasoned bread crumbs; sautéed in
extra virgin olive oil, garlic and fresh herbs.   11.25

51 ▶ Homemade Tortellini — half stuffed with veal and prosciutto, half with
ricotta; served with parmesan cream sauce or with bolognese
(tomato meat sauce) on request.   10.95

52 ▶ Potato and Three Cheese Homemade Ravioli — filled with caramelized
onions, roasted garlic, ricotta, smoked mozzarella and parmesan; served with:
pancetta*, fresh basil pomodoro and spinach — _or_ — with
pesto and mushrooms cream sauce.   12.50

53 ▶ Porcini Mushroom Ravioli — sage brown butter sauce,
fresh grated parmesan.   11.25

House Specialties

54 ▶ Polenta Lasagne 1 — Tri-colored polenta layered with fresh ling cod,
fontina and mozzarella in a spicy fresh basil cream pomodoro.   11.95

55 ▶ Polenta Lasagne 2 — Tri-colored polenta layered with fresh-roasted
Niman-Schell pork, cilantro, red bell pepper pomodoro, fresh corn, roasted red
bell peppers, jalapeño jack cheese.   11.95

56 ▶ Pesto Lamb Shank Cassoulet — Baked with 15 beans, fresh vegetables,
fresh tomato pomodoro, puréed and encrusted with mint pesto and
seasoned breadcrumbs.   12.50

57 ▶ Roasted Turkey Tenderloin — encrusted with pancetta*, roasted garlic,
roasted red bell pepper purée, parsley, sage, rosemary and thyme,
served with seasonal fresh vegetables and potatoes.   12.95

58 ▶ Niman-Schell Rib Eye — 8 oz., pan-roasted in extra virgin olive oil,
salt and black pepper; served with roasted garlic purée, served with
seasonal fresh vegetables and potatoes.   15.95

WELCOME
Our Dinners are served "Family Style" and include
A Tureen of Minestrone Soup
Green Salad with Italian Vinaigrette
Pasta of-the-day (except Pasta Entrees)
Your Choice of Entree
Sauteed Fresh Vegetables
and
Dessert

ENTREES FOR 10.50

MEAT RAVIOLI BOLOGNESE
   Meat Ravioli with Fresh Basil, Tomato & Meat Sauce

CHEESE RAVIOLI MARINARA
   Ricotta Ravioli with Tomato & Fresh Basil

TORTELLINI ALLA PANNA
   Veal Tortellini in Cream Sauce

STEAMED MUSSEL & CLAMS WITH LINGUINE
   Fresh Manilla Clams & Prince Edward Island Mussels
   in a Spicy Tomato Sauce with Fresh Basil

FETTUCINI WITH BAY SHRIMP
   Egg Fettucini & Fresh Bay Shrimp in Tomato
   Sauce with Fresh Basil

LINGUINI CALAMARI
   Calamari in a "HOT" Red Sauce with Linguini

LINGUINI PESTO
   Linguini in a Fresh Basil & Walnut Pesto

1600 Powell St • North Beach • (415) 989-2589 • (Call for Additional Locations)

ENTREES FOR 12.50

CHICKEN BREAST
Lemon Butter Wine Sauce & Capers

VEAL T-BONE 8 OZ CHOP
Marinated in Rosemary & Grilled to Order

CHOICE NEW YORK STEAK
Grilled to Order

LEG OF LAMB
Roasted on the Bone and served Au Jus
(Yes we have Mint Jelly, but it goes best on toast)

ROAST VEAL
Sliced Leg of Veal served Au Jus

PORK LOIN ROAST
Roasted Pork Loin with Mushroom Sauce

SAUSAGE & PEPPERS
Housemade Spicy Sicilian Sausage with
Fire Roasted Peppers

ROAST GARLIC CHICKEN
Half Chicken Roasted with Fresh Garlic & Rosemary

FRESH FISH OF THE DAY
San Francisco's Finest prepared alla Capp's

OSSO BUCO PIEDMONTESE
Braised Veal Shanks served with Baked Polenta

EGGPLANT PARMAGIANA
Eggplant baked en casserole with a Tomato
and a Cream Sauce

BAKED VEAL CANNELLONI
Handmade Crepes filled with ground Veal & Cheese
Baked with Tomato and a Cream Sauce

BAKED LASAGNA
Meat & Cheese Lasagna with a Tomato and
a Cream Sauce, topped with Mozzarella

SIMPLY SOUP, SALAD, PASTA & DESSERT IS **8.50**

KIDS DINNER (Under 12)
Minestrone Soup, Pasta of-the-Day,
Portioned Entree and Dessert
7.50

Dinner: Sun - Thur 4:30 - 10:30, Fri - Sat 4:30 - 11

Menu Changes Seasonally

Antipasti

Insalata "Ciao„ ‹	4.95
lettuce, mushrooms, tomato, provolone cheese, garbanzo beans, salame, onions	
Antipasto assortito	5.50
assorted appetizer platter for two or more	per person
Insalata di fagioli e pollo	6.75
assorted chilled beans, homemade pesto, shredded chicken, tomato	
Insalata di riso	4.95
arborio rice salad of the day	
Insalata mista	4.95
mixed greens, balsamic vinaigrette and gorgonzola crostini	
Piatto campagnola	4.75
frisée salad with feta cheese, olives, onions, anchovy, lemon, extra virgin olive oil	
Mozzarella alla caprese	6.95
sliced tomatoes, fresh mozzarella, olive oil, fresh basil	
Ortaggi saporiti	5.50
grilled marinated eggplant, fried zucchini, roasted peppers, extra virgin olive oil	

Pasta

Capellini al pomodoro e basilico	8.95
angel hair pasta, fresh tomato, basil; garlic, olive oil	
Fusilli al pesto Genovese	9.25
pasta spirals; homemade pesto, green beans, potato	
Farfalle con zucchine	8.75
bow-tie pasta, fried zucchini; milk, parmesan, olive oil, bread crumbs	
Gnocchi alla sorrentina	8.95
light potato pillows; simmered tomato sauce, basil, fresh mozzarella	
Tortelli ai carciofi	10.75
pasta filled with fresh artichoke, parmesan cheese; butter and sage	

Ravioli di magro al limone   9.95
ravioli filled with ricotta, basil and parsley; lemon butter

Fedelini tuttomare   11.75
thin pasta with today's fresh seafood; spicy tomato sauce

Fettuccine ai quattro formaggi   9.25
flat pasta; cream, butter, fontina, pecorino, gruyère
and parmesan cheeses

Fedelini alle vongole   10.95
thin pasta; fresh Manila clams, garlic, olive oil

Fettuccine alla crema di scampi   10.75
flat pasta, shrimp; creamy tomato sauce

Lasagnette riccie   8.75
wide pasta; ricotta cheese, tarragon, mint, basil, virgin olive oil

Paglia e fieno   9.75
spinach and egg fettuccine; pancetta, peas, cream

Lasagne alla Bolognese   9.95
thin sheets of fresh pasta layered with meat sauce,
bechamel and parmesan cheese

Risotto del giorno   A.Q.
creamy arborio rice of the day

Secondi

Pesce fresco del giorno   A.Q.
today's selections of fresh fish

Petti di pollo alla cacciatora   9.95
sautéed chicken breast with rosemary, vinegar, olives
and soft polenta

Paillard di pollo   12.95
mesquite-grilled chicken breast with roasted garlic,
lemon, olive oil, tomatoes and basil

Gamberi in padella   16.75
sautéed prawns with lemon, garlic, parsley, white wine

Stufato di salsiccie   9.95
Italian sausages with stewed peppers, onions and potatoes

Cotoletta al prosciutto   14.95
breaded and sautéed veal paillard with prosciutto, fontina and
parmesan; served with green beans and lemon

Agnello alla griglia   14.50
mesquite-grilled lamb loin chops with Swiss chard
and roasted potatoes

Lombata di vitello   16.75
large mesquite-grilled natural-fed veal chop with virgin olive oil
and lemon; served with fresh spinach

Piatto di verdure   7.50
fresh spinach, soft polenta, roasted garlic, potatoes, eggplant,
fire-roasted peppers, glazed onions and marinated zucchini

CIRCOLO

RESTAURANT & CHAMPAGNERIA

Menu Changes Semi-Annually

SQUEEZE PLAY

Selection of Freshly Squeezed Juices and Cocktails...A.Q.

ANTIPASTI

Focaccia (filled with fontina cheese) $4.95
Polenta (with roasted peppers and feta cheese) $5.50
Melanzane Arrostite (roasted Japanese eggplant with gorgonzola, proscuitto, fresh basil
and sour cream, with tomato sauce)...$4.95
Salmone (Faz's smoked salmon)...$6.50
Calamari Marinati (with olive oil, lemon juice, garden vegetables and spices).........................$4.95
Carpaccio (thin sliced raw beef with homemade mustard sauce and capers)............................$5.25
Ricotta al Forno (brick oven baked fresh ricotta served on a bed of greens
with roasted walnuts and balsamic vinegar and olive oil) $4.95

ZUPPA DEL GIORNO $3.25

INSALATA

Insalata Circolo (baby lettuce with tomato and raspberry vinaigrette).......................................$3.50
Insalata Caesar (Caesar salad of Romaine hearts) $4.95
Insalata di Spinaci (warm spinach salad with pancetta, mushrooms, onions, pine nuts
and pomegranate vinaigrette...$5.50
Insalata Mediterranea (arugula and baby spinach, with roasted eggplant, kalamata olives,
cherry tomatoes and feta cheese)..$5.95
Insalata di Ricotta (fresh ricotta cheese with roasted peppers, pine nuts and radicchio)...........$6.50
Petti di Anatra alla Griglia (grilled breast of duck with spinach, fresh orange
and pomegranate vinaigrette)...$8.95

PIZZA

Margherita (tomato, basil, oregano and mozzarella) $7.95
Melanzane (grilled eggplant with garlic, tomato, basil and mozzarella)...............................$7.95
Frutti di Mare (gulf shrimp with mozzarella cheese and tomato)..$9.95
Salcicce (spicy Italian sausage with tomato and fresh herbs)...$8.95

ALLA GRIGLIA

Pesce Fresco del Giorno (fresh fish of the day) ....A.Q.
Gamberoni (jumbo prawns with basil butter sauce) $14.95
Coniglio (braised and sauteed fresh rabbit with pomegrenate sauce, served with spaghettini) $12.95
Pollo alla Mo (grilled boneless chicken with saffron and fresh herbs, served with
pasta and wild mushrooms) $9.95
Quaglia (boneless whole quail stuffed with chicken, prosciutto and gorgonzola
cheese, served on a bed of capellini with spinach) $9.95
Anatra Arrosto (split side of roasted duck with pomegranate sauce, served with
roasted potatoes and vegetables)..$12.95
Braciola di Maiala (grilled pork chop with sauteed apple and spinach)...............................$12.95
Braciola di Vitello (grilled 14oz veal chop)...$15.95
Agnello Arrosto (loin of lamb served on a bed of grilled eggplant with roasted potatoes
and vegetables)..$15.95
Bistecca alla Griglia (grilled New York steak) $15.95

DOLCI

Frutta Fresca di Stagione (fresh berries in season) ....A.Q.
Gioia Mia (semi-sweet chocolate with pecan crust served with caramel sauce).......................$4.50
Flan del Circolo (served with fresh fruit) $3.95
Tiramisu (lady fingers, espresso, frangelico and cream) $3.95
Gelati Assortiti (homemade ice cream) $3.25
Dolce di Formaggio (cheesecake served with fresh berry sauce)..$3.95

PASTE FRESCA DELLA CASA

Fettuccini Marco Polo (flat noodles with jumbo prawns, arugula and curry) $12.95
Tagliatelle Vegetariane (broad noodles with roasted peppers, mushrooms, spinach and
tomatoes)..$8.95
Linguini al Pettini (oval noodles with sea scallops and sun dried tomatoes) $9.95
Fettuccine al Salmone (whole wheat flat noodles with snow peas, dill and cream).................$9.95
Linguini Misti (oval noodles with clams, calamari, scallops, mushrooms,
spinach and tomato sauce) $10.95
Capelli d'Angelo (angel hair pasta with scallops, baby artichokes,
shitake mushrooms, spinach, tomatoes and herbs) $9.95
Pappardelle con Prosciutto (pasta with prosciuto, fresh basil, parmesan and romano cheese) $8.95
Ravioli del Giorno...A.Q.

Gli Antipasti

Rosette di salmone al basilico 12.00
Rosettes of salmon in a basil coulis on a bed of green lettuce

Insalatina di anatra e lenticchie all'aceto balsamico 13.00
Duck salad with lentils in a balsamic vinaigrette

Filetto di vitello in salsa leggera di tonno e capperi 12.00
Cold fillet of veal in a light sauce of tuna fish and capers

Capesante e gamberi con rucola e cannellini 14.00
Sauteed scallops and prawns with arugula and cannellini beans

Carpaccio di manzo con sedano e tartufi neri 14.00
Thinly sliced raw beef with celery and black truffles

I Primi

Risotto al peperone dolce e astice 16.00
Risotto with sweet red peppers and lobster

Tortellini di piccione e verze in brodo leggero 9.00
Squab tortellini in its own broth with green cabbage

Ravioli di ricotta e mozzarella ai carciofi 11.00
Ricotta and mozzarella cheese ravioli with artichoke

Trenette al pesto con fagiolini e patate 9.00
Trenette pasta with pesto, green beans and potatoes

Lasagne leggere di capesante con finocchi e anice 14.00
Scallop lasagne with fennel in a light cream of anise sauce

Rigatoni al ragu di cacciagione e funghi 12.00
Rigatoni in a sauce of game and wild mushrooms

---

501 Post St • Union Square • (415) 441-7182

Prix fixe menu

Capesante e gamberi con rucola e cannellini
Sauteed scallops and prawns
with arugula and cannellini beans

Risotto "primavera"
Risotto with spring vegetables and parmesan
* * * * *
Fagiano con spinaci pinoli e uvetta
Wild pheasant with spinach, pinenuts and raisins
or
Branzino grigliato al basilico
con zabaglione all'olio d'oliva
Grilled striped bass with olive oil zabayon and basil puree
* * * * *
Pera brasata al barolo con panna cotta
Braised pear in barolo wine with cream flan

Caffe

Price $52.00 per person
Tax and gratuity not included

I Secondi

Branzino grigliato al basilico con zabaglione all'olio d'oliva 25.00
Grilled striped bass with extra virgin olive oil zabayon and basil puree

Filetto di San Pietro con ravioli ai carciofi 26.00
Lightly sauteed filet of John Dory with artichoke raviolis

Capesante al pomodoro fresco e caponata 25.00
Pan-fried scallops with fresh tomato and ratatouille

Scaloppa di salmone con cipolla rossa e scorza d'arancia 24.00
Fillet of salmon with red onions and orange zest

Astice al forno con funghi, patate e porri 33.00
Braised whole Maine lobster with mushrooms and potatoes

Fagiano con spinaci pinoli e uvetta 25.00
Wild pheasant with spinach, pinenuts and raisins

Vitello farcito agli asparagi, patate all'erba cipollina 26.00
Loin of veal filled with asparagus
and served with quenelles of potatoes and chives

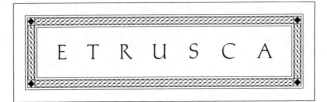

Menu Changes Daily

ANTIPASTI

Salmone al Balsamico	*Pacific salmon marinated in balsamic vinegar served with homemade gallets and horseradish cream*	9.25
Prosciutto e Melone	*Prosciutto di San Leo served with anisette and mint marinated melon*	8.75
Mozzarella alla Romana	*Mozzarella served with baby romaine lettuce and a relish of roasted bell peppers*	7.75
Lattughe Miste	*Organically grown lettuces, fresh fennel, extra virgin olive oil and red wine vinegar*	6.50
Insalata Populonia	*Vine-ripened tomatoes, sweet onions, green and black olives, feta and fresh oregano in a lemon vinaigrette*	6.25
Riscaldata	*Timbale of fresh vegetables, Tuscan bread and herbs baked in a wood-burning oven*	5.00
Carpaccio d'Agnello	*Lamb carpaccio with whole grain mustard and sour cream dressing*	8.75
Insalata di Arance Rosse	*Fennel and blood orange salad with raspberry vinegar dressing*	7.50
Gamberoni Gratinati	*Jumbo shrimp gratinee with fresh herbs served on a bed of mixed baby greens*	9.75
Melanzane alla Greca	*Timbale of grilled eggplant, artichokes and spinach on a bell pepper puree*	8.00

ZUPPE E MINESTRE

Crema di Finocchi	*Cream of fennel soup with a reduction of Cabernet garnished with vegetable brunoise*	4.75
Zuppetta di Pomodori Gialli	*Golden tomato soup with onions, garlic and fried sage*	5.00

PASTA

Agnolotti di Vitellone	*Raviolis filled with veal, Italian bacon and mortadella with a sauce of green peas, demi-glace and cream*	11.75
Crespelle di Ricotta	*Crepes stuffed with ricotta cheese and mint baked in the oven with Bechamel sauce*	11.00
Umbrichelle all'Etrusca	*Square pasta tubes, sausage, peas, field mushrooms and fresh tomato sauce*	9.75
Tortelloni di Coniglio	*Homemade pasta filled with rabbit and ricotta cheese in a fresh tomato sauce*	11.50
Risotto alle Pere	*Italian rice with d'Anjou pear and Taleggio cheese*	11.25
Fettuccine alla Carrettiera	*Fettuccine with a sauce of mushrooms, olive paste and fresh tomatoes*	10.50
Cannelloni Penelope	*Cannelloni filled with sausage and spinach baked in the oven with Bechamel sauce*	11.50
Fusilli alla Cacciatora	*Corkscrew pasta with a Bolognese and imported Porcini mushroom sauce*	10.75

SECONDI PIATTI

Salmone al Pesto di Prezzemolo	*Sauteed salmon served with a pesto of Italian parsley and basil*	17.75
Quaglie con Risotto	*Roasted quail served on Italian rice with Parmesan cheese*	17.50
Storione al Finocchio	*Grilled sturgeon served with fresh fennel, tomato basil and balsamic vinaigrette*	18.00
Petto di Pollo Saturnia	*Grilled chicken breast in a fresh tomato and vegetable sauce served with grilled corn*	14.00
Coniglio al Forno con Funghi	*Boneless roasted rabbit served with field mushrooms and soft polenta*	17.25
Carre di Vitello	*Roasted rack of veal served with imported Porcini mushroom sauce*	19.75
Pesce Etrusca	*Striped bass with fresh herbs encrusted in Kosher salt baked in the wood-burning oven* *(serves two)*	29.50
Anatra ai Pinoli	*Roasted half duckling with pinenut sauce*	18.50

Dinner: Mon - Fri 5:30 - 12, Sat - Sun 5 - 12

RISTORANTE EST. 1886 FIOR d'ITALIA

Pasta Fatta in Casa
FRESH PASTA
MADE DAILY IN OUR KITCHEN

Pasta del Giorno   **8.95**
PASTA OF THE DAY

Paglia e Fieno con Salsicia Funghi e Crema   **8.95**
FINE STRANDS OF SPINACH AND EGG PASTA WITH A
SAUCE OF SAUSAGE, MUSHROOM, CREAM AND GARLIC

Cannelloni   **8.95**
PASTA CREPE FILLED WITH CHICKEN AND VEAL

Ravioli di Pollo   **8.95**
PASTA STUFFED WITH CHICKEN AND PROSCIUTTO
SERVED WITH A MEAT SAUCE

Lasagne Verdi al Forno   **8.95**
LAYERED PASTA WITH CHEESE, PROSCIUTTO AND MEAT

Trenette con Pesto   **8.95**
FINE PASTA TOSSED WITH BASIL, PINENUTS,
GARLIC AND OLIVE OIL SAUCE

Insalate
SALADS

Insalata di Cesare Augusto Per Due   **9.50**
FIOR CAESAR SALAD FOR TWO

Insalata di Crescione Pomodori Cipola a Gorgonzola Condita al Dragoncello   **8.95**
SALAD OF WATERCRESS, TOMATO, ONION AND
GORGONZOLA WITH TARRAGON DRESSING

Insalata di Serra con Mozzarella e Pomodori Secchi   **9.95**
BABY GREENS WITH MOZZARELLA AND DRY CURED TOMATOES

Mozzarella e Pomodoro   **9.25**
MOZZARELLA SERVED WITH TOMATOES,
FRESH BASIL AND VIRGIN OLIVE OIL

---

601 Union St • North Beach • (415) 986-1886

Polli e Caciagione
CHICKEN AND GAME

Medaglioni di Cervo al Vino Rosso e Ginepro — 18.50
MEDALLION OF VENISON WITH A SAUCE OF RED WINE
AND JUNIPER BERRY – SERVED RARE

Quaglie alla Griglia — 16.75
QUAIL BROILED AND SERVED WITH POLENTA

Coniglio all Vino Rosso con Polenta — 16.50
RABBIT STEW IN RED WINE SERVED WITH POLENTA

Pollo al Mattone — 15.25
1/2 CHICKEN FLATTENED AND ROASTED
WITH GARLIC AND ROSEMARY

Parmigiana di Pollo — 15.25
BREAST OF CHICKEN BREADED AND TOPPED WITH
CHEESE AND SERVED ON TOMATO SAUCE

Petto di Pollo Vuldo Stana — 15.25
BREAST OF CHICKEN SAUTEED AND TOPPED
WITH PROSCIUTTO AND CHEESE

Costoletta di Pollo al Mascotte — 15.25
BREAST OF CHICKEN SAUTEED WITH MUSHROOMS
AND ARTICHOKE

Pesci
FISH

Pesce Spada alla Griglia — 17.50
SWORDFISH BROIL

Capesante in Brodo — 16.25
SCALLOPS IN A SAFFRON BROTH

Calamari Milleottocentoottantasei — 12.75
CALAMARI 1886, LIGHTLY FRIED AND THEN TOSSED
WITH SAUTEED MUSHROOMS, ONIONS AND GARLIC

Sogliola Dorata — 13.75
PETRALE SOLE DORE LEMON BUTTER

Verdure
VEGETABLES

Parmigiana di Melanzane — 9.50
EGGPLANT SAUTEED, THEN BAKED WITH
TOMATO SAUCE AND TOPPED WITH CHEESE

Zucchini Saute — 4.00
ZUCCHINI SAUTEED WITH GARLIC AND OLIVE OIL

Pure di Spinaci — 4.00
CREAMED SPINACH

Sunday Brunch; Dinner: Sun - Thurs until 10:30, Fri - Sat until 11:30   ●ⓁⒹ

ANTIPASTI

Misto d'estate.. $5.50
Vine-ripened tomatoes with diced fresh mozzarella, olives, basil, oregano, extra virgin olive oil and garlic

Involtini di bresaola..6.75
Bresaola rolled with herbed goat cheese and pears, served with caponata and grilled zucchine

Insalata di carpaccio.......................................7.50
Thin slices of raw beef served with arugula, endive, radicchio, celery hearts, and shaved parmesan, topped with a dressing of pureed artichoke hearts, lemon, balsamic vinegar and extra virgin olive oil

Antipasto Fornelli (for two)................................9.50
Crostini, rolled stuffed eggplant, caponata, grilled peppers with eggplant and anchovies, grilled marinated shrimp and stuffed calamari

INSALATE

Insalatina..5.50
Mixed baby greens, balsamic vinegar, extra virgin olive oil

Insalata di Cesare..6.25
Caesar salad, Forenlli style

Insalatina arcobaleno.......................................6.75
Salad of fresh mozzarella, pears, baby greens and pecans in a dressing of walnut oil and champagne vinegar

---

5891 Broadway Terrace • Oakland • (510) 652-4442

PRIMI PIATTI (First Courses)

Capellini alla rucola e pomodoro............................$10.25
*Angel hair pasta with arugula, sundried tomatoes, cherry
tomatoes, basil, garlic and olive oil*

Tagliarini alla Norma......................................10.75
*Homemade tagliarini with sauteed eggplant in a fresh
tomato sauce*

Tagliatelle ai gamberoni....................................12.50
*Homemade tagliatelle with prawns, parsley, garlic, and
olive oil in a light shrimp sauce*

Risotto del giorno..A.Q.
Risotto of·the day

SECONDI PIATTI (Second Courses)

Rotolo di pollo alla bresaola...............................14.50
*Chicken breast rolled with bresaola, fontina and grilled
marinated peppers, sauteed in a Dijon mustard sauce*

Coniglio in agrodolce.......................................17.25
*Braised rabbit in a Sicilian sweet-sour sauce with
pinenuts, raisins and green olives*

Pesce fresco del giorno.....................................A.Q.
Fresh fish of the day

DOLCI

Cannolo siciliano..$4.75
*Homemade cannolo shell filled with sweetened ricotta
and bits of chocolate*

Torta gelato..5.75
*Base of Italian sponge cake infused with rum, layered
with chocolate and hazelnut ice cream, sweetened
whipped cream and bits of chocolate*

Biscotti con Malvasia.......................................7.00
*Homemade almond biscotti served with Malvasia delle
Lipari, a Sicilian dessert wine*

VINI DA DESSERT AL BICCHIERE (Dessert wines by the glass)

Marsala Superiore	*1984 De Bartoli, Sicilia*	4.25
Malvasia delle Lipari	*1987 Hauner, Sicilia*	5.00
Bukkuram Moscato Passito	*1986 De Bartoli, Sicilia*	6.00

Half Roasted Chicken .... 11.95   Quarter Roasted Chicken 7.95
Served with Palermo potatoes, and fresh vegetable.

Gira Polli Special

Half of our delicious wood-fired roasted chicken
served with Palermo potatoes, fresh vegetable
and choice of garden fresh salad or soup of the day.
12.95

APPETIZERS – SALADS – SOUP

ANTIPASTO MISTRO DELLA CASA ....
(for one) ....   5.25   (for two) 9.75
Roasted peppers, cannellini beans, artichoke hearts, prosciutto and
Sicilian olives

*MOZZARELLA FRESCA, POMO D'ORO E BASILICO ....
(for one) ....   4.25   (for two) 7.75
Fresh mozzarella cheese, tomatoes and basil with imported olives
and capers

CUORI DI LATTUGA ROMANA 4.75
Hearts of romaine with gorganzola cheese and toasted pine nuts

INSALATA VERDE MISTA 3.75
Star Route Farms garden fresh salad

VERDURA FRESCA DEL GIORNO 3.75
Fresh vegetable of the day

ZUPPA DEL GIORNO 2.75
Fresh homemade soup of the day

PASTA (also served as an appetizer for two)

*MANICOTTI CON TRE FORMAGGI 11.50
Fresh pasta filled with three cheeses; fresh mozzarella, fresh ricotta,
and parmigiano baked in tomato sauce

TORTELLINI AL PESTO 12.50
Pasta rings filled with veal and prosciutto

RAVIOLI CON SUGO DI CARNE ALLA SICILIANA 11.50
Ricotta filled ravioli with sicilian meat sauce

PENNONI CON SALSICCIA AL FINOCCHIO 9.75
Pennoni pasta with fennel sausage

DOLCE

*CANNOLI DI CASA 4.50
The most famous dessert of Sicily, a light and flaky pastry filled
with fresh sweetened ricotta cheese

YOLANDA'S CHEESE CAKE 3.25
A creamy and light lemon flavored cheesecake (Michele's recipe)

BISCOTTI DELLA MAMMA 3.50
An assortment of homemade Sicilian cookies
"made exclusively for Gira Polli"

TIRAMISU 4.50
Lady Fingers soaked in espresso and Amaretto with mascarpone cheese
(Dilizioso)

TORTA DI GELATO 4.50
Please ask for today's flavor

CAFFE

ESPRESSO	1.50
CAFFE LATTE	1.75
CAPPUCCINO	1.75

*We are proud to serve fresh Ricotta and Mozzarella cheeses from the Ferrante Cheese Co.

HYDE *Bistro* STREET

APPETIZERS

Soup of the Day
A.Q.

Warm Mozzarella and Tomato Salad with Buendnerfleisch
$6.25

Warm Vegetable Strudel with Herb Sauce
$5.25

Bistro Garden Salad with Seasonal Field Greens
$4.75

Grilled Country Sausage with Polenta
$6.25

PASTA

Spinach Fettuccine with Fresh Tomatoes and Basil
$7.95

Viennese Spinach Gnocchi Gorgonzola and Pancetta Sauce
$8.95

Ravioli with Wild Mushroom Sauce
$9.75

Penne with Sausage, Peppers, Tomato and Eggplant
9.75

Spaetzle with Smoked Ham Gruyere, Mozzarella and Parmesan
$10.75

Spaetzle with Scallops Chardonnay Cream Sauce
$10.95

Pasta Pesto and Chicken
$9.80

GRILLS — MAIN COURSES

GRILLED RED SNAPPER
with Mustard Herb Mayonnaise spaetzle Gratin
$13.75

GRILLED HALIBUT
on a Bed of Spinach with Tagliarini
$14.75

FISH OF THE DAY
A.Q

ROASTED SONOMA CHICKEN
with Potato Pancakes and Double Blanched Garlic
$13.90

WIENER SCHNITZEL
Lightly Breaded Veal Cutlet with Lingenberry and Potato Pancake
$15.75

Pumpernickel Sour Dough Rye Bread is baked locally by Patisserie Francaise
Fresh Viennese Coffee is roasted by Caffé Trieste

ANTIPASTI

BOMBA! 7.50
Dome-shaped focaccia baked in the oakwood-burning oven, covered with speck (smoked prosciutto)

BRUSCHETTA 3.95
Filone bread toasted with garlic and olive oil, topped with chopped fresh tomatoes, basil

MELANZANE AL FORMAGGIO DI CAPRA 6.50
Grilled eggplant, goat cheese, sun-dried tomatoes, sweet onions, capers

CARPACCIO 6.95
Thinly sliced beef, grana, capers, arugula

INSALATA MISTA DELL'ORTAGLIA 5.95
Organically grown lettuces, tomatoes, extra virgin olive oil, wine vinegar

INSALATA DEL FORNAIO 4.95
Mixed greens, toasted garlic croutons, parmesan, vinaigrette

CALAMARETTI FRITTI 6.75
Baby squid, lightly floured

GAMBERI CON ENDIVIA 7.95
Cold marinated shrimp, Belgian endive, fresh mozzarella, walnuts; basil-lemon vinaigrette

CARCIOFO RIPIENO 5.95
Cold artichoke stuffed with marinated artichoke hearts, chopped fresh tomato, radicchio
and Il Fornaio bread; lemon vinaigrette

FILONE DI MOZZARELLA FRESCA 7.25
Fresh mozzarella rolled with speck, ricotta, arugula, toasted pinenuts

PIZZA DAL FORNO A LEGNA

PIZZA MARGHERITA 6.95
Tomato sauce, mozzarella, oregano, basil

PIZZA MARINARA (senza formaggio) 7.50
Tomato sauce, grilled eggplant, red onion, garlic, basil, olive oil, fresh herbs (no cheese)

PIZZA AI QUATTRO FORMAGGI 8.75
Tomato sauce, provolone, ricotta, gruyere, smoked mozzarella, oregano

PIZZA CON BROCCOLI E SALSICCIA D'ANATRA 9.25
Fresh tomatoes, broccoli, goat cheese, smoked duck sausage

PIZZA VEGETARIANA 8.50
Fresh seasonal vegetables, tomatoes, low-fat mozzarella

PIZZA CON LA LUGANEGA 8.95
Tomato sauce, mozzarella, sausage, roasted peppers, oregano

CALZONE 10.95
Folded pizza filled with mozzarella, ricotta, sausage, pancetta, garlic, peppers, onions

FOCACCIA AL GORGONZOLA, BASILICO E PIGNOLI 8.95
Thin pizza filled with gorgonzola, roasted pinenuts, basil, sweet onions

PASTE E MINESTRE

ZUPPA D'ORZO E FAGIOLI 4.25
Barley and bean soup with fresh herbs

PAPPA COL POMODORO 4.25
Fresh tomato soup with Tuscan bread, herbs, cold-pressed olive oil

FETTUCCINE ALLA FRIULIANA 8.95
Flat noodles with sausage, onions, fresh tomato sauce, red wine

FARFALLE AL MASCARPONE, GORGONZOLA E BASILICO 9.25
Bow tie pasta with mascarpone and gorgonzola cheeses, basil, cream

CAPELLINI AL POMODORO NATURALE 8.95
Angel hair pasta, chopped fresh tomatoes, basil, garlic

FUSILLI AI VEGETALI (senza olio o burro) 8.75
Corkscrew pasta, fresh vegetables, herbs (no oil or butter)

MEZZELUNE ALLE ERBE AMARE 9.50
Half-moon ravioli, ricotta, dandelion greens, brown butter, sage

PAGLIA E FIENO CON GAMBERETTI 10.95
Spinach and egg linguine, marinated shrimp, garlic, parsley

GRIGLIA, GIRARROSTO E SPECIALITA

POLLO DAL GIRARROSTO TOSCANO 11.95
Free range chicken from the rotisserie
GALLETTO AL FORNO IN TERRACOTTA 11.75
Whole game hen oakwood-roasted in a clay pot with pancetta, garlic, rosemary, lemon
PIATTO DI VEGETALI AL FORNO 8.95
A selection of seasonal vegetables and garlic roasted in the oakwood-burning oven, with polenta
POLLO AL'AGLIO E ROSMARINO (senza burro o sale) 9.95
Grilled pounded chicken breast with puree of roasted garlic and rosemary (no butter or salt)
PETTI DI POLLO "TRATTORIA SOSTANZA" 10.75
Double boneless chicken breast pan roasted in butter
LOMBATA DI VITELLO AL CARBONE 17.95
Large charcoal-grilled veal chop with sage and rosemary
SALSICCIE CON POLENTA E PEPERONATA 8.95
Italian sausages, stewed peppers, grilled polenta
BISTECCA ALLA FIORENTINA 17.95
Dry-aged, Porterhouse steak, marinated in olive oil and rosemary, with Tuscan beans and sauteed spinach
TAGLIATA DI MANZO 11.75
Flank steak grilled rare and sliced, rosemary, fresh peppercorns; balsamic vinegar
AGNELLO SCOTTADITO 17.50
Baby lamb chops sauteed with fresh thyme

DOLCI

BISCOTTI ASSORTITI 3.75
Assortment of cookies from the Il Fornaio bakery
TORTE DI MELE E NOCI AL CARAMELLO 4.75
Apple and walnut torte with caramel sauce
GELATI MISTI 3.50
Assortment of Italian ice creams and sorbets
VALENTINO VESTITO DI NUOVO 4.75
Three-layer terrine of Italian white, Swiss milk, and Belgian dark chocolates
AFFOGATO AL CAFFE 4.50
White chocolate ice cream, espresso, whipped cream
TIRAMISU 4.95
Ladyfingers, rum, zabaglione, mascarpone cheese, espresso, cocoa powder
MERINGATA ALLA FIORENTINA 4.50
Meringue, whipped cream, shaved Belgian chocolate
ZUPPA ITALIANA 4.50
Genoise, marsala, chocolate and vanilla cream
BUDINO DI PANE 3.95
Warm bread pudding with raisins and rum
BACCHE DI SOTTOBOSCO ALLA CREMA FRESCA ...... A.Q.
Seasonal berries

BEVANDE

Espresso	1.25	Cioccolata Calda (hot chocolate)	1.95
Doppio Espresso	1.95	Latte Caldo (steamed milk)	1.50
Cappuccino	2.25	Latte	1.50
Cappuccino con Vov	3.00	Te (herb or black)	1.50
Caffe Macchiato	1.35	Te Freddo	1.75
Caffe Latte	2.25	Espresso Freddo	1.95
Caffe Latte Scremato	2.25	Acqua Minerale 1/2 liter	3.25
(with lowfat milk)		750 ml	5.50
Cafe au Lait	2.00	Limonata Fresca (fresh lemonade)	2.75
Caffe Mocha	2.50	Italian Soda (Torani syrup, soda)	2.50
Caffe Americano	1.50	Cremosa (Torani syrup, soda, cream)	2.50
Caffe Corretti	add 1.25		
con grappa, sambucca, brandy			

(Coffee drinks available with lowfat milk)

You are kindly requested to smoke cigars or pipes only in the bar. Thank you.
We accept American Express, Visa and Mastercard. Sorry, no personal checks.

JACKSON FILLMORE
t r a t t o r i a

ANTIPASTI

Fried Mozzarella	5.75
Spiedini alla Romana	6.25
Stuffed Artichoke	6.50
Prawns Arreganato	6.75
Zuppa di Cozze e Vongole	6.75
Spec	4.50
Eggplant al Forno	4.75
Artichokes (cold)	5.00
Cold Antipasto	7.00
Bruschetta (per piece)	1.00

PRIMI PIATTI

Linguini Marinara or Pesto	7.50
Linguine Pescatore	9.75
Fusili con Funghi	8.25
Ravioli al Pesto	7.75
Ravioli Della Casa	7.75
Risotto con Funghi	9.50
Pasta Alla Verdura	8.00
Ziti con Spec	7.50
Tortellini al Forno	8.25
Tortellini Della Casa	8.25
Linguini with Prawns (G.O.A.)	9.50
Risotto Alla Milanese	9.25
Risotto Pescatore (for two)	17.50

SECONDI PIATTI

Prawn Alla Jack	13.25
Seafood Composition, Marinara or Fra' Diavolo	13.00
Calamari Fritti	9.50
Jack's Roast Chicken	9.75
Chicken (G.O.V.)	10.25
Chicken with Olives, Onions and Anchovies	10.50
Eggplant Parmigiana or Pesto	8.25
Veal di Noci	13.75
Veal Sardegna	13.75
Lombata di Vitello	16.00
Sausage Alla Contadino	9.75
Salsiccie con Fagioli	9.25
Peppercorn Steak	13.50
Mixed Contadino (Chicken, Steak, Sausage for two)	26.50
Mixed Vegetables	6.00

INSALATA

Insalata Jack	7.25
Mixed Vegetables	6.50
Insalata Tri Colore	6.50
Prawns and Arugula	7.75

SPECIAL FEATURES:

Radicchio Al Forno — wedges of radicchio wrapped in pancetta and baked briefly
7.00

Carpaccio Di Zucchini — shredded zucchini tossed with garlic virgin olive oil, toasted almonds and pecorino cheese
6.50

Minestra Rustica — Tuscan soup of white beans, sage, swiss chard, artichokes and polenta
4.50

Spagaetti All`Amatriciana — pasta with pancetta, onion, peppers, garlic and spicy tomato sauce
8.25

Tortelli Di Asparagi E Prosciutto — large squares of homemade pasta, stuffed with asparagus and prosciutto
9.75

Branzino Pappa Giovanni (Seabass) — with anchovy, parsley, and butter
14.00

JOE LOCOCO'S

RISTORANTE

Gli *Antipasti*	**INSALATA DI POLLO** *Grilled marinated chicken served with baby greens*	$ 8.50
	INSALATA DI SALMONE *Cold poached salmon salad*	$ 8.95
	INSALATA CESARE *Caesar salad*	$ 5.25
	POMODORI E MOZZARELLA *Bufala mozzarella, tomatoes and balsamic vinaigrette*	$ 6.95
	ANTIPASTO MISTO *Selections from our antipasto table*	$ 7.50
	BISTECCA CARPACCIATO *Thinly sliced rare filet, served with arugola, capers, and grana*	$ 5.95
Pastasciutte *E Risotti*	**CAPELLINI AL POMODORO** *Angel hair pasta with fresh basil and tomatoes*	$ 8.25
	PENNE CON MELANZANE *Pasta tubes with eggplant, fresh tomatoes, and basil*	$ 8.95
	FETTUCCINE CON SALSICCE E BROCCOLI RABE *Fettuccine with housemade sausage,* *sun dried tomatoes and broccoli rabe*	$ 9.75
	FETTUCCINE AI QUATTRO FORMAGGI *Four cheese: Fontina, Mozzarella, Bel Paese, Parmigiana*	$ 8.95
	SPAGHETTI CON POMODORI ARROSTITI *Spaghetti with roasted roma tomatoes and fresh herbs*	$ 8.75
	SPAGHETTI CARBONARA *Spaghetti with garlic, parmigiana, eggs and pancetta*	$ 8.95

300 Drake's Landing Rd • Greenbrae • (415) 925-0808

Il Secondo		
SCALLOPPINE PICCATA *Veal with lemon and capers*		$14.50
POLLO ALLA ROSMARINO *Breast of chicken with wild mushrooms,* *pancetta, fresh tomatoes and rosemary*		$11.95
OSSO BUCO DI AGNELLO *Braised lamb shanks with soft polenta*		$10.95
PETTO DI POLLO VALDOSTANA *Chicken breast with prosciutto, mozzarella,* *sage, mushrooms and cream*		$11.50
SALTIMBOCCA *Veal with prosciutto, sage and mozzarella*		$14.95
GAMBERONI AL LIMONE *Prawns sauteed with lemon and garlic*		$14.95
GAMBERI MEDITERANEO *Prawns with garlic, chili peppers, tomato and marsala*		$14.95
MISTO GRIGLIA DI CARNE *Mixed grill of lamb, housemade sausage, veal, and quail*		$14.95
LOMBATA DI AGNELLO *Grilled rack of lamb with rosemary sauce*		$15.95
COSTOLETTA DI VITELLO *Grilled range fed veal chop*		$17.95
SPIEDINO DI GAMBERI *Prawns wrapped with pancetta and grilled*		$14.95
DALLO SPIEDO *Selections from our rotisserie*		A.Q.
POLLASTRINO ALLE ERBE *Young chicken marinated in herbs*		$11.50

Piattini		
SPIEDINI ALLA ROMANA *Mozzarella grilled on skewers Roman style*		$ 6.75
CROSTINI DI FUNGHI *Grilled Tuscan bread with wild mushrooms and fresh herbs*		$ 7.50
LA BRUSCHETTA *Grilled Tuscan bread rubbed with garlic and* *topped with fresh tomatoes and virgin olive oil*		$ 4.50
RADICCHIO E SALSICCE *Grilled radicchio and duck sausage with* *balsamic vinegar, and virgin olive oil*		$ 6.95
CALAMARI FRITTI *Deep fried calamari with caper aioli and cocktail sauce*		$ 8.95

LA FIAMMETTA RISTORANTE

ANTIPASTI E INSALATE

ZUPPA IMMAGINATIVA-make your own soup. We have chicken broth,
seafood, chicken, vegetables, beans, and pasta

PROSCIUTTO DI PARMA CRUDO CON PERA-ripe in-season pears with thinly   7.00
sliced prosciutto

CARPACCIO DI ZUCCHINI-shredded zucchini topped with toasted almonds   6.00
and pecorino cheese

INSALATA DI VERDURA MISTA-salad of Italian greens and garden   6.00
vegetables

INSALATA DI MELANZANE-grilled eggplant, roasted pepper dressing,   6.75
olives, and arugula

SORRENTINO DI PESCE-grilled blue nose seabass with lemon, over   7.50
Italian greens

VONGOLE E COZZE AL VAPORE CON AGLIO E VINO-clams and mussels steamed   7.00
with garlic and white wine

RADICCHIO CON PANCETTA ALLA GRIGLIA-radicchio wrapped with pancetta,   6.50
grilled and served with balsamic vinegar

P A S T E

GNOCCHI AL PESTO-homemade potato dumplings in a walnut-mint-basil   10.00
virgin olive oil pesto

GNOCCHI CON PESCE ALLA ROMANA-homemade potato dumplings with a   10.00
seabass-tomato sauce

RISOTTO PESCATORE ALLO ZAFFERANO-rice cooked in a chicken broth with 11.00
assorted seafood

RISOTTO CARNEVALE-rice cooked in a chicken broth with artichokes,   10.00
prosciutto, fresh tomatoes, and fresh oregano

PENNE CON POLLO AL AGLIO E OLIO DI MONTALCINO-tubular shaped pasta   9.00
with saute chicken tidbits in garlic, virgin olive oil,
and olive paste

PENNE MARINARA-tubular shaped pasta with a marinara sauce, (choice   8.50
of mild or hot)

CASARECCIA CON SALMONE E LENTICCHIA-pasta swirls with local salmon,   11.00
simmered with tomatoes, virgin olive oil, garlic, and
lentils

1701 Octavia St • Pacific Heights • (415) 474-5077

LINGUINI CON VONGOLE E COZZE AL CAPERI-thin ribbon pasta with clams and mussels in a caper marinara sauce ... 9.50

LINGUINI GAMBERI A FRA'DIAVOLO-linguini with prawns in our hot/spicy tomato sauce ... 11.00

SPAGHETTI CON FUNGHI PORTOBELLO-spaghetti with imported Italian Portobello mushrooms ... 9.50

SECONDI PIATTI

PETTI DI POLLO TOSCANA-breast of chicken with sausage, white beans, Portobello mushrooms and swiss chard ... 13.50

MISTO ALLA GRIGLIA-grilled chicken and sausage, radicchio in pancetta, artichoke heart, and mushroom ... 13.50

CANESTRELLI ALLA GRIGLIA-grilled jumbo scallops in a virgin olive oil-garlic marinade ... 16.00

SALMONE SFRIGOLATO-sizzled salmon filet studded with garlic, fresh herbs, and virgin olive oil ... 15.00

BRASATO D'ANATRA ALLA FRAGALA-braised duck with onion, garlic, tomatoes, herbs, and virgin olive oil ... 12.50

PETTI DI POLLO CON LE NOCE-saute chicken breast in a walnut/cream sauce ... 12.00

LOMBATA DI VITELLO AFFUNGATO-grilled veal chop with a mushroom sauce ... 15.50

SALSICCE ALLA GRIGLIA-grilled Italian sausages with braised swiss chard in a tomato sauce ... 12.00

FUNGHI PORTOBELLO ALLA GRIGLIA-Italian mushrooms grilled with virgin olive oil and balsamic vinegar ... 14.50

PESCE SPADA ALLA GRIGLIA-grilled swordfish in a tomato sauce with olives and fresh herbs ... 16.00

****

WINE BUYS

White: 1990 Libbaio,   1989 Cuprese

Red: 1988 Montepulciana D'Abruzzo, 1989 California Nebbiolo

Bottle: 19.00
Glass: 5.00
****

DESSERTS

ZABAGLIONE-hot marsala dessert
TIRAMISU-"pick me up, unlike you've ever tasted"
DOUBLE DUTCH CHOCOLATE CAKE-"a flourless cake"
PERA IN PASTICCINO-filo dough-wrapped pears with
    creme chantilly

Remember, Our Restaurant Is Available For Private Parties.

LA PERGOLA

Antipasti é Insalate

BRODETTO Assorted seafood in spicy tomato sauce $ 8.00

FUNGHI Sauteed seasonal fresh mushrooms served on soft polenta 8.00

PEPPERONI Sauteed red and yellow peppers in a sauce of anchovies and garlic 8.00

VERDURE Fresh grilled vegetables marinated in olive oil, garlic and herbs 8.00

DUETTO Thinly sliced cold salmon and tuna served with olive oil, lemon and herbs 8.00

CARPACCIO Thinly sliced raw beef with arrugola, mustard and caper dressing 8.00

ROMANA Baby romaine with gorgonzola and parmigiano with mint and lemon dressing 5.00

SPINACI Spinach, endive, green apple and avocado salad with a mustard dressing 5.00

NOSTRANA Assorted fresh baby lettuce with house vinaigrette 5.00

CETRIOLI Cucumbers, tomato, and spring onions in a balsamic vinegar dressing 5.00

Pasta

RAVIOLI Pasta filled with ricotta and beets in a lemon and chive cream sauce $ 10.50

MEZZALUNA Half moon pasta filled with squash is browned butter and sage 10.50

AGNOLOTTI Oval pasta filled with salmon in a dill, caper and saffron sauce 12.50

2060 Chestnut St • Marina • (415) 563-4500

TORTELLONI Hat shaped pasta filled with duck and rabbit in light tomato sauce   **12.50**

CAPELLINI Angel hair pasta with olive oil, tomato, basil and garlic   **9.50**

TAGLIOLINI Black and white pasta served with seafood in light cream fish stock   **12.50**

TAGLIATELLE Egg pasta served with cream, pancetta and arrugola   **10.00**

LINGUINE Long egg pasta served with fresh clams, olive oil, garlic and basil   **12.50**

PAGLIA E FIENO Spinach and egg pasta with a seasonal mushroom and tomato sauce **12.50**

BIGOLETTI Long bread pasta with ragout of the day   **10.00**

MALFATTI Potato and cheese dumplings in a sauce of the day   **A.Q.**

RISOTTO Italian rice of the day   **A.Q.**

Pietanze

GALLETTO Sauteed free-range baby chicken with olive oil and lemon   **$14.50**

FILETTO Grilled beef tenderloin with wild seasonal mushrooms and thyme   **18.50**

CONIGLIO Marinated rabbit, roasted and served with green and black olives   **16.50**

MEDAGLIONI Sauteed medallions of veal with rosemary and green peppercorns   **18.00**

AGNELLO Grilled lamb loin with a mustard, mint and balsamic vinegar sauce   **18.00**

ANATRA Roasted duck breast served with stuffing and a juniper and grappa sauce   **18.50**

SALMON Poached fresh salmon with basil, pink pepper and pernod   **16.50**

BATTUTA Think veal scaloppina served in a sauce of the day   **15.00**

MENU CHANGES REGULARLY

ANTIPASTI

BRESAOLA	8.50
Sliced cured beef	
PROSCIUTTO E MELONE	8.50
Parma Ham with Melon	
INVOLTINI DI PEPPERONI ALLA SICILIANA	10.50
Red Peppers with Chopped Olive	
INSALATA CALDA DI CANNELLINI E GAMBERETTI	12.50
Warm bean Salad with Shrimp	
TORTINA PASQUALINA	13.50
Vegetable Pie with One Egg	
CARPACCIO DI PESCE	13.50
Fish Thinly Sliced	

MINESTRE

ZUPPA DEL GIORNO	5.90
Soup of the Day	

601 Van Ness Ave • Civic Center • (415) 928-0400

INSALATE

INSALATA TIEPIDA DI CALAMARI E ERBE 11.50
    Warm Squid Salad with Herbs
INSALATA MISTA TUTTO VERDE 6.50
    Mixed Baby Greens and Balsmaic Vinaigrette
INSALATA TIPO CESARE CALIFORNIA 6.90
    Caesar Style Salad
POMIDORI CON MOZZARELLA ALLA CAPRESE 9.50
    Tomatoes with Mozzarella Cheese

PRIMI

TRENETTE AL PESTO FRAMURESE 13.50
    Flat Spaghetti with Original Pesto Sauce
PANSOTI DE RECCU 14.50
    Spinach Pasta Stuffed with greens and Ricotta Walnut Sauce
TORTELLI ROTONDI DI CINGHIALE AI FUNGHETTI 15.50
    Round Wild Boar Ravioli with Mushroom Sauce
CARAMELLE DI TACCHINO SALSA LIMONCELLO-GRAPPA 14.50
    Turkey Stuffed Pasta with Lime and Grappa Sauce
GNOCCHI MAMA DIVA 13.50
    Modest's Mother's Recipe
CORDELLE AL SUGO DI POLLO 12.50
    Large Fetuccine with Chicken Sauce
GUANCIALI AI FUNGHI 14.50
    Squid Sauteed in Red Wine Sauce

SECONDI

CAPESANTE AL PROSECCO 17.50
    Scallops Cooked with Prosecco Wine Sauce
COSTATA DI AGNELLO CON CIPPOLLE E MELE 22.50
    Rack of Lamb with Apples and Onions

SPECIAL DEL GIORNO

LUNEDI FIORENTINA DI VITELLO
Veal Chop Broiled 16.50

GIOVEDI TORTINO DI GRANCHIO SU POLENTA
Crab Cake and Polenta 14.50

MARTEDI TRIPPE CON CECI (ZIMMINO)
Stewed Tripe with Garbonzos 14.50

VENERDI BURIDDA FRAMURESE
Rich Ligurian Seafood Stew 18.50

DOMENICA PETTO DI TACCHINO BURRO-MANDORLE LIMONE
Breast of Turkey with Butter, Almonds and Lemon 18.50

MERCOLEDI SPIEDINO DI GAMBERONI
Prawns on Skewer, Broiled 19.50

SABATO OSSO BUCO ALLE ERBE CON RISO
Veal Shanks Sauteed with Rice 16.00

Appetizers

Mixed Green Salad 3.25
Salad Alla Brooks 6.50
Spinach Salad 6.50
Mussels Della Casa . . . 10.50
Escargot 5.95
Prawn or Crab Cocktail . . 9.50
Our own Specialty — Calamari Vinaigrette . . . 5.95
Caesar Salad 8.75

Shrimp Cocktail 6.95
Antipasto for Two 14.75
Mixed Green Salad with
    Shrimp or Crab 7.95
Sliced Tomatoes with
    Anchovies 6.95
Half Caesar Salad 4.50

Hearts of Romaine with
    Crab or Shrimp 8.95
Sliced Tomatoes with
    Crab or Shrimp 9.50
Combination
    Carpaccio & Prosciutto . . 7.95
Our Famous Home-Cured Prosciutto and Melon . . 7.50
Carpaccio Alla Veneziana . 7.25

Soup

Polenta – *House Specialty* . . . 4.95   Minestrone . . . 3.75   Maritata Alla Bruno (for Two) . . . 9.50

Pasta

Ravioli Toscana – Homemade 10.95
Lasagne – Made to Order (20 Min.) 10.95
Linguine Con Vongole – Baby Clams . . . 11.95
Linguine Con Vongole Alla Marinara . . . 11.95
Tortellini Supreme – Cream Sauce 11.50
Pasta Della Casa 9.95
Cannelloni – Homemade 10.95
Spaghetti All' Amatriciana 10.95
Tagliatelle Luigi – Marinara Sauce 9.95
Risotto Pescatora – Seafood 15.50
Risotto Porcini – Wild Mushrooms 15.50
Pasta Con Gamberi 22.50

Spaghetti Smirnoff – *Our Own Specialty* . . 11.95
Fettuccine Della Casa – Homemade 10.95
Tagliatelle Bolognese – Meat Sauce 10.95
Tagliatelle Al Pesto – Basil Sauce 10.95
Tagliatelle Alla Pescatora – Seafood 15.50
Pasta Mare Chiaro – *Chef's Creation* 14.95
Spaghetti Carbonara – *House Specialty* . . 10.95
Spaghetti Fleishell 9.95
Gnocchi Piemontese – Homemade 10.95
Creste Di Gallo Marinara – *Chef's Creation* 12.50
Linguine Fresh Clams, White Wine
    and Tomato 16.50

♥ Spaghettini Lorenzo — *No cholesterol, 247 calories as tested by UC Berkeley* . . . 11.50

Entrees

All Entrees Cooked To Order and Served with Fresh Vegetable. Dinner includes Antipasto:
(Salame Toscano, Salsa Verde, Kidney Beans Vinaigrette, Veal Shank Vinaigrette, Calamari Marinati)
Mixed Green Salad-Italian Dressing, Minestrone or Soup du Jour, Pasta Della Casa Con Prosciutto Sauce.

Ask about the Chef's Daily Special

From the Sea

	A La Carte	Dinner
Petrale-Mugnaia (Amandine, add $1.75)	15.95	24.95
Rex Sole Mugnaia (Amandine, add $1.75)	12.95	21.95
Sand Dabs from the Bay (Amandine, add $1.75)	12.95	21.95
Petrale Portofino Stuffed with Shrimp and Crab	16.95	25.95
Calamari Livornese, Doré or Mugnaia	12.95	21.95
Cioppino Alla Pescatora - *Our Own Specialty*	16.50	25.50
Combination of Filet of Veal and Prawns - Lemon and Butter Sauce	17.50	26.50
Abalone Doré Mugnaia or Combination - *Chef's Pride*	Market Price	
Scampi Della Casa - Lemon and White Wine Sauce	Market Price	
Prawns Provinciale - Fresh Tomatoes and White Wine Sauce	17.95	26.95
Scallops Sautéed with Lemon, White Wine and Mushrooms	17.50	26.50
Broiled Swordfish, plain, served with Fresh Lemon	17.95	26.95

From the Land

	A La Carte	Dinner
Eggplant Parmigiana - Fresh Tomato and Mozzarella	11.95	20.95
Chicken Livers Sautéed with Mushroom Sauce	11.75	20.75
Sweetbreads Sautéed with Mushroom Sauce or Supreme	12.95	21.95
Roast Caponette with Italian Herbs	11.95	20.95
Chicken Toscana - *Our Own Creation*	12.50	21.50
Pollo Ruspante Alla Salvia and Aglio	12.50	21.50
Chicken Al Mattone - *House Specialty*	12.50	21.50
Veal Scaloppine Piccata Con Capperi	14.50	23.50
Veal Scaloppine Alla Sorrento - *House Specialty*	14.50	23.50
Veal Scaloppine All'Agro with Lemon Sauce	14.50	23.50
Veal Scaloppine with Marsala Wine	14.50	23.50
Veal Milanese served with Fresh Lemon	14.50	23.50
Veal Scaloppine Alla Bruno Con Pinoli and Mushrooms	14.95	23.95
Veal Portafoglio with Grand Marnier Sauce	18.95	27.95
Veal Cutlets Parmigiana with Fresh Pomodoro and Mozzarella	14.50	23.50
Saltimbocca Alla Nerone - *Chef's Creation*	15.50	24.50
Veal Chops, Milanese, Broiled or Sautéed	17.75	26.75
Lamb Alla Bruno with Barolo Sauce - *House Specialty*	17.95	26.95
Broiled New York Steak	17.25	26.25
Broiled Filet Mignon	17.25	26.25
Steak Caruso with Prosciutto, Funghi and Pomarola Sauce	17.25	26.25
Pepper Steak with Grappa Sauce - *Chef's Creation*	17.95	26.95

(All our Entrees are cooked to order, please allow time for your order to be prepared.)

Beverages

Dinner includes choice of
Coffee, Tea or Milk

Sanka, Coffee, Tea or Milk	1.50
Caffe Espresso	2.25
Caffe Lorenzo House Specialty	4.00
Cappuccino	2.50

Desserts

Dinner includes choice of Spumoni, Sherbet, or Semifreddo
House

Cold Zabaglione dela Casa	3.50	Torta di Gelato, *Specialty*	3.75
Sherbet	2.95	Spumoni	3.25
Cream Caramel	3.50	Semifreddo - Homemade	3.25
Parmigiano Grana	4.50	Zabaglione for Two	8.50
Tiramisú	4.50	Tray of Cheese, Walnuts, Figs and Apples	9.75

Dinner: 7 Days a Week until 11:45

Cafe & Restaurant

DINNER MENU

Antipasti

Baccala: **salt cod fritters** with a spinach salad and aioli 5.75

Insalata rinfrescante: **frisee, fennel, and blood orange salad** with asiago cheese 6.50

Pomodori marinate: **marinated tomatoes,** red onion, black cabbage, and ricotta salata cheese 5.50

Formaggio fondente: **deep-fried fontina,** cherry tomatoes, and onions with spinach and a pancetta vinaigrette 7.00

Minestra: **seafood soup** with shrimp, clams, chickpeas, and saffron 5.75

Primi piatti

Polenta alla griglia: **grilled polenta** with a green olive relish 7.75

Penne: **penne pasta alla bolognese** 11.00

Pasta e fagioli: **pasta and bean "soup"** with spring peas, asparagus, and ham 7.50

Fusilli alla vongole: **fusilli pasta** with clams, tomatoes, and mint 11.75

Risotto: **smoked chicken risotto** with asparagus and bacon 12.50

Secondi piatti

Agnello brasato: **braised lamb** with ceci beans and Spanish chorizo 15.25

Salmone in padella: **sauteed salmon** with a piquant green bean salad 16.50

Salsiccie al modo nostro: **grilled house-made sausages** with vinegared braised greens, bintje potatoes, and fruit mustard 14.75

Cape sante alla griglia: **grilled scallops and shrimp** with polenta and eggplant salad 17.50

Piccione sulla brace: **grilled squab** with red currant sauce, roasted garlic, and a straw-potato cake 17.75

I Dolci

Torta di mandorla: **almond butter cake** served with caramel sauce and orange segments 5.00

Fragole: **vine-ripened strawberries** with sweetened whipped cream 4.75

Torta vellata: **chocolate mousse cake** with rum sauce anglaise 5.00

Gelato all' amarena: vanilla bean and amarene cherry **ice cream** with chocolate sauce 4.75

Sorbetto tropicale: **mango and pineapple sorbets** with macaroon cookies 4.50

Biscotti: cardamom, orange and pistachio biscotti 2.25

DESSERT WINES

Porto, Warre's Vintage Character	3.25	glass
Madeira, Malmsey, Blandy's 10-yr-old	7.00	glass
Porto, Graham 10-yr-old Tawny	6.50	glass
Muscato d'Andrea Pecota 1990	11.00	tenth
Late Leap, Frog's Leap 1989	24.00	tenth
Vin Santo di Carmignano, Baccherto 1983	25.00	tenth
Cuvee d'Or, Kalin Cellars 1989	33.00	tenth
Malvasia, Hauner 1988	35.00	tenth
Torcolato, Maculan 1988	38.00	tenth

In tribute to this glorious culinary tradition, Gianni Fassio celebrates the Gastronomia of his ancestors in San Francisco with the creation of Palio d'Asti.

Il Palio is a bareback horse race dating back to Medieval times. In Asti, the race was historically run in homage to its patron saint, San Secondo, or as a celebration of victory in battle. There are twenty entries in the race representing Asti's neighborhoods and outlining villages. The race takes place in the triangular Piazza Alfieri - a particularly difficult test for the talented jockeys.

ANTIPASTI

Antipasti del Giorno, Assorted Traditional Antipasti
    Piatto Normale, Regular Size $ 8.50
    Piatto Grande, Large Size   12.50

Carpaccio di Vitella all'Astigiana, Veal Carpaccio, Celery, Shaved Parmigiano Cheese
    and White Truffle Oil   9.75

Prosciutto di Parma con Pere Ubriache, Prosciutto from Parma with Pears,
    Poached in White Wine and Grappa, Gorgonzola Cheese and Hazelnuts   9.50

Bresaola con Piccola Insalata di Funghi e Arrugula, Cured Beef with Arrugula and
    Marinated Wild Mushrooms with Citronette Dressing   8.25

Affettati Misti, Assorted Italian Cured Meats and Oil-Cured Olives   6.75

Frittura di Mare, Lightly Fried Assorted Seafood with "Bagnet Rosso"   8.75

Piatto di Verdura con Bagna Caôda, Assorted Seasonal Vegetables with
    Traditional Piemontese Sauce Prepared with Garlic, Anchovies,
    Extra Virgin Olive Oil and White Truffles   8.50

PIZZE

Pizza Margherita alla Regina di Savoia, Tomato Sauce, Mozzarella, Oregano and Basil   7.75

Pizza ai Funghi Trifolati e Olive, Sautéed Mushrooms, Italian Oil-Cured Olives,
    Tomato Sauce, Mozzarella and Fontina Cheese   8.25

Pizza Capricciosa, Tomato Sauce, Mozzarella, Artichoke Hearts, Mushrooms,
    Black Olives, Capers and Cooked Prosciutto   9.25

Pizza alla Siciliana, Fennel Sausage, Roasted Sweet Bell Peppers, Red Onions,
    Mozzarella, Tomatoes and Fresh Basil   9.75

Pizza alla Scozzese, Cured Salmon, Ricotta and Goat Cheese, Red Onions and Fresh Dill   9.75

Pizza ai Porri Grigliati, Grilled Leeks, Smoked Mozzarella, Tomatoes, Oregano and Basil   9.25

Calzone al Prosciutto, Folded Pizza Filled with Mozzarella, Ricotta,
    Mountain Herbs and Mushrooms, Topped with Prosciutto   9.25

Pizza Trevisano, Radicchio Trevisano, Gorgonzola Cheese and Pine Nuts   9.25

---

640 Sacramento St • Financial District • (415) 395-9800

INSALATE

Insalata con Pollo Arrosto, Roasted Shredded Chicken with Gorgonzola Cheese, Walnuts and Mixed Greens with Citronette Dressing   7.25

Insalata della Nonna, Red Leaf, Butter Leaf, Romaine, Curly Endive and Italian Field Mushrooms with Citronette Dressing   5.25

PRIMI PIATTI (Pasta is made Fresh on the Premises Daily)

Zuppa del Giorno, Soup of the Day   A/Q

Risotto del Giorno, Risotto of the Day   A/Q

Radiatori al Ragù di Verdura, Radiator Shaped Pasta with Vegetables (no Oil or Butter) $ 8.50

Stelle Filanti Gialle, Verdi e Rosse, Yellow, Red and Green Pasta, Served with Gorgonzola Sauce and Roasted Pine Nuts   9.50

Tagliatelle ai Funghi Misti, Wide Pasta Ribbons with Porcini, Chanterelle, Shitake and Oyster Mushrooms, Butter, Parsley Garlic and White Wine   9.25

Mezzelune alla Monferrina, Ravioli Filled with Fontina Cheese and Toasted Almonds, Served with Sautéed Spinach, Butter and Essence of White Truffles   12.75

Gnocchi di Ricotta, Ricotta and Spinach Dumplings with Tomato Sauce   9.75

Penne all'Arrabbiata, Quill Shaped Pasta with Spicy Tomato Sauce   8.50

Farfallette alla Russa, Bowtie Pasta with Smoked Salmon, Vodka, Mascarpone and Caviar   10.75

Cannelloni di Granchi, Spinach and Egg Cannelloni Filled with Dungeness Crab, Ricotta Cheese and Pine Nuts   12.50

Tagliolini alle Vongole, Thin Pasta Ribbons with Fresh Clams, Garlic and White Wine   11.50

Agnolotti di Grasso alla Piemontese, Pasta Filled with Roasted Veal and Beef, Served with Roasting Juices   12.75

SECONDI PIATTI

Spiedini di Gamberi con "Bagnet Verd", Grilled Prawns Wrapped in Pancetta and Baby Artichokes, with Grilled White Polenta   17.75

Salmone ai Ferri, Grilled Salmon with Virgin Olive Oil and Fine Herbs   15.25

Pollo al Finocchio, Roasted Half Chicken with Braised Fennel and Polenta   14.75

Quaglia alla Griglia, Grilled Semi-Boned Quail Marinated in Fine Herbs with Soft Polenta and "Bagnet Rosso e Verde"   16.50

Rotolino di Coniglio, Saddle of Sonoma Rabbit Filled with Chanterelle Mushrooms and Pancetta   16.50

Vitello alla Valdostana, Veal Loin Filled with Prosciutto and Fontina Cheese   17.25

Costoletta di Vitello, Grilled Veal Chop Marinated in Sage   17.50

Animelle ai Fungi Misti, Sautéed Sweetbreads with Assorted Mushrooms   15.25

Salsiccia d'Anitra, Home Made Duck Sausage with Soft Polenta and Gorgonzola Cheese   13.50

Costolette di Maiale alla Senape e Salvia, Grilled Pork Chops with Mustard and Sage   14.75

Costolette di Agnello ai Ferri, Grilled Lamb Chops Marinated in Thyme and Juniper Berries   16.75

Arrosto del Giorno, Roast of the Day   A/Q

Dinner: Mon - Fri until 11, Sat 5:30 - 11

TRATTORIA

LISTA DEL GIORNO:

MINESTRA CASALINGA 3.50
daily made fresh soup

ANTIPASTI:

CARPACCIO 5.95
thin slices of raw beef, lemon juice, mustard sauce
MOZZARELLA E POMODORI 5.95
fresh mozzarella, tomatoes, basil, cold pressed olive oil
GAMBERETTI MARINATI 7.95
grilled shrimp, chilled, feta cheese, lime & mint vinaigrette
VITELLO TONNATO 8.00
roasted veal, sliced, capers, lemony tuna sauce
TIMBALLO DI MELANZANE E SALMONE AFFUMICATO 7.50
grilled eggplant stuffed with salmon mousse, goat cheese, tomato sauce
CARCIOFO RIPIENO, FREDDO 6.95
cold artichoke, stuffed w/bread, artichoke heart, tomatoes, vinaigrette
BRESAOLA CON RUCOLA 7.25
dry cured beef, arrugola, sweet onions, vinaigrette
INSALATA PANE E VINO 3.95
mixed lettuces, garlic croutons, parmesan, vinaigrette
INSALATA MISTA 4.50
daily picked baby lettuces, tomatoes, leeks, oil & vinegar
ANTIPASTO ASSORTITO 7.50
assorted meats and marinated vegetables

PASTA:

CAPELLINI AL POMODORO NATURALE 7.50
angel hair pasta, fresh tomatoes, basil, garlic, extra virgin olive oil
TAGLIATELLE VERDI ALLA BOLOGNESE 8.50
spinach noodles, Italian style meat sauce
LINGUINE ALLE COZZE AFFUMICATE 8.95
thin flat noodles, smoked mussels, spicy tomato sauce
ZITI ALLA PUTTANESCA 8.25
short tube pasta, capers, olives, oregano, tomato sauce
FUSILLI CON MELANZANE E SCAMORZA 8.50
corkscrew pasta, smoked mozzarella, eggplant, tomato sauce

(pasta)

BUCATINI ALL'AMATRICIANA 7.95
hollow straw pasta, tomato sauce, pancetta, hot pepper
FETTUCCINE AL FORMAGGI 8.50
flat noodles, fontina, parmesan, smoked mozzarella, cream, peas
PENNETTE ALA BOSCAIOLA 9.25
pasta tubes, porcini mushrooms, pancetta, tomato sauce, cream
RIGATONI AL POMODORA E BASILICO 7.25
short tubes, fresh tomato sauce, basil
RISOTTO DEL GIORNO. . . . . A.Q.
creamy Italian rice; ask server for daily special

GRIGLIA:
PESCE FRESCO . . . . A.Q
fresh fish
POLLO MARINATO ALLA GRIGLIA 10.50
charbroiled chicken breast, marinated in lime juice and herbs
SALSICCE CON POLENTA E PEPERONATA 9.75
Italian sausages, stewed peppers, grilled polenta
BISTECCA ALLA FIORENTINA 15.95
grilled rib-eye steak, served with Tuscan beans
BRACIOLINE D'AGNELLO ALLE ERBE 15.95
grilled lamb loin chops marinated in sage-rosemary
LOMBATA DI VITELLO AL ROSMARINO 16.50
large veal chop, rosemary butter

SPIEDO:
SPECIALITA DAL GIRARROSTO. . . . . A.Q.
meats and fowl from the rotisserie

DOLCI:
GELATI MISTI 3.75
assorted Italian ice creams
AFFOGATO AL CAFFE 4.50
white chocolate ice cream, espresso, whipped cream
TIRAMISU 4.00
lady fingers, mascarpone cheese, espresso, cocoa
CREAM CARAMEL 4.00
cream custard, caramel sauce
BACCHE DI STAGIONE . . . . A.Q.
berries in season (with cream or zabaglione add .50)
CANTUCCI DI PRATO CON VINSANTO 5.50
almond dipping cookies, aged Trebbiano wine

RISTORANTE PIATTI

ZUPPA
Zuppa Del Giorno (soup of the day)   3.95

INSALATE
Insalata Mista (mixed green salad)   4.50

Insalata Della Salute (endive, arugola, shaved parmesan cheese,   5.75
lemon olive oil dressing)

Caesar Salad (classic style)   6.95
Small Caesar Salad   4.25

Insalata di Pollo Capricciosa (Piatti cobb salad)   7.50

Mozzarella Tricolore (fresh mozzarella, roasted bell peppers, tomatoes,   6.95
red onion and anchovies)

GLI ANTIPASTI
La Bruschetta (grilled Piatti bread with tomatoes, garlic, basil and olive oil)   4.50

Il Carpaccio con Arugola (thinly sliced raw beef, with olive oil,   6.95
grana cheese and arugola)

Calamari Fritti (fried calamari)   6.75

Le Verdure Alla Griglia (fresh grilled vegetables with whole roasted garlic   6.25
and olive oil)

Le Animelle (sauted fresh sweetbreads with assorted mushrooms)   7.50

Involtini di Melanzane (warm grilled eggplant rolled with goat cheese,   6.95
arugola and sun dried tomatoes)

PIZZE E CALZONE DAL FORNO A LEGNA
La Marinara (fresh tomatoes, oregano, garlic and olive oil)   7.95

La Margherita (tomatoes, mozzarella and basil)   7.95

Pizza Del Giorno (pizza of the day)   A.Q.

Il Calzone "Torrese" ("Torre del Greco" style calzone, filled with ham,   9.75
mushrooms, ricotta, smoked mozzarella , basil and garlic)

Focaccia Del Giorno (sandwich of the day)   A.Q.

6480 Washington St • Yountville • (707) 944-2070 • (Call for Additional Locations)

LE PASTE

I Capellini in Bagna Di Pomodoro (angel hair pasta with fresh tomatoes, basil, garlic and olive oil) — 8.75

Lasagna Al Pesto (layers of fresh spinach pasta, grilled zucchini, sundried tomatoes, pinenuts and assorted Italian cheeses) — 10.95

I Ravioli Al Limone O Al Pomodoro (homemade ravioli filled with spinach and ricotta cheese with lemon cream or tomato sauce) — 9.95

Paglia e Fieno alla "Patrizia" (green and white fettuccine with fresh spinach, oven roasted eggplant, onions and peppers, no oil or butter) — 10.50

Pappardelle "Fantasia" (wide saffron fettucine with shrimp, arugola and fresh tomatoes) — 12.95

Penne e Polpette (penne pasta with homemade meatballs in a rich tomato sauce) — 9.75

Cipolla "Pazza" (spaghetti with onions, anchovies, garlic and chili flakes) — 9.50

Fusilli alla "Campagnola" (corkscrew pasta with fresh baby artichoke hearts, toasted garlic, tomatoes, olives, capers and chili flakes) — 10.95

Conchiglie al Salmone Affumicato (shell pasta with smoked salmon, asparagus, red onions in a light dill cream sauce) — 11.95

Linguine Alle Vongole (linguine pasta, fresh clams, olive oil, garlic, and fresh tomatoes) — 11.95

Pasta Per Bambini (child's plate: pasta, butter and cheese, no green stuff) — 5.00

Il Risotto Del Giorno (a creamy Italian rice dish, changes daily) — A.Q.

SPECIALITÁ DELLA CASA

Zimino Di Cozze E Vongole (fresh mussels and clams cooked in a rich tomato broth, served with garlic bread) — 13.50

Cannelloni "Mamma Concetta" (homemade cannelloni filled with spinach, ground meat, ricotta, mozzarella cheese and wild mushrooms) — 11.25

Arista di Maiale con Purée (rotisseried pork chop with mashed potatoes and porcini mushroom gravy) — 13.95

GRIGLIA E ROSTICCERIA

Il Pollo Arrosto (spit roasted chicken with rosemary potatoes and fresh vegetables) — 11.95

Salsicce Con Fagioli (grilled homemade hot italian sausage, served with Tuscan beans) — 10.50

Petto Di Pollo Ai Ferri (grilled skinless chicken breast with sauteed greens and caponata) — 11.75

Il Pesce Del Giorno (fresh fish of the day) — A.Q.

Bistecca e Fettuccine Alfredo (grilled steak served with fettuccine Alfredo) — 16.95

ZUPPE

Minestrone (fresh vegetable soup) 4.50

Brodo di Pesce (fresh fish and shellfish; fish broth) 6.75

ANTIPASTI

Insalata Prego (chopped romaine, carrots, celery, bell pepper, mushrooms;
    lemon vinaigrette) 4.95

Carpaccio G. Cipriani (thinly-sliced raw beef, parmesan, capers, olive oil,
    lemon) 7.25

Carciofi Marinati (steamed artichokes marinated with lemon and goat
    cheese) 6.75

Antipasto Misto (a platter of assorted Prego appetizers) 6.95

Involtini di Melanzane (ricotta, mozzarella, and goat cheese wrapped in
    eggplant and prosciutto; tomato, basil, and garlic sauce) 6.95

Scottata di Pesce (thinly sliced and marinated salmon, Ahi tuna and
    swordfish with lemon zest and parsley; warmed in the pizza oven 8.75

Bocconcini in Camicia (grilled radicchio and lettuce filled with fresh
    mozzarella, sun-dried tomatoes, black olives and capers; polenta) 7.50

Insalata Mista (radicchio, watercress, tomato, leek, fennel, arugula) 6.50

Mozzarella alla Caprese (buffalo mozzarella, tomato, olive oil, basil,
    oregano) 6.95

FORNO E PIZZERIA

Focaccia al Formaggio (thin layers of pizza dough filled with robiola
    cheese and mozzarella) 7.50

Pizza alla Margherita (fresh tomato sauce, mozzarella, basil, oregano) 8.25

2000 Union St • Marina • (415) 563-3305

Pizza con Gamberi e Salmone (marinated shrimp and salmon, mozzarella, fresh tomatoes, garlic, olive oil, basil) 10.95

Pizza alla Salsiccia (sausage, hot salami, fresh tomato sauce, mozzarella, oregano) 9.85

Pizza alle Quattro Stagioni (prosciutto, mushrooms, artichokes, fresh tomato sauce, mozzarella) 9.95

Calzone di Formaggi e Salsiccia (filled with ricotta, mozzarella, goat cheese, sausage, basil) 10.95

PASTA FATTA IN CASA (homemade)

Tagliolini al Pomodoro e Basilico (thin pasta; fresh tomato sauce, basil) .. 8.95

Ravioli di Carne ai Funghi Porcini (spinach pasta filled with veal, lamb, goat cheese; porcini mushrooms, veal stock, cream) 11.75

Trenette alla Rustica (flat pasta; olives, sun-dried tomatoes, capers, feta cheese, roasted garlic) 9.25

Conchiglie al Carciofo e Spinaci (tiny pasta shells; artichoke, spinach, pancetta, cream, parmesan) 9.95

Fusilli con Luganega (corkscrew pasta; sausage, wild mushrooms, onions, tomato sauce, aged ricotta) 9.95

Gnocchi all Vaccinara (potato pillows; tomato-meat sauce, carrots, celery) . 9.85

Tortelloni alle Melanzane (saffron pasta filled with eggplant, tomatoes, ricotta, parmesan; butter and sage) 10.95

Agnolotti d'Aragosta (half-moons filled with lobster, prosciutto, ricotta; lemon-lobster sauce) 11.95

Capellini Vegetariani (angel hair pasta; seasonal vegetables, vegetable stock - no oil or butter) 8.95

GRIGLIA E SECONDI

Pesce Fresco (today's selections of fresh fish) .... A.Q.

Costoletta di Maiale (pork chop; roasted garlic sauce, roasted potatoes) ... 12.50

Pollo all'Aglio e Rosmarino (boneless double chicken breast; garlic, rosemary, roasted potatoes) 11.50

Carré d'Agnello (spit-roasted rack of lamb; white cannellini beans, fresh vegetables) 17.95

Bistecca alla Fiorentina (aged T-bone steak; white beans) 17.95

Costata di Vitello (natural-fed veal chop; rosemary, red wine, roasted potatoes) 17.95

Le Carni dal Gioarrosto (meat or fowl from the rotisserie) .... A.Q.

SPIEDINI

DAL FORNO

FOCACCIA AL PESTO
(thin layers of pizza dough, mozzarella, pine nuts, pesto, parmesan) 6.95

PIZZA SEMPLICE
(tomato, fresh mozzarella, basil) 7.50

PIZZA CON SCAMORZA E RUGHETTA
(smoked mozzarella, arugula, virgin olive oil) 8.95

PIZZA AI GAMBERI
(prawns, pancetta, tomato, mozzarella, garlic, hot peppers) 10.75

PIZZA ALLE QUATTRO STAGIONI
(prosciutto, mushrooms, fresh artichoke, mozzarella, tomato sauce) 9.25

PIZZA ALLA SALSICCIA
(homemade sausage, pepperoni, tomato sauce, onions, mozzarella) 9.95

CALZONE ALLA PARMIGIANA
(filled with eggplant, parmesan, fontina, tomato sauce, basil) 10.95

PASTA

RIGATONI AL POMODORO
(pasta tubes, fresh tomato sauce, basil) 7.75

CAPELLINI ALLA RUGHETTA
(angel hair pasta, arugula, garlic, sun-dried tomatoes, hot peppers) 9.75

FETTUCCINE CON SCAMPI E SPINACI
(ribbon pasta, scampi., fresh spinach, light curry sauce) 11.95

VERMICELLI ALLE VONGOLE
(thin spaghetti, fresh clams, tomato sauce) 10.95

GNOCCHI AL SUGO DI POLLO
(potato dumplings, roasted chicken, sausage, tomato sauce, mascarpone, sage) 9.95

PAPPARDELLE ALLA PAPALINA
(wide pasta, prosciutto, peas, cream, parmesan, basil) 9.75

---

101 Ygnacio Valley Rd • Walnut Creek • (510) 939-2100

SPAGHETTI ALL' AMATRICIANA
(thin pasta, pancetta, onions, tomato sauce, hot peppers) 8.75

AGNOLOTTI D' ANITRA E FUNGHI
(hat-shaped pasta filled with duck; wild mushrooms, cream,parmesan) 11.75

RAVIOLI DI GAMBERI
(ravioli filled with shrimp; prosciutto, ricotta, basil) 10.95

BACI DI DAMA
(spinach pasta filled with shrimp; prosciutto, ricotta; wild mushroom, prosciutto, cream) 11.95

CAPELLINI VEGETALI - SENZA OLIO
(angle hair pasta, fresh vegetables, vegetable stock, no oil or butter) 8.95

DAILY SPECIALS

GRIGLIA E SECONDI

GUAZZETTO CON PIZZETTA
(cioppino with fresh fish, prawns, mussels, and clams in spicy tomato broth with pizza bread) 12.95

PESCE DEL GIORNO
(fresh fish - selection changes daily) A.Q.

SPIEDINI DI GAMBERI
(skewered prawns; artichokes, olives, lemon, olive oil) 14.75

PAILLARD DI POLLO
(pounded double breast; olive oil, lemon) 10.75

SPIEDINI DI POLLO ALL' AGLIO E ROSEMARINO
(skewered chicken breasts, rosemary, garlic, sun-dried tomatoes; wrapped in pancetta) 11.95

SPIEDINI DI MAIALE ALL' ACETO BALMASICO
(skewered pork loins, pancetta, shallots; balsamic-herb marinade) 12.95

SPIEDINI DI VITELLO ALLE ERBE
(skewered domestic veal filets, pancetta; fennel-rosemary marinade) 16.75

SPIEDINI DI MEDAGLIONO AL MANZO
(skewered filet mignon medallions; sun-dried tomato oil marinade) 16.75

COSTATINE D' AGNELLO
(Sonoma lamb chops; sage, mint, garlic) 16.95

SPIEDO

SPECIALITÁ DALLO SPIEDO
(daily selection of meats and fowl from the rotisserie) A.Q.

S·P·U·N·T·Ī·N·O sm

LUNCH MENU

PANINI

SPUNTINO Chicken breast, roasted peppers, watercress,
caper mayonnaise on toscano bread — 4.95 half / 6.95 whole

TONNO Tuna salad, arugula, tomatoes on toscano bread — 4.95 half / 6.95 whole

VERDURE Grilled to order - eggplant, spinach, roasted peppers, mushrooms,
and sun-dried tomatoes, with fontina on focaccia bread — 5.50 half / 7.50 whole

TACCHINO Smoked turkey, onion, tomato, romaine, mustard and mayonnaise
on a rosemary roll — 7.50 whole

SALMONE Smoked salmon, dill, mascarpone, red onion on focaccia bread — 4.95 half / 6.95 whole

DEL GIORNO:

PIZZA - FROM OUR WOOD-FIRED OVEN

MARGHERITA Tomato sauce, mozzarella, basil, oregano	7.95
SALAME TOSCANO Tuscan salami, tomato sauce, onions, mozzarella	8.25
QUATTRO STAGIONI Prosciutto, artichokes, mushrooms, tomato sauce, mozzarella	8.25
ORTO Roasted peppers, tomato sauce, smoked mozzarella	7.95
FUNGHI Wild and domestic mushrooms, tomato sauce, mozzarella	7.95
CALZONE Prosciutto, spinach, ricotta, mozzarella, fontina	8.95
CALZONE PRIMAVERA Artichoke, spinach, mushrooms, tomato, basil, fontina, ricotta	8.75

DEL GIORNO:

PASTA

CAPELLINI ALLA CHECCA Angel hair pasta, fresh tomato, basil, garlic, olive oil, parmesan	7.25
FETTUCCINE ALLA CAMPAGNOLA Flat pasta, sausage, onions, roasted peppers, tomato sauce	8.25
LINGUINE AL PESTO Thin pasta, basil, garlic, pine nuts, parmesan	7.95
LASAGNE AL FORNO Baked pasta layered with zucchini, spinach, mushrooms, ricotta, mozzarella, tomato sauce	8.95
LINGUINE ALLE VONGOLE Thin pasta with clams, olive oil, garlic, white wine, tomato sauce	9.95
RAVIOLI DI RICOTTA Spinach pasta filled with ricotta, and spinach, tomato sauce	8.95

DEL GIORNO:

---

524 Van Ness Ave • Civic Center • (415) 861-7772

DINNER MENU

ANTIPASTI

CARPACCIO SPUNTINO Thinly sliced raw beef, shaved pecorino cheese, capers, virgin olive oil, lemon   5.75

MOZZARELLA E POMODORI Fresh mozzarella, tomato, basil, olive oil   5.95

ANTIPASTO MISTO Assorted Italian meats, cheeses, marinated vegetables   6.75

PANINI

SPUNTINO Chicken breast, roasted peppers, watercress, caper mayonnaise on toscano bread   6.95

TONNO Tuna salad, arugula, tomatoes on toscano bread   6.95

VERDURE Grilled to order - eggplant, spinach, roasted peppers, mushrooms, and sun-dried tomatoes, with fontina on focaccia bread   7.50

TACCHINO Smoked turkey, onion, tomato, romaine, mustard and mayonnaise on a rosemary roll   7.50

SALMONE Smoked salmon, dill, mascarpone, red onion on focaccia bread   6.95

DEL GIORNO:

PIZZA - FROM OUR WOOD-FIRED OVEN

MARGHERITA Tomato sauce, mozzarella, basil, oregano   7.95

SALAME TOSCANO Tuscan salami, tomato sauce, onions, mozzarella   8.25

QUATTRO STAGIONI Prosciutto, artichokes, mushrooms, tomato sauce, mozzarella   8.25

ORTO Roasted peppers, tomato sauce, smoked mozzarella   7.95

FUNGHI Wild and domestic mushrooms, tomato sauce, mozzarella   7.95

CALZONE Prosciutto, spinach, ricotta, mozzarella, fontina   8.95

CALZONE PRIMAVERA Artichoke, spinach, mushrooms, tomato, basil, fontina, ricotta   8.75

DEL GIORNO:

PASTA

CAPELLINI ALLA CHECCA Angel hair pasta, fresh tomato, basil, garlic, olive oil, parmesan   7.25

FETTUCCINE ALLA CAMPAGNOLA Flat pasta, sausage, onions, roasted peppers, tomato sauce   8.25

LINGUINE AL PESTO Thin pasta, basil, garlic, pine nuts, parmesan   7.95

LASAGNE AL FORNO Baked pasta layered with zucchini, spinach, mushrooms, ricotta, mozzarella, tomato sauce   8.95

LINGUINE ALLE VONGOLE Thin pasta with clams, olive oil, garlic, white wine, tomato sauce   9.95

RAVIOLI DI RICOTTA Spinach pasta filled with ricotta and spinach, tomato sauce   8.95

DEL GIORNO:

Sunday Brunch; Dinner: Sun until 9, Mon until 10, Tu - Th until 11, Fri - Sat until 12   Ⓑ Ⓛ Ⓓ

Soup Of The Day $5
Zuppa Del Giorno

Calamari Filled With Prawns & Radicchio $9
Calamari Ripieni di Gamberoni e Radicchio

FINALE

Grilled Tuna & Cannellini & Thyme $19
Tonno Grigliato al Profumo di Timo

Rolled Breast Of Chicken With Wild Mushrooms $16
Fagottini di Pollo ai Funghi Selvatici

Veal Scaloppine Sauteed With Lemons & Capers $19
Scaloppine di Vitello al Limone e Capperi

Roasted Pork Chop With Prunes & Balsamic Vinegar $18
Lombatina di Maiale con Prugne al Balsamico

Grilled Lamb Chops With Fine Herbs $21
Costolette d'Agnello Alle Erbe Fini

Beef Fillet With Cabernet Sauce $19
Filettini di Manzo al Cabernet

OVERTURE

Smoked Salmon & Mascarpone Terrine $10
Terrina di Salmone Affumicato e Mascarpone

Beef & Veal Carpaccio $10
I Due Carpacci

Air Cured Beef With Baby Greens $9
Bresaola e Insalatine Miste

Mozzarella & Prosciutto di Parma $12
Mozzarella e Prosciutto di Parma

Mixed Baby Greens With Vinaigrette $7
Insalatine Miste

Asparagus With Vegetable Vinaigrette $9
Asparagi Vinaigrette di Vegetari

INTERMEZZO

Risotto Of The Day   A.Q.
Risotto Del Giorno

Crab Ravioli Lobster Sauce $10
Ravioli di Granchio, Salsa Aragosta

Spaghetti With Fresh Tomatoe & Basil $8
Spaghetti al Pomidoro e Basilico

Vegetable Tortelloni $10
Tortelloni di Vegetali

Gnocchi With Meat Sauce $10
Gnocchi al Sugo di Carne

Rainbow Pappardelle With Basil $10
Arcobaleno di Pappardelle al Basilico

OF SAN FRANCISCO

A Rustic Neopolitan Specialty Restaurant

PIZZAS

	SMALL	LARGE
1. Pizza a la Neapolitan *(Cheese and Tomato Sauce)*	10.50	14.00
2. Pizza With Ham	11.50	15.00
3. Pizza with Ham and Mushrooms	12.50	16.00
4. Pizza with Anchovies	11.50	15.00
5. Pizza with Black Olives	11.50	15.00
6. Pizza with Mushrooms	11.50	15.00
7. Pizza with Sliced Italian Sausage	11.50	15.00
8. Pizza with Bell Peppers	11.50	15.00
9. Pizza with Salame	11.50	15.00
10. Pizza with Prosciutto	12.50	17.00
11. Pizza with Mushrooms and Sliced Italian Sausages	12.50	16.00
12. Pizza with Italian Pepperoni	11.50	15.00

	SMALL	LARGE
13. Italian Turnover Specialty (Calzone Imbottito) *(Folded Pizza with Ricotta and Mozzarella Cheese, Prosciutto Ham and Spices)*	13.50	18.00
14. Italian Turnover, Mushrooms, Sausage and Sauce *(Folded Pizza with Ricotta and Mozzarella Cheese, Tomato Sauce, Sausages and Mushrooms)*	14.50	19.00
15. Pizza with Clams and Garlic	12.50	17.00
16. Vegetarian Pizza *(Bell Pepper, Green Onions, Mushrooms Garlic and Olives)*	13.50	18.00
17. Pizza with Sauce, Oregano, Garlic and Basil *(Cheese optional)*	12.50	16.00
18. Pizza, with Meat Balls	11.50	15.00
19. Pizza Super Deluxe *(Mushrooms, Anchovies, Peppers Ham and Italian Sausage)*	13.50	18.00

Above pizzas with any extra item $1.00 more

DESSERTS

Cannoli	3.00
St. Honore Cake	3.50
Spumoni	2.50

BEVERAGES

Decaf, Coffee, Milk, Tea, Coke, 7-Up	1.25
Italian Roast Coffee, per pot	3.50
S. Pellegrino Small	1.75
S. Pellegrino Large	4.00

BEERS Corona ... 2.50   Beck's ... 2.50   Miller Lite ... 2.25   Moretti ... 2.50

1042 Kearny St • North Beach • (415) 398-9696

SEA FOODS

Baked Fresh Coo-Coo Clams, Specialty 8.50
Baked Marinated Oysters 8.00
Calamari (Squid) Saute (Marinara Sauce) 9.00
Shrimp a la Marinara 11.00
Clams, (red or white sauce)
on toasted French Bread 8.00
Calamari (Squid) Fried 10.00

SALADS
(When Available or in Season)

Broccoli, Chilled, with Olive Oil, Lemon 4.50
Chilled String Beans with Olive Oil, Lemon 4.50
Toasted Pepper with Olive Oil, Lemon 4.50
Zucchini a la Vinaigrette 4.50
Dinner Salad 4.00
Garbanzos (Ceci Beans) 4.50

PASTA and SPAGHETTI

Spaghetti Marinara Sauce 8.00
Spaghetti with Meat Sauce 9.00
Spaghetti Meat Balls 9.00
Spaghetti with Meat Sauce and Mushrooms 9.50
Half Spaghetti and Half Ravioli 9.00
Half Spaghetti, Half Ravioli with Meat Balls or Sausage 10.00
Stuffed Manicotti (Homemade) 9.00
Stuffed Manicotti with Meat Balls or Sausage 10.00
Ravioli, Homemade 9.00
Ravioli with Meat Balls or Sausage 10.00
Spaghetti with Sausage 9.50
Spaghetti with Butter 8.00
Spaghetti with Olive Oil, Garlic and Parsley 9.00
Linguine with Clams — Red or White Sauce 10.00
Spaghetti with Calamari (Baby Squid) in Marinara Sauce 10.00
Spaghetti with Shrimp in Marinara Sauce 12.00
Spaghetti with Fresh Broccoli, Saute Olive Oil and Garlic 10.00
Macaroni with Mushrooms, Olive Oil, Garlic, Parsley & Sausage 10.00

TOMMASO'S OVEN-BAKED SPECIALITIES and ENTREES

Veal Scaloppine Marsala 13.50
(Imported Italian Wine)

Veal Scaloppine Fiorentina 13.50
(Coated with Egg Yolk)

Baked Eggplant Parmigiana 10.00

Veal Scaloppine Piccante 13.50
(Lemon base)

Veal with Fresh Pepper and Mushrooms 13.50
(Saute in Marinara Sauce)

Veal Scaloppine Parmigiana 13.50
(With Melted Cheese)

Chicken Cacciatore 12.00

Chicken Marsala 12.00
(Imported Italian Wine)

Stuffed Veal Rolletini 14.00
(Broiled, stuffed with Prosciutto Ham and Cheese)

(Veal and Chicken dishes served with Rigatoni a la Marinara)

ANTIPASTI

ZUPPA DEL GIORNO
Today's soup .... $ A.Q.

PIZZETTA CON AGLIO
Rosemary flat bread with roasted garlic and cambazola cheese 5.40

INSALATA DI SALMONE AFFUMICATO CON FAGIOLINO
House smoked salmon tartare on crostini with green beans and chive vinaigrette 6.25

VONGOLE ALLA CALABRESE
Pan roasted manilla clams with white beans and spicy dried sausage 5.95

POLENTA ARROSTO CON FUNGHI
Oven roasted polenta with wild mushrooms and balsamic game sauce 6.70

SPIEDINI DI GAMBERI
Prawns wrapped in pancetta with roasted garlic vinaigrette 5.35

INSALATA DI FORMAGGIO DI CAPRA
Warm salad of winter greens, goat cheese, grilled pears and pancetta dressing 6.50

CALAMARI FRITTI
Fresh squid dusted in arborio rice flour, fried, served with mustard seed vinegar 5.50

CARPACCIO DI CERVO
Seared slices of spiced raw venison with chestnuts, dried cherries, pecarino cheese and greens .. 6.95

INSALATA CESARE
Romaine with caesar dressing, roasted garlic anchovy crouton 6.25

LASAGNETTE DI MELANZANE
Eggplant lasagnette with goat cheese and fresh tomato sauce 6.50

INSALATA MISTO
Mixed lettuces with house made vinegar & extra virgin olive oil dressing 4.95
with warm gorgonzola bruschetta 5.95

PASTE

PAPPARDELLE ALLA MATSUTAKE
Wide flat spinach pasta ribbons, fresh matsutake mushrooms, baby spinach and artichokes ... 11.95
ORECCHIETE CON BROCCOLI RABE E SALSICCIA
Spicey "Little ear" pasta with broccoli rabe and Sicilian sausage 8.95
POLLO NANO ARROSTO CON RAVIOLONI DI ZUCCA
Pan roasted half of young chicken with butternut squash ravioloni and mollases brown butter . 10.95
CAVATAPPI CON CONIGLIO E FUNGHI
Corkscrew pasta with braised rabbit , pancetta, wild mushrooms and rabbit broth 11.95
FUSILLI MICHAELANGELO
Spiral pasta with arugula, house dried tomatoes, wild mushrooms and fresh tomato sauce 9.75
BRODETTO DI VONGOLE E TORTELLONI DI ARAGOSTA
Lobster tortellini and clams in a tomato saffron shellfish broth 12.95
RAVIOLI DI MAGRO AL BURRO
Pasta filled with homemade ricotta, spinach and red chard, sage butter 9.50
RAVIOLONI SALSICCIA DI CASA
Huge ravioli with homemade sausage and roasted tomato basil sauce 10.95
RISOTTO DEL GIORNO
Italian style rice prepared as described on your daily menu .... A.Q.

AL FORNO

PIZZA SFOGLIATINA
Cracker thin crust with carmelized onions, thyme and gorgonzola 7.10
PIZZA MARGHERITA
Fresh tomato sauce, Mozzarella Fresca and basil 7.50
PIZZA SALSICCIA
Home cured sausage, Mozzarella Fresca, tomato onion herb sauce 8.25
PIZZA DI PARMA
Parma prosciutto, Mozzarella Fresca, fresh tomato sauce and gaetta olive paste 9.25
PIZZA DI FUNGHI MISTI
Assorted wild mushrooms with roasted garlic and teleme cheese 9.70
PIZZA AI GAMBERI
Prawns, sliced tomatoes, garlic paste and basil pesto 9.25
LA BELLE LUNA
Calzone stuffed with artichokes, prosciutto, four cheeses and mixed herbs 9.30

PIATTI del GIORNO

PESCE FRESCO
Fresh fish daily .... $ A.Q.
COSTOLETTA DI MAIALE
Grilled boneless pork chop, smoked wild mushroom sauce and tellegio scalloped potatoes 12.95
PESCE SPADA CON PASTA PUTTANESCA
Swordfish on pasta with sundried tomatoes, olives and capers 13.95
SALSICCIA E POLENTA
Grilled pork and apple sausage with soft polenta and game sauce 10.35
BOLLITO MISTO
Braised oxtail, duck confit, sicilian sausage, white beans and baby vegetables 13.50
LOMBATA DI AGNELLO CON POLENTA ARROSTO
Grilled lamb loin served with roasted pepper polenta and smoked tomato lamb jus 16.50
PETTO DI ANITRA AFFUMICATO
Duck breast, pan roasted and house smoked with aromatic black rice risotto and duck jus 14.25

Sunday Brunch; Dinner: 7 Days a Week until 10:30   ●ⓁⒹ

CUCINA IMMAGINATIVA
Menu Changes Daily

ANTIPASTI

ALICI MARINATE
imported anchovies marinated in vinegar $4

CAPONATA
sweet and sour Sicilian style eggplant with tomatoes,
capers, golden raisins and olives $6

INSALATA DI MARE
fresh seafood salad with cucumber, celery, basis and mint $8

INSALATA MISTA
radicchio, watercress, arugula, endive, fennel, cherry
tomatoes, virgin olive oil $5

INSALATA ALLA NATALINO
romaine, escarole; virgin olive oil, anchovy, parmesan,
garlic, crouton $7

ASPARAGI E TROTA AFFUMICATA
asparagus, smoked trout, dijon, lemon and olive oil $8

PIATTO ASSORTITO (platter for two or more)
caponata, insalata di more, bresaola, crostini with marinated
zucchini, asparagi $7 *each*

BRESAOLA CON RADICCHIO E CAPRINO
thinly-sliced air-dried beef with radicchio, goat cheese and
garlic-olive oil $7

PROSCIUTTO DI PARMA E MELONE
Parma ham with selected melon $8

CARPACCIO CON RUCOLOA E TARTUFO
dry-aged sirloin with arugula, celery, reggiano and white
truffle aioli $9

SPIEDINI DI MOZZARELLA
grilled rosemary-skewered bread and fresh mozzarella,
anchovy, olive oil and butter $6

SPIEDINI DI POLLO
grilled skewered chicken with Sicilian pesto $6

CROSTINI MISTI
grilled walnut bread topped with wild mushrooms;
marinated zucchini; smoked salmon; arugula and sun-dried
tomatoes; chicken salad $8

2080 Van Ness Ave • Russian Hill • (415) 673-3500

PASTA (FATTA IN CASA)

MINESTRONE
spring vegetable soup with beans and pasta — $5

FEDELINI AL SAPORE DI MARE
thin pasta with olive oil, garlic, anchovy, parsley and lemon — $8

CAPELLINI DEL CAMPO
angel hair pasta with spring greens, red pepper flakes, garlic, lemon and virgin olive oil — $9

SPAGHETTI ALLA CARBONARA
thin pasta with pancetta, egg, butter, parmesan cheese and black pepper — $10

GNOCCHI ALLO ZAFFERANO
light saffron-potato pillows with venison and pork ragu — $11

MEZZELUNE ALLE MELANZANE
spinach half moons filled with ricotta cheese on eggplant with fresh tomato and basil — $12

RAVIOLINI CON VONGOLE
artichoke stuffed ravioli with clams, tomato, corn and beans — $13

RISOTTO DEL GIORNO
creamy carnaroli rice, selection changes daily (please allow 30 minutes cooking time) — A.Q.

SECONDI PIATTI

MAIALE ALLA GRIGLIA
grilled pork chop with celery root and Swiss chard — $14

COTOLETTE ALLA BOLOGNESE
breaded veal and pork paillard filled with fontina and prosciutto; green beans — $17

ANATRA COTTA ALLE DUE MANIERE
grilled duck breast and leg confit, frisee, spiced walnuts, citrus, balsamic vinegar — $18

AGNELLO ALLA BRACE
grilled lamb loin with juniper, fennel and garlic; white beans — $18

PESCE DI GIORNATA
fresh fish, changing by availability and inspiration of the day — A.Q.

VERDURE

PATATE ARROSTO
roasted small potatoes with garlic, rosemary, sage and thyme — $3

SPINACI IN AGRO
fresh spinach with lemon and virgin olive oil — $3

FAGIOLI CON FOGLIE DI SENAPE
small Tuscan white beans with mustard greens — $4

POLENTA
soft polenta with taleggio cheese and sage; whole roasted garlic — $4

PIATTO DI VERDURE
platter of vegetables — patate arrosto, spinaci in agro, polenta, grilled leeks, white beans, and whole roasted garlic — $9

Dinner: Tues - Thurs 5 - 11, Fri - Sat 5 - 12 ●●Ⓓ

 V A N E S S I ' S

A P P E T I Z E R S

Prosciutto and Melon 8.25   Steak Tartare 7.95

Escargot 8.00   Calamari Basket 5.25

Crab Cocktail 7.95   Zucchini Basket 4.95

Shrimp Cocktail 7.95   Eggplant Parmigiana 4.50

Prawn Cocktail 7.95   Steamed Clams 10.95

Smoked Salmon 9.25   Vanessi's Hors d'Oeuvres 11.95

S A L A D S

Baby Greens 5.95   Mixed Green 4.25

with Seafood — A.Q.   with Seafood — A.Q.

Hearts of Palm 6.95   Hearts of Romaine 5.75

Spinach with Bacon and Mushrooms 7.50   Sliced Tomatoes 4.00

Caesar Salad 8.25   for two 12.95   with Mozzarella and Ricotta 6.50

Roquefort Dressing 1.50

S E A F O O D

Gamberoni 15.75   Scallops Agrodolce 15.75

Filet of Calamari 11.25

FRESH FISH OF THE DAY — A.Q.

F R O M   V A N E S S I ' S   B R O I L E R

Double French Lamb Chops 19.75   Filet Mignon 19.95

Rack of Lamb for two 39.50   Chateaubriand for two 39.50

Loin of Veal Chops 17.50   Top Sirloin 15.75

New York 19.75   Grilled Half Chicken 13.75

1177 California St • Nob Hill • (415) 771-2422

V A N E S S I ' S   S P E C I A L T I E S

Veal Agrodolce 16.95
Veal Saltimbocca 17.95
Veal Piccata 17.25
Veal Cutlet 16.25
Veal Parmigiana 17.25
Veal Parmigiana Bartolomeo 17.25
Veal Scallopini 17.25
Calves Liver with Onions and Bacon 14.75
Breast of Chicken Parmigiana 14.50

Chicken Saute Vanessi 14.75
Chicken Cacciatora 14.75
Chicken Saltimbocca 14.95
Chicken Dijon 14.50
Chicken Piccata 14.50
Joe Vanessi's Special 11.75
with mushrooms 12.75
Grilled Hamburger 8.95
with Cheese 9.25

P A S T A

with choice of sauces: Bordelaise, Napolitano, Alfredo,
Marinara, Mushroom, Bolognese, Della Casa
Pesto 1.50

Spaghetti 8.75
Spaghetti with Meatballs 9.75
Spaghetti Carbonara 11.25
Gnocchi 10.95
Tortellini Triangolo 10.95
Fettucini 10.25
Lasagne 10.95
Chicken Cannelloni 10.50
Cannelloni Supreme 10.50

Capellini 9.95
Linguini 9.95
Linguini with Clams 10.50
Linguini with Fresh Clams 13.75
Seafood Pasta 16.95
Meatballs and Ravioli 10.95
Cheese or Meat Ravioli 10.25
Swiss Chard and Ricotta Ravioli 10.50
Pasta Primavera 10.95

Capellini with Prosciutto and Peas 10.25

S I D E   O R D E R S

Half Order Vegetables 4.50
Half Order Spaghetti 4.95
French Fries 2.75
Shoestring Potatoes 3.75

Garlic Bread 3.50
Baked Potato 2.25
Creamed Spinach 5.95

Minimum Service 8.00 per person
All split orders 2.25
Personal checks not accepted
Cigar and pipe smoking permitted in bar area only

Dinner: Mon - Thurs until 10, Fri until 11, Sat 4:30 - 11, Sun 4:30 - 10 ●ⓁⒹ

Venticello Ristorante

Antipasti

Pizza Margherita: Tomato sauce, basil and mozzarella	8.95
Pizza Gamberetti: Shrimp, pesto and goat cheese	9.50
Insalata Mista: Young lettuce with balsamic vinaigrette	5.95
Insalata Venticello: Young lettuce with gorgonzola, toasted walnuts and honey mustard vinaigrette	6.50
Insalata Cesare: Hearts of romaine with creamy parmesan dressing and herbed croutons	6.95
Carciofo Brasato: Artichoke stuffed with garlic and herbs, served with parmesan crostini	6.50
Carpaccio: Pounded and sliced raw angus beef with arugula, shaved parmesan and extra virgin olive oil	8.25
Antipasti Mista del Giorno: An array of cured meats, seafood, grilled and marinated vegetables and cheeses	small 7.95 large 12.95

Paste

Capellini Primavera: Angel hair pasta with artichoke hearts and marinara	9.50
Fettucine con Funghi e Panna: Homemade egg fettucine in wild mushroom cream sauce	11.95
Tagliarini Neri: Fresh black pasta with daily changing array of shellfish and seafood	14.95
Ravioli del Giorno: Homemade ravioli with chef's choice of fillings and sauce	12.95

Secondi

Petti di Pollo alla Griglia: Boneless chicken breast grilled with lemon and rosemary	13.95
Animelle Saltati: Natural veal sweetbreads sauteed with brandy, caper and basil	15.95
Agnello al Ferri: Grilled leg of lamb served with Chianti wine sauce	16.50
Vitello Saltimbocca: Scaloppine topped with mozzarella, sage and prosciutto	16.95
Vitello Marsala: Scaloppine with wild mushrooms and marsala wine sauce	16.95

Antipasti

Pizza Margherita: Tomato sauce, basil and mozzarella	8.95
Pizza Gamberetti: Shrimp, pesto and goat cheese	9.50
Insalata Mista: Young lettuce with balsamic vinaigrette	5.95
Insalata Venticello: Young lettuce with gorgonzola, toasted walnuts and honey mustard vinaigrette	6.50
Insalata Cesare: Hearts of romaine with creamy parmesan dressing and herbed croutons	6.95
Carciofo Brasato: Artichoke stuffed with garlic and herbs, served with parmesan crostini	6.50
Carpaccio: Pounded and sliced raw angus beef with arugula, shaved parmesan and extra virgin olive oil	8.25
Antipasti Mista del Giorno: An array of cured meats, seafood, grilled and marinated vegetables and cheeses	small 7.95 large 12.95

Paste

Capellini Primavera: Angel hair pasta with artichoke hearts and marinara	9.50
Fettucine con Funghi e Panna: Homemade egg fettucine in wild mushroom cream sauce	11.95
Tagliarini Neri: Fresh black pasta with daily changing array of shellfish and seafood	14.95
Ravioli del Giorno: Homemade ravioli with chef's choice of fillings and sauce	12.95

Secondi

Petti di Pollo alla Griglia: Boneless chicken breast grilled with lemon and rosemary	13.95
Animelle Saltati: Natural veal sweetbreads sauteed with brandy, caper and basil	15.95
Agnello al Ferri: Grilled leg of lamb served with Chianti wine sauce	16.50
Vitello Saltimbocca: Scaloppine topped with mozzarella, sage and prosciutto	16.95
Vitello Marsala: Scaloppine with wild mushrooms and marsala wine sauce	16.95

VINOTECA

JACKSON FILLMORE

PRIMI

Ziti con Spec   7.75
pasta tubes with smoked proscuitto, cream, parmesan and an egg yolk

Gnocchi al Pesto   8.00
homemade potato dumplings with basil-mint pesto and walnuts

Ravioli al Forno   9.50
ricotta filled ravioli with mushrooms, cream and proscuitto

Bombolotti al Sugo Coniglio   8.50
*large pasta tubes with rabbit-tomato ragout, sage, cannolini beans
and ricotta*

Spaghetti Funghi   8.50
spaghetti with portobello mushrooms, garlic and olive oil

Rustici con Salmone   9.00
pasta shapes with salmon, lentils, garlic, and a touch of tomato

Penne alla Siciliana   7.75
pasta tubes in a spicy tomato-eggplant sauce with capers and olives

Linguine Fra Diavolo   12.00
prawns and scallops in "Vinoteca's" spicy tomato sauce

Riso Pescatore   12.00
arborio rice simmered with mixed seafood and tomato

Riso del Giorno   A.Q.
Italian arborio rice ~ featuring seasonal ingredients

586 Bush St • Union Square • (415) 983-6200

SECONDI
CARNE

Coniglio all Toscana — 11.00
braised leg of rabbit with Roman beans, swiss chard, and portobello mushrooms

Pollo in Casseruola ~ O.O.A. — 13.00
chicken simmered in a sauce of caramelized onion, olives, and anchovies

Involtini di Tacchino — 12.00
turkey scallopine rolled with proscuitto and mozzarella, topped with marinara and served over polenta

Pollo all Griglia ~ G.O.V. — 12.50
half chicken, grilled and served with a garlic, olive oil and balsamic vinegar on a bed of spinach

Coniglio e Salsicce Contadino — 13.00
rabbit and sausage roasted with potatoes, peppers, mushrooms, garlic cloves, and rosemary

Bistecca all Griglia — 15.00
charbroiled New York steak with garlic and herbs

Lombata di Vitello al Trastevere — 18.00
grilled choice veal chop served with Italian greens, pancetta and balsamic dressing

Contadino Misto ~ for two — 26.00
chicken, steak, and sausage roasted with potatoes, peppers, garlic and mushrooms

FRUTTI DI MARE

Pesce Spada Fra Diavolo — 14.00
swordfish sauteed in "Vinoteca's" spicy tomato sauce

Salmone alla Moda — 14.00
grilled salmon served over Italian greens, with capers and green onions

Gamberi al "Timo" — 14.75
Chef Tim's combination of prawns and scallops sauteed with fennel and mushrooms

Saltimbocca di Pesce — 14.00
swordfish topped with house cured tuna "proscuitto," in a sage brown butter sauce

Salmone Agrigento — 14.50
local salmon baked in the oven with garlic, and oregano breadcrumbs

Pesce al Vapore — 15.00
steamed mixed seafood with saffron, fennel, tomato and white wine

---

Dinner: Mon - Thurs 5 - 10:30, Fri - Sat 5 - 11, Sun 4:30 - 10   Ⓑ Ⓛ Ⓓ

ALLA CARTA
CALDO (hot): Daily 11:30 - 4:00
Minimum $9.00 Food Charge Per Person
Visa, Mastercard, American Express, Diners

PIATTI DA FARSI (Cooked to Order) BUON APPETITO

UOVA (Egg Dishes)
Frittata Tre Colore (Pan omelette, marinara, bell pepper and cheese)..........9.75
Frittata Di Verdure (Baked timbale, grilled with fresh house-made
                              sausage and potatoes)...................................9.75

PANINI IMBOTTITI (Sandwiches)
Fresh oysters, fried, in a trencher of bread; spinach salad..................11.50
Fresh house-made sausage, grilled, in a trencher of bread; spinach salad.....11.50

PASTA (Made fresh daily of durum flour, semolina and egg)
          The chef prepares pasta garnished with cheese when traditional in Italy.
Aglio Olio (Garlic and Extra Virgin olive oil)...............................11.50
  Carbonara (Pancetta, parmesan, egg)...11.50
   Primavera (Fresh vegetables in season).....................................11.50
    Romana (Cream, butter, parmesan)...11.50
     Pesto (House-made w/ fresh basil, parmesan, Extra Virgin olive oil)......11.50
      Salsiccia (House-made sausage, bell peppers, marinara)..................11.50
       Fresh oysters, fried, served with Pasta al Pesto.......................13.00

SAUSAGE SPECIALTY
Boscaiola ("of the forest"); a saute of our sausages with potato, bell peppers,
          mushrooms, onions, wine and garlic.................................13.50

INSALATA (Salad)
Main course spinach salad, with Feta cheese, pine nuts, tomato, hard boiled
 egg, pancetta, fresh lemon juice and Extra Virgin olive oil vinaigrette.....10.00

CONTORNI (Side dishes, served with main course only)
Small spinach salad, Feta Cheese, pine nuts, lemon vinaigrette................5.00
    Salads from the delicatessen..5.00 to 8.00
      Pates, Cheeses...from 6.00
        Parmigiano Reggiano cheese with walnuts...........................7.00

ZUPPA (Today's soup)..4.75

2125 Fillmore St • Pacific Heights • (415) 346-4430

* SPECIALS * Additions to our menu, and prices, are listed on our chalkboard. Featured daily are selected wines available by the bottle or glass. A complete list of fine Italian wines, aperitivi and other beverages is available.

COLD PLATES

Assembled from our fabulous collection of Carry-Out Cuisine. Served weekdays and Saturdays 11:30 - 5:00 and Sunday 11:30 - 4:00.

<u>Spit</u> <u>Roast</u> <u>Chicken</u>, one quarter; with fettuccine salad of vegetables and cheese, roast onion with Balsamic vinegar sauce..........................11.50

<u>Torta</u> <u>Milanese</u>, savory layers of ham, spinach frittata and cheese, in a deep crust; baked "sandwich" of eggplant, mortadella and provolone; Napa cabbage or coleslaw, fresh house-made mayonnaise...................11.50

<u>Onion</u> <u>Cheese</u> <u>Tart</u>, with sliced pepper ham and celery and mushroom salad in a mustard vinaigrette..11.50

<u>Chicken</u> <u>Pie</u> or <u>Mushroom</u> <u>Pie</u>, luscious individual pastry crust; Napa cabbage or coleslaw, fresh house-made mayonnaise.......................11.50

<u>Roast</u> <u>Beef</u>, with Fusilli pasta salad, fresh basil, tomato, in vermouth mayonnaise dressing; roasted onion with Balsamic vinegar sauce..........11.50

<u>Vivande's</u> <u>Fresh</u> <u>Smoked</u> <u>Breast</u> of <u>Turkey</u>, (no pre-brining); prosciutto, new potato salad, mayonnaise; zucchini & onion salad....................11.50

<u>Stuffed</u> <u>Breast</u> of <u>Veal</u>, with farce of veal and pistachio nuts; white bean and caviar salad; capunatina, Sicilian eggplant relish with raisins and pine nuts; tree oyster mushroom pate with walnuts...........11.50

<u>Chicken</u> <u>Galantina</u>, boned rolled chicken, farce of veal with juniper berries, pasta Puttanesca salad with anchovies, black olives; celery mushroom salad in a mustard vinaigrette.........................11.50

<u>Vivande's</u> <u>Fresh</u> <u>Smoked</u> <u>Chicken</u> <u>Salad</u>, (no pre-brining), peas, cucumber, fresh mayonnaise; hard boiled egg, sliced apple, spinach and tomato......12.75

<u>Vivande's</u> <u>Special</u> <u>Selection</u> of <u>Contorni</u> ("Contours" or side dishes)..........28.00

* * *

Please ask for information about Vivande's Carry-Out Cuisine; complete catering and party planning service; wine and food banquets featuring knowledgeable speakers; private evenings in the Vivande Cafe; gift baskets, local and national delivery; private register for special interests and requests.

We reserve the right to refuse service to anyone. We are not responsible for lost articles. Corkage fee for customer's own wine is $10.00; $15.00 for sparkling wines. 15% service charge added for parties of six or more.

No Smoking Allowed

THANK YOU

Sunday Brunch; Lunch: 7 Days a Week 11:30 - 4

cafe ORItalia

Soup of the Day . . . .   A.Q.

APPETIZERS

Antipasto Plate . . . .   A.Q.

Crabcakes with Tobiko & Crème Fraîche in Roasted
Red Pepper Cream Sauce 8.95

Poached Prawns & Scallops with Spicy Caper
Aioli 7.75

Fried Calamari 6.75

Grilled Lamb Tenderloin Wrapped with Prosciutto
& Mint Pesto 6.75

SALADS

Mixed Green Salad 4.25

Caesar Salad with Sun-dried Tomatoes 4.95

Fresh Seasonal Marinated Vegetables 5.25

Tomato & Basil Salad 5.25

PASTA

Penne with Smoked Cod, Tomatoes, Garlic, Red
Onions & Olives 8.75

Pasta Primavera
(Vegetables, Garlic & Olive Oil) 8.50

Ancho-Chili Angel Hair Pasta with Manila Clams,
Tomatoes, Basil & Garlic 9.25

Cheese Tortellini with Pesto Cream Sauce 8.95

Penne with Bolognese Sauce (Tomato Meat Sauce). .   8.75

ENTREES

Crab, Ricotta Cheese & Spinach in Puff Pastry . .   11.95

Poussin with Polenta & Porcini Mushroom Cream
Sauce 10.95

N.Y. Steak with Pink Peppercorn Tomato Salsa with
Roasted Potatoe & Garlic 12.75

Cioppino with Pasta 12.75

Baked Polenta with Grilled Eggplant & Herbed
Ricotta with Tomato Sauce 10.50

Hamburger on Focaccia Bread with French Fries . .   6.50
With Cheese — Add 75¢
With Sauteed Mushrooms & Onions — Add 75¢

DESSERTS

Apple Ginger Crisp with Vanilla Ice Cream 4.50

Brownie Sundae 4.95

Ice Cream 3.00

Chestnut Tiramisu 4.95

ÓRITalia

Garlic Bread 1.75

Olive Oil & Rosemary Bread 1.95

Fresh Tomato Salsa Bread 3.50

Wilted Spinach Salad with Mushrooms, Red Onion,
Pickled Ginger & Cilantro 5.95

Oriental Chicken Noodle Salad 6.50

Caesar Salad with Ginger & Sun-Dried Tomatoes . . 4.95

Smoked Trout & Cucumber Salad with Horseradish
Cream 6.25

Marinated Grilled Vegetables with Herbed Goat
Cheese 6.75

ENTREES

Satsuma Potato w/ Crème Fraîche & Tobiko Caviar. . 7.50

Sliced N.Y. Steak with 4-Mushrooms Sauce 9.95

Mu-Shu Duck with Whole Wheat Tortilla 7.95

Fried Calamari 6.75

Crispy Fried Shrimp & Pork Dumplings with
Cilantro-Mint Sauce 6.50

Korean Barbecued Beef with Lettuce Wrap 7.75

Enoki-Shiitake-Oyster-Mushrooms in Sake-Butter-
Ginger Sauce 7.80

Indonesian Chicken Saté with Spicy Indonesian
Peanut Salad 7.25

Fish of the Day . . . .   A.Q.

Crabcakes with Tobiko & Crème Fraîche in Roasted
Red Pepper Cream Sauce 8.95

Fried Brown Rice with Vegetables 4.95

Fried Brown Rice with Shrimp 5.95

Angel Hair Pasta with Mussels 8.75

Angel Hair Pasta Oriental Style with Chicken . . .   8.75

Fettuccine with Spicy Mabo-Tofu, Shiitake &
Sun-Dried Tomatoes 8.75

Fettuccine with Vegetables, Garlic & Olive Oil . .   8.25

Squid Ink Linguine with Smoked Tuna & Green Beans
in Dijon Mustard Sauce 9.25

Spaghettini with Shrimp in Sake-Creme Sauce . . .   9.50

DESSERTS

Fruit Compote with Pound Cake & Mascarpone 4.95

Bread Pudding with Vanilla Ice Cream
(Varies Daily) 4.75

Apple Ginger Crisp with Vanilla Ice Cream 4.50

Chocolate Almond Butter Pot de Crème 3.95

Ice Cream 3.00

Chestnut Tiramisu 4.95

BAYWOLF
R E S T A U R A N T

A P P E T I Z E R S

Butternut squash soup with lemon, rice and parsley 3.50

Baked polenta appetizer with mushroom sauce 5.00

Duck liver flan with currants, madeira and thyme 4.75

Tossed greens 4.00 : with aged goat cheese 4.50

Baby Caesar salad 6.25

"S A L A D S"

Duck tostada with avocado, cheese, lettuce,
black beans and mango salsa 9.25

Greek salad with feta cheese, tomatoes, olives and greens 8.75

Pork loin salad with stuffed squash,
grilled eggplant, peppers and couscous 9.25

E N T R E E S

Grilled fish with mustard/caper sauce,
mint pilaf and grilled squash A.Q.

Lasagna with various mushrooms,
spinach, ricotta cheese and tomato sauce 9.25

Sausage sandwich with roasted peppers
and corn/tomato salad 8.75

Roast top sirloin with basil mashed potatoes,
asparagus and red wine sauce 9.50

*   *   *

3853 Piedmont Ave • Oakland • (510) 655-6004

*　　*　　*

* Antipasto plate: prosciutto wrapped greens, grilled balsamic onions,
baked tomato, baby leeks and carrot salad 7.25 *

Salad of grilled tuna with frisee, fava beans,
cucumbers and olive vinaigrette 6.75

* Appetizer of grilled portabello mushrooms with gorgonzola,
arugula and fennel 6.50 *

Romaine salad with garlic, anchovies, croutons and parmesan cheese 6.50

Baby spinach salad with goat cheese, hazelnuts and pears 6.50

Six oysters on the half shell
with Champagne mignonette 8.00

Duck liver flan with green peppercorns,
madeira, and thyme 5.50

Tossed green salad 4.75 : with aged goat cheese 5.25

* Oxtail soup with barley, mushrooms and escarole 4.50 *

Fresh pasta with smoked trout, garden peas,
creme fraiche and dill 12.75

* Grilled swordfish "peperonata" with new potatoes
and grilled squash 17.00 *

* Pan roasted salmon with artichokes, asparagus,
spring carrots and sorrel sauce 16.75 *

Grilled duck with with blood oranges, pesto and morel-potato pancakes 16.75

* Roast loin of pork stuffed with pistachio nuts, garlic & herbs;
served with baked polenta, pickles and mustard sauce 16.50 *

Braised short ribs with various mushrooms,
green garlic mashed potatoes and "gremolata" (parsley/lemon/garlic) 17.00

* Northern Italian dishes. *

*　　*　　*　　*

:CHEZ:PANISSE:

DOMAINE TEMPIER AT CHEZ PANISSE
CELEBRATING THE VISIT OF LULU PEYRAUD & PAULE PEYRAUD

Typical Daily Menus

· $35
Anchoïade croûtons
Mesclun salad à la Panisse
Bouillabaisse for Lulu
Meyer lemon sherbet with calissons

· $45
Petit aïoli
Sea bass grilled in its scales
Spit-roasted Gibbs Farm lamb; potato gratin with lamb juices
Pear tart Tatin with Beaumes-de-Venise

· $45
Marinated sardines
Stuffed baked snapper
Maurer chicken flattened and grilled with tapenade
Strawberries and oranges in rosemary syrup

· $45
Red wine octopus confit with aïoli
Lamb chops and lamb sausages grilled with thyme; potatoes baked with olives
Curly endive salad with walnuts
Bandol wine jelly with fresh peaches

· $65
Brandade fritters
Soupe au pistou
Grilled sea bream with black olives and anchovies
Mesclun salad
Lemon verbena snow ice

· $65
Warm wild asparagus with olive oil
Little fish baked in grape leaves
Grilled squab with peas and basil
Mesclun salad
Candied orange soufflé

1517 Shattuck Ave • Berkeley • (510) 548-5525

• *$35*

MONDAY NIGHT THREE-COURSE DINNER
Onion galette with garden salad
Lyonnaise-style truffled sausage with leeks and potatoes
Chocolate sherbet and tangerine sherbet

• *$45*
Sautéed oysters with leek and shallot sauce
Spit-roasted duck with truffled celery root and potato purée
Bob's radicchio salad with old balsamic vinegar and Parmesan cheese
Poached pears with walnut ice cream

• *$45*
Warm curly endive salad with pancetta, garlic croûtons, and pickled chanterelles
Pasta with squid and leeks
Bellwether Farm leg of lamb stuffed with rosemary
    Tuscan-style beans
Roald Dahl's pecan and orange mousse

• *$45*
Paine Farm pigeon salad
Potato gnocchi gratin with veal and wild mushroom *ragù*
Skillet-roasted Columbia River salmon with spinach and Meyer lemon sauce
Upside-down red wine pear tart

• *$65*
Salmon prepared three ways
Winter vegetable and herb soup
Roast truffled breast of guinea hen
    Angel hair potato and celery root cake
Garden lettuces vinaigrette
Tangerine soufflé

• *$65*
Tête de veau with tiny clams, green onions, watercress, and horseradish
Guinea hen consommé with vegetable julienne and black truffles
Grilled Columbia River winter run salmon with red wine sauce and fennel gratin
Garden salad
Warm apple tart with vanilla ice cream and apple sherbet

CHEZ PANISSE CAFÉ

Menu Changes Daily
Typical Selections Are Listed

Minestrone, $4.50

Pizzetta with sausage, stewed onions & rosemary, $9.00

Six Hog Island oysters, mignonette, $9.00

Smoked trout & tuna confit with cucumber salad, $8.50

Caesar salad, $8.00

•

Pizza with spicy sausage & curly endive, $13.00

Calzone with goat cheese, mozzarella, prosciutto & garlic, $13.00

•

Whole wheat fettucine with greens, onions, ricotta salata
& toasted crumbs, $13.75

Grilled mako shark with spicy tartar sauce, asparagus
& roasted potatoes, $15.50

Sauteed shrimp with carrots, squash, leeks
& Meyer lemon sauce, $17.00

Grilled Niman-Schell filet steak with bacon
& potato turnip gratin, $18.00

DESSERTS
Apple polenta tart, $5.00

Mocha Cake with whipped cream, $5.00

Grand Marnier custard with strawberries, $5.25

Strawberry-orange sherbet with fruit compote, $5.50

Coffee almond praline ice cream puffs with warm chocolate sauce, $5.50

1517 Shattuck Ave • Berkeley • (510) 548-5525

Tuscan white bean soup with fried sage, $4.50

Garden lettuce salad, $6.00

Baked goat cheese with Heidi's garden lettuce, $7.50

Pizzetta with tomato sauce, onions, anchovies & egg, $9.00

Smoked salmon with cucumber, dill, crème fraîche
& pickled onion, $8.75

Vegetables vinaigrette with olive & eggplant toasts, $7.50

Spinach salad with bacon & gruyère cheese, $6.50

•

Pizza with spicy sausage & curly endive, $13.00

Calzone with goat cheese, mozzarella, prosciutto & garlic, $13.00

•

Whole wheat fettucine with greens, sun-dried tomatoes,
olives & onion, $14.50

Steamed clams with garlic toast & gremolata, $15.00

Grilled tuna with radicchio, leeks, purple potatoes & Meyer
lemon mayonnaise, $16.75

Spring Pot-au-Feu: beef brisket, chicken,
stuffed chard & horseradish, $15.50

DESSERTS
Rhubarb crisp with vanilla ice cream, $5.75

Mocha cake with whipped cream, $5.00

Caramelized almond & pinenut tar, $5.00

Grand Marnier crème brulée, $5.00

Strawberry-orange sherbet with fruit compote, $5.50

Candied orange-prune ice cream with chocolate sauce, $5.25

R E S T A U R A N T & B A R

Menu Changes Daily

Selection of Freshly Squeezed Juices   A.Q.

Appetizers

MEDITERRANEAN PLATTER *dolmas, hummas, tabouleh, eggplant, olives, tomato, feta and cucumber* $6.95
GRILLED PASSILLA PEPPER *filled with Sonoma jack, cheddar and feta, served with fresh salsa* $4.95
FAZ's SMOKED SALMON *served with cucumber dill salad** $6.50
CARPACCIO *thinly sliced raw beef with mustard and capers* $5.25
FOCACCIA *filled with fontina cheese, baked in the wood-burning oven* $4.95
CALAMARI *quick fried, served with fresh lemon and spicy tomato sauce* $4.95
MOZZARELLA *cheese filled with sundried tomato and basil; deep fried and served*
with roma tomato sauce $5.50
CANNELLONI *pasta filled with ricotta, spinach, fresh fennel and pinenuts* $4.50
SOUP OF THE DAY $2.95

Salads

SUMMER BABY GREENS *with tomatoes and lemon vinaigrette* $3.25
CAESAR *salad of romaine hearts, parmesan and creamy anchovy dressing* $3.75
GREEK *salad of roma tomatoes, cucumbers, olives and feta cheese* $3.50

*Faz's house-smoked salmon is available to take home. Please ask your server for details.

600 Hartz Ave • Danville • (510) 838-1320

Pizzas

TOMATO-BASIL *mozzarella and oregano*	*$6.25*
CALZONE *filled with ricotta, feta, mozzarella, parmesan and sausage*	*$7.95*
ROASTED EGGPLANT *smoked mozzarella, chopped tomato, basil and garlic*	*$6.95*
ITALIAN SAUSAGE *roasted peppers, caramelized onions, tomato sauce and mozzarella*	*$7.95*
MUSHROOM *olives, artichoke hearts, pancetta, tomato sauce and mozzarella*	*$8.25*
PEPPERONI *tomato sauce, mozzarella and oregano*	*$6.50*
SHRIMP *marinated tomatoes, feta, basil and mozzarella*	*$9.95*

Pastas

ANGEL HAIR *tossed with chopped tomato, roasted peppers, spinach, basil, virgin olive oil and garlic*	*$7.50*
FETTUCCINE *with gulf shrimp*	*$10.95*
CANNELLONI *filled with ricotta, spinach, fresh fennel and pinenuts*	*$8.50*
FETTUCCINE MARCO POLO *with large shrimp, fresh tomatoes and curry*	*$12.95*
LINGUINE *noodles with sea scallops, sun dried tomatoes and creamy tomato-basil sauce*	*$10.95*
RAVIOLI *filled with chard, ricotta, parmesan and romano cheese, served with sage butter and fresh tomato*	*$9.95*
HOUSE-SMOKED SALMON *with vermicelli pasta, snow peas, dill and cream*	*$9.95*
SPAGHETTINI *tossed with fresh clams, shrimp, scallops, mussels, calamari and spicy tomato sauce*	*$11.95*

Entrees

FRESH CATCH *today's selection of fresh fish*	*A.Q.*
JUMBO SHRIMP *marinated in fresh lime, mint and cilantro grilled and served with basmati rice*	*$14.95*
SPIT-ROASTED *daily selection from our rotisserie*	*A.Q.*
CHICKEN BREAST *grilled boneless, skinless breast with lemon, basil and virgin olive oil*	*$8.95*
EGGPLANT PARMESAN *grilled eggplant, tomatoes and mozzarella baked in wood-burning oven*	*$7.95*
CHICKEN KABOB *marinated in olive oil, lemon juice and mint, served with basmati rice*	*$8.95*
VEAL CHOP *grilled to order and served with rosemary butter*	*$16.95*
RACK OF LAMB *grilled to order with mint chutney*	*$15.95*
RIB EYE STEAK *grilled to order*	*$15.95*

Desserts

BOMBA PASTRY *puff filled with ice cream; berry puree*	*$4.50*
TIRAMISU *lady fingers, espresso, frangelico, mascarpone cheese and cream*	*$3.95*
FRESH SEASONAL BERRIES *topped with creme fraiche*	*$3.95*
CHOCOLATE PECAN TART *served with caramel sauce*	*$4.50*
BAKLAVAH *made with almond and pistachio*	*$2.95*
NEW YORK STYLE CHEESECAKE *served with fresh berry sauce*	*$4.50*

Please inquire about our banquet facilities and catering services.

Dinner: Mon - Thurs 5 - 10, Fri - Sat 5 - 11, Sun 4 - 10

Soupes

Soupe du Jour 3.95
Soup of the Day

Soupe à l' Oignon Gratinée 4.95
French Onion Soup

Salades

Petite Salade 3.95
Butter lettuce, chopped walnuts and house dressing
With French Roquefort Cheese 4.95

Salade César 7.95
Romaine lettuce, garlic croutons, Parmesan cheese and anchovy dressing

Salade d' Epinards 7.95
Spinach, mushroom, tomato and bacon salad

Salade Fermière.. 8.95
French Feta cheese, apples, celery, romaine lettuce and walnuts

Avocat Fourré aux Petites Crevettes 8.95
Avocado with bay shrimp

Salade Niçoise.. 11.95
A classic favorite, we serve it with fresh grilled Ahi tuna

Salade de Crevettes 12.95
Jumbo prawns sald with avocado, oranges, cucumber and snow peas

---

À la Carte

Light Specialities

Pasta of the Day. Ask your server about varieties .... A.Q.

Pâté Maison 6.50
House-made pâté

Epinards Aux Crêpes Fourrées au Fromage 7.95
Warm cheese crêpes served on a bed of spinach with garnishes

Saumon Fumé 8.95
Smoked salmon with garnish

Steak Tartare 12.95
Freshly ground New York steak served raw with condiments and spices

Les Escargots du Café de Paris 6.25

Hot Dog Parisien 6.95
Baguette filled with grilled French sausage, served with pommes frites

Hamburger Parisien 7.95
Served with grilled onions, tomatoes, lettuce, cornichons and pommes frites
With Sautéed Mushrooms, Onions and Tomatoes 8.95

Coquillages

Seafood Specialties

Oysters (1/2 dozen) Fresh daily varieties. Ask your server for details 7.50

Petit Plateau Oysters, mussels, clams 8.95

Grand Plateau Oysters, mussels, clams, prawns 12.95

Jumbo Prawns Cocktail 8.95

Moules Marinières Steamed mussels in shallot sauce 7.95

Oyster Brian Baked oysters w/garlic butter sauce 8.95

Spécialité de la Maison

House Specialty

L'Entrecôte de Paris 16.95
Delicate Eye of New York charbroiled.
Served with the original recipe of the renowned Sauce "Café de Paris."
Includes Pommes Frites and Petite Salade.

LALIME'S

Pre-set dinner menu

Marinated quail grilled and served on sauteed foie gras

Rack of lamb chops cooked on the iron, served on stuffed
portabello mushrooms

Sauterne poached pears, served on a sauterne flavored flan

$ 25.00

Wine Selection

1989 Le Haut-Lieu, Vouvray	6.50/26.00
1989 Bonny Doon, Cigare Volant	8.00/32.00
1979 Chateau Sigalas Rabaud, Sauternes, 1er Cru	6.00
Complete wine selection	**$ 14.75**

We also recommend a 1980 Joselph Phelps,
Cabernet Sauvignon with the rack of lamb   4.50/3oz.
(We only have a 6 litre bottle so it's while it lasts!)

Aperitives by the Glass

Lillet(Blonde)	3.75
Kir	4.75
Kir Royale	5.00
Dubonnet	3.25
Williams and Humbert, Dry Sack Medium Dry	3.50

1329 Gilman St • Berkeley • (510) 527-9838

Appetizers, soups and lighter dishes

Seafood bisque
$ 6.25
Garden greens with balsamic vinaigrette
$ 5.75
Quesadilla with fennel, zucchini, eggplant and black beans
$ 6.50
Marinated grilled quail served on sauteed foie gras
$ 9.25
Calamari stuffed with scallops served on grilled radicchio,
with a spinach and red bell pepper romesco
$ 8.75
Hog Island oysters with a mignonette dip
$ 7.75
Pizzetta with artichokes, roast garlic, fennel and aioli
$ 7.25
A platter with olives, roast garlic and onion, crostini,
tapenade, and lamb and vegetable skewers
$ 9.25

More substantial dishes

Stuffed vegetables with a tuscan white bean sauce
$ 10.75
Grilled seabass served with black beans, and a szechuan
vegetable sauce
$ 14.75
Juniper berry cured pork chop roasted and served with
garlic mashed potatoes & roasted balsamic red onions
$ 15.50
Rack of lamb chops cooked on the iron and served on a
stuffed portabella mushroom
$ 16.75

Water is served upon request

Beer Selection
Pacific Brewing Company On Tap
Grey Whale Ale   1.75/glass
Killer Whale stout 1.75/glass
Bottled Beers
Lager

Moretti, Birra Friulana, Italy 2.25
Kronenbourg, France   2.25
Sapporo(633 ML.)   5.50
Ales
Sierra Nevada Pale Ale 2.00
Molson, Export Ale   2.00
Orval, Belgium   4.75
Anchor Steam   2.00

Menu Changes Daily

LASCAUX
Bar & Rotisserie

DINNER MENU CHANGES DAILY

APPETIZERS

HERB POLENTA
with fried leeks, feta cheese and roasted tomato sauce   *$5.75*

GRILLED PRAWNS
with white bean salad and garlic-mint vinaigrette   *$7.25*

GRILLED VEGETABLES
with radicchio and caper vinaigrette   *$5.00*

SAUTEED CALAMARI
with garlic, tomatoes and fresh mint   *$5.50*

HOUSE SMOKED MUSCOVY DUCK BREAST
with a French lentil salad and basil-walnut vinaigrette   *$6.50*

SALMON TARTARE
with cucumbers and a lemon dill vinaigrette   *$7.50*

EMPANADA
Spanish style turnover, stuffed with spinach, raisins, pine nuts
and sheep's milk cheese   *$4.75*

MUSSELS BAKED IN PARCHMENT
with onions, sausage, lemon zest and fresh coriander   *$6.25*

SOUPS AND SALADS

MIXED GREEN SALAD
with lemon-thyme vinaigrette and eggplant-tomato crostini   *$4.00*

HEARTS OF ROMAINE
with sundried tomato vinaigrette, cured olives and parmesan   *$4.50*

ASPARAGUS SOUP
with lemon zest and basil   *$3.75*

WHITE BEAN AND ARUGULA SOUP
with smoked pork   *$4.50*

---

248 Sutter St • Union Square • (415) 391-1555 • (Call for Additional Locations)

PASTA

TAGLIERINI
with smoked chicken, sundried tomatoes and oregano — $12.00

FETTUCCINE
with rabbit ragout, parsley and parmesan cheese — $11.50

PENNE
*with tomatoes, red onions, baby artichokes and
crushed chilies* — $10.00

ENTREES

PROVENCAL FISH STEW
with saffron onion, new potatoes and gremolata — $13.50

SPIT ROASTED SADDLE OF LAMB
with its natural juices (as available) — $18.75

GRILLED BRADLEY RANCH NEW YORK STEAK
with a red wine and black peppercorn glace — $20.00

ROASTED HOUSE SMOKED CORNISH HEN
with a roasted garlic, lemon and basil scented jus — $16.50

ROASTED DUCK BREAST
with shallots, apples and chestnuts — $16.50

SAMPLE DAILY SPECIAL SELECTIONS

GRILLED SALMON
with a lemon and saffron sauce — $18.00

GRILLED HALIBUT
with tarragon and fennel oil — $16.75

GRILLED AHI TUNA
with artichokes, prosciutto and fennel — $19.00

ROASTED VEAL CHOP
with a wild mushroom and roasted garlic sauce — $26.00

GASTON STYLE LEG OF LAMB
with garlic and sage — $17.00

GRILLED VENISON LOIN
with braised leeks and red wine sauce — $21.00

ROASTED LOIN OF RABBIT
with asparagus, prosciutto and shiitake mushrooms — $19.50

DESSERTS

A selection of freshly made desserts and pastries — $4.50 – $6.50

♣ All the artwork in Lascaux is for sale at the Montgomery gallery.

LUNCH

ANTIPASTO	Yellow Split Pea soup with creme fraiche	$3.75
	Mixed Greens with balsamic vinaigrette	$4.25
	Caesar Salad with parmesan cheese and croutons	$6.25
SALADS	Smoked Chicken with endive, escarole, celery, olives & watercress with a roasted onion vinaigrette	$7.75
	Grilled Flank Steak with roast potatoes and pickled eggplant, tomato- sherry vinaigrette & greens	$8.25
SANDWICHES ON CIABATTA	Grilled Marinated Lamb with red onions, mint , cilantro & greens	$7.25
	Grilled chicken breast & pancetta with mustard aioli and marinated olives	$7.00
PIZZA	Grilled radicchio, walnuts, basil & gorgonzola	$9.75
	Prosciutto, mushrooms, basil, mozzarella, goat cheese & gremolata	$9.75
	Umbrian Sausage with ricotta, mozzarella, fennel & arugula	$9.75
CALZONE	Roasted eggplant, caramelized onions, salami & olives with ricotta & mozzarella	$10.75
PASTA	Spaghettini with spinach, lemon zest, caciovalle cheese & cream	$9.00
	Fusilli with grilled tuna, onions, mint, lemon & tomatoes	$10.25
	Linguini with clams, green olives, capers, parsley, garlic & olive oil	$9.95
	Baked Penne with Greek meatballs & tomato-feta sauce	$9.75

3909 Grand Ave • Oakland • (510) 601-0500

DINNER

ANTIPASTO

Portuguese chicken soup with spinach, rice and mint	$3.75
Mixed Greens with balsamic vinaigrette	$4.25
Caesar Salad with parmesan cheese and croutons	$6.25
Terrine of goat cheese & green olives with green beans & tomato vinaigrette	$5.95
Charcuterie with olives, cornichons and mustard	$7.25
Antipasti plate	$8.25

PASTA

Fusilli with escarole, olives, anchovies & breadcrumbs	$9.75
Linguini with bacon, tomatoes, arugula & clams	$10.25
Baked Penne with Greek meatballs & tomato-feta sauce	$9.75

PIZZA

Asparagus, pancetta, pinenuts, caciovalle and mozzarella	$9.75
Provencal Duck Sausage with eggplant, olives & mozzarella	$9.75
Potatoes, sage, caramelized onions & ricotta salata	$9.75

CALZONE

Grilled radicchio, mushrooms, prosciutto, mozzarella, goat cheese & basil	$10.75

ENTREES

Grilled Beef Tenderloin with tomato-tarragon-caper salsa and potato gratin	$16.25
Fish & Mussel ragout with garlic croutons & mustard greens	$14.95

DESSERTS

Warm Apple and Pine Nut Crisp with brandy sauce	$4.25
Chocolate Pot De Creme served with shortbread & whipped cream	$4.25
Strawberry and Rhubarb Galette with cream chantilly	$4.25
Chocolate Almond Date Cake with pear mascarpone	$4.25

Sunday Brunch; Dinner: Mon - Thurs 5:30 - 9:30, Fri - Sat 5:30 - 10, Sun 5:30 - 9 ●ⓁⒹ

L u n c h e o n

Roast tomato soup with garlic croutons	$5.00
Asparagus with Italian parsley vinaigrette	5.00
Antipasto of Toscano salami, Parma proscuitto, fresh mozzarella, red and yellow tomatoes, olives and grissini	8.00
Primavera salad of asparagus, favas, English peas, carrots and red peppers with butter lettuce and lemon vinaigrette	8.00
Prawns with cannelini beans, arugula and a roast red pepper vinaigrette	9.00
Niçoise salad of tuna, potatoes, green beans, tomato, red onion, hard boiled egg, croutons, hearts of romaine and red wine vinaigrette	11.00
Grilled marinated eggplant on warm tomato focaccia with provolone, roasted red peppers, basil and mesclun salad	8.00
Applewood smoked bacon, gruyère, roma tomatoes, and butter lettuce on toast with basil mayonnaise and shoe string fries	9.00
Roast pork loin on sliced toasted brioche with watercress, sliced apples, horseradish mayonnaise and a carrot mint salad	10.00
Grilled chicken breast on a green and yellow zucchini salad with a basil tomato vinaigrette	12.00
Grilled flank steak, radicchio, mushrooms and garlic toasts	12.00
Chef's desserts of the day	A.Q.

S. Pellegrino mineral water	small	2.00	large	5.00
Fiuggi still spring water				5.00
Assorted beer				A.Q.
Illycaffé espresso				2.00
Cappuccino				2.50
Caffé latté				3.00
Coffee, regular or decaffeinated				1.50
Tea service				2.00
Iced Tea				2.00
Milk	1.00	juice	2.00	soda	1.50

Dinner

Carrot soup with sherry and fennel	$6.00
Fresh mozzarella, red and yellow tomatoes, roasted peppers and basil	7.00
Crispy eggplant "fans" with roast tomato purée	6.00
Chili lemon prawns with white beans and arugula	8.00
Soufflé of feta and mint with a saffron cream	8.00
Garden lettuces with croutons and a mustard vinaigrette	5.00
Grilled quail with radicchio, spinach and a warm shallot pancetta vinaigrette	8.00
Risotto with asparagus and reggiano	12.00
Conchiglie with salmon, peas and tomatoes in a sherry broth	12.00
Fettucine with basil almond pesto and fresh ricotta	12.00
Mussels, clams and scallops in a fennel orange broth	15.00
Grilled salmon with herbed basmati rice and red pepper coulis	17.00
Chicken breast with basil aioli and a provençal "Tian"	15.00
Ragoût of rabbit with tomatoes, olives and bacon on grilled polenta	16.00
Grilled rib-eye steak with horseradish cream and pomme boulanger	17.00

Brunch

Fruits – berries or citrus salad	$5.00
Cereals – raisin bran, granola, müeslix or hot steel cut oats with fruit add $1.50	4.00
All cereals are 100% natural and preservative-free	
Eggs – scrambled, poached, fried or 'scrambled-in' served with potatoes and toast	5.00
Oeufs Specialité:	
Omelette du jour served with home-fried potatoes and toast	7.00
Provençal vegetable gratin with poached eggs and red pepper purée served with garlic toast	8.00
Frittata with prawns and artichoke hearts served with mesclun salad	9.00
Lemon soufflé pancakes with strawberry compote served with pure maple syrup	8.00
Raisin brioche french toast served with hot orange slices and pure maple syrup	8.00

Sunday Brunch; Dinner: Tues - Sat 5:30 - 10   ●ⒶⒹ

Splendido

STARTERS

MEDITERRANEAN FISH & SHELLFISH SOUP WITH ROUILLE AND CROUTONS
5.50

CURRY SOUP WITH SPICED CHICKEN, PINEAPPLE, TOASTED ALMOND AND MINT
4.95

HOUSE SALAD WITH LEMON, VIRGIN OLIVE OIL, PARSLEY & SHALLOTS
4.75

STEAMED MUSSELS WITH SORREL, TOMATO & GARLIC
6.95

WARM GOAT CHEESE AND RATATOUILLE SALAD WITH ARUGULA & RADICCHIO
7.75

HEARTS OF ROMAINE WITH CAESAR VINAIGRETTE, GORGONZOLA CHEESE
AND SUN-DRIED TOMATO TAPENADE ON FOCCACIA
8.50

SCALLOPS WITH DILL CURED SALMON AND CREAMY HERB VINAIGRETTE
8.75

FRIED OYSTER SALAD WITH TOASTED FENNEL REMOULADE AND BRIOCHE
8.95

RAVIOLI WITH PROSCIUTTO AND MASCARPONE
9.25

FUSILLI COL BUCO WITH BABY ARTICHOKES, ROAST TOMATO
AND TAPENADE
9.75

---

4 Embarcadero Center • Financial District • (415) 986-3222

PIZZA

GRILLED EGGPLANT PIZZA WITH CAPRINI CHEESE,
PESTO AND ROAST TOMATO
9.50

PIZZA WITH DUCK CONFIT AND ROAST SHIITAKE MUSHROOMS
12.50

SMOKED CHICKEN PIZZA WITH FETA CHEESE, ROAST TOMATO & CILANTRO
10.95

ENTREES

PAN ROAST CHICKEN BREAST WITH CIOFATTA
"VEGETABLE RAGOÛT" AND COUS COUS
14.95

GRILLED SWORDFISH WITH CINNAMON CAP MUSHROOMS,
PANCETTA AND ROSEMARY BROTH
16.50

SEARED TUNA SALAD WITH NICOISE OLIVE VINAIGRETTE
14.75

GRILLED SALMON WITH ZUCCHINI, LEEK, ROAST TOMATO AND THYME TARTLET
15.95

SAUTEED LAMB TENDERLOIN SALAD WITH CREAMY CUMIN VINAIGRETTE,
MARINATED LENTILS AND GRILLED FLATBREAD
13.50

GRILLED VENISON SAUSAGE WITH WILD MUSHROOMS,
CELERY ROOT AND APPLE COMPOTE
12.75

SAUTEED SHRIMP "SCAMPI"
14.50

GRILLED STEAK WITH FRIED ONIONS AND HORSERADISH
18.50

DUNGENESS CRAB RISOTTO WITH TOMATO, LEMON & CAPERS
11.75

SQUARE ONE

THE RESTAURANT AT
GOLDEN GATEWAY COMMONS
190 PACIFIC AT FRONT
SAN FRANCISCO 94111
TELEPHONE 415 788-1110

■ SALADS & LIGHT ENTREES ■

Sopa de cilantro: Mexican zucchini and cilantro soup with fried tortillas, chiles and cheese	$ 4.75
Lentil and spinach soup with rice avgolemono	$ 4.75
> Mixed garden lettuce salad with garlic croutons	$ 6.00
> Six oysters on the half shell, served with black pepper mignonette, Square One cocktail sauce, or tangerine salsa	$ 8.00
Cæsar salad	$ 8.50
Grilled leeks and roasted beets with prosciutto, mint, hazelnuts and balsamic vinaigrette	$ 8.50
Celery, mushrooms, favas, pecorino cheese and arugula salad, with black pepper vinaigrette, served with mushroom crostini	$ 9.00
Grilled polenta, smoked salmon and asparagus with crème frâiche	$ 9.50
Avocado, papaya and watercress salad with lime-ginger vinaigrette	$ 8.00

We also have our fabulous Square One sandwiches with soup and salad combinations available in our Bar only. Please ask your waiter or the host to show you the Bar menu.

■ DAILY SPECIALS ■

Rigatoni with Sicilian meatballs, artichokes, peas, tomatoes and lemon zest	$14.00
> Linguine with tuna, saffroned onions, greens, currants and sun dried tomatoes	$14.00
Sauteed prawns with garlic, hot pepper, wine and toasted almonds, served with saffron rice and asparagus	$19.00
Roast chicken with a Moroccan sweet and hot tomato sauce with cinnamon, honey, cayenne and onion, served with couscous and grilled eggplant	$18.00
> Grilled salmon with tarragon and mint salsa verde, served with oven roast potatoes and broccoli	$20.00
Grilled swordfish in a Yucatecan marinade of orange, lime, chiles, oregano, and allspice, served with black beans, rice, cauliflower with avocados and tomatoes, and grilled pineapple	$21.00
Bistecca alla fiorentina: grilled rib eye steak with virgin olive oil, and black pepper, served with white bean ragout with tomatoes, garlic and sage, and sauteed greens	$23.00
Grilled lamb loin chops in an Afghani marinade of yoghurt, onion, curry, cinnamon, garlic, tumeric and nutmeg, served with cracked wheat pilaf, spiced apricot chutney and spinach and zucchini borani	$21.00

Vegetarian entrees:

> Linguine with saffroned onions, greens, currants and sun dried tomatoes	$11.00
Couscous, grilled eggplant with sweet and hot tomato sauce and greens	$10.00
> Rigatoni with artichokes, peas, tomatoes and lemon zest	$12.00

DESSERTS

Frozen nougat terrine served with bitter orange chocolate sauce and berries	$ 5.75
Vanilla crème brûleé served with walnut clouds	$ 5.75
Banana brown sugar tartlette served with toasted pecan brown sugar ice cream and caramel sauce	$ 5.75
Dark chocolate torte filled with white chocolate ganache and raspberries, served with raspberry sauce	$ 5.75
Coconut truffle ice cream served with hot fudge sauce and macadamia nut cookies	$ 5.75
Sorbet plate served with lemon violet cookies	$ 5.75
Mixed berries served with whipped cream and assorted cookies	$ 6.00
Assorted dessert platter for two or more, per person	$ 7.50

TERRA

Appetizers

Pear and Goat Cheese Salad with Warm Pancetta and
Sherry Wine Vinaigrette
7.00

Home Smoked Salmon with Garden Greens and Golden Caviar,
Sour Cream
8.75

Fresh MIYAGI Oysters in Ponzu Sauce and Daikon Radish
7.50

Terrine of Foie Gras with Apple Walnut Frisée Salad
13.50

Fried Rock Shrimp with Calistoga Field Greens and
Chive Mustard Sauce
7.75

Radicchio Salad with Parmesan Balsamic Vinaigrette
6.50

Crab and Savoy Cabbage Egg Roll with Saffron Tomato Cream
7.25

Tripe and White Bean Stew with Basil
6.50

Clam and Potato Leek Chowder
5.00

1345 Railroad Ave • St Helena • (707) 963-8931

Main Courses

Grilled Filet of Salmon with Thai Red Curry Sauce and Basmati Rice
15.50

Malfatti with Ragoût of Rabbit and Mushroom
14.50

Grilled Tuna Steak with Grilled Eggplant, Cucumber Tomato Salad,
and TAHINI Sauce
15.50

Lamb Shank braised in Cabernet Sauvignon and Black Mission Fig
15.50

Grilled Marinated Pork Chop with Yam Purée and Spicy Red Onion Salad
15.00

Spaghettini with Bottarga
12.50

Grilled Breast of Duck with Sun Dried Cherry Sauce
17.50

Fricassée of Catfish in Tomato Garlic Caper Sauce with Polenta
14.50

Grilled Wolfe Ranch Quail with Pithivier of Mushroom and Foie Gras
18.50

Desserts

Warm Chocolate Bread Pudding with Créme Fraîche 5.50

Tirami sù 4.50

Pecan Tart with Chocolate Bourbon Ice Cream 5.50

Gratin of Fresh Berries 5.50

Apple Almond Tart with Vanilla Ice Cream and Caramel Sauce 5.50

Selection of Sorbet with Coconut Tuile 5.00

Cheese Plate with Fruit and Grilled Crouton 7.50

ASPARAGUS, ROASTED POTATOES AND MOREL MUSH-
ROOMS with mustard and walnut oil vinaigrette
6.00

SALAD OF MIXED GREENS
with basil and lemon oil vinaigrette
5.00

CAESAR SALAD
7.00

SPINACH AND RICOTTA GNOCCHI
with sage butter and fried sage
6.00

SCALLOP, SQUID AND CHICKPEA SALAD
with tomato and rosemary
7.00

DUCK CHARCUTERIE PLATE
duck ham with rhubarb pickle, confit gizzard salad and foie gras
8.00

BRANDADE OF SALT COD
with melted sweet peppers and onion
6.00

395 Hayes St • Civic Center • (415) 864-4824

CARROT AND FENNEL SOUP
with a mint cream
5.00

SPAGHETTI PUTTANESCA
spicy tomato sauce with fried capers
13.00

ORECCHIETTE PASTA
with anchovies, broccoli rabe, garlic and hot pepper flakes
14.00

ROASTED STRIPED BASS
with leek and asparagus ragout
16.00

GRILLED GULF PRAWNS
with grilled eggplant and olive salad
19.00

AHI TUNA SEARED RARE
with roasted beets and horseradish creme fraiche
18.00

CASSOULET
cranberry beans with duck confit, smoked pork sausage and bacon
15.00

GRILLED NATURAL RIB EYE STEAK
with potato-leek pancake and roquefort butter
19.00

PAN ROASTED SQUAB
with a pickled cherry clafouti
18.00

RABBIT CONFIT
with artichokes, sundried tomatoes and pickled lemon
15.00

ZOLA'S OLIVES ARE AVAILABLE FOR $10.00 PER JAR

Dinner: Tues - Sat 5:30 - 10:30, Sun 5 - 9

Aperitivos

NACHOS- Refried pinto beans, fresh tomatoes, sliced jalapño, guacamole,
sour cream, lettuce and cheese ... 5.95   with crab ... 7.95

PANCHOS- Individual nachos with chicken and beef ... 6.40

ONGOS RELLENOS- Seared mushroom caps filled with shrimp
and cilantro salpicón ... 4.75

QUESADILLAS- Monterey jack cheese and pico de gallo melted in
whole wheat tortillas ... 5.40   with fresh spinach ... 5.95

Sopas Y Ensaladas

	CUP	BOWL		
TORTILLA SOUP	1.50	2.75	GRINGO SALAD	2.65
SOPA DEL DIA	1.50	2.75	CAESAR (for two)	6.75
MARISCO'S SOPA	--	6.50	CEVICHE	5.50

ENTREE ENSALADAS

ENSALADA MATADOR- Thinly sliced sirloin, mesquite broiled, served on a
bed of romaine, tomatoes, pimentos, radish and olives ... 7.95

ENSALADA de MARISCO'S- Prawns, scallops, jicama, hearts of palm,
tomatoes and avocado- tossed tableside with cilantro vinaigrette ... 8.20

Cadillac Botana Platters

CADILLAC BOTANA PLATTER- Our complete combination of regional specialties para todos; carnitas, fajitas, pollo jalapeño, flautas, chile con queso or queso flameado, corn chowder, frijoles borrachos, pico de qallo, fresh tortillas, bolillos, chips and salsa ... 2-3 persons 23.95 4-5 persons 43.50

PLATILLO de SIETE MARES- A collection of our seafood specialites; steamed Alaskan king crab, camarones verdes, pescado fresco, camarones al tocino, ceviehe, marisco's rojos, Cadillac Rice and fresh vegetables ... 2-3 persons 32.95

Entrees

POLLO LAREDO- Chicken breast stuffed with cheese, olives chiles and bacon - a Mexican cordon bleu!
.... 10.75

POLLO YUCATAN- Half chicken baked in pipian ranchero sauce. Served with rice, beans and fried bananas 9.75

HOT MARISCO PASTA- Fresh fish and shellfish, simmered in red chile sauce, over cilantro pasta
.... 11.50

FILET al CHIPOTLE- Filet mignon, broiled to perfection, topped with chipotle sauce, monterey cheese and cilantro 13.95

FAJITAS ASADAS- Choice of broiled beef of chicken, served with guacamole, sour cream and pico de gallo 9.70

CREPAS de CARNITAS- Pork loin sautéed in ancho chile, sesame and orange. Rolled in corn crepes
.... 8.95

CHILE RELLENO de ELOTE- Flame-roasted peppers filled with sweet corn, vegetables and cheese
.... 8.75

CAMARONES al TOCINO- Prawns and jalapeños, wrapped in bacon, broiled over mesquite
.... 10.95

CAMARONES en SALSA ASSAFRAN (Sunrise Shrimp)- Large prawns sautéed in Spanish saffron sauce 11.95

SOPAPILLAS del MAR-Prawns-Scallops and fresh fish in madeira cream sauce. Baked in homemade pastry 10.75

CABRITO-
La especialidad de la casa! Cadillac Bar serves only the choicest kidgoat available.
A.Q.

VISTA del MAR-
Prawns, chicken and fish, simmered in salsa Espanola, baked with cheese.
10.95

ANTOJITOS
(Appetizers)

NACHOS
Jalapeños and Cheese	1/2 order 3.95	5.95
Spicy Beef and Cheese	1/2 order 4.95	6.95
Fajita Nachos (Beef, Chicken, or Combo)	1/2 order 5.95	7.95

QUESOS   Skillets of melted Monterey Jack cheese, poblano peppers, onions and mushrooms, served with Fresh flour tortillas hot off EL MACHINO – our Tortilla Machine

Vegetable	5.95
Fajita Queso (Beef or Chicken)	7.95
Rock Shrimp Queso	7.95

QUESADILLAS   Your choice of Flour or Whole Wheat Tortillas

Cheese	Small 3.95	Large 5.95
Vegetable	Small 4.95	Large 6.95
Fajita Beef or Shredded Chicken	Small 5.95	Large 7.95

CALDOS Y ENSALADAS
(Soups and Salads)

SOPA DE TORTILLA . . . . Cup 2.25 . . . . Bowl 3.25
Mexican vegetable soup with fresh zuchini, corn, peppers, tomatoes and onions.
Topped with crisp tortilla chips and Monterey Jack cheese

FAJITA GRANDE SALAD 8.95
As the name suggests, a very large handmade tortilla shell stuffed with crispy lettuce
and slices of tomato, cucumber, green pepper, onion and mushrooms. Topped with
cheese and Mesquite broiled Beef or Chicken

TOSTADA SALAD 6.95
Spicy Beef or Chicken served on a bed of lettuce with guacamole, sour cream, salsa,
beans, and cheese in a crispy flour tortilla shell

CEVICHE SALAD 6.95
White fish gently marinated in Fresh lime juice, mixed with tomatoes, onions and
Fresh cilantro. Served on a bed of crispy lettuce with cucumbers, tomatoes and limes

CHICKEN FIESTA SALAD 6.95
Mesquite Broiled Chicken Breast with cucumbers, tomatoes and green peppers.
Served on a bed of lettuce in a crispy flour tortilla shell

PLATILLOS TRADICIONAL
(Traditional Platters)

CHEESE ENCHILADA with Chili Meat Sauce . . . . 2 for 6.95

BEEF ENCHILADA with Chili Meat Sauce . . . . 2 for 6.95

CHICKEN ENCHILADA with Spicy Red or Green Sauce. . . . . 2 for 6.95

ENCHILADA COMBINATION Beef, Chicken and Cheese. . . . . 3 for 8.45

FAJITA BURRITO Mesquite Broiled Beef, Chicken or Vegetable. 7.45

CRISPY TACOS Beef or Chicken . . . . .3 for 6.95

SOFT TACOS Beef or Chicken . . . . 3 for 6.95

FLAUTAS Beef, Chicken, Cheese or Combo . . . . 3 for 7.45

COMBINADOS TRADICIONAL
(Traditional Combinations)

Your choice of a Soft or Crispy Taco and a Chicken or Pork Tamale

SUPER CHEVYS 10.95
  Beef AND Chicken Enchiladas, Beef Taco, Tamale and Chili Relleno

LAREDO 8.95
  Beef AND Chicken Enchiladas, Chicken Taco and Tamale

SONORA 8.45
  Beef Enchilada, Beef Taco and Tamale

REYNOSA. 8.45
  Chicken Enchilada, Chicken Taco and Tamale

YUCATAN 8.45
  Chicken Enchilada, Beef Taco and Tamale

CHIHUAHUA 8.45
  Beef Enchilada, Chicken Taco and Tamale

FRESH MEX® FAJITAS

Beef, Chicken, or a Combination of the two, marinated and Mesquite Broiled.
Our Fajitas are served sizzling with our soft, Fresh flour tortillas hot off EL MACHINO,
pico de gallo, guacamole, our own unique rice and BEANS A LA CHARRA.
Roll these yourself at the table to make any taste combination you wish.

We are dedicated to serving the best FAJITAS !

Single Portion 10.95   Double Portion 19.95

SUPER SIZE PLATTERS are available – 9.95 for each additional person

Please specify Beef, Chicken or a Combination

Monterey Jack or Cheddar Cheese. . . .65¢

PLATILLOS COMBINADOS
(Sizzling Combinations)

CANCUN   Chicken Fajitas and Jumbo Shrimp 13.95

TIJUANA   Beef Fajitas and Jumbo Shrimp 13.95

SAN LUIS   Mesquite Broiled Quail and Jumbo Shrimp. 13.95

Dinner: Sun - Thurs until 10, Fri - Sat until 11   ●ⓁⒹ

Corona Bar & Grill

Menu Changes Monthly

LUNCH

SANDWICHES

HAMBURGER on Housemade Bolillo Bun with Escabeche Vegetables and Fries ... 5.95

HOUSEMADE CHORIZO SAUSAGE SANDWICH on Soft Roll with Jack Cheese,
Salsa Verde and fries ... 6.95

TACOS

PIT COOKED CHICKEN TACO fajita style with Black Beans, Tomatillo-Chipotle Salsa
and Tortilas ... 8.95

BEEF CARNITAS & CHEESE TAQUITOS with Roast Tomato & Chile Basil Salsas
and Beans. ... 5.95

GRILLED PRAWN TACO in Crisp Taco Shells with Achiote Marinade,
Tomato Pico de Gallo Salsa and Chile Aioli ... 10.95

BURRITOS

CORONA DUCK BURRITO
with Roasted Corn, Pasilla Pepper, beans, Ranchero Salsa and Jicama. 9.95

VEGETARIAN STYLE Roasted Peppers, Corn, Squash and Sonoma Goat Cheese,
with Salsa Verde. ... 8.95

ENCHILADAS

SHRIMP & TOMATO with Avocado-Tomatillo Salsa and Pico de Gallo ... 8.95

CHICKEN with Corn, Cheese, Mole Colorado, Queso Fresco and Jicama Salad ... 9.50

CHILE VERDE & BEEF CARNITAS with Jack Cheese and Black Beans ... 7.95

ANAHEIM CHILE RELLENO with PumpkinSeed and Cheese Filling
Roasted Tomato Salsa and Tortilla Salad. ... 5.95

CHICKEN TAMALE with Red Chile Salsa, Black Bean Salad and Salsa Verde. ... 6.95

PAELLA VALENCIANA baked Mixed Shellfish, Chicken and Chorizo Sausage with
Saffron Rice And Onion-Tomato Sofrito. ... 14.95

FISH OF THE DAY ... A.Q

DINNER

SOUPS / SOPAS

TORTILLA SOUP roasted Tomato Broth with Avocado-Tomatillo Salsa and Tortillas ... 3.95

SOUP OF THE DAY traditional and Contemporary ... 4.95

QUESADILLAS

CURED HAM and JACK CHEESE with Guacamole ... 5.25

SPICED SHRIMP and CRAB EMPANADA on Minted Corn Salsa ... 7.25

ASSORTED ANTOJITO PLATTER of Flauta, Chile Relleno, Ceviche and Quesadilla ... 10.50

88 Cyril Magnin St • Union Square • (415) 392-5500

APPETIZERS / COMIENSOS

TORTILLA CHIPS with SALSAS (3)	3.25
GUACAMOLE with Tomato, Cilantro and Tortilla Chips	3.95
CEVICHE of LOCAL REDSNAPPER in Tortilla Cup with, Lime Marinated Onions and Chiles	3.95
PACIFIC COLD WATER OYSTERS ON THE HALF SHELL with Serrano-Lime Mignonette	1.35 Each
CHILE RELLENO With Jack Cheese and Pumpkin Seed Filling and Roast Tomato Salsa	5.50
CHILE SMOKED CHICKEN WINGS with Chile Aioli and Queso Fresco	4.50
TAQUITOS Of Beef Carnitas and Cheese with Tomatillo-Serrano Salsa	5.00
TAMALE Red Chile Chicken filling with Salsa Verde	5.95

SALADS

BABY GREENS with Ranch Style Dressing and Chile Spiced Mixed Nuts	4.25
CAESAR SALAD with Dry Jack Cheese and Mexican Oregano Croutons	5.50
NOPALES CACTUS SALAD with Roasted Red Peppers, Sun Dried Tomatoes in Tostada	4.25
WARM ASPARAGUS SALAD with Tortillas, Jicama, Pineapple Vinaigrette & Sun-Dried Tomatoes	5.95

ENTREES / ENTREMESES

PIT COOKED CHICKEN TACO with Black Beans, Tomatillo-Chipotle Salsa, Nopalitos and Tortillas	11.75
CHILE DUCK BURRITO Reichardt Farm Duck, Corn and Black Beans with Ranchero Salsa and Jicama	12.50
VEGETARIAN STYLE BURRITO Roasted Peppers, Corn, Squash and Sonoma Goat Cheese with Salsa Verde	10.95
BEEF & CHEESE TAQUITOS with Roast Tomato & Chile Basil Salsas and Beans.	5.95
PASTA EN CAZUELA housemade Corn Pasta with Sun-dried Toamato-Chile Filling Lemon-Sage Sauce and Quese Ranchero	

ENCHILADAS

YUCATAN with Shrimp, Avocado-Tomatillo Salsa and Pico de Gallo	13.95
CORONA chicken, Roasted Corn and Jack Cheese with Mole Coloradito and Jicama-Black Beans Salad	11.95

SEAFOOD / MARISCOS Y PESCADOS

STEAMED CLAMS MARISCADA Manila Clams Steamed with Sherry, Garlic, Tomato and Served with Basil-Chile Salsa, Tortillas and Rice	11.95
GRILLED SPICED PRAWNS VERACRUZANA with Tomato, Caper and Olive Salsa and Cumin Rice	15.95
PAELLA VALENCIANA baked Mixed Shellfish, Chicken and Chorizo Sausage with Saffron Rice And Onion-Tomato Sofrito.	16.95
FISH OF THE DAY A.Q	

OAK WOOD GRILLED

HUSEMADE CHORIZO SAUSAGE Chicken and Pork Sausage with Ancho Vinaigrette and Vegetable-Rice Tostada	10.50
LAMB CHOPS with Argentine Spice Marinade, Potato Tortilla and Red Chile Salsa	17.50
TAMPICO STYLE NEW YORK STEAK with Lime-Garlic Marinade, Chipotle Salsa Fries and Corn on the Cob	16.95
UN PLATO GRANDE DE NUESTROS FAVORITOS Platter of Assorted Entree Selections Shrimp Veracruzano, Chicken Enchilada and Housemade Chorizo	16.95

Sunday Brunch; Dinner: Sun - Wed until 10, Thurs - Sat until 11

 FRESH SEAFOOD APPETIZERS

Fresh fish marinated in lime and lemon juices with chopped   Chica 3.95
onions, tomato, jalapeño chiles, cilantro, avocado.   Grande 5.95

Fresh fish and shrimp marinated in lime and lemon juices with   Chica 4.50
chopped onions, tomato, jalapeño chiles, cilantro, avocado.   Grande 6.75

 SALADS

Romaine lettuce, jicama, tomato, avocado, goat cheese with
lime-oregano vinaigrette. 4.25

Thin slices of jicama, cucumber, fresh fruit in season with lemon-chile dressing. 4.50

Marinated cactus strips, onions, fresh cheese with cilantro-chile vinaigrette. 4.50

Shrimp, squid, avocado, lettuce and tomatoes with vinaigrette. 8.95

 SOUP

Chipotle flavored chicken broth with tortilla strips, avocado, fresh cheese. 3.95

Cold black bean soup with sour cream, lime, cilantro. 3.85

Corn kernels in chicken and pork broth served with radishes, lettuce, lemon. 5.75

 STUFFED FRESH CORN MASA

Two tamales of chicken with green and red chile sauce, served in corn husks. 7.95

Two tamales of pork with guajillo chile sauce, served in banana leaves. 7.75

Green corn masa stuffed with cactus, plantain, salsa cruda, steamed in green
corn husks and topped with fresh Mexican cream (two). 7.95

An assortment of three tamales - one of each of the above. 9.95

For parties of 7 or more, a 15% gratuity will be added.

5 Main St • Tiburon • (415) 435-6300

 MEXICAN FAVORITES

Half chicken with sauce of chocolate, chiles, fruits and spices. 10.75

Two large green poblano chiles stuffed with chicken and raisins;
walnut sauce and pomegranate seeds. 9.25

Slowly roasted pork sirloin served with tomato, chopped onions, cilantro,
serrano chiles, warm corn tortillas. 10.25

Shrimp sautéed with chipotle sauce, garlic, onions, sour cream. 14.25

Pan-seared fresh water fish; sautéed onions and tomatoes. 10.95

Fresh seasonal fish and shellfish in fish broth with chayote, cabbage,
red potatoes. 8.95

Roasted duck, pumpkin seed sauce. 12.95

Fresh Pacific snapper sautéed with mushrooms, jalapeño chiles, onions,
tomato, garlic, served on a banana leaf. 11.50

Strips of chicken breast sautéed with achiote chile and onions. 10.95

Thinly-pounded sautéed veal with peanut-serrano chile sauce. 12.75

Above served with fresh corn tortillas, epazote rice and black beans.

 MESQUITE CHARCOAL-GRILLED

Giant shrimp marinated in lime juice and cilantro. 15.75

Fresh fish served with güero chile-tomato butter (daily selection). A.Q.

Shrimp, squid, baby octopus marinated in lime juice and cilantro. 10.75

Large platter of assorted fresh seafood (for two or more). A.Q.

Game hen; tomatillo-jalapeño chile sauce. 10.50

Skewers of marinated chicken and beef. 11.95

Butterflied filet mignon with spring onions. 13.95

Medallions of pork tenderloin with chayote and marinated red onions. 10.50

Strips of marinated skirt steak with onions, on a sizzling platter. 10.95

Spit-roasted meats and fowl (daily selection). A.Q.

Marinated top sirloin steak, sautéed onions and mushrooms; grilled corn. 12.50

Double breast of chicken; peanut-serrano chile sauce. 10.95

Above served with fresh corn tortillas, epazote rice and black beans.

 DESSERTS

Chocolate "sin." 4.75

Fritter with "drunken" bananas and vanilla ice cream. 4.75

Avocado and lime pie. 3.95

Sunday Brunch; Dinner: Sun - Thurs until 10, Fri - Sat until 11   ●ⓁⒹ

¡Salud!

ENTREMESES
(appetizers)

SOPES
two handmade corn masa cups filled with:

    zucchini and fresh cheese   4.50

    chicken, cheese and red onions   4.50

    black beans, nopales and cheese   4.50

PLATILLO DE SOPES
an assortment of sopes, one of each of the above 6.50

CEVICHE DEL DIA
daily selection of fresh seafood marinated with lime, cilantro, red onions, and jalapeño chilies 6.50

QUESADILLAS SURTIDAS
three corn tortilla turnovers filled with seafood; cheese and potato; mushrooms and herbs 6.50

ENSALADAS
(salads)

¡ENSALADA SALUD!
*romaine lettuce, tomato, cucumber, jicama and fresh cheese with
oregano-lime vinaigrette* 4.25

¡SALUD CESAR!
romaine and escarole lettuces, roasted corn, Salud Caesar dressing, chili croutons and parmesan 6.50

TAMALES
(stuffed fresh
corn masa)

TAMALES DE PECHUGA DE POLLO
two tamales of chicken with green and red chili sauces; steamed in a corn husk 8.50

TAMALES DE MASA A LA OAXAQUENA
two tamales of pork with guajillo chili sauce; steamed in banana leaves 8.50

TAMALES DE ELOTE CON NOPALES Y PLATANO
two tamales of green corn masa stuffed with cactus and plantain; steamed in a corn husk 8.50

---

500 Van Ness Ave • Civic Center • (415) 864-8500

PLATILLOS FAVORITOS

(Regional favorites
served with
black beans)

PASILLA RELLENO
two roasted green pasilla chilies stuffed with simmered chicken and raisins;
walnut-goat cheese sauce with pomegranate seeds 8.95

PESCADO DEL DIA
today's fresh seafood, changing by availability and inspiration of the day A.Q.

HUACHINANGO MAZATLAN
sautéed fresh snapper with shrimp, tomato, mushrooms, chilies and garlic with pasilla rice 11.50

CAMARONES A LA SAL DE ROCA
giant shrimp cooked over rock salt with pasilla rice 15.95

DON CACAHUATE
mesquite-grilled double breast of chicken with peanut-chili sauce and pasilla rice 10.95

POLLO EN MOLE
poached double breast of chicken with traditional dark mole sauce and pasilla rice 10.95

FILETE A LA PARILLA
grilled marinated beef tenderloin with chipotle butter, rajas and smashed potatoes 15.95

BORREGO CON CEBOLLITAS
cumin and cilantro-marinated lamb, slow-roasted and served with onions, spicy tomatoes
and avocado on a sizzling platter; soft tortillas 13.50

CARNITAS URUAPAN
slowly roasted pork with onions, cilantro, serrano chilies, salsa cruda and soft tortillas 10.50

ACOMPAÑAS

(sides)

ESPINACA
spinach sauteed with olive oil and garlic 3.95

RAJAS
roasted chilies, caramelized onions, cream and cheese 3.95

PLATILLO DE VEGETALES ASADOS
platter of assorted vegetables - green corn tamale with cactus and plantain, pasilla rice,
chayote, spinach, spicy tomatoes, rajas, yucca, grilled scallions and black beans 9.95

POSTRES

(desserts)

PASTEL DE CHOCOLATE
dark chocolate flourless cake with cajeta sauce and rice ice cream 4.75

TRES HELADOS
selection of almond nougat, rice and strawberry ice creams 3.95

¡SALUD FLAN!
traditional caramelized custard with fresh pineapple 3.95

TORTA DE MAIZ CON FRESAS EN MEZCAL
cornmeal cake with strawberries in mezcal, strawberry ice cream and mango ice 4.75

ALI'S

FROM THE GRILL
Served with rice and vegetables

Shish Taouk
Chunks of chicken breast marinated in our lemon sauce and herbs ... $14.75

Shish Kebab
Top round lamb marinated in fresh herbs ... $17.75

CURRY DELIGHTS
*All dishes are prepared with our own blend of mild spices
and are served with rice and vegetables.
Spicy Harisa sauce is available upon request.*

Chicken Breast
Sauteed chicken breast topped with mild curry sauce ... $13.75

Lamb
Sauteed lamb blended with mild curry sauce .., $16.50

Prawns
Jumbo prawns sauteed in sherry wine, blended
in mild curry sauce ... $19.50

VEGETARIAN SPECIALS
Fantasia Couscous

A variety of fresh steamed vegetables served on a bed of couscous and
topped with basil and tomato sauce ... $11.75

Magali
Mixed vegetables sauteed in olive oil blended in garlic and lemon sauce,
served on a bed of rice ... $12.50

ALI'S SPECIALS
Chef's Platter
Your choice of Bastilla or Harira
Combination of lamb, chicken and jumbo prawn kebabs, served with rice and vegetables
(for two) .. $59.00

385 Colusa Ave • Berkeley • (510) 526-1500

POULTRY SELECTIONS
Served with rice and vegetables

Chicken Magli
Chicken breast sauteed with green olives in lemon sauce ... $13.50

Chicken Oasis
Braised chicken in light honey sauce, sprinkled with almonds and raisins ... $14.00

Battah
Half duck roasted with fresh herbs, topped with light honey sauce and sprinkled with almonds and raisins ... $18.75

LAMB AND BEEF SPECIALTIES
Served with rice and vegetables

Marouzia
Braised lamb with fresh herbs, blended in light honey sauce, topped with raisins and almonds ... $18.00

Lahem Ghanem
Poached lamb topped with light sauce, served with sauteed eggplant .. $17.75

Filet Magli
Filet mignon sauteed in olive oil, topped with raisins, walnuts, and pomegranate sauce ... $25.00

COUSCOUS DISHES
Imported fine semolina, steamed over a rich both to enhance its flavor

Lamb
Chunks of lamb topped with light sauce, mixed vegetables, raisins, and chickpeas, served on a bed of couscous ... $17.75

Chicken
Braised chicken breast, topped with sauce, vegetables, and chickpeas, served on a bed of couscous ... $13.50

Seafood
Jumbo prawns, scallops sauteed in wine and blended in lobster sauce with vegetables, served on a bed of couscous ... $22.00

Dinner: 7 Days a Week 6 - 9:30

FROM THE LAND OF MESOPOTAMIA

LUNCH MENU

SALADS

MIXED GREEN SALAD *with cucumber, red onion, tomato and goat, blue or feta cheese* $4.50

MEZA *tabbouleh, baba ghanoush, pickled turnips and cucumber served with pita bread* $5.00

FATOOSH *onion marinated with sumac, cucumber, mint, Italian parsley, cilantro,*
grilled eggplant and tomato in lemon vinaigrette $4.75

RAVIOLI *stuffed with dates, cardamom and cinnamon, topped with parmesan cheese*
and chopped walnuts in olive oil, surrounded with roasted red bell pepper $5.50

ENTREES

CHICKEN KEBE *stuffed with chicken and cumin, served with whole apricot sauce and vegetables*........ $6.75
(Kebe is a typical Middle Eastern dish consisting of a rice shell which is stuffed and baked)

LAMB KEBE *stuffed with lamb and coriander, served with a carmellized onion and potato sauce* $7.25

BEEF KEBE *stuffed with beef and curry served with a grilled eggplant and tomato sauce*......................$6.50

VEGETARIAN KEBE *stuffed with mushroom, cheese, and tomato, served*
on a bed of warm spinach salad. $6.00

VEGETARIAN DOLMA *stuffed zucchini, tomato and wrapped swiss chard with bulgar,*
cilantro, Italian parsley, and jalapeno pepper served with yogurt and mint sauce..............$7.25

GRILLED TROUT *marinated with thyme and served with a curry sumac aioli*......................$7.50

SPECIAL OF THE DAY..............*ask waiter*

DESSERTS..............*ask waiter*

DINNER

APPETIZERS

GRILLED JAPANESE EGGPLANT *with pomegranate sauce and Mesopotamian salsa* $4.00

BOURAK *ground beef with parsley and cilantro wrapped in phyllo dough,*
served with tahini date syrup... $4.25

RAVIOLI *stuffed with dates, cardamom and cinnamon, topped with parmesan cheese*
and chopped walnuts in olive oil, surrounded with roasted red bell pepper $4.50

BASTERMA *Mesopotamian carpaccio served with pickled mango aioli* $4.00

SALADS

MIXED GREEN SALAD *with cucumber, red onion, tomato and goat, blue or feta cheese* $5.00

MIXED HERB SALAD *with mustard vinaigrette* $5.00

MEZA *tabbouleh, baba ghanoush, pickled turnips and cucumber served with pita bread* $6.00

FATOOSH *onion marinated with sumac, cucumber, mint, Italian parsley, cilantro,*
grilled eggplant and tomato in lemon vinaigrette $6.00

ENTREES

BABY CHICKEN *stuffed with rice , golden raisins, cashews, Italian parsley and cumin,*
served with kasy (whole apricot sauce) $12.50

DOLMA *stuffed zucchini, onion and wrapped swiss chard with rice, diced lamb, tomato*
and allspice, served with tamarind sauce $10.50

VEGETARIAN DOLMA *stuffed zucchini, tomato and wrapped swiss chard with bulgar,*
cilantro, Italian parsley, and jalapeno pepper served with yogurt and mint sauce............................... $9.50

MUKLOOBA *curried scallops, fried eggplant, cauliflower, zucchini and rice, served*
with sun-dried lime and black bean sauce $12.50

BIRIANI *lamb and rice mixed with potato, onion,raisons, garlic,cumin, cinnamon, cardomom,*
and chopped sun-dried lime , served with kashk sauce $11.00

PERDAPLOW *chicken , rice, almonds, golden raisins and cardomon wrapped in phyllo*
dough served with berry cinnamon sauce. $12.50

MEZGOOF *whole grilled fish of the day* .... market price

RICE DISHES

(all of these dishes are served with rice mixed with fava beans and peas)

SHEIK MAHSHE *Japanese Eggplant stuffed with lamb, coriander, and pine nuts served with a*
tamarind and tomato sauce... $9.50

PRAWNS *served with a Mesopotamian sweet and sour sauce (raisins and limes)*.............................. $11.50

SPECIAL OF THE DAY.. *ask waiter*

*or yesterday is but a dream and tomorrow is only a vision, but today well lived
makes every yesterday a dream of happiness and every tomorrow a vision of hope.
Look well, therefore to this day! Such is the salutation of the dawn.*

Salutation of the dawn from the Sufi 1200 BC

HUMOS	3.75	**CHEESE FLAMBÉ**	5.00
Chickpeas pureé, sesame paste		*with cognac*	
FALAFEL	4.00	**BUREK**	5.50
Fried patties of crushed beans		*Pastry stuffed with minced meat or cheese*	
DOLMA	3.75	**ARAYES**	6.00
Stuffed grapeleaves		*Pita stuffed with spicy meat sauce*	
EGGPLANT SALAD	4.50	**MERQUEZ**	6.00
Baba Ghannoug		*Spicy Tunisian Sausage*	
MUSAKKA	4.50	**KIBBEH**	9.00
Sautéed eggplant, zucchini, and green peppers		*Lebanese steak tartar with cracked wheat*	
TABBOULEH SALAD	4.50	**B'STILLA**	8.50
Parsley, cracked wheat		*Fillo pie with chicken almonds, topped with powdered sugar, cinnamon*	
MEDITERRANEAN SALAD	4.50		
Fattoush		**PIYAZ**	4.00
		Mediterranean white beans	
FETTA CHEESE, OLIVES	4.50		

1516 Broadway St • Marina • (415) 885-4477

A ROYAL FEAST

Includes Hummas, Falafel, Dolma, Piyaz, Fried Pita, Tabbouleh, B'Stilla,
Dessert & Tea • $ 6.00 over price of entrée.

RACK OF LAMB *Charbroiled or baked with pomegranate and honey*	18.50	**LAMB WITH HONEY** *Almonds & Raisins*	18.00
GULF PRAWNS BROCHETTE *Lemon Butter*	18.50	**VEAL WITH EGGPLANT** *Tomato Sauce, sun dried mint*	17.50
QUAILS CHARBROILED *Lime & Sage*	16.50	**CHICKEN TANGINE** *Pickled lemon & olives*	16.50
SHISH KEBAB *Tender lamb marinated*	16.00	**CHICKEN WITH HONEY** *Onions, raisins & sesame*	17.00
FILET OF BEEF BROCHETTE *Cumin, cilantro*	16.00	**HARE WITH PAPRIKA** *Tomatoes & onions*	17.50
KEFTA *Minced lamb with parsley, onions & cardamom*	15.00	**COUSCOUS VEGETABLES** *Harissa "cumin cayennes sauce"*	14.50
CHICKEN FILETS BROCHETTE *Lemon, Greek Oregano*	16.00	**COUSCOUS** *with choice of Seafood, Lamb, Chicken, or Merquez*	18.50
MIDDLE EASTERN COMBINATION	28.00	**MOROCCAN COMBINATION**	25.00

CALIFORNIA
Red Wines

Cabernet Sauvigon 28.00
Robert Mondavi-Napa Valley

Cabernet Sauvignon 22.00
Grand Cru-Sonoma

Merlot 21.00
Madroña-El Dorado

IMPORTED
Red Wines

Chateau Duhart-Milon-Rothschild ..40.00
Bordeaux

Fontvillac Grand Cru 24.00
St. Emilion-Bordeaux

Beaujolais Villages 17.00
Armand Roux

CALIFORNIA
White Wines

Chardonnay - Reserve 36.00
Robert Mondavi - Napa

Chardonnay 27.00
Lawrence J. Bagetto-Santa Cruz Mountains

Chardonnay 22.00
Gundlach-Bunschu-Sonoma Valley

Fume Blanc....................................21.00
Robert Mondavi-Napa Valley

Sauvignon Blanc 19.00
Guenoc Winery-Lake County Estate

Chevrignon.....................................19.00
Vichon-Napa Valley

LUNCH TIME SPECIAL

Served With
Benihana Salad
Hibachi Vegetables, Rice and Green Tea

Chicken Tropicana   **6.25**
With Fresh Pineapple and Ham

Luncheon Hibachi Steak   **7.75**

Luncheon Filet Mignon   **8.50**

Chef-San's Choice   **8.75**
Chicken and Teriyaki Steak

Shogun Special   **10.75**
Hibachi Steak and Shrimp Appetizer

Ocean Catch   **12.50**
Shrimp and Ocean Scallops

TRADITIONAL

Served With
Japanese Onion Soup, Benihana Salad, Shrimp Appetizer,
Hibachi Vegetables, Rice and Tea.

Hibachi Chicken   **13.25**

Teriyaki Steak   **16.00**

Hibachi Steak   **16.25**

Filet Mignon   **17.75**

Hibachi Shrimp   **16.75**

1737 Post St • Japantown • (414) 563-4844 • (Call for Additional Locations)

SPECIALITIES

Served With
Japanese Onion Soup, Benihana Salad, Shrimp Appetizer,
Hibachi Vegetables, Rice, Tea, and Fresh Pineapple

Rocky's Choice   19.25
Steak and Chicken.

Imperial Steak   22.00
14 ounces of Hibachi Steak.

Benihana San Francisco   21.25
Teriyaki Beef Julienne and Shrimp.

Benihana Delight   19.50
Chicken and Shrimp.

Land and Sea   21.50
Beach Feast with Tenderloin and Ocean Scallops.

Benihana Special   25.50
Steak and Cold Water Lobster Tail.

Benihana Marina   23.50
Cold Water Lobster Tail and Ocean Scallops.

 Benihana is a Poetic Word for Red Flower and
to Millions in Japan who know the
Benihana Chain of Restaurants it also signifies a
Tradition of Fine Dining

Dinner: Mon - Thurs 5 - 10, Fri - Sat 5 - 11, Sun 4:30 - 10   ●ⓁⒹ

CHO-CHO
JAPANESE RESTAURANT

LUNCH

Appetizers —

Yaki Tori	7.00
Teba (Chicken Wings)	4.00
Sashimi	(Seasonal)
Beef Sashmi	8.50
Spinach Salad	3.50

Luncheon —

Shabu-Shabu	11.00
Beef Sukiyaki	11.00
Beef Butter-Yaki	11.50
Rib Steak Teriyaki	9.00

Chef's Special —

Farmer's new York Steak	9.50
Farmer's Chicken	7.50
Chicken Yakitori	7.50
Assorted Tempura, Shrimp, Vegetables	9.50

Donburi-Mono (Rice Casseroles) —

Oyako Donburi, chicken vegetables, eggs	5.50
Ten Don, shrimp tenpura with sauce	6.50
Yakitori Donburi, chicken yakitori, rice	5.50

Nabe-Mono —

Gyu Nabe, beef, onion and egg	7.75
Torinabe, chicken, onion and egg	7.25

1020 Kearny St • North Beach • (415) 397-3066

Salads —
    Spinach   3.50
    Green Salad   4.50

DINNER

A. Niku Teriyaki Dinner	B. Sashimi Dinner
Chicken Soup	Miso Soup
Green Salad	Shnomono
Yakitori	Sashimi
Tempura	Yakitori
Beef Teriyaki 17.50	Tempura 18.00

Shabu-Shabu Dinner   15.00
Okaribayaki Dinner   15.00
Beef Butter-Yaki Dinner   14.00
Chicken Yakitori Dinner   8.50

Tempura Dinners —
    Shrimp Tempura   11.00
    Assorted Tempura   10.50

Tempura Bar (Custom Service) Salmon Dinners: —
    Salmon Shioyaki   12.00
    Salmon Teriyaki   12.00
    Salmon Butter-Yaki   13.00

• All Dinners include soup, sunomo and rice •

Side Orders —
    Sashimi   (Priced by Day)
    Chicken wings or Teba   4.00
    Miso Soup   1.00
    Nameko-wan, with Nameko Mushrooms 1.75
    Chicken Soup   1.00

Dinner: Mon - Fri 5:30 - 9, Sat 5 - 10   ● Ⓛ Ⓓ

KANSAI COMBINATION DINNER   18.00
Dinner includes rice, Japanese pickles and green tea.

CHEF'S SPECIAL APPETIZER
CLEAR SOUP or MISO SOUP
ENTREE   Enjoy your selection from any two items.
SASHIMI
TEMPURA
CHICKEN TERIYAKI
BEEF TERIYAKI
CHICKEN TATSUTA-AGE
marinated and deep-fried
HAMACHI Shiokayi or Teriyaki
SALMON Shiokayi or Teriyaki
SUSHI

TABLE-TOP COOKING

SUKIYAKI   16.50
Thinly sliced beef, vegetables, noodles and
Tofu cooked in our own Sukiyaki sauce.

SHABU-SHABU   16.50
Thin sliced beef, vegetables, Tofu and yam
noodles cooked in a light broth. Served with
two kinds of delicious dipping sauce.

UDON SUKI DINNER   16.50
Noodles cooked in delicately seasoned broth
with fresh clam, chicken, prawns and assorted
vegetables.

ISHIKARI NABE   15.00
Salmon and assorted vegetables cooked in a
miso based delicious broth.

YOSENABE   15.00
Assorted seafood, vegetables and chicken in a
tasty broth.

KANSAI SELECTED DINNER

SASHIMI ASSORTMENT	13.50
SASHIMI Tuna Only	15.00
SALMON TERIYAKI or SHIOYAKI	13.50
TEMPURA Assortment	12.50
TEMPURA VEGETARIAN	10.00
HAMACHI (Yellowtail)	14.50
TERIYAKI New York Beef Striploin	15.00
CHICKEN TERIYAKI	12.50
TONKATSU	11.50
DEEP FRIED SEAFOOD COMBINATION	15.00

OTHER SPECIALITIES

UNA-JU   13.50
Barbecued eel basted with our special sauce.
Served with rice in a delicate lacquered tray.

ZOSUI   6.00
Rice in broth cooked with your choice of crab,
shrimp, chicken or vegetables.

ONIGIRI   5.75
Three rice balls filled with salmon, plum and
Okaka

YAKI-ONIGIRI   6.75
Three rice balls grilled with light soy sauce.

OCHAZUKE   5.75
Tasty light broth over rice with your choice of
salmon, plum or seaweed.

NOODLES

CHA-SOBA   8.50
Green tea noodles served with delicious
dipping sauce.

UDON   6.00
White flour noodles

SOBA   6.00
Wholewheat brown noodles

NABEYAKI UDON   6.75

Kyo-ya Set Dinners

Sakana-Misoyaki	20.50
Grilled fish with miso sauce	
Wafu-Steak	19.50
New York steak with two special dipping sauces	
Nizakana	19.25
A special soup of simmered fish	

From the Sushi Bar

Sashimi-Teishoku	25.00
Assorted sashimi dinner	
Served with kobachi, soup, pickles, rice and dessert	
Chirashi Sushi	20.00
Served with miso soup	
Omakase (Kiku-Chrysanthemum)	60.00
Deluxe assortment of sashimi (Chef's choice)	

Skewered Grilled Dishes

Sakana-Misoyaki	13.00
Grilled fish with miso sauce (Fresh fish of the day)	
Mirugai-Moromiyaki	8.25
Grilled giant clam topped with sweet moromi sauce	
Komochi-Shishamo	6.75
Grilled smelt with lemon	

Unagi-Kabayaki   12.75
Barbecued fresh eel with tsume sauce

Deep Fried Dishes

Isoage   11.75
Deep fried fresh sea food of the day

Sakana-Oroshini   13.00
Simmered fish topped with grated radish

Tempura   11.75
Assortment of seafood and vegetable tempura

Ebi-Kakiage   12.75
Minced shrimp and trefoil

Karei-Karaage   12.75
Fresh karei sole deep fried

Tori-Karaage   9.25
Japanese style fried chicken

Nabemono
One pot dishes cooked at the table.

Sukiyaki   35.00 *per person*
*Beef with vegetables and noodles cooked with sukiyaki sauce
served with soup*

Shabu-Shabu   35.00 *per person*
*Vegetable soup served with thin slices of beef cooked at your table
with two special dipping sauces*

Udonsuki   35.00 *per person*
A sukiyaki soup of chicken, clam & vegetables with udon noodles

Yosenabe   35.00 *per person*
Bouillabaisse Japanese style with assorted fish

Kyo-ya Nabe   50.00 *per person*
Lobsterbouilla baisse Japanese style

SANPPO RESTAURANT

NABE

Chanko - Nabe **8.25**
Fish, Chicken, Vegetable, and Egg Cooked in Broth, Served
with Lemon Flavored Sauce

Oyster - Nabe **7.75**
Oyster, Vegetable, and Egg Cooked in Broth and Served
with Lemon Flavored Sauce

Gyoza - Nabe **7.75**
Seasoned Ground Pork, Warpped in Thin Pastry
Cooked with Vegetable in Broth, Served with
Lemon Flavored Sauce

Seafood Nabe **7.95**
Assorted Seafood, Bean Cakes, Egg and Vegetables
Cooked in Broth and Served with Ponzu
Dipping Sauce (Lemon Flavored soy sauce)

Shabu Shabu **7.75**
Beef and Vegetables Cooked in Broth and
Served with a Special Dipping Sauce

Sukiyaki (Beef) **7.95**
Thinly Sliced Beef, Bamboo Shoots, Bean Cakes, Egg
and Vegetables Cooked in a Soy Flavored Broth

Tori Nabe **7.75**
Chicken, Vegetables, Egg, and Soy Bean Cakes,
Cooked in Broth.

PORK

Tonkatsu **7.50**

Pork Teriyaki **7.50**

Pork Ginger Yaki **7.75**

Roast Pork **7.50**
Roast Pork Pan Fried with Vegetables

Gyoza **6.50**
Seasoned Ground Pork, Wrapped in Thin
Pastry and Fried

1702 Post St • Japantown • (415) 346-3486

ENTREES

BEEF

Butter - Yaki **7.95**
Sliced Beef, Vegetables Cooked with Butter

Nasu Hasamiyaki (in season) **7.95**
Sliced Beef, Japanese Egg Plants, boiled with (ginger)
Seasoned Sauce

Ginger - Yaki **7.95**
Sliced Beef Cooked with a Shoga (ginger)
Seasoned Sauce

Shoyu Steak **8.25**
Mushroom Butter, Soy Sauce

Lemon Steak **8.50**
Sliced Beef and Vegetables cooked in Butter with Orange and
Lemon flavored soy sauce. (May we suggest eating this dish
with rice)

Top Sirloin Teriyaki **7.95**

Rib Eye Teriyaki **9.25**

CHICKEN

Garlic - Chicken **8.25**
Chicken Broiled and Basted with Garlic Seasoned
Sweet Soy Sauce

Chicken Teriyaki **7.95**
(Fried and Basted)

Broiled Chicken Teriyaki **8.25**

Shioyaki Chicken **7.95**

YAKITORI AND KUSHIYAKI

Yakitori (Chicken) **7.50**

Beef Kushiyaki **7.95**

Squid Kushiyaki **7.50**

Combination Kushiyaki **8.25**

Above Orders Served with Soup, Rice, Pickled Vegetable and Green Tea

Yoshi's
Restaurant & Nitespot

DINNER MENU

FIRST FLAVORS

MIXED SALAD With wakame seaweed and Yoshi's house vinaigrette	3.25
OHITASHI Lightly blanched spinach with soy sesame dressing	3.95
GRILLED MUSHROOMS (two skewers)	3.25
GRILLED JAPANESE EGGPLANT With fresh ginger and fried bonito flake	3.75
AH-EMONO Asparagus and shrimp with sesame miso vinaigrette	5.00
TEMPURA Batter fried shrimp and vegetables	5.00
BBQ CHICKEN WINGS With Thai chili sauce	4.00
SOFT SHELL CRAB Batter fried soft shell crab with *PONZU* sauce	5.50
YAKITORI Chicken skewered and grilled with teriyaki sauce	5.25
GYOZA-JAPANESE POTSTICKERS Ground chicken, mushroom and water chestnut	4.75
SUSHI CALIFORNIA ROLL Crab and avocado in seaweed inside-out roll	5.75

SUSHI CHEF'S RECOMMENDATION

ASSORTED SUSHI of Tuna, Yellowtail & Eel Nigiri, California Roll and Spicy Tuna Roll	9.00
ASSORTED SASHIMI & SUSHI Chef's Choice Sashimi; and Tuna, Yellowtail, and Eel Nigiri Sushi	12.00

Yoshi's **DINNERS**

Served with Sunomono, Miso Soup and Rice

SUKIYAKI with TEMPURA & YAKITORI	13.50
TEMPURA and YAKITORI	11.50
YOSHI'S FAMOUS DINNER FOR TWO A Large Platter Featuring Tuna Sashimi, Tempura, Teriyaki Chicken, Beef Yakitori, Salmon, Mixed Sauteed Vegetables and Fresh Fruits	29.50
YOSHI'S BENTO A box dinner with chicken, seafood and vegetables	13.75
VEGETABLE BENTO A box dinner with a special assortment of vegetables and served with brown rice	11.50

*———— The Following Items may be served with Yoshi's Traditional ————
Teriyaki Sauce or Chef's Special Sauces*

NEW YORK STEAK With garlic teriyaki sauce, served on a sizzling platter	11.50
CHICKEN Grilled and served with lemon butter soy sauce	9.50
SALMON Grilled and served with spicy soy ginger sauce	13.00
AHI TUNA Grilled and served with mushroom teriyaki sauce	13.50
YAKITORI Skewered chicken, beef and seafood with mustard soy bean sauce	11.50

DINNER SALAD A plentiful serving of mixed greens and marinated vegetables	9.00
SEAFOOD YOSE-NABE Japanese-style bouillabaisse and vegetables cooked in *KOMBU* broth	13.00
SUKIYAKI Thinly sliced beef and seasonal vegetables cooked in soy-mirin broth – *Vegetarian Sukiyaki is also available*	11.00
YOSHI'S TEMPURA UDON NOODLE	9.00
TON KATSU Pork tenderloin breaded and fried, served with vegetables	10.00
TEMPURA Batter fried prawns and vegetables – *Vegetarian Tempura is also available*	11.00
UNA JU Fresh water eel, grilled with Teriyaki sauce and served over rice, with assorted Japanese pickles	13.00
SASHIMI ASSORTMENT Tuna, white tuna, mackerel, salmon, snapper, etc. with julienned daikon	15.00

Khayyam's

APPETIZERS

Dolmeh
Grape leaves stuffed with meat, rice, and vegetables 3.95

Kofteh
Mid-Eastern meat ball made with vegetables, rice, meat & beans 3.95

Cucco
Delicious patty of chopped vegetables, eggs & wheat flour 3.95

Mirza Ghasemi
Slow fried mashed eggplants, tomatoes, eggs and garlic 3.95

Combination Platter
A little of everything above 8.95

Torshi
Vegetables, processed with vinegar and spices 1.50

Moust O Moosir
Yogurt and shallots 2.00

Moust O Khiar
Yogurt and Cucumber 2.00

Panir va Sabzi
Sweet basil, mint, radish, green onions, and Bulgarian cheese 2.00

Tah-Dig 2.50

Sear Torshi 2.50

SOUP & SALAD
(we offer marvelous home-made soup every day)

Cup of Soup 1.50

Bowl 2.95

Salad Shirazi 1.50

Dinner Salad 1.75

Soup and Salad with bread & butter 5.50

ENTREES

(All entrees served with perfectly textured white rice.)

Khoresht Fesenjone
*Slowly cooked ground walnuts, chicken legs, pomegranate sauce
and saffron* 7.95

Khoresht Gheimeh Budemjone
*Delicious cut beef, yellow split peas, eggplant, tomatoes, lemon juice
and saffron* 6.95

Khoresht Ghormeh Sabzi
*Our Chef's favorite finely chopped green vegetables, red beans, beef stew,
lemon juice and saffron* 7.75

Combination Khoresht
*Smaller servings of Khoresht Fesenjone, Khoresht Gheimeh, and Khoresht
Ghormeh Sabzi* 10.95

Chelo Kabab Koobideh
Two skewers of charbroiled ground beef blended in mid-eastern spices 7.95

Chelo Kabab Barg
One skewer of tender cut pounded beef filet 9.45

Chelo Kabab Soltani
*Combination of one skewer of Koobideh and one skewer of Barg
(complimentary raw yolk of egg upon request)* 10.95

Joojeh Kabab
Marinated boneless chicken breast on skewer 9.95

Shish Kabab
*Steeped tender lamb cuts, tomatoes, mushrooms, onions and green peppers
on skewer. Broiled* 9.95

Four Season Red and White
*One skewer Koobideh & one skewer of marinated Persian Classic Joojeh
Kabob* 10.95

Maykadeh
Persian Cuisine

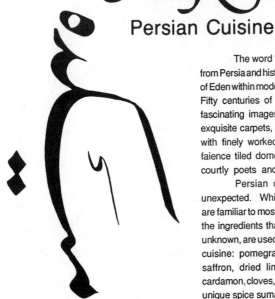

The word "paradise" comes to us from Persia and historians place the Garden of Eden within modern Persia's boundaries. Fifty centuries of Persian culture evoke fascinating images of brilliant peacocks, exquisite carpets, nomad caravans laden with finely worked gold and silver, blue faience tiled domes, graceful minaretes, courtly poets and an aromatic cuisine.

Persian cuisine is one of the unexpected. While its basic ingredients are familiar to most, such as lamb and rice, the ingredients that enhance it, while not unknown, are used infrequently in Western cuisine: pomegranates, pistachio nuts, saffron, dried lime, rosewater, yogurt, cardamon, cloves, barberry, fenugreek, the unique spice sumak—the list is endless.

Mazeh Appetizer

Salad Shirazi	diced tomato, cucumber, onion, in lemon dressing	$ 3.00
Kashke Bademjan	eggplant with mint garlic sauce	$ 5.50
Hot Dolma	stuffed grape leaves	$ 5.50
Lamb Tongue	lamb tongue with lime juice, sour cream, saffron	$ 6.00
Brain	mesquite broiled brain	$ 6.00
House Salad	green salad	$ 4.00
Mast-o-Khiar	homemade yogurt and cucumber	$ 3.00
Mast-o-Musir	yogurt with dried elephant garlic	$ 3.00
Mast	homemade yogurt	$ 2.50
Pickles	baby cucumber, prepared in garlic, vinegar and a little salt	$ 3.00
Torshee	pickled vegetables	$ 3.00
Aash	soup	$ 3.00
Sabzee	traditional garnish, onions and feta cheese	$ 3.00
Feta Cheese		$ 3.00
Tah Digh		$ 4.50

Desserts

Bastani	Persian ice cream	$ 3.00
Baklava	traditional Persian pastry	$ 2.00

470 Green St • Telegraph Hill • (415) 362-8286

From the Mesquite

Chelo-Kabab Koobideh	skewered mixture of ground lamb, beef with Persian spices	$ 8.50
Chelo-Kabab Barg	skewered thin slices of filet mignon, marinated in lime juice and onion	$12.50
Chelo-Kabab Soltani	combination of Kabab-Koobideh and Kabab-Barg	$13.75
Joojeh Kabab	pieces of boneless chicken marinated in home made yogurt and saffron	$ 9.75

Items Below Include Rice and Vegetable

Poussin	baby chicken marinated in onion and saffron served with bones	$ 9.75
Kabab Bare	baby lamb loinchops, garlic, mint	$13.50
Prawns Kabab	mesquite broiled in shell	$13.50

House Specials

Ghorme Zabzee	lamb shank cooked in finely chopped onion, scallions, leeks, chives, herbs	$ 9.50
Khoresht Bademjan	eggplant braised with saffron, fresh tomato dried lime, lamb shank	$ 9.50
Ta-Chin	rice cake made with yogurt, saffron, eggplant, barberry, and chicken thighs	$10.50
Zereshk Polo	steamed rice with barberry, saffron, and chicken thighs	$ 9.50
Baghali Polo Sunday	lima beans, dill, rice, served with lamb shank and saffron	$ 9.00

CHARDONNAY

Maykadeh, California 14.00
by the glass 4.00
Rutherford Ranch, Napa 18.00
Pars, Carneros 19.00
ZD, California 32.00

SAUVIGNON BLANC

Rutherford Ranch, Napa 14.00

WHITE ZINFANDEL

Grand Cru, California 11.00

CABERNET SAUVIGNON

Maykadeh, California 16.00
Pars, Carneros 18.00
ZD, California 25.00

PINOT NOIR

ZD, Napas Carneros 25.00

IMPORTED WINES

Cotes-Du-Rhone, Thorin 16.00
Shiraz 16.00

Dinner: Sun - Thurs 5 - 10, Fri - Sat 5 - 11

A.Sabella's
RESTAURANT

APPETIZERS

— COLD —

Shellfish Medley 9.75
  Two prawns, two oysters, smoked salmon and
  a crab leg with cocktail sauce, onions, capers,
  and lemon.
Combination Cocktail 8.00
  Bay shrimp and Dungeness crabmeat in our
  zesty cocktail sauce.
Crab Cocktail 8.00
Bay Shrimp Cocktail 7.25
Jumbo Shrimp Cocktail 8.75
Fresh Shucked Oysters 8.00
  on Ice (6)
Fresh Shucked Clams 6.50
  on Ice (6)
Smoked Salmon 9.75
  Fresh Scottish smoked salmon with Vodka
  Creme Fraiche, American Golden Caviar and
  chives.
Smoked Mussels
  with warm Chevre 7.75
  Applewood-Smoked Atlantic mussels on
  a bed of Arugula with warm goat cheese
  and roasted red peppers.

— HOT —

Baked Clams Oreganato 8.00
Baked Bay Shrimp Oreganato 8.00
Steamed Clams Bordelaise 7.75
Steamed Mussels Bordelaise 6.50
Oysters Rockefeller 9.00
  Six fresh oysters baked with spinach and
  pernod. Topped with champagne mousseline.

PASTA

LINGUINI WITH CRAB ALFREDO ... 19.50
  Dungeness crab with cream, butter and
  Parmesan.

LINGUINI CON SALMONE 18.50
  Linguini and salmon sauteed with
  mushrooms, fresh tomato and spices.

NANA'S PASTA 15.50
  With scallops, zucchini, tomato and
  mushrooms. Spicy!

FETTUCCINE ANGELINA 15.50
  Bay shrimp and cauliflower enhanced with
  garlic, then simmered in a delicate white
  sauce. Served with spinach fettuccine.

LINGUINI CON COZZE 15.50
  Linguini and fresh mussels steamed with
  onion, tomato and garlic.

ANGEL HAIR PASTA
WITH BUTTER CLAMS 16.50
  Fresh butter clams steamed with scallions
  and garlic.

ANGEL HAIR PASTA AND CRAB 19.50
  Served in a marinara sauce with scallions.

ANGEL HAIR PASTA 10.50
  Served in a marinara sauce or Italian
  meat sauce.

SOUPS

San Francisco-style
Clam Chowder (white or red) 4.75

2766 Taylor St • Fisherman's Wharf • (415) 771-6775

SALADS

Sabella's Special Pirate Salad 18.75
  Crab, Shrimp, garnished with Jumbo Shrimp
  and Lobster on shredded Lettuce,
  served with 1,000 Island dressing.
Crab Louis 17.75
Bay Shrimp Louis 15.75
Seasonal Green Salad 4.75
Dinner Salad with Crab 8.50
Dinner Salad with Shrimp 7.25
Fresh Tomato,
  Onion & Anchovy 5.00
Tossed Green Salad
  a la Lucien 9.50
  Tossed with crab, shrimp, avocado,
  mushroom, tomato. House dressing.
Caesar Salad with Shrimp 7.50
Warm Maine Lobster Salad 16.50
Orange, Avocado, and Shrimp Salad 7.25

CALAMARI
Squid sautéed with Olive Oil,
Mushrooms, Tomato and Garlic
or
Deep-Fried Alla Danilo (Spicy!)
$17.00

FRESH FILET
OF SOLE GRENOBLOIS
Fresh Local Sole Pan-Fried in Butter
Topped with Lemon Butter Sauce and
Almonds, then Garnished with
Shrimp and Capers
$20.25

FRESH WHOLE
BABY ABALONE
Delicate Shellfish from
our California Coast
Served Doré Meunière
$37.00

SHELLFISH

Shrimp

THAI CURRY 22.00

DEEP-FRIED 22.00

SAUTEED 22.00
  With garlic, tarragon and lemon

Scallops

FRIED, Tartar Sauce 20.75

SAUTEED BORDELAISE 20.75

BROILED MEUNIERE 20.75

STEAK, VEAL AND LAMB

FILET MIGNON 24.00
  With green peppercorns and tarragon.

NEW YORK CUT STEAK 24.00
  With shiitake mushrooms and onion rings.

VEAL PICCATA 20.00
  Milk-fed veal sautéed with lemon and capers.

VEAL PARMIGIANA 20.00
  Breaded veal cutlet topped with tomato
  sauce and Dofino cheese.

ROASTED BONELESS LAMB LOIN ... 22.25
  With polenta croutons.

ALIOTO'S

FRESH FISH

FILLET OF HALIBUT
    Halibut Bollito (Poached) *Served with a lemon butter sauce and garnished with diced tomatoes, capers, and basil.*   19.75
    Baked *Served with a light tomato sauce, eggplant and cheese.*   19.75
    Pan Fried *Seasoned, flavored, and pan fried in olive oil.*   19.75

FILLET OF SALMON
    Sautéed or Grilled (Broiled) *Served with a lemon butter sauce.*   17.50
    Poached *Served with a Hollandaise sauce.*   17.50

FILLET OF SWORDFISH
    Sautéed or Grilled (Broiled) *Served with a lemon butter sauce.*   22.00

FILLET OF TUNA
    Grilled (Broiled) *Served with a caper sauce.*   17.75
    Grilled (Broiled) *Served with virgin olive oil.*   17.75

MEAT & FOWL

BREAST OF CHICKEN PARMIGIANA *Boneless breast of chicken floured, sautéed, and topped with tomato sauce, Parmesan and Monterey Jack cheese.*   14.75

GRILLED (Broiled) CHICKEN *Chicken marinated in garlic oil and rosemary, and grilled (broiled).*   14.50

NEW YORK STEAK *grilled (broiled).*   21.00

NEW YORK STEAK SICILIAN STYLE *Coated with olive oil and bread crumbs, seasoned with garlic, parsley, grated cheese, and fresh ground pepper.*   21.00

VEAL SCALLOPINI *Sautéed with fresh mushrooms, prosciutto, peas, and diced tomatoes in a light brown sauce.*   22.00

VEAL MILANESE *Breaded veal cutlets.*   22.00

---

8 Fisherman's Wharf • Fisherman's Wharf • (415) 673-0183

PASTA

	Appetizer/Entree
SPAGHETTINI AGLIO E OLIO *Spaghettini tossed with oil, garlic and red pepper flakes.*	5.75/11.50
SPAGHETTINI WITH CLAMS *Your choice of red or white sauce.*	7.25/14.50
SPAGHETTINI FRUTTA DI MARE *A combination of seafood in a Cioppino-style sauce.*	7.50/15.00
CAPELLI D'ANGELO *Angels' hair pasta served with fresh tomato, basil and grilled marinated shrimp.*	7.25/14.50
FETTUCCINE ALLA CARBONARA *Ribbon pasta served with a mixture of ham, peas, and cheese in a cream sauce.*	6.75/13.50
TORTELLINI *Pasta stuffed with Prosciutto and Mortadella, served with a cream and tomato sauce.*	7.50/15.00
PASTA ALLA NORMA *Spaghettini tossed with tomatoes, garlic, basil and eggplant.*	6.25/12.50
PERCIATELLI PASTA *Long pasta tubes garnished with diced tomatoes, basil, bay shrimp, grilled scallop, and a light fish stock.*	13.50
CANNELLONI AI GRANCHI *Homemade pasta filled with a savory stuffing of crab, onions, red pepper and Parmesan, served with an herbed tomato sauce and melted Jack cheese.*	15.50

SHELLFISH

MUSSELS

Marinara *Served with a tomato sauce.*	14.50

PRAWNS

Prawns Alioto's *Seasoned with breadcrumbs, herbs, a generous amount of garlic, and oven baked.*	19.25
Sautéed *With garlic, white wine, tomatoes, lemon and butter.*	19.25
Deep Fried	19.25

ABALONE *(when available)*

Doré *Dipped in egg batter and griddle fried.*	40.00

CLAMS

Steamed *Served with drawn butter.*	18.75
Steamed *With a garlic-flavored broth.*	18.75

BABY LOBSTER TAILS

Broiled *Served with drawn butter*	28.00
Sautéed *With garlic, white wine, lemon, butter and parsley*	28.00

Dinner: 7 Days a Week until 11   ●ⓁⒹ

Ă Q U Ă

Appetizers

Savory Black Mussel Soufflé
Chardonnay, Garlic, Parsley $8.50
(Please allow fifteen minutes)

Dungeness Crab and Fennel Soup
Assorted Spring Vegetable Raviolini, Fava Beans $12.50

Aqua Fruitwood Smoked Salmon Salad
Warm Potato Pancakes Vonnas $11.00

Tasting of Ahi Tuna
Parfait of Tartare, Pepper-Crusted Loin $12.50

Cherrywood Smoked Idaho Trout
Spicy Walnut-Pear Vinaigrette, Watercress Salad $8.00

Seared Scallop and Foie Gras Salad
Belgian Endive, Carmelized Rhubarb-Lime Compote $14.00

Fried Oysters with Curry Essence
Frisée & Red Apple Salad, Green Apple Chutney $9.00

Salad of Field Lettuces with Potato Croutons
Champagne Vinaigrette, Snipped Herbs $7.50

Entrees

Aqua Paella
Smoked Chorizo Broth $19.00

Filet of Striped Bass
Oyster, Watercress and Salsify Stew $20.00

One and One-Half Pound Sweet Maine Lobster
Thai Coconut Broth, Sweet Potato Fritters (Market Price)

Grilled King Salmon
Asparagus, Potatoes Baked with Foie Gras Fat, Citrus Syrup $22.00

Swordfish Lightly Smoked & Wrapped in Prosciutto
Tuscan White Bean Purée, Honey-Thyme Sauce $24.00

Farmed Monterey Bay Red Abalone
Herb Egg Batter, Spinach Fettucine, Caper-Artichoke Brown Butter $29.00

Seared Atlantic Monkfish
Grilled Octopus Tabbouleh, Roasted Eggplant Turnover $20.00

Medallions of Ahi Tuna
Domestic Foie Gras, Pinot Noir Sauce $25.00

Desserts

Tasting of Three Soufflés
Orange, Banana, Espresso
Sauce Anglaise

Glazed Pear and Roquefort Tart
Black Peppercorn Caramel, Port Wine Jellies

Pineapple Ricotta Fritters
Frozen Spiced Glacé, Coconut Rum Sauce

Hot Chocolate Obsession
Cinnamon-Chocolate Ice Cream, Brandied Cherry Sauce

$6.50

BENTLEY'S

SEAFOOD GRILL & OYSTER BAR
SAN FRANCISCO

OYSTERS ON THE HALF SHELL (Market Price)

DABOB BAY (WASHINGTON) - A small oyster delicate in texture. Mildly salty, fruity flavor with a coppery aftertaste.

GOLDEN MIYAGI (BRITISH COLUMBIA) - Very delicate in flavor and texture. The flavor is like mild watermelon with a clean aftertaste.

HOOD CANAL (PUGET SOUND) - A salty oyster, firm and plump in texture. Fruity aftertaste.

HAMA HAMA (WASHINGTON) - A delicate oyster. Only slightly salty, with a mild, fruity aftertaste.

MALPEQUE (PRINCE EDWARD ISLAND) - Firm texture with a crisp lettuce-like flavor.

HOG ISLAND (CALIFORNIA) - Plump and salty with smoky-sweet flavor.

KUMAMOTO (HUMBOLDT BAY) - The "oyster virgin's favorite." Small oyster with a buttery texture, sweet in flavor and not very salty.

FANNY BAY (BRITISH COLUMBIA) - Firm texture and very salty. Very sweet in flavor with a strong aftertaste, similar to a cucumber.

SNOW CREEK (WASHINGTON) - Small deep cup - fruity and mildly salty.

SKOOKUM (WASHINGTON) - Firm in texture - almost crunchy. Less salty with a mild aftertaste.

QUILCENE (WASHINGTON) - Very delicate in texture, slightly salty and sweet, with a cucumber aftertaste.

TOMALES BAY (CALIFORNIA) - Firm, plump, and medium size with a briny, crisp clean flavor.

STARTERS

CHOWDER - Changes daily	Cup 3.50	Bowl 5.25
LOUISIANA GUMBO - With Andouille sausage and seafood. Served with a corn muffin.	Cup 3.95	Bowl 8.2
HOUSE SALAD - Organic lettuces with Sherry Vinaigrette With Roquefort Cheese and Toasted Walnuts.		4.95 6.00
CAESAR SALAD - With Croutons, Anchovies and Parmesan.		6.00
CRAB, SHRIMP & SCALLOP CAKES - A Bentley's tradition - sauteed and served with a spicy remoulade sauce.		7.25

185 Sutter St • Financial District • (415) 989-6895

SMOKED SALMON & CRAB CORNOCOPIA - Fresh Crabmeat mixed with Ginger, Lime Juice, Celery and Seaweed, rolled in Smoked Salmon and drizzled with Wasabi. — 9.25

HANGTOWN FRY - Freshly shucked Oysters baked with Parmesan, Bacon, and Toasted Bread Crumbs - served in the skillet. — 8.95

GRILLED TUNA & ALMOND SALAD - Chunks of lime-marinated Tuna mixed with Toasted Almonds, Wine Poached Pears, Red Onions and Watercress. — 10.25

GRILLED SCALLOP AND TANGERINE SALAD - With baby Spinach, Crispy Rice Noodle, and Pinenuts. Tossed with a mild Jalapeno-Tangerine Vinaigrette. — 10.75

DEEP FRIED BEER BATTER CALAMARI - With Chile and Cocktail sauces. — 5.75

DINNER ENTREES

GRILLED WARM SALMON SALAD - Served on a bed of Garden Greens with Pancetta-Cognac dressing. — 12.95

CLAMS PROVENCALE - Manilla Clams simmered in Tomato, White Wine, and Garlic Broth, drizzled with extra virgin olive oil. — 12.95

LOBSTER PASTA WITH SEA SCALLOPS - Chunks of Maine Lobster and Sea Scallops with sauteed Mushrooms, Leeks, Dill and Lemon Cream sauce. Tossed with Fresh Egg Linguini. — 17.00

TUNA CONFIT PASTA - House cured Ahi Tuna marinated with Fennel and Caraway Seeds; Tossed with Capers, Black Olives, Roasted Tomatoes and Penne. — 12.95

SEAFOOD STEW - Shrimp, Scallops, Clams, and Mussels simmered in a Saffron broth with aromatic Vegetables, Tomatoes, and Pernod; Topped with Rouille. — 18.95

GRILLED PACIFIC SNAPPER - Topped with Fresh Fruit Salsa and served over smoky Yucatan Black Beans. — 12.95

GRILLED MAHI MAHI - With Rosemary Balsamic Vinaigrette. Served with Argula and Roasted Potatoes. — 15.95

GRILLED SEA BASS - With preserved Lemon-roasted Olive Sauce, served over spiced Couscous. — 15.95

HERB-CRUSTED PACIFIC HALIBUT - Grilled and served with marinated Leeks and topped with Aioli. — 16.95

GRILLED PACIFIC SWORDFISH - Marinated in Thyme and served with a Wild Mushroom Caper Sauce and grilled Polenta. — 18.50

GRILLED HAWAIIAN TUNA TERIYAKI - Line caught Ahi Tuna, topped with housemade Teriyaki Sauce and served with a Vegetable Noodle Pillow. — 17.95

OVEN-ROASTED PACIFIC SWORDFISH - Stuffed with Monterey Jack, Pinenuts, Oregano and Jalapenos. Served with Tequila Lime Sauce and Ancho Mashed Potatoes. — 18.95

BROILED SALMON - With fresh Horseradish-Citrus glaze. Served with vegetable and Basmati Rice. — 17.95

GRILLED NIMAN-SCHELL NEW YORK STEAK (10 oz.) - Served with Oregano Butter, fresh Vegetables, and Ancho Mashed Potatoes. — 19.95

Just For Starters...
Appetizers

DUNGENESS CRAB COCKTAIL	7.75	OYSTERS ROCKEFELLER	7.95
BAY SHRIMP COCKTAIL	6.75	DEEP FRIED OYSTERS	7.45
PRAWNS SAUTEED WITH		OYSTERS ON HALF SHELL	
FETA CHEESE	9.45	– 3 Each 4.25 1/2 Dozen 7.95	
DEEP FRIED CALAMARI	7.95	STEAMED CLAMS	9.95
CLIFF HOUSE POT STICKERS	7.25	SPICY SALMON AND CRAB CAKES	8.95

Small Salads

THE CLIFF HOUSE DINNER SALAD
– Assorted California Greens   4.50
– with Bay Shrimp   5.95
CAESAR SALAD
with Garlic, Parmesan Croutons   6.25

MARINATED CALAMARI
Garnished with Red and Green
* Bell Pepper, Basil Vinaigrette*   6.45
TOMATO, ONIONS, AVOCADO
with Olive Oil and Oregano   5.75

Salad Creations

GRILLED BUTTERFLIED PRAWNS
with Field Lettuces and Walnut
* Vinaigrette*   15.75

MEDITERRANEAN CHICKEN SALAD
Marinated Chicken Breast on Mixed
* Greens with Pine Nuts and Feta Cheese*   13.45

Sandwiches

MARINATED BREAST OF CHICKEN
Grilled, Sliced and Served
* with Onion Rings*   8.45
THE CLIFF HOUSE BURGER
Charcoal Broiled on Onion Roll
* Served with Steak Fried Potatoes*   7.95
CHEESEBURGER   8.95

THE BEN BUTLER
Crab Meat Topped with Cheddar
* Cheese on Rye Bread Served*
* with Green Salad*   12.45
GRILLED FILET OF RED SNAPPER
Topped with Tartare Sauce, Tomato
* and served with Green Salad*   8.95

1090 Point Lobos • Ocean Beach • (415) 386-3330

Soups

BOSTON CLAM CHOWDER   SOUP DU JOUR

CUP 3.45   BOWL 4.75

Cliff House Favorites

SEAFOOD LOVER'S FEAST
Scallops, Oysters, Filet of Sole,
Clams and Prawns   17.25

DEVILED CRAB
Spicy Dungeness Crab in
Puff Pastry Shell   16.25

STUFFED FILET OF SOLE
with Dungeness Crab and Bay
Shrimp with Lobster Sauce   16.95

CURRIED SHELLFISH
Shrimp, Scallops and Prawns
with Mango Ginger Chutney   16.75

Shellfish

PRAWNS
– Deep Fried with Bread Crumbs   16.25
– Sauteed with Mushrooms and wine   17.25
– Sauteed with Feta Cheese   17.25

OYSTERS
– Deep Fried with Spicy Hollandaise   12.95

SCALLOPS
Sauteed with Tomatoes,
Mushrooms and wine   16.45

JUMBO PRAWNS (Scampi)
Sauteed with Garlic, Shallots and
Butter Sauce   19.75

Fish

SWORDFISH
Charcoal Broiled, plain or
with Teriyaki Baste   17.75

FILET OF SOLE
Just Grilled   13.25

PETRALE SOLE DORE
A Treat from San Francisco   15.45

SALMON
– Charcoal Broiled or Grilled   17.25
– Poached with Hollandaise   17.25

CALAMARI
Deep Fried   12.95

PACIFIC RED SNAPPER
– Charcoal Broiled or Grilled   13.45
– Grilled with Dungeness Crab
and Hollandaise Sauce   14.95

Meat – Poultry – Pasta... Etc...

HALF AND HALF
New York Steak and Jumbo Prawns   21.95

BROILED NEW YORK STEAK – 12 oz. 17.95

BROILED DOUBLE LAMB CHOPS (3)
Herb Sauce   17.75

TODAY'S FRESH PASTA
Please ask your server

BREAST OF CHICKEN MARSALA
Mushrooms and Marsala Wine   13.25

CHICKEN OSCAR
Sauteed with Crab Meat and
Topped with Hollandaise   14.95

"GARDEN VEGETABLES"
Assorted Seasonal Fresh Vegetables
Sauteed with Garlic, Shallots and Herbs   11.95

Sunday Brunch; Dinner: 7 Days a Week until 2am   Ⓑ Ⓛ Ⓓ

Fishermen's Grotto
M. Geraldi & Sons

Luncheon Specials by Chef Pietro

Rex Sole: With Rigatoni Pasta, Fresh Vegetable, and Tartar Sauce **8.50**
Pacific Red Snapper: With Rigatoni Pasta, Fresh Vegetable and Tartar Sauce **8.50**
Mussels: Steamed to Order à la Bordelaise **8.50**
Spaghetti or Ravioli Italiano: Meat Sauce **8.50**
Calamari Steak: With Rigatoni Pasta, Fresh Vegetable and Tartar Sauce **8.50**
Special of the Day: Ask Your Waiter   Bread and Butter Included

Filet of Sole Sandwich: On Sour Dough Bread
with Tartar Sauce and French Fries **8.75**
Tuna Sandwich: On Sour Dough Bread
with French Fries **5.75**

Crab or Shrimp Sandwich: On Sour Dough Bread
with Louis Dressing and French Fries **10.25**
Hamburger Sandwich: On a Sesame Seed
Bun with French Fries **5.75**

CHEF'S SPECIAL: Crab, Shrimp and Lobster
Salad, Louis Dressing and Mayonnaise **18.75**
Lobster Salad: Louis Dressing .... *
Mixed Green Salad: **6.75**
  with Shrimp or Crab Meat **16.75**
Crab Salad: Louis Dressing **16.75**
Shrimp Salad: Louis Dressing **16.75**
          Roquefort Dressing: Extra

Tomato Stuffed with Crab or Shrimp **16.75**
Combination Crab and Shrimp Salad:
Louis Dressing or Mayonnaise **16.75**
Avocado Stuffed with Crab or Shrimp:
Louis Dressing or Mayonnaise **16.75**
Jumbo Prawn Salad:
Louis Dressing or Mayonnaise **16.75**
.... **1.00**

Prawns: French Fried or Sauteed with
Mushrooms, Garlic, Wine, and Butter **16.75**
Eastern Scallops: Fried with
Lemon Butter Sauce **16.25**
Prawns à la Newburg: Served in a
Cream Sherry Wine Sauce **16.75**
Baked Crab au Gratin: In a Cream Sauce,
with Parmesano Cheese and
Lightly Seasoned .... **15.25** ••
Adventure Omelette à la "Hines":
Crab, Shrimp and Mushrooms,
"An Adventure in Good Eating" **13.75**
Crab Cioppino: Crab, Prawns and Clams in a
Seasoned Italian Tomato Sauce. You Pick
It Out of the Shells. We Provide the Bib **18.75**
Crab Del Monico: Cream Wine Sauce,
Bell Peppers, Potatoes, Mushrooms
and Parmesano Cheese **15.25**
Crab or Shrimp à la Creole:
Seasoned Tomato Sauce, served on a
Bed of Rice en Casserole **15.25**
Scalone Steak: A Combination of Ground
Scallops and Abalone, Lightly Breaded and Pan
Fried. Served with Pasta and Vegetables **15.25**

Crab or Shrimp à la Newburg:
Served in a Cream Sherry Wine Sauce **15.25**
Crab Cakes: Egg and Crab Meat Patties
Pan Fried with a Touch of Garlic **14.25**
Clams, Steamed to Order:
Coo Coo Clams from Washington State.
Fresh via Air Daily **14.25**
Mussels Bordelaise: Steamed to Order with
Garlic, Butter, Parsley, Fresh via Air Daily **8.50**
Eastern Oyster Hangtown Fry: This
Omelette Originated in California
Mining Camps in 1849. .... **13.25**
Eastern Oysters Broiled or
Eastern Oyster Stew: From Long Island **10.25**
Crab Legs: Sautéed in Wine Sauce,
or Butter with Mushrooms, and
Basilico, an Italian Herb Sauce .... •
Crab Legs Mornay: Special
Fisherman's Cream Sauce .... •
Abalone: Lightly Breaded and Pan Fried:
Served with Meuniere and Tartar Sauce .... •

Rex Sole or Sanddabs: Weather Permitting,
Caught Fresh Daily **12.20**

Rainbow Trout: From the Trout Farm
to You—A Camper's Favorite **13.25**

Calamari Steak: Lightly Breaded
and Pan Fried and Tartar Sauce **12.75**

Mahi Mahi Amandine: Pan Fried with
Lemon Butter Sauce and Almonds.
Via Air from Hawaii to You **14.25**

Petrale Filet Amandine: Grilled with
Lemon Butter Sauce and Almonds.
Caught in Local and Northern Waters **13.75**

Calamari: Sautéed in Wine or French Fried.
Caught in Monterey, Different and Pleasing ... **12.75**

Pacific Red Snapper: Pan Fried with
Lemon Butter and Tartar Sauce.
Caught daily by our Local Fishermen **12.20**

Swordfish: Grilled (Broiled)
Caught in Southern Waters. Tasty! **17.25**

Filet of Sole: Pan Fried and Served with
Meuniere and Tartar Sauce. From
Local and Northern Pacific Waters **12.20**

Sea Bass: Grilled and Served with Tartar Sauce.
Caught Locally and in Southern Waters **15.20**

Halibut: A Local White Textured Fish.
Grilled and Served with Lemon Butter
and Tartar Sauce **15.20**

Salmon Grilled: A Local Fish,
Extremely Good Tasting **15.20**

Salmon à la Sicilia: Poached with Garlic and
Parsley, Served with Boiled Potatoes **15.20**

Poached Halibut: Served with Cream Sauce
or à la Scandia, a Mustard Sauce .... **15.20 ‧‧**

Filet of Sole Marquery: Stuffed with Shrimp
in a Cream Wine Sauce with Mushrooms ...... **15.50 ‧‧**

Small Mixed Green Salad with Louis Dressing (when served with Entrees only, **extra**) **3.00**
Roquefort Dressing, extra **1.00**

Lobster à la Newburg: Served in a
Cream Sherry Wine Sauce .... *

Lobster Thermidor: Cubed Lobster, in a
Cream Wine Sauce with Mushrooms,
Parmesano Cheese and Butter, then Baked in
Its Own Shell. Allow 25 Minutes. Delicious! .... *

Lobster Tail (Imported): Broiled
and Served with Melted Butter .... *

Lobster (Imported) **and Steak Brochette:**
Broiled with Onions, Bell Peppers and
Mushroom. Served with Rice Pilaf .... *

Priced According to Availability

Fishermen's Dinner

(Price of Entree Determines Price of Dinner)

Choice of One: Clam Chowder, or Mixed Green Salad, or Shrimp Salad with Louis Dressing

17.95 Entrees (Choice of One)
PAN FRIED FILET OF SOLE
PAN FRIED REX SOLE
PAN FRIED SAND DABS
or
PAN FRIED PACIFIC RED SNAPPER

20.95 Entrees (Choice of One)
GRILLED SEA BASS
GRILLED HALIBUT
GRILLED SALMON
or
ASSORTED SHELLFISH PLATE À LA GROTTO
(Fried Crab Legs, Prawns, Oysters and Scallops)

Pasta and Fresh Vegetables Included
Coffee • Tea • Milk

New York Cut: French Fried Potatoes **18.25**
Broiled Tenderloin Steak: Maitre d'Hotel **18.25**
Veal Scaloppine **15.25**

Ham or Bacon and Eggs **7.25**
Broiled Breast of Chicken .... **11.75 ‧‧**

Broiled Ground Round Steak **11.25**

Ravioli Italiano: Meat Sauce **8.50**
Spaghetti Italiano: Meat Sauce **8.50**
Cannelloni (Sea Food) **11.75**

Spaghetti with Crab Meat: Tomato Sauce **13.75**
Linguini Vongale: (Baby Clams) White Sauce ... **12.25**
Cannelloni à la Milanese (Veal) **11.75**

Spumoni: Italian Ice Cream — 3 Flavors **2.50**
Ice Cream or Sherbet **2.00**

Chocolate or Amaretto Mousse Cake **3.50**
French or Italian Pastries or Cheese Cake **3.50**

Filet of Sole **4.75**
Hamburger Steak or Sandwich **5.75**

Chardonnay   Glass........... **3.75**
Drinks House Wine - Chablis, Rosé, Burgundy or
White Zinfandel

Dinner: Sun - Fri until 11, Sat until 12

●ⓁⒹ

Menu Changes Daily

LUNCH

T O D A Y ' S   L U N C H   S P E C I A L
Tagliarini Calabrese with Cauliflower and Green Beans 9.50

S A L A D S   A N D   S P E C I A L   A P P E T I Z E R S
Grilled Quail Salad 7.50
Greens with Sherry-Shallot Vinaigrette 4.75
Romaine, Croutons and Blue Cheese 5.50
Caesar Salad (for 2) 9.75
Warm Spinach and Bacon Salad (for 2) 9.75
Spinach Salad with Feta Cheese and Black Beans 5.50/8.50
Warm Goat Cheese with Greens and Toasted Pecans 7.50
Smoked Chicken Salad 9.25
Chinese Chicken Salad 9.25

G R I L L E D   F I S H
Mako Shark 13.25 Puget Sound Salmon 15.75 Mahi Mahi 15.50
Pacific Snapper 10.75 Pacific Halibut 15.50 Swordfish 16.75
Yellowfin Tuna (line caught) 16.25 Sturgeon 16.25

S A U T E E D   F I S H
Petrale Sole with Morels and Fresh Peas 12.25
Crab Cakes with Pasilla Beurre Blanc and Frisee 15.75
Shad Roe with Bacon and Brown Butter, served with New Potatoes
12.75
Steamed Clams with Chinese Black Beans and Ginger 6.75/11.50

G R I L L E D   M E A T S
Niman-Schell Hamburger 8.50; with Vermont Cheddar 9.25
Whiskey Fennel Sausages with Dijon Mustard 9.50
Dry Aged New York Steak 21.50
Marinated Poussin (Young Chicken) 11.50
Whole Chicken Breast (with choice of sauce) 10.25

S P E C I A L   E N T R E E S
Crab and Asparagus Salad with Red and Green Endive 12.75
Smoked Chicken, Mango and Avocado Salad with Lime Cream 9.75

S O U P
Celery and Celery Root
Cup 3.50   Bowl 4.50

A   L A   C A R T E   V E G E T A B L E
Red Chard
3.50

DINNER

S P E C I A L   A P P E T I Z E R S
Six Dabob Bay Oysters on the Half Shell 8.00
Grilled Shrimp, Arugula and Fava Bean Salad with Shaved
Parmesan 7.75
Grilled Asparagus with Anchovy Vinaigrette 6.75
Fritto Misto of Calamari, Red Onions and Artichokes with Salsa
Verde 7.25
Crab Tostaditos 7.75

S A L A D S
Spinach Salad with Feta and Black Beans 6.25
Warm Goat Cheese with Greens and Toasted Pecans 7.75
Caesar Salad (for 2) 11.50
Warm Spinach and Bacon Salad (for 2) 11.50
Smoked Chicken Salad (for 2) 11.50

G R I L L E D   F I S H
Atlantic Salmon 16.75 Yellow Tuna 17.25 Mako Shark 13.75
Swordfish 17.75 Pacific Snapper 12.25 Pacific Halibut 16.50
Shrimp with Roasted Tomatoes and Soft Polenta 17.75 Oysters
with B.B.Q. Sauce and Cole Slaw 13.25

S A U C E S   F O R   G R I L L E D   F I S H (please choose one)
Herb Shallot Butter - Sichuan Peanut - Extra Virgin Olive Oil
- Tartar - Pasilla Beurre Blanc - Tomatillo Salsa (Served on
the Side)

S A U T E E D   F I S H   A N D   S H E L L F I S H
Crab Cakes with Pasilla Beurre Blanc and Frisee 16.75
Steamed Clams with Sweet Italian Sausage & Extra-Virgin Olive
Oil 7.75/13.50
Steamed Mussels with Lemon, Garlic & Extra-Virgin Olive Oil
7.75/13.50
Trout with Pecan Butter and Cajun Spices 12.50
Petrale with Scallions 15.50
Shad Roe with Bacon, Browned Butter and New Potatoes 13.75
Pan Poached Halibut with Chinese Black Beans, Ginger, Bok Choy
& Basmati 16.50

G R I L L E D   M E A T S
Niman-Shell Hamburger 8.75, with New York Cheddar 9.75
Marinated Poussin (Young Chicken) 14.50
Dry-Aged New York Steak 23.75
Bradley Ranch Rib-Eye Steak with Mustard Butter and Roasted
Onions 17.25
Whiskey Fennel Sausages 10.25

McCORMICK&KULETO'S
SEAFOOD RESTAURANT

HALFSHELLS

Westcott Bay Belon Oysters *Washington* 12.00
Westcott Bay Petite Oysters *Washington* 9.95
Hog Island Oysters *California* 8.95
Preston Point Oysters *California* 7.50
Kumamoto Oysters *California* 8.50
Skookum Bay Oysters *Washington* 7.75
Hood Canal Oysters *Washington* 7.95
Large Sampler *two of each* 17.95
Small Sampler *one of each* 9.95

APPETIZERS

Dungeness Crab Cakes .... 9.95   Smoked Salmon Cakes 7.95
Rock Shrimp Popcorn .... 6.40   Smoked Mussels Vinaigrette 4.95
Fried Calamari .... 5.25   Tuna Tartare 7.25
Prawn Cocktail .... 11.50   Seafood Potstickers 5.80
California Brie with Fresh Fruit Chutney 7.25
Roast Garlic with Herb Toast Points 4.45
Wild Rice Griddle Cakes with Duck Confit 7.25
MooShu Seafood with Scallions and Hoisin 6.65
Dungeness Crab and Shrimp Quesadilla with Tomatillo Salsa 5.85
Seared Rare Ahi with Wasabi and Soy 8.10
Chilled Seafood Sampler 22.95

SHELLFISH AND STEAMERS

Prince Edward Island Mussels in Red Wine Tomato Broth 8.50
Crayfish in Crushed Red Chilies and Garlic 7.95
Green Lip Mussels in Warm Red Pepper-Basil Vinaigrette 9.90
Half Dunguness Crab 8.95
Manila Clams with Garlic, Wine and Parsley 9.95
Mixed Shellfish Steam with Mussels, Clams, Crayfish, Crab 11.75

SOUPS, SALADS AND VEGETABLES

	Cup	Bowl
McCormick's Clam Chowder	1.95	2.95
Fennel and Bean Soup	1.95	2.95

Oyster Stew with Garlic Croutons 5.75
Spring Mixed Greens 3.75
Spring Mixed Greens with Bleu Cheese and Glazed Walnuts 4.50
Romaine Salad with Anchovie-Garlic Dressing 4.50
Mozzarella, Basil and Tomato Salad with Kuleto's Olive Oil 7.90
Lemon Pepper Prawn Salad 11.85
Nicoise Salad with Seared Rare Ahi 9.50
Hot Seafood Salad with Hot Bacon Dressing 8.70
Dungeness Crab Louie with Thousand Island Dressing 12.95

900 Northpoint St • Ghirardelli Square • (415) 929-1730

SPECIALTIES

Grilled Jumbo Scallops
with Saffron Chive Butter Sauce
and Roasted Red Pepper Basmati Rice 17.75
Oven Roasted Canadian Halibut
Stuffed with Crab and Brie
Served with Lemon Thyme Beurre Blanc 19.95
Peppercorn Seared Thresher Shark
with Roast Red Pepper and
Basil Vinaigrette 14.50
Ahi Tuna "Black and Blue"
Served Very Rare and Spicy
with Wasabi and Soy 18.50
Grilled Hawaiian Ono
With Lime Shallot Oregano Sauce
and Fried Maui Onion Rings 17.50
Alder Smoked King Salmon
Lightly Smoked and Served with
Saffron Chive Butter Sauce 18.75
Mesquite Grilled Swordfish
With Tamarind Sesame Baste
and Fried Young Ginger 19.50
Alaskan White King Salmon
Mesquite Grilled with
Tomato Tarragon Coulis 18.95
Pacific Seafood Stew
Dungeness Crab, Green Lip Mussels, Prawns and
Butter Clams simmered in a Red Wine Tomato Broth 18.50

MESQUITE GRILLED

Canadian Halibut with Red Pepper Oregano Butter 18.50
Ahi with Nori and Pickled Ginger 16.95
King Salmon with Tobiko Caviar Creme Fraiche 17.95
Idaho Trout with Toasted Almonds 9.90
Thresher Shark with Coriander Peanut Sauce and Fried Leeks 13.75
Sea Bass with Tomatillo Salsa and Chestnut Lima Beans 15.45

SAUTEED & PAN FRIED

Pan Fried Catfish with Crispy Potato and Jalapeno Crust 11.25
Prawn and Bay Scallop Ragout with Chipotle Polenta 17.75
Linguini with Smoked Mussels and Radicchio 10.70
Pan Fried Ling Cod with Crayfish Tails and Sweet Peppers 12.95
Spicy Fried Wild Rice with Bay Shrimp and Scallops 9.80
Fettucini with Pesto, Rock Shrimp and Scallops 9.50
Sea Scallops Sauteed with Mushrooms, Tomato and Pancetta . 16.25
Petrale Sole Parmesan with Lemon-Caper Butter 14.25

Daily Menu

Sample Menu . . . Our Menu Changes Daily!

O Y S T E R S

	each	1/2 dz		each	1/2 dz
Snow Creeks (Wa.)	1.25	7.45	Olympias (Wa.)	1.10	6.50
Hog Islands (Ca.)	1.25	7.45	Kumamotos (wa.)	1.25	7.45
Fanny Bays (B.C.)	1.25	7.45	Samish Bays (Wa.)	1.25	7.45
Totten Bays (Wa.)	1.25	7.45	Hood Canals (Wa.)	1.25	7.45
Eagle Creeks (Wa.)	1.25	7.45	Skookums (Wa.)	1.25	7.45
Dabods (Wa.)	1.25	7.45			

CAVIARS: Sevruga 27.00, Golden 7.95
AQUA GEM CLAMS ON THE HALF SHELL: each 1.25, 1/2 dz 7.45
FRESH!!! OREGON DUNGENESS CRAB: whole 13.25, 1/2 6.75

C O L D S T A R T E R S

WILD MIXED GREENS SALAD
    balsamic vinaigrette or creamy blue cheese   4.50
CAESAR SALAD WITH GARLIC CROUTONS   4.50
SHRIMP "LITTLE LOUIE"
    with baby mixed greens   5.95
HAWAIIAN AHI TUNA CEVICHE
    lime juice, cilantro, jalapenos   5.95
SHRIMP COCKTAIL WITH COCKTAIL SAUCE   6.50
HAWAIIAN AHI TUNA PATE
    creamy pate with cognac, dill and pistachios · 4.95
HOUSE-CURED KING SALMON GRAVLAX
    mustard-dill sauce and toast points   6.95
FRESH DUNGENESS CRAB (OREGON) house cocktail sauce,
    whole...   13.25
    half...   6.75

H O T S T A R T E R S

NEW ENGLAND CLAM CHOWDER   4.25
INDIVIDUAL PIZZA smoked salmon, pesto, mozzarella,
    provolone and asiago cheese   6.95
DEEP FIRED CALAMARI housemade tartar sauce   5.75
DUNGENESS CRAB CAKES spicy remoulade and straw potatoes 6.75
BARBECUED OYSTERS spicy housemade barbecue sauce 6.95
GRILLED PRAWNS (IN SHELL) WITH SPICY PEANUT SAUCE
    oriental cabbage salad   5.95
STEAMED PRINCE EDWARD ISLAND, NEW ZEALAND GREEN LIP MUSSELS
    in a savory saffron-garlic broth with garlic toast 7.25

DEEP FRIED OYSTERS IN MEXICAN CORN FLOUR
  tomato salsa, jalapeno cream   6.95
Baked Brie With Roasted Garlic and Grape-Jalapeno Salsa
  toast points   5.75
GRILLED HERB POLENTA WITH WILD MUSHROOM SAUCE
  asiago cheese   5.95
SEARED RARE AHI TUNA
  oriental cabbage salad, orange-sesame vinaigrette   7.25

M A I N   C O U R S E S

MESQUITE GRILLED KING SALMON, HAWAIIAN SWORDFISH, HAWAIIAN
AHI TUNA OR PACIFIC MAHI MAHI   A.Q.
  with french fries and sauteed vegetables
  sauces: lemon dill butter, tomato salsa, spicy
  remoulade, sun-dried tomato butter, spicy peanut sauce
SEAFOOD RAVIOLIS
  salmon, halibut, prawns, ricotta, herb cream sauce   8.75
MESQUITE GRILLED PRAWNS (IN SHELL):
  herb-marinated prawns, herb and caramelized onion
  polenta, roasted eggplant relish, tomatoes   12.50
PACIFIC HEIGHTS PAELIA
  mussels, shrimp, chicken, housemade beef and pork
  chorizo, Pacific rock fish, linquisa and green peppers
  in a tomato sofrito, with saffron rice   12.95
SHRIMP AND SPICY ITALIAN SAUSAGE PASTA WITH
TOMATO-BASIL SAUCE
  Bruce Aidells' sausage with garlic fettucini and
  asiago cheese   9.75
PAN-FRIED PACIFIC SNAPPER
  with housemade spicy barbeque sauce, french fries
  and sauteed fresh corn   9.75
GRILLED PACIFIC MAHI MAHI WITH BLACK BEAN CHILI
  fresh tomatillo salsa, sour cream cucumber sauce and
  chile relleno   12.75
GRILLED PETITE FILET MIGNON WRAPPED IN PANCETTA WITH
CARAMELIZED ONIONS AND SUN-DRIED TOMATO BUTTER
  sauteed asparagus and roasted potatoes   13.25
CIOPPINO WITH GARLIC TOAST
  mussels, pacific rock fish and shrimp in a savory
  tomato, herb and mushroom broth   11.95
MESQUITE GRILLED BURGER
  with french fries and cheddar or jack cheese   6.95
  ...with bacon   7.50

DAILY SPECIALS

BLACKENED PACIFIC HALIBUT WITH LEMON BUTTER SAUCE
  roasted rosemary potatoes and fresh asparagus   14.50
GRILLED HAWAIIAN SWORDFISH WITH ROASTED TOMATILLO
AND AVOCADO SALSA
  potato-jalapeno-cheese pie and sauteed fresh corn   15.75

Sunday Brunch; Dinner: Sun - Thurs 5:30 - 9:30, Fri - Sat 5:30 - 10:30 ●●Ⓓ

SAM'S
Grill

and

Seafood

Restaurant

California
Wine List

Gary F. and Walter G. Seput
Established 1867

Appetizers

Fried Eggplant or Zucchini 3.00
Bay Shrimp Cocktail 5.25
Crab Cocktail 7.50
Crab Leg Cocktail 9.50
Prawn Cocktail 6.50
Olympia Oyster Cocktail 8.00
Clam Cocktail 7.00
Baked Clams Elizabeth (For Two) 13.00
Linguine with Clams, Red or White Sauce (For Two) 10.50

Soups

Minestrone .... Cup 2.00 .... Bowl 2.50
Clam Chowder .... Cup 2.25 .... Bowl 2.75
Mock Turtle .... Cup 2.25 .... Bowl 2.75

Salads

Mixed Greens 5.75
   with Shellfish 12.50
Hearts of Romaine 6.00
   with Red Beans 6.50
   with Shellfish 13.75
   with Avocado and Shellfish 14.25
Bay Shrimp Salad or Louie 10.00
Crab Salad or Louie 14.00
Prawn Salad or Louie 12.25
Marinated Calamari and Mixed Greens 9.00
Avocado .... 6.00 ...... with Shellfish 13.50
Tomato .... 5.75 ...... with Shellfish 13.50
Artichoke Heart .... 7.25 ...... with Shellfish 14.50
Vegetable .... 6.50 ...... with Shellfish 14.00
Anchovy 8.00
Celery Victor 8.00
Sam's Special Seafood Salad 14.00

Pasta

Linguine with Red Sauce, Clams, Bay Shrimp and Blue Cheese 11.50
Linguine with Clams — Red or White Sauce 10.50
Linguine with Calamari and Red Sauce 11.00
Linguine with Shellfish and Red Sauce 15.50

Vegetarian Items

Mushroom Omelette 7.50
Spanish Omelette 7.00
Hot Vegetable Platter 7.50
Spinach Florentine 7.00
Linguine with Tomato Sauce 7.50

---

374 Bush St • Financial District • (415) 421-0594

Fish

Boned Rex Sole a la Sam	10.25
Boned Sand Dabs a la Sam	10.50
Fried Filet of Sole	7.50
Smoked Alaskan Cod	12.00
with Scrambled Eggs	13.00
Poached Salmon	13.25
with Egg Sauce	13.75
Charcoal Broiled	
Ahi Tuna	15.00
Baby Steelhead	10.00

Shellfish

Fried Seafood Platter	14.00
Shellfish Sauté	16.50

Prawns

Fried	12.50
Sauté	14.00
Curry or Creole	13.00

Dungeness Crab

Half Cracked Crab	10.50
Whole Cracked Crab	18.00
Deviled, baked en Casserol	13.50
Au Gratin	14.25
Newberg	14.25

Littleneck Clams

Fried	11.00
Steamed with Garlic	11.50
Elizabeth – Baked	13.00

Olympia Oysters

Fried	13.00
Milk Stew	13.00
Hangtown Fry	13.50

Abalone

Meuniere	30.00

Calamari

Fried	9.00
Sauté – Red Sauce and Mushrooms	9.50
Steak, Pan Fried a la Sam with Garlic	10.00
Steak, Pan Fried Dore with Capers	11.00

Chicken

One Half Chicken per Order

Roasted	7.50
Charcoal Broiled	7.50
Elizabeth	9.50
Sauté with Mushrooms	8.50

Meats

New York Steak	15.50
New York Minute with Bercy Sauce	13.50
Top Sirloin Steak	14.00
Salisbury Steak with Mushroom Sauce	8.50
Veal Chop with Bacon	12.00
Veal Porterhouse with Bacon	13.00

SHELLFISH

21. **_Scoma's Special Lobster Tail_**
Priced According to Availability . . . . *Please Ask Waiter*

37. **DOUBLE LOBSTER TAIL WITH DRAWN BUTTER & LEMON**
Priced According to Availability . . . . *Please Ask Waiter*

38. **STEAMED CLAMS BORDELAISE** 14.25
When in Season

39. **HANGTOWN FRY** 13.25

40. **OYSTERS ROCKEFELLER** 14.25
Fashioned alla Scoma

41. **SCOMA'S DEVILED CRAB** 15.75
Dungeness Crab in a Cream Sauce en Casserole

42. **COMBINATION SEAFOOD PLATE** 17.25
French Fried Scallops, Filet of Sole, Oysters & Prawns

43. **CREOLE SHELLFISH** 14.75
The Old South comes to San Francisco

44. **CURRIED SHELLFISH** 15.25
Always Exotic and Delicious

45. **FRENCH FRIED PRAWNS** 17.25
A Golden Browned Treat

46. **FRENCH FRIED SCALLOPS** 16.25

Pier 47 • Fisherman's Wharf • (415) 771-4383 • (Call for Additional Locations)

FROM the BROILER

When Available

52.	SALMON STEAK	17.25
	Tender, Juicy, Flavorful	
53.	HALIBUT STEAK	14.25
54.	Baked alla Cardinale or alla Via Reggio'	14.50
55.	SWORDFISH	18.25
56.	Alla Via Reggio'	18.50
56A.	Blackened	18.25

SCOMA'S FISH

80.	REX SOLE	12.95
	King of Flatfish, Succulent	
81.	With Amandine Sauce	13.95
82.	SAND DABS *(when available)*	12.95
	Delightfully Different	
83.	With Amandine Sauce	13.95
84.	FILET OF SOLE MEUNIERE	13.95
	Light, Delicate, Delicious	
85.	With Amandine Sauce	14.95
86.	SOLE MARGUERY	16.25
	Petrale Sole topped with Crab & Shrimp and Hollandaise Sauce	

SCOMA'S SAUTES

69.	PRAWNS	18.75
	Sauteed with Wine & Mushrooms Sec	
70.	DUNGENESS CRAB LEGS	22.75
	Sauteed with Garlic, Wine & Mushrooms Sec	
74.	SHELLFISH SAUTE SEC	23.25
75.	SCAMPI – Genuine Scampi Tails	23.25
	Sauteed with Wine & Mushrooms Sec	
73.	SCALLOPS	18.50
	Sauteed with Wine & Mushrooms Sec	

Fresh Seafood Specials Change Daily

STARTERS AND SALADS

BOSTON CLAM CHOWDER   Cup 2.50   Bowl 3.75
Prepared in the Scott's Tradition

BAY SHRIMP, TOMATO AND AVOCADO SALAD   6.00
With Balsamic Vinaigrette

STEAMED WASHINGTON STATE MANILA CLAMS   10.25
Cooked in Wine, Garlic and Lemon Butter

PACIFIC PRAWNS   7.95
Six, Served Chilled, with Cocktail Sauce

HOUSE SALAD   3.75
Hearts of Romaine with Tomato and Cucumber

SCOTT'S CAESAR SALAD   4.95
Romaine Lettuce, Garlic Croutons, Grana Cheese

SPINACH SALAD   5.25
With Smoked Bacon, Feta Cheese, Balsamic Vinaigrette

SHRIMP LOUIS   11.50
Bay Shrimp on a Bed of Shredded Mixed Lettuces
With Sliced Tomatoes and Cucumbers, Hard Boiled Egg, Fresh Vegetable

SCOTT'S SEAFOOD SALAD   13.25
A Variety of Shellfish, with Avocado, Tomato and Hard Boiled Egg,
Served with a Choice of Dressing

Dressings: Vinaigrette, Louis, Roquefort Vinaigrette or Creamy Blue Cheese

2400 Lombard St • Marina • (415) 563-8988

SCOTT'S SPECIALTIES

EASTERN SCALLOPS SAUTÉ   15.95
With Fresh Tomato, Mushrooms, Lemon Butter

FRIED MONTEREY BAY CALAMARI   12.25
Tossed in Garlic, Shallots, Wine, Lemon Butter

GRILLED PACIFIC PRAWNS   16.25
On a Bed of Grilled Garnish and Saffron Rice

SEAFOOD SAUTÉ   17.50
Eastern Scallops, Pacific Prawns and Dungeness Crab Legs
Sautéed in Wine, Garlic, Shallots and Lemon Butter

FISHERMAN'S STEW   14.95
Fresh Fish, Prawns, Clams, Mussels, Scallops, Bay Shrimp Cooked in a Hearty Broth

PRAWNS SAUTÉ   16.50
Sautéed in Wine, Garlic, Shallots and Lemon Butter

MEATS

NEW YORK STEAK   Petite Cut   14.95   Regular Cut   18.95

FILET MIGNON   Petite Cut   15.50   Regular Cut   19.50
Steaks cut to order from Black Angus Beef, Served with Bearnaise Sauce

FRESHLY GROUND HAMBURGER   6.50   CHEDDAR CHEESEBURGER   6.95

DESSERTS

NEW YORK STYLE CHEESECAKE   4.50
CHOCOLATE MOUSSE TORTE   4.50
CREME CARAMEL   3.50
RASPBERRY JACK   4.00
FRENCH VANILLA ICE CREAM   2.50
GHIRARDELLI CHOCOLATE SUNDAE   4.00
CHOCOLATE - CARAMEL CRUNCH GELATO   3.50

Sunday Brunch; Dinner: Sun - Thurs until 10:30, Fri - Sat until 11   ●ⓁⒹ

CHILLED SEAFOOD COCKTAILS

Shrimp Cocktail 4.25
Crab Cocktail 4.75
Crab Leg Cocktail 5.75
Combination Shell Fish Cocktail 6.75
Marinated Herring with Sour Cream 4.25
Tossed Green Salad (choice of Dressing) ..2.50
Lettuce and Tomato Salad (choice of Dressing) 3.75

Oysters on the Half Shell ....3/3.25 ....6/5.25
Chilled Prawns in Shell 4.50
Oyster Cocktail 4.25
Prawn Cocktail 4.95
Lobster Cocktail 7.25

COLD CRISP SALADS

Combination Shell Fish Salad Lobster, Prawns, Crabmeat, Shrimpmeat..........(½ - 9.00) 12.00
Shrimp Salad...(½ - 6.50) 8.50
Crab Meat Salad..(½ - 8.25) 10.50
Crab Leg Salad...(½ - 9.50) 12.50
Prawn Salad..(½ - 7.50) 9.50
Lobster Salad..(½ - 10.50) 14.00
Combination Shrimp and Crab Salad.................................(½ - 8.25) 10.50

OYSTERS

Oysters on the Half Shell ....3/3.25 ....6/5.25
Deep Fried Oysters, French Fries with Cole Slaw 9.50
Oyster Hangtown Fry (with Bacon) 9.50
Oysters Stewed ....(in Milk) 7.50 - (in Cream) 8.00
Baked Oysters Rockefeller (baked in their Shells with Chopped Spinach) 9.50
Oysters, baked in their Shells, Kirkpatrick (Tomato Sauce and Bacon) 9.50
Curried Oysters with Rice in Casserole 9.50
Three-Egg Oyster Omelet 7.50

LOBSTERS

Steak & Lobster 17.50
Broiled Lobster Tail..16.00
Pan Fried Whole Lobster Tail (Wine Butter) 16.00
Baked Lobster Thermidor 16.00
Lobster a la Newburg 16.00
Lobster in Creole Sauce with Rice 16.00
Curried Lobster with Rice in Casserole 16.00
Cold Boiled Lobster tail; Garni....................................16.00

1919 4th St • Berkeley • (510) 845-7771

GRILLED FISH

Salmon, Lemon Butter 11.00
Halibut Steak 11.00
Sea Bass Steak, Maitre d'Hotel 11.00
Deep Fried Fillet of Rex Sole 9.75
Whole Rex Sole 8.75
Fillet of Rex Sole, Saute Meuniere 9.75
Swordfish Steak (no bones) 11.00

Orange Roughy 10.50
Fillet of Pacific Red Snapper 8.50
Fillet of Sole...........................10.50
Sand Dabs 9.75
Fresh Rainbow Trout 9.75
Fish'n Chips with Cole Slaw.............9.75

(Above orders served with tartar sauce, cole slaw and French fried potatoes.)

SHARK CATALINA
Fillet of Shark, served with Butter Lime &
Mushroom Sauce, au gratin Potatoes & Vegetables..................................9.50

POACHED AND BAKED FISH

Poached Salmon with Egg Sauce...11.00
Baked Fillet Salmon, Tomato Sauce 11.00
Poached Fillet of Halibut, Egg Sauce 11.00
Baked Fillet of Halibut, Au Gratin..11.00
Baked Halibut, Florentine (with Creamed Spinach) 11.00
Steamed Kippered Cod with Drawn Butter 9.50
Steamed Finnan Haddie with Drawn Butter 8.50

(Above served with choice of Potatoes or Rice)

SHELL FISH

CAPTAIN'S PLATE — A combination of Fine Seafood —
Including Scallops, Prawns, Oysters and Fillet of Fish —
Served with Cole Slaw, Tartar Sauce and French Fries 12.00
Combination Shellfish, sauteed in sherry wine sauce, including
Lobster, Prawns and Scallops 12.00
Eastern Fried Clams with Tartar Sauce, French Fries and Cole Slaw 9.50
Scallops (Deep Fried) with Tartar Sauce, French Fries and Cole Slaw 12.00
Steamed Clams (Plain or Bordelais) with Cup of Broth and Melted Butter 12.00
Steamed Mussels (Plain or Bordelais) with Cup of Broth and Melted Butter 10.50

CRABS

Crab Legs Sauteed in Butter with Sherry Wine, Mushrooms and Green Onions 15.00
Baked Crab Meat Au Gratin in Casserole 10.50
Baked Crab Legs Au Gratin in Casserole 14.00
Crab Meat a la Newburg...............10.50   Creamed Crab in Three-Egg Omelet.....8.75
Curried Crab Meat with Rice...........10.50   Baked Deviled Crab in Casserole........10.50
Crab Meat in Creole Sauce with Rice 10.50
Chilled Cracked Crab (in season) ....(½ - 7.75) 11.25

PRAWNS AND SHRIMPS

SHRIMP SCATTER, French Fries, Cole Slaw 8.50
Jumbo Prawns French Fried...........10.50   Prawn a la Newburg 10.50
Baked Prawns Au Gratin ....10.50   Shrimp a la Newburg.................9.25
Prawn Omelet ....10.50   Shrimp Omelet 9.25
Prawn Creole.....................10.50   Shrimp Creole 9.25
Curried Prawns ....10.50   Curried Shrimp 9.25
Prawns Sauteed in Butter with Sherry Wine, Mushrooms and Green Onions 12.50

STEAKS — *We use only superior quality Beef aged to perfection in our own refrigerator rooms*

Special Cut New York—14 oz. ....15.00   Ground Sirloin Steak 7.75
T-Bone Steak—16 oz. ....12.00   Breaded Veal Cutlet, Country Gravy 9.50

(Above orders served with French Fried Potatoes)

Steaks smothered with Onions ....1.50 (extra) — Fresh Mushrooms ....2.50 (extra)
HAM or BACON and EGGS (any style) 4.25

Dinner: Sun - Thurs until 11, Fri - Sat until 12   Ⓑ Ⓛ Ⓓ

OYSTER DEPOT
Quality Shell Fish

SALADS
served with bread and butter
& a choice of louie sauce or oil & vinegar

shrimp	10.50
prawn	11.25
crab	11.75
combination	11.25
lobster	13.50

SEAFOOD COCKTAIL

crab	6.25
shrimp	5.25
prawn	5.75
olympia oyster	7.50
eastern oyster	4.95
clam	4.95
combination	5.75
lobster	6.95

SPECIALTIES

Clams and Oysters on the Half Shell   5.75
Cherry Stone Clams or Blue Point Oysters

1517 Polk St • Polk Gulch • (415) 673-1101

West Coast Little Necks on the Half Shell   5.75

Smoked Trout or Smoked White Fish   10.50
served with salad, bread & butter

Half Cracked Crab   9.95
served with bread & butter, choice of
cocktail sauce, louie sauce or mayonnaise

Lobster   25.00
served with drawn butter cooked to order

One Half Cold California Lobster   A.Q.
served with salad, french bread

Smoked Salmon   11.25
served on rye of french bread with shrimp salad

Boston Clam Chowder   bowl - 3.25   cup 1.75
bread & butter .50

BEVERAGES

anchor steam	2.00
heineken draft	2.00
wine	2.50
lemon lime	1.00
pepsi	1.00
coffee	1.00
tea	1.00
milk	1.00

Menu Changes Daily

Appetizers

Crab Cocktail	6.75
Crab Leg Cocktail	10.25
Seafood Cocktail	7.25
Prawn Cocktail	7.75
Bay Shrimp Cocktail	6.50
Oysters Rockefeller	11.75
1/2 Doz. Eastern Oysters on the Half Shell	8.50
Fried Calamari (Squid), Tartar and Cocktail Sauce	8.75
Manila Clams, Steamed or Garlic Butter	
One Doz.	6.50
Two Doz.	12.50
Smoked King Salmon Garnished	7.95
Tadich Platter, Garni (For Two)	10.75

Soups

Lentil	Cup 2.95	Bowl 3.95
Boston Clam Chowder	Cup 2.95	Bowl 3.95
Coney Island Clam Chowder	Cup 2.95	Bowl 3.95
Clam Broth	Cup 2.25	Bowl 2.95

A LA CARTE SALADS

Cosmopolitan Salad	
Vegetable, Crab, Prawns and Bay Shrimp	**13.95**
Crab Legs	16.95
Crab or Prawn Louie	12.95
Bay Shrimp Louie	11.75
Mixed Seafood	13.25
Sliced Tomato	
with Crab or Prawns	11.50
with Bay Shrimp	10.95
Vegetable Combination	8.75
with Seafood	13.95
Half Avocado, Crab	11.95
Half Avocado, Bay Shrimp	10.25
Whole Avocado	8.25
Extra Seafood	2.00
Extra Garnish	1.50

CHARCOAL BROILED

Served with Long Branch Potatoes, Butter Parsley and Tartar sauce

Pacific Rex Sole (Boned on request) 10.95
Filet of Petrale Sole 14.95
Filet of Pacific Red Snapper 10.95
Boneless Rainbow Trout 10.75
Halibut Steak 13.95
Salmon Steak or Filet 14.95
Swordfish Steak .14.95

GRILLED (PAN-FRIED)

Served with Long Branch Potatoes and Butter Sauce

Pacific Rex Sole or Sanddabs
   (Boned on request) 10.95
Filet of Petrale Sole, Tartar Sauce 14.95
Filet of Pacific Red Snapper with Sautéed
   Crab or Bay Shrimp 12.50
Boneless Rainbow Trout, Meuniere Sauce 10.75
Hangtown Fry (Oysters, Bacon and Eggs) 11.50
Calamari Steak (Squid) with Garlic Butter 11.75
Filet of English Sole, Tartar Sauce 10.75

SAUTÉ

In White Wine and Mushrooms with Rice and Vegetables

Seafood Sauté (Scallops, Prawns
   and Crab Legs) 16.75
Scallops 13.95
Jumbo Prawns 15.95
Crab Legs 17.95

HOUSE SPECIALS

Filet of English Sole all'Agro, Potato
   and Vegetable .11.25
Baked Avocado and Bay Shrimp Diablo
   with Rice, en Casserole 11.50
Crab and Prawns a la Monza with Rice,
   en Casserole 12.95
Seafood Cannelloni Florentine, Cheese Sauce 11.75
Seafood Cioppino with Garlic Bread, includes clams,
   prawns, scallops, bay shrimp, crabmeat and white fish . .15.50
Pacific Oyster Stew in Milk or Half and Half 10.50
Oysters Rockefeller .11.75
Lobster Thermidor Baked in Shell with Potato 17.25
Broiled California Lobster (Langouste), Garnished 24.75

THE WATERFRONT

Menu Changes Daily

BRUNCH

Eggs Benedict *Grilled Canadian Bacon & Poached Eggs on English Muffin with Hollandaise Sauce*..............6.95

Scrambled Eggs *with Italian Sausage, Polenta Marinara, Peppers & Onions*..7.25

Eggs San Francisco *Fettuccine and Bacon in Cream Sauce topped with Poached Eggs & Hollandaise Sauce*.....7.25

Eggs Waterfront *Filet Mignonettes on English Muffin with Mushroom Sauce topped with Poached Eggs
& Bearnaise Sauce*..9.25

Hangtown Fry *Sauteed Fresh Pacific Oysters and Bacon in Barbeque sauce with scrambled Eggs on the Side*.....7.25

The Waterfront Crab Cakes *Tender Blue Crab Meat with Hot & Spicy Seasonings topped with
Poached Eggs & Hollandaise Sauce*...10.75

Penne Pasta *with Dungeness Crab, Gulf Prawns, Smoked Sausage, Mushrooms, Tomatoes, Spinach,
Balsamic Vinegar & Olive Oil*...10.75
As an Appetizer..8.95

Chinese Smoked Chicken Salad *with Crispy Rice Noodles, Roasted Peanuts, Toasted Sesame Seeds,
Sweet Peppers, Shiitake Mushrooms, Shredded Cabbage & Sesame Vinaigrette*...................................8.50

LUNCH SPECIALS

Cajun Gulf Shrimp Popcorn Appetizer *with Creole Tartar Sauce*..5.75

Medley of Penne & Fusilli Pasta *with Dungeness Crab, Gulf Prawns, Sundried Tomatoes, Arugula,
Spinach, Basil & Toasted Pinenuts*...10.75
As an Appetizer..8.95

Chinese Smoked Chicken Salad *with Crispy Rice Noodles, Roasted Peanuts, Toasted Sesame Seeds,
Sweet Peppers, Shiitake Mushrooms, Shredded Cabbage & Sesame Vinaigrette*...................................8.50

Waterfront Seafood Chili *with Gulf Prawns, Bay Scallops, Red Snapper & Spicy Seasonings.
Served with Caesar Salad*...8.75

Sauteed Hawaiian Onaga *with Maine Lobster, Fennel, Leeks, Tomatoes, Yellow Roasted Peppers
& Fresh Tarragon*...12.95

Broiled Hawaiian Ono *with a Toasted Peanut Chili Sauce, Sugar Peas, Grilled Japanese Eggplant,
Shiitake Mushrooms & Radicchio*..12.95

Broiled California Sturgeon *with a Puree of Italian Parsley, Dill, Capers & Anchovy*..........................16.50

One Half Dungeness Cracked Crab *Served with Seasonal Greens Vinaigrette*...................................9.00

Whole Dungeness Cracked Crab *Served with Dijon Mustard Mayonnaise*......................................16.50

Pier 7 • Financial District • (415) 391-2696

FRESH FISH & SHELLFISH
*Our Fish Can be Prepared Broiled, Sauteed Meuniere or Dore, Steamed, Blackened, or Poached
Served with Seasonal Vegetables*

Sturgeon	*California*	16.50	Swordfish	*Hawaii*	17.75
Pacific Snapper	*California*	11.00	Ahi	*Hawaii*	16.00
Red Abalone	*California*	29.95	Ono	*Hawaii*	15.75
Petrale Sole	*California*	12.50	Mahi Mahi	*Hawaii*	14.75
Sanddabs	*California*	11.25	Onaga	*Hawaii*	15.75
Rex Sole	*California*	11.25	Dungeness Crab	*California*	16.50
King Salmon	*Washington*	16.00	Sea Scallops	*Maine*	15.75
Monkfish	*Maine*	14.75	Cockle Clams	*New Jersey **	
Halibut	*Canada*	14.75	P.E.I. Mussels	*Canada **	
Sea Bass	*Mexico*	14.75	Cherrystone Clams	*New Jersey **	
Ivory Salmon	*Alaska*	17.00			

*** See Shellfish Section*

OYSTERS
Assortment on Request

Six Oysters on the Half Shell, Iced, with Oriental Mignonette.................................7.25
Twelve Oysters on the Half Shell, Iced, with Oriental Mignonette.........................13.50
Six Baked Skookum Oysters...7.95
    with Bacon, Sweet Corn, Bell Pepper, Onion & Parmesan Cheese

Skookum	*Washington*	Dabob	*Washington*	Kumamoto	*California*
Hama Hama	*Washington*	Indiana Island	*Washington*	Hog Island	*California*
Quilcene	*Washington*	Hood Canal	*Washington*	Fanny Bay	*British Columbia*

FIRST COURSES
Medley of Penne & Fusilli Pasta *with Dungeness Crab, Gulf Prawns, Sundried Tomatoes, Arugula,*
    Spinach, Basil & Toasted Pinenuts..8.95

Six Baked Skookum Oysters *with Bacon, Sweet Corn, Bell Pepper, Onion & Parmesan Cheese*.............7.95

One Half Dungeness Cracked Crab *Served with Seasonal Greens Vinaigrette*...................10.00

Waterfront Seafood Chili *with Gulf Prawns, Bay Scallops, Red Snapper & Spicy Seasonings*.................3.50

Cajun Gulf Shrimp Popcorn *with Creole Tartar Sauce*..5.75

DINNER SPECIALS
Medley of Penne & Fusilli Pasta *with Dungeness Crab, Gulf Prawns, Sundried Tomatoes, Arugula,*
    Spinach, Basil & Toasted Pinenuts.. 11.75

Sauteed Mexican Sea Bass *with Maine Lobster, Leeks, Shiitake Mushrooms, Chives, Brandy,*
    & Lemon Cream..16.25

Broiled Canadian Halibut *with Basil Aioli & Saffron Rice*.. 16.00

Broiled California Sturgeon *with a Puree of Italian Parsley, Dill, Capers & Anchovy*...........17.50

Whole Dungeness Cracked Crab *Served with Dijon Mustard Mayonnaise*.......................17.50

Sunday Brunch; Dinner: 7 Days a Week until 10:30

Fresh Squeezed Juice Of The Day ....A.Q.

Appetizers

BLACK BEAN GIETA   served in a bread bowl from our wood burning oven with sour cream,
cilantro and two cheeses...$4.95

GRILLED MARINATED VEGETABLES   in balsamic vinegar with shallots and fresh basil,
served with black bean salad $4.25

POLENTA   with feta and bell pepper topped with herbed goat cheese and served on tomato sauce $4.95

FAZ'S SMOKED SALMON   cured over alderwood, served with cucumber dill salad $6.50

GRILLED PASSILLA PEPPER   filled with Sonoma jack, cambozola, cheddar cheese,
served with fresh salsa..$4.95

CARPACCIO   served with mustard sauce and capers $5.25

JAPANESE EGGPLANT   roasted Japanese eggplant filled with shallots and garlic,
served on tomato coulis, topped with yogurt and mint $5.25

Soup of The Day..$3.50

Salads

CAESAR SALAD   hearts of romaine with Caesar dressing...$4.25

SEASONAL GREENS   with fresh herbs and raspberry vinaigrette $3.50

MIXED GREENS   with feta cheese, walnuts, bell peppers and basil, tossed with olive oil
and lemon juice $4.95

WARM GOAT CHEESE   rolled in toasted pecans and served with roasted bell peppers,
seasonal greens, and black bean salad...$6.50

Pastas

FETTUCCINE   with curried jumbo prawns, shallots, fresh cilantro and mushrooms $12.95
LINGUINI   with sea scallops and sun dried tomatoes..$10.95
ANGEL HAIR   with mushrooms, arugula and roasted bell peppers $9.95
RAVIOLI   filled with swiss chard, ricotta cheese, and fresh sage $8.95

Pizzas

VEGETARIAN   with grilled seasonal vegetables..$7.95
GOAT CHEESE PIZZA   with black olives, onions and fresh herbs $8.95
SPICY ITALIAN SAUSAGE   with tomato sauce, mozzarella, mushrooms,
   red bell peppers and onions...$7.95
SEAFOOD PIZZA   fresh seafood with tomato concasse, mozzarella, onions, black olives,
   garlic and fresh herbs $9.95

Rotisserie and Wood Burning Grill

FRESH FISH OF THE DAY..A.Q.

JUMBO PRAWNS   served with potatoes and vegetables, lemon, and basil butter $14.95

ROASTED CHICKEN   with fresh squeezed lemon and herbs, served with vegetables
   and roasted baby potatoes...$10.95

SMOKED STUFFED QUAIL   filled with chicken mousse, served with
   roquefort mushroom sauce, saffron rice and vegetables $12.95

ROASTED RACK OF LAMB   served on eggplant coulis and demi glace
   with herb polenta and vegetables $15.95

CLAY POT..A.Q.

DRY AGED NEW YORK STEAK   grilled to order..$16.95

Smoker

DOUBLE BONE PORK CHOP   on seasonal fruit relish with roasted potatoes and vegetables..................$11.95

PETALUMA DUCK   served with saffron rice and pomegranate sauce...$12.95

BABY BACK PORK RIBS   half rack, served with french fries and cole slaw $9.95

Desserts

VANILLA ICE CREAM   with caramel sauce $2.95

COBBLER $3.95

FRESH FRUIT FLAN $3.95

CHOCOLATE PIE   semi sweet chocolate with pecan crust, served with caramel sauce $4.25

CHEESECAKE   with blueberry sauce...$3.50

FRESH FRUIT   (upon availability) $3.95

Alejandro's

·SOCIEDAD GASTRONOMICA·

Enchiladas Verdes   10.75
Choice of beef, chicken or cheese, topped with our special
green sauce, sour cream, parmesan cheese served with rice,
beans, and salad.

Enchiladas Rancheras   10.75
Choice of beef, chicken or cheese, on rolled tortilla covered
with onion, peppers, tomatoes, melted cheese served with
rice, beans, and salad.

Enchiladas Suizas (SG)   10.90
Choice of beef, chicken or cheese, topped with sour cream
sauce served with rice, beans and salad.

Chiles Rellenos (SG)   10.90
Pepper stuffed with cheese topped with a special relleno
sauce and melted cheese served with rice, beans and salad.

Pollo al Jerez   13.95
Breast of Chicken sauteed in sherry, saffron rice.

Conejo en Salsa de Mani (SG)   14.95
Tender young Rabbit cooked in its natural juices and peanut
sauce. A delicious and unusual dish. Worth trying!!!

Filet de Res   15.95
Choice New York steak, 14 ounces after trimming.
Served with rice, beans and salad.

Bisteck a la Chorrillana   14.95
Top Sirloin topped with onions, tomatoes, mild chiles, herbs,
and a sprinkle of wine. Served with rice, beans and salad.

1840 Clement St • Richmond District • (415) 668-1184

Filete de Lenguado al Ajo (SG)   14.45
Filet of Snapper sauteed lightly and topped with crisp
roasted garlic.

Filete de Pescado (SG)   15.60
a lo Macho
Filet of Snapper topped with sauteed Shellfish and covered
with a hearty sauce.

Trucha (SG)   14.95
"Meson de Candido"
Trout cooked with serrano ham. Thanks to Master Candido
we are able to present this dish as it is served at El Meson
in Segovia.

Steak Picado (SG)   14.95
Top Sirloin strips sauteed with onions, tomatoes, ortega
chiles in a sauce well spiced but not hot. Served with rice,
beans and salad.

Lomo Saltado (SG)   14.95
Top Sirloin strips sauteed with onions, tomatoes,
potatoes, herbs. Served with rice, beans and salad.

Carne Asada   14.95
Center cut Top Sirloin pan fried with bell peppers, tomatoes,
onion in our special sauce. Served with rice, beans and salad.

Zarzuela di Mariscos (SG)   15.60
Assorted Seafood and Shellfish sauteed with shallots,
tomatoes, aromatic herbs and a touch of Jerez.

Parrillada de   15.60
Mariscosy Pescados
Fish and Shellfish grilled and served on a bed of saffron rice.

Arroz con Mariscos   15.60
a lo Macho (SG)
Shellfish simmered in a spiced semi-hot sauce blended in a
special sauce.

A FINE STEAKHOUSE WITH AN ITALIAN TOUCH
APPETIZERS
ALFRED'S ANTIPASTO

Calamari Vinaigrette, Pickled Pigs feet,
Dry Salami, Mild Coppa, & Mortadella,
Garbanzo & Kidney Beans Vinaigrette
Marinated Artichokes, Stuffed Grape Leaves,
Italian Green Olives & California Ripe Olives,
Italian Pepperoncini, Garden Relishes

8.50 *(serves two)*

WARMED
CRISPO MISTO Crisp Onion Rings,
Zucchini Sticks, Lemon Slices 4.45
CRISP CALAMARI FRITTI 4.95
ESCARGOTS Bourguignonne 7.25
ITALIAN SAUSAGE Mesquite Grilled,
White Bean Vinaigrette 4.15

CHILLED
PICKLED PIGS FEET housemade 3.95
ROCK SHRIMP COCKTAIL 5.75
PROSCIUTTO & SEASONAL FRUIT 6.25
JUMBO SHRIMP on ICE 8.25
SLICED TOMATOES Onions,
Gorganzola Crouton 5.25

GARLIC BREAD 2.95

SALADS & SOUPS
CLASSIC CAESAR SALAD
Prepared at the Table
Minimum Service For Two or More
5.25 *(per person)*

MIXED GREENS Tomato
choice of dressing 3.75
HEARTS OF ROMAINE
Anchovies 5.25
SOUP of the DAY 3.45
(Friday, Clam Chowder)

PASTAS
(appetizer portion)

CANNELLONI alla Toscana
Whole Milk Ricotta Cheese, Meat, Jack Cheese 5.45
FRESH LINGUINE with ROCK SHRIMP
Light Primavera Sauce 7.25
SPINACH & MEAT RAVIOLI Meat Sauce 4.75
TORTELLINI della CASA Creamy Pesto Sauce 4.75
FRESH FETTUCINE ALFREDO
Fresh Cream, Butter & Imported Parmesan Cheese 5.45

886 Broadway St • North Beach • (415) 781-7058 • (Call for Additional Locations)

ENTREES
ALFRED'S WORLD FAMOUS STEAKS
From Our Broiler - Genuine Mesquite Charcoal

STEAKS FROM THE SKILLET

FILET TIPS TOSCANA Polenta *12.55*
FILET TIPS & TORTELLINI Tomato Sauce *14.65*
WHISKEY STEAK Jack Daniels Sauce, French Fries *18.10*
PEPPER STEAK Petite New York, Cracked Peppercorns, French Fries *18.10*
GARLIC STEAK Petite New York, Crushed Garlic Cloves, French Fries *18.10*

All Steaks are served with a choice of baked Idaho* potato,
french fries, or ravioli unless otherwise stated
*Seasonal
Not responsible for steaks ordered cooked more than medium.

CHATEAUBRIAND
Of Beef Tenderloin
Bernaise Sauce, Duchess Potatoes,
Mushroom Cap & Broiled Tomato,
Carved at the Table, Service for two or more
18.85per person

ALFRED'S STEAK Bone-in Strip Steak, aged 21 days *19.90*
MEDALLIONS of Beef Tenderloin
Bernaise Sauce, Rice *17.80*
NEW YORK CUT STRIP STEAK Boneless, aged 21 days *18.85*
FILET MIGNON Most Tender Steak of Them All *19.90*
FILET MIGNON & GOLDEN FRIED JUMBO SHRIMP
French Fries *20.95*
CHICAGO RIB EYE STEAK Bone-in, aged 21 days *19.90*
T-BONE STEAK Center Cut of the Shortloin, aged 21 days *25.15*
PORTERHOUSE STEAK King of Steaks, aged 21 days *27.25*

OTHER HOUSE SPECIALITIES

CANNELLONI alla Toscana *10.45*
HALF FRESH CHICKEN Broiled, Roasted Garlic Sauce *11.50*
RACK OF LAMB Mesquite Broiled, Whole Mustard Sauce *17.80*
OSSO BUCCO Braised Veal Shank, Polenta *12.55*
VEAL PICCATA Imported Capers, Lemon & White Wine *14.65*
FRESH SALMON Mesquite Broiled, Sweet Red Pepper Sauce *16.75*
GOLDEN FRIED JUMBO SHRIMP French Fries *15.70*
JUMBO SHRIMP SAUTEED Light Mustard Sauce, Rice *15.70*

Dinner: 7 Days a Week 5:30 - 10

Harris'

Appetizers

Our own spreadable Beef Paté 5.75
Served with house-made melba toast

Fresh Oysters on the Half Shell 8.25   Steak Tartare (½ portion) 9.50

Smoked Salmon 8.25   Crab Cocktail 9.75   Prawn Cocktail 9.75

Imported Prosciutto di Parma with seasonal fruit 8.25

Fried Zucchini 5.75   Fried Mushrooms 5.75   Fried Onion Rings 4.75

Raw Vegetables with Curry Dip 5.25

Beluga Caviar 55.00

Soups
Served with house-made melba toast

Hot Soup of the Day 4.25   Cold Soup of the Day 4.25

Traditional Onion Soup 4.25

Salads

Crabmeat, Grapefruit & Avocado 8.50   Papaya with Bay Shrimp 8.50

Fresh Spinach 6.25   Mixed Green 5.75, with Bay Shrimp 9.95

Caesar 6.50   Sliced Tomato, Onion & Green Chile 5.75

Desserts

Cakes and Pastries from Our Cart   Seasonal Fresh Fruit

Sherbet or Ice Cream 3.00, Topped with your favorite liqueur 4.00

Dine with Beef

We serve carefully selected Midwestern Beef, dry aged in our lockers twenty one days at 33°.
Entrees accompanied by fresh vegetables and baked potato

The Harris Steak 22.75
A bone-in New York

Filet Mignon 22.75   Petit Filet 19.25   Petit New York 21.75

T-Bone 23.50   Ribeye Steak 21.75   Calf's Liver 17.75

Pepper Steak 22.50
A petit New York with black pepper and Brandy Sauce

Steak Tartare 19.00   Sliced Roast Filet, Bordelaise sauce 19.50

Sweetbreads 19.50
Broiled, or with Mushroom Cream Sauce

Brains Sauteed in Brown Butter 17.25

All steaks may be served Pepper Style, 2.00 extra.

Roast Prime Rib
With our freshly grated horseradish
Harris Cut 21.50   Executive Cut 23.50

Harris Selections

Served with fresh vegetables and rice pilaf

Our Chef prepares a Fresh Catch daily

Roast Duckling a la Baie 18.50   Grilled Breast of Chicken 16.95
In a light Orange Sauce   Topped with a light wine sauce

Domestic Lamb Chops 22.00

Mixed Grill: Petit Filet, Lamb Chop, Calf's Liver 23.75

Sliced Pork Tenderloin 19.50
With green peppercorn sauce & fried apples

ROAST PRIME RIB of BEEF

THE CITY CUT   18.75
A smaller cut for those with a
lighter appetite.

HOUSE OF
PRIME RIB CUT   19.75
A hearty portion of juicy, tender beef.

THE ENGLISH CUT   19.75
Some feel that a thinner slice produces
the better flavor.

KING HENRY VIII CUT   22.25
Extra-generous thick cut of prime beef,
for king-size appetites.

CHILDREN'S
PRIME RIB DINNER   8.45
Complete with milk and ice cream.
(For children 10 and under.)

1906 Van Ness Ave • Nob Hill • (415) 885-4605

FRESH FISH

Ask your server for today's special catch and price.

DINNER

ACCOMPANIMENTS
INCLUDED WITH PRIME RIB DINNERS

THE SALAD BOWL
A colorful mixture of healthy, crisp, seasonal greens prepared at your table, tossed in our unique house dressing.

MASHED POTATOES
A generous, steaming helping of the all American favorite, served with thick brown gravy.

OR BAKED POTATO
A superior sized Idaho potato served with butter and sour cream, with a sprinkling of chives.

YORKSHIRE PUDDING
Straight from merry olde England! Light, airy batter baked to a golden brown dome, with a fluffy interior to soak up those savoury beef juices.

FRESH, CREAMED SPINACH
A light dish of garden spinach whipped with fresh cream and pieces of bacon.

Fresh cream of horseradish sauce

Dinner: Mon - Fri 5 - 10, Sat - Sun 4 - 10

RUTH'S CHRIS STEAK HOUSE®
HOME OF SERIOUS STEAKS

APPETIZERS

Garlic Cheese Bread	2.50	Escargot & Hearts of Artichoke	8.75
Shoestring Potatoes	3.50	Shrimp Cocktail	7.75
French Fried Onion Rings	3.75	Shrimp Remoulade	7.75
Mushrooms Stuffed with Crabmeat	7.25	Barbecued Shrimp	7.75
		Blackened Tuna	7.95

SALADS

Italian	small 3.25 large 4.50	Spinach Salad	
Dinner (Mixed Greens)	small 2.75 large 3.75	with Hot Bacon Dressing	5.00
Heart of Lettuce	small 2.75 large 3.75	Fresh Asparagus	6.50
Sliced Tomato and Onion	4.50	Fresh Garden Salad (crisp seasonal	
Caesar	small 3.75 large 5.00	vegetables topped with shrimp)	9.95

Bleu Cheese, Remoulade, Thousand Island, Ranch, Creole French, Italian, Vinaigrette
(all made fresh daily from our exclusive recipes.)

POTATOES

Au Gratin (in cream sauce, topped		Steak Fries (big and rough cut)	3.25
with thick sharp melted cheddar)	4.25	Julienne (fried long and thin)	3.25
Baked (with butter, sour cream,		Shoestring (fried crispy, cut extra-thin)	3.25
bacon, cheese and chives)	3.25	Cottage (thick round slices)	3.25
Lyonnaise (sauteed with onions)	3.25		

VEGETABLES

Fresh Steamed		Broiled Tomatoes	3.50
Broccoli or Cauliflower	3.50	Sauteed Mushrooms	4.25
Au Gratin	4.50	Fresh Asparagus (in season)	
Spinach	3.50	with Hollandaise	6.50
Creamed	4.00	French Fried Onion Rings	3.75
Au Gratin	4.50		

1700 California St • Nob Hill • (415) 673-0557

OUR STEAKS ARE SERVED SIZZLING IN BUTTER. SPECIFY EXTRA BUTTER OR NONE.
SORRY, WE ARE NOT RESPONSIBLE FOR STEAKS ORDERED WELL DONE.

FILET 12-14 oz. 20.50
A thick cut of the tenderest corn-fed Midwestern beef.
So tender it practically melts in your mouth.

PETITE FILET 8 oz. 17.00
A smaller but equally tender filet.

NEW YORK STRIP 16 oz. 21.95
This specially aged U.S. Prime sirloin strip is the favorite of many steak
connoisseurs. It is a little firmer than a ribeye, and has a full-bodied flavor.

RIBEYE 16 oz. 20.50
An outstanding example of U.S. Prime at its best. This steak has the most
marbling of all prime cuts, which makes the ribeye flavorful and tender.

PORTERHOUSE (Per Person) 22.50
A massive cut of finest quality beef, suitable for sharing, combining the
rich flavor of the strip steak with the tenderness of the filet. *(Minimum 2 people)*.

T-BONE 20 oz. 29.95
This hearty portion of U.S. Prime beef is a classic cut which combines full flavor
with ideal tenderness. It's really two pieces of mouth watering steak, joined by the
famous "T". *(For 1 person)*.

PRIME VEAL CHOP 16 oz. 23.00
White tender milk-fed veal. This chop is so delicately flavored,
we simply broil it to release all the flavor. Served sizzling.

LAMB CHOPS 23.00
Two double cut U.S. Prime chops, hand cut extra thick. Extremely tender,
thanks to the natural marbling. Broiled and brought to your table
sizzling; served with mint jelly.

CENTER CUT PORK CHOPS 16.00
Two 8 oz. center cut chops, extra-fine grained and served
sizzling with sweet and spicy apple slices.

LOBSTER 2-5 lbs. Market Price
Fresh live Maine lobster, flown in daily. This lobster is a gourmet's delight.
Served with hot butter.

STEAK AND LOBSTER 29.95
A 6 oz. cut of our tender U.S. Prime filet, combined with
Australian Lobster tail. An unbeatable combination!

SALMON FILET 18.50
The aristocrat of North American fish caught in cold Northwestern waters.
Broiled and served sizzling, with a little lemon and parsley.

GRILLED TUNA 18.50
Fresh tuna grilled or blackened in hot spices in the famous New Orleans style.

CHICKEN CALIFORNIA 16.00
Fresh broiled double breast of chicken, marinated and seasoned with herbs.

Khan Toke
Thai House
Traditional Thai Cuisine

Complete Dinner Thai Royal Style
*Includes Appetizer, Soup, Choice of Salad, Two Entrees,
Thai Dessert, and Hot Tea or Hot Coffee*

$14.95 per person

Choice of Salads *(Select one)*

SALAD NEUA (Beef)
*Green salad, served with sliced beef
& lemon dressing*

SALAD KHAI (Egg)
*Served with broiled egg &
egg yolk dressing*

Entrees *(Select two items)*

1. **MUS-AMUN**
Beef with red curry, peanuts, onions and coconut milk

2. **KA REE KAI**
Chicken with Thai curry, potatoes and coconut milk

3. **SA-TE**
Sliced and marinated beef, served with peanut and cucumber sauce

4. **MOO KA TIEM**
Marinated tender pork with fresh garlic, black pepper, pan fried

5. **PED KA REE**
Duck, deep fried to crispy and cooked until tender in special mild curry

6. **GOONG TOD**
Fresh prawns, deep fried and served with honey sauce

7. **NUR KA PROU**
Beef, sauteed with mint leaves and hot chili sauce

8. **PLA MUK PAD PHED**
Squids, sauteed with spicy chili sauce and fresh mint leaves

9. **PLA LONG HON**
Fillet of fish, deep fried, topped with ginger sauce

10. **KAI YANG**
Marinated Bar-B-Q chicken Thai style, served with honey sauce

5937 Geary Blvd • Richmond District • (415) 668-6654

Dinner A La Carte

Entrees Served with Steamed Rice 75¢ Per Person

Appetizers

1. NEUA NUM TOK (Northeast Style) 5.50
Sliced beef steak mixed with onion, hot peppers, mint leaves

2. NAM SOD (Northern Style) 5.50
Ground pork with fresh ginger, green onions, peanuts

3. TOD MUN 5.75
Fish cakes with green beans, fried, served with cucumber sauce

4. PLA GOONG 5.75
Fresh prawns mixed with lemon grass, onion, hot chili, mint leaves

5. SA-IE 5.95
*B-B-Q sliced and marinated beef on skewers, served with cucumber and
peanut sauces*

6. LOOK CHIN MOO YANG 5.95
Pork balls, diced Thai fine herbs, tamarind sauce. You wrap them in rice paper

7. YAM PLA MUK 5.75
Squids with onions, hot chili, lemon grass, mint leaves

8. MEING COM 5.95
*Seven favorite Thai ingredients diced, lemon grass sauce. You wrap them in
butter lettuce*

9. KHANOM BEUNG 6.25
*Thai crepe, Shrimps, Pork, Shredded coconut, ground peanuts, Thai Turnip and
bean sprouts served with cucumber sauce*

10. YAM MA KHOUR 6.25
*Thai eggplant, char-broiled, mixed with fresh prawns, onion, mint leaves and
lime sauce*

11. YAM TA HAN ROUR (Navy Salad) 6.25
*Salad mixed with prawns, squids, clams, toasted coconut, red onions and
spicy navy sauce*

12. LAAB PED YANG 5.95
*Sliced roast duck, mixed with red onions, toasted rice, mint leaves and spicy
lime sauce, served with garnishes*

Salads

13 KHAN TOKE SALAD 5.95
*Green salad with bean sprouts, potato chips, hard boiled eggs and
Khan Toke dressing*

14. SOM TAM 4.95
Shredded green papaya, carrots, tomatoes, green beans and shrimp powder

greens
RESTAURANT

WEEK NIGHT DINNER
Menu Changes Daily

APPETIZERS

Mesquite grilled shiitake mushrooms, Japanese
eggplant and yams with green curry and spiced
peanuts.

6.25

Fall salad of golden and chioggia beets, Sierra
Beauty apples, fennel, walnuts and watercress in
orange vinaigrette with warm roquefort croutons.

6.50

O Konomi Yaki, Japanese vegetable pancakes with
shiitake mushrooms, napa cabbage, scallions,
carrots, ginger, cilantro and chilies. Served with
dipping sauce and sesame cucumbers.

6.75

Garden lettuces, watercress and Belgian endive with
red blush pears, pecans and pomegranates
champagne vinaigrette.

6.00

Spinach salad with radicchio, frisee, feta cheese,
kalamata olives, croutons, red onions, mint, garlic,
sherry vinegar and hot olive oil.

7.00

Marinated French lentils with goat cheese, lemon,
mint and croutons.

4.75

Carrot leek soup with gruyere cheese and chervil.
Cup   3.50   Bowl   4.50

Fort Mason, Bldg A • Marina • (415) 771-6222

ENTREES

Tart with Japanese eggplant, leeks, sun dried
tomatoes, asiago cheese, creme fraiche and eggs.
Served with sauteed chanterelle mushrooms and
roasted Green Gulch Farm rosefir potatoes.

11.50

North African vegetable stew with mushrooms, new
potatoes, butternut squash, peppers, carrots and
zucchini stewed with tomatoes, ginger, chick peas
and North African spices. Served with raisin almond
couscous.

10.75

Mesquite grilled brochettes with mushrooms, cherry
tomatoes, garnet yams, peppers, red onions,
zucchini and marinated tofu. Served with basmati
and wild rice pilaf.

10.00

Fettucine with Green Gulch Farm spinach and red
chard, currants, pinenuts, brown butter and
parmesan cheese.

10.50

Pizza with shiitake, domestic and porcini
mushrooms, tomatoes, gruyere, fontina cheese
and thyme.

9.75

Pizza with roasted pepper sauce, leeks, asiago,
mozzarella cheese and Green Gulch Farm marjoram.

9.50

Menu Changes Seasonally

Starters

SALADS

House Salad   4.75
Organic mixed Baby Field Greens, Carrots, Cucumbers and Toasted Sunflower Seeds with House Dressing. (Oil Free)

Insalata Caesar   5.75
Romaine Lettuce, Carrots, and Croutons tossed with our special Caesar Dressing. (Asiago cheese upon request)

Thai Salad   5.75
Grated Carrots and Jicama served on Organic Field Greens with Asian Pears and a Spicy Ginger Dressing. (Oil Free)

Spinach Salad   5.75
Organic Spinach, Mushrooms, Red Onions, Garlic, and Roasted Walnuts braised in Olive Oil with Croutons and Balsamic Vinegar. (Oil Free upon request)
With Feta Cheese or Smoked Tofu add 1.50

APPETIZERS

Filo Butterflies   5.75
Filo Pastry filled with Broccoli, Spinach, Onions, Walnuts, and Currants, with Pomegranate-Burgundy Sauce.

Los Ninos Tamales   6.25
Baby Tamales filled with Southwestern Barbecue Tempeh and served on Rojo Sauce and Jalapeno-Lime Sauce.

Smoked Shiitake Mushrooms   4.50
Alder Smoked Shiitake Mushrooms braised with Balsamic Vinaigrette and served with Roasted Garlic Toast.

SPECIALTY ITEMS
Milly's Ceasar Salad Dressing 4.95
Milly's Organic Purple Basil Vinegar 4.95

1613 Fourth St • San Rafael • (415) 459-1601

Seasonal Entrees

The Great Macro Plate 12.95
Millet Croquettes, Gingered Azuki Beans, Marinated Braised Beets, Arame and Seapalm Salad, Steamed Organic Vegetables and Housemade Pickles. (Wheat and Oil Free)

Tempeh Normandy 13.75
Marinated and Baked Tempeh sauteed with Apple-Brandy-Mushroom Sauce, Beets, Blue Lake Green Beans and Garlic Potato Pie. (Oil Free upon request) (Wheat Free)

Tangy Yaki Soba 12.95
Soba Noodles prepared Japanese style with Ginger, Garlic, Smoked Tofu, Organic Shiitake Mushrooms, Snowpeas, Red Bell Peppers, Burdock Root, Broccoli and Slivered Cucumbers.
(Spicy upon request.) (Oil Free upon request.)

Polenta Torte 11.75
Herbed-Polenta Lasagne filled with layers of Red Lentil Mushroom Duxelle, Pesto, Roasted Pepper- Mochi Confit served on Puttanesca Sauce with Swiss Chard and Broccoli.

Southwestern Kachina Tempeh 12.95
Marinated Tempeh served with a Smokey Pinto Bean Sauce, Jalapeno Cilantro Rice, Pisto Manchego Vegetables and Salsa Fresca. (Wheat Free) (Oil Free upon request)

Shiitake Steaks 14.50/13.50
Marinated and pan-sauteed medallions of Seitan or Tofu served with a rich Shiitake Mushroom Sauce, Red Onion Marmalade, Baby Organic Carrots, Snowpeas and choice of Baked New Potatoes or a mixture of Brown Basmati and Wehani Rice.

Catalan Pasta 9.95
Paella Fettucini sauteed with Garlic, Oyster Mushrooms, Fresh Seasonal Vegetables and served with Caper-Pepperoncini Sauce. (Oil Free)

Enchiladas De Casa 10.95
Blue Corn Tortillas filled with Tempeh Chili and Housemade Tofu Cheese, served on Rojo Sauce and topped with Tomatillo Sauce and Chipotle Tofu Creme, served with Fiesta Vegetables, Black Bean Chili, and Salsa Fresca. (Spicy upon request.) (Wheat and Oil Free) (Cheddar Cheese upon request.)

Ragout Provencale 10.95
A savory stew of Organic Vegetables, Potatoes and Crimini Mushrooms served over a Creamy Rosemary Polenta. (Wheat, Oil and Dairy Free)

Tanjore Crepes 13.75
Delicate Chickpea Crepes filled with Curried Tempeh, served with dairy-free Cucumber Raita, Housemade Spicy Chutney, Brown Basmati Pilaf, and Organic Vegetables. (Wheat and Oil Free)

Jean Louis Pasta 13.50
Penne Pasta, Seitan Prosciutto, Organic Baby Vegetables, Zucchini, Sweet Baby Tomatoes, and Oyster Mushrooms with an elegant Carrot-Cashew Chardonnay Sauce. (Oil Free)

Thai Basil Curry 9.95
Spicy Basil Curry sauteed with Baked Tofu, Snowpeas, Carrots, Jicama, Broccoli, Enoki Mushrooms and served with Basmati Rice and Eggplant Chutney.

Milly's is committed to using organic grains and organically grown fresh produce as available. (As locally grown organic produce seasonally changes, so does our menu.) Please let us know if you have special dietary concerns so we can do our best to accommodate them.

Afghanistan
Helmand, The, 24

American
Asta, 26
Bette's Oceanview Diner, 28
Buck Eye Roadhouse, 30
Campton Place, 32
Casa Madrona, 34
Cypress Club, 36
Embarko, 38
L' Avenue, 40
Lark Creek Inn, The, 42
MacArthur Park, 44
Max's Opera Cafe, 46
Mo's, 48
Mustards Grill, 50
Paragon, 52
Stars, 54
Stars Cafe, 56
Suppers, 58
Table 29, 60

Asian
Monsoon, 62

Bar & Grill
Buena Vista Cafe, 64
Tommy's Joynt, 66

Burmese
Mandalay, 68

Cajun-Creole
Elite Cafe, The, 70

Californian
231 Ellsworth, 72
Atrium, 74
Auberge du Soleil, 76

Balboa Cafe, 78
Bix, 80
Brasserie Savoy, 82
Brava Terrace, 84
Café Mozart, 86
Café Pastoral, 88
Caffe Esprit, 90
Chateau Souverain, 92
Christopher's Café, 94
Domaine Chandon, 96
Fog City Diner, 98
Fournou's Ovens, 100
Fourth Street Grill, 102
French Room
   (Four Seasons Clift), 104
Fringale, 106
Madrona Manor, 108
Masons (Fairmont), 110
Napa Valley Wine Train, The, 112
Nob Hill (Mark Hopkins), 114
Pacific Grill (The Pan Pacific), 116
Postrio, 118
Ritz-Carlton Restaurant, 120
Seltzer City Cafe, 122
Sherman House, The, 124
Showley's At Miramonte, 126
Silks (Mandarin Hotel), 128
Sonoma Mission Inn & Spa, 130
Trudys, 132
Victor's (St. Francis), 134

Cambodian
Angkor Palace, 136

Caribbean
Miss Pearl's Jam House, 138

Chinese
Brandy Ho's, 140
China Moon Cafe, 142
Great Eastern, 144

Harbor Village, *146*
Hong Kong East Ocean
    Seafood, *148*
Hong Kong Flower Lounge, *150*
House of Nanking, *152*
Hunan Village, *154*
Mandarin, The, *156*
New Asia, *158*
North Sea Village, *160*
Taiwan Restaurant, *162*
Tommy Toy's, *164*
Wu Kong, *166*
Yank Sing, *168*
Yuet Lee, *170*

Continental
Beethoven, *172*
Big Four, The, *174*
Carnelian Room, *176*
Garden Court, The
    (Sheraton Palace), *178*
Meadowood,
    The Restaurant at, *180*
Tourelle, *182*
Washington Square
    Bar & Grill, *184*

French
Amelio's, *186*
Bistro Clovis, *188*
Bistro Roti, *190*
Brasserie Chambord, *192*
Café Jacqueline, *194*
Ernie's, *196*
Fleur de Lys, *198*
French Laundry, The, *200*
L' Olivier, *202*
La Folie, *204*
Le Castel, *206*
Le Central, *208*
Le Trou, *210*

Masa's, *212*
Remillard's, *214*
Ritz-Carlton Dining Room, *216*
Rodin, *218*
South Park Cafe, *220*

Indian
Gaylord India, *222*

Indonesian
Rice Table, The, *224*

International
Cava 555, *226*
Jack's, *228*
Trader Vic's, *230*

Italian
Academy Grill, The, *232*
Acquerello, *234*
Albona, *236*
Alexander Lanzone, *238*
Bella Voce (Fairmont), *240*
Blue Fox, The, *242*
Bontà, *244*
Buca Giovanni, *246*
Caffe Macaroni, *248*
Caffé Roma, *250*
Calzone's Pizza Cucina, *252*
Capp's Corner, *254*
Ciao, *256*
Circolo, *258*
Donatello, *260*
Etrusca, *262*
Fior d' Italia, *264*
Fornelli, *266*
Gira Polli, *268*
Hyde Street Bistro, *270*
Il Fornaio, *272*
Jackson Fillmore Trattoria, *274*
Joe LoCoco's, *276*

La Fiammetta, *278*
La Pergola, *280*
Modesto Lanzone's, *282*
North Beach, *284*
Oliveto Cafe, *286*
Palio, *288*
Pane e Vino, *290*
Piatti, *292*
Prego, *294*
Spiedini, *296*
Spuntino, *298*
Teatro, *300*
Tommaso's, *302*
Tra Vigne, *304*
Tutto Bene, *306*
Vanessi's, *308*
Venticello, *310*
Vinoteca, *312*
Vivande Porta Via, *314*

Italian Oriental
Cafe Oritalia, *316*
Oritalia, *318*

Mediterranean
Bay Wolf, *320*
Chez Panisse, *322*
Chez Panisse Café, *324*
Faz, *326*
L' Entrecôte de Paris, *328*
Lalime's, *330*
Lascaux Bar & Rotisserie, *332*
Piemonte Ovest, *334*
Rosmarino, *336*
Splendido, *338*
Square One, *340*
Terra, *342*
Zola's, *344*

Mexican
Cadillac Bar, *346*
Chevys, *348*
Corona Bar & Grill, *350*
Guaymas, *352*
Salud, *354*

Middle Eastern
Ali's, *356*
Ya Ya Cuisine, *358*

Moroccan
Pasha, *360*

Japanese
Benihana,
    The Japanese Steakhouse, *362*
Cho-Cho, *364*
Kansai, *366*
Kyoya (Sheraton Palace), *368*
Sanppo, *370*
Yoshi's, *372*

Persian
Khayyam's, *374*
Maykadeh Persian Cuisine, *376*

Seafood
A. Sabella's, *378*
Alioto's, *380*
Aqua, *382*
Bentley's, *384*
Cliff House, *386*
Fishermen's Grotto, *388*
Hayes Street Grill, *390*
McCormick & Kuleto's, *392*
Pacific Heights Bar & Grill, *394*
Sam's Grill & Seafood, *396*

Scoma's, *398*
Scott's Seafood Grill & Bar, *400*
Spenger's, *402*
Swan Oyster Depot, *404*
Tadich Grill, *406*
Waterfront, The, *408*

Southwest
Santa Fe Bar & Grill, *410*

Spanish
Alejandro's, *412*

Steak House
Alfreds, *414*
Harris', *416*
House of Prime Rib, *418*
Ruth's Chris Steak House, *420*

Thai
Khan Toke Thai House, *422*

Vegetarian
Greens, *424*
Milly's, *426*

EAST BAY

Albany
Khayyam's, *374*

Berkeley
Ali's, *356*
Bette's Oceanview Diner, *28*
Café Pastoral, *88*
Chez Panisse, *322*
Chez Panisse Café, *324*
Fourth Street Grill, *102*
Lalime's, *330*
Santa Fe Bar & Grill, *410*
Spenger's, *402*
Trudys, *132*

Danville
Faz, *326*

Emeryville
Hong Kong East Ocean
   Seafood, *148*

Layfayette
Tourelle, *182*

Oakland
Bay Wolf, *320*
Fornelli, *266*
Oliveto Cafe, *286*
Piemonte Ovest, *334*
Yoshi's, *372*

Orinda
Alexander Lanzone, *238*

Walnut Creek
Spiedini, *296*

MARIN

Greenbrae
Joe Lococo's, *276*

Larkspur
Lark Creek Inn, The, *42*
Remillard's, *214*

Mill Valley
Buck Eye Roadhouse, *30*

San Rafael
Milly's, *426*
Rice Table, The, *224*

Sausalito
Casa Madrona, *34*
North Sea Village, *160*

Tiburon
Guaymas, *352*

PENINSULA

San Mateo
231 Ellsworth, *72*

SAN FRANCISCO

China Basin
Caffe Esprit, *90*

Chinatown
Great Eastern, *144*
Helmand, The, *24*

Hunan Village, *154*
New Asia, *158*
Yuet Lee, *170*

Civic Center

Academy Grill, *232*
Bistro Clovis, *188*
Christopher's Café, *94*
Hayes Street Grill, *390*
Max's Opera Cafe, *46*
Miss Pearl's Jam House, *138*
Modesto Lanzone's, *282*
Monsoon, *62*
Salud, *354*
Spuntino, *298*
Stars, *54*
Stars Cafe, *56*
Tommy's Joynt, *66*
Zola's, *344*
Big Four, The, *174*
Fournou's Ovens, *100*
House of Prime Rib, *418*
Masons (Fairmont), *110*
Nob Hill (Mark Hopkins), *114*
Ritz-Carlton Dining Room, *216*
Ritz-Carlton Restaurant, *120*
Ruth's Chris Steak House, *420*
Vanessi's, *308*
Venticello, *310*

Financial District

Aqua, *382*
Asta, *26*
Atrium, *74*
Bentley's, *384*
Bistro Roti, *190*
Bix, *80*
Blue Fox, The, *242*
Brasserie Chambord, *192*
Carnelian Room, *176*

Chevys, *348*
Ciao, *256*
Circolo, *258*
Cypress Club, *37*
Ernie's, *196*
Fog City Diner, *98*
Garden Court, The
   (Sheraton Palace), *178*
Harbor Village, *146*
House of Nanking, *152*
Il Fornaio, *272*
Jack's, *228*
Kansai, *366*
Kyoya (Sheraton Palace), *368*
L'Olivier, *202*
Le Central, *208*
MacArthur Park, *44*
Palio, *288*
Sam's Grill & Seafood, *396*
Silks (Mandarin Hotel), *128*
Splendido, *338*
Square One, *340*
Tadich Grill, *406*
Tommy Toy's, *164*
Waterfront, The, *408*
Wu Kong, *166*
Yank Sing, *168*

Fisherman's Wharf

A. Sabella's, *378*
Alioto's, *380*
Buena Vista Cafe, *64*
Gaylord India, *222*
Scoma's, *398*

Ghirardelli Square

Cafe Oritalia, *316*
Mandarin, The, *156*
McCormick & Kuleto's, *392*

Japantown

Benihana, The Japanese
  Steakhouse, *362*
Sanppo, *370*

Marina

Angkor Palace, *136*
Balboa Cafe, *78*
Bontà, *244*
Greens, *424*
L'Entrecôte de Paris, *328*
La Pergola, *280*
Pasha,*360*
Pane e Vino, *290*
Paragon, *52*
Prego, *294*
Rodin, *218*
Scott's Seafood
  Grill & Bar, *400*

Mission District

Le Trou, *210*

Nob Hill

Acquerello, *234*
Bella Voce (Fairmont), *240*

North Beach

Albona, *236*
Alfred's, *414*
Amelio's, *186*
Beethoven, *172*
Brandy Ho's, *140*
Buca Giovanni, *246*
Café Jacqueline, *194*
Caffe Macaroni, *248*
Caffè Roma, *250*
Calzone's Pizza Cucina, *252*
Capp's Corner, *254*
Cho-Cho, *364*

Fior d' Italia, *264*
Fishermen's Grotto, *388*
Gira Polli, *268*
Mo's, *48*
North Beach, *284*
Teatro, *300*
Tommaso's, *302*
Washington Square
  Bar & Grill, *184*

Ocean Beach

Cliff House, *386*

Pacific Heights

Elite Cafe, *70*
Harris', *416*
Jackson Fillmore Trattoria, *274*
La Fiammetta, *278*
Le Castel, *206*
Oritalia, *318*
Pacific Heights Bar & Grill, *394*
Sherman House, The, *124*
Suppers, *58*
Vivande Porta Via, *314*

Polk Gulch

Swan Oyster Depot, *404*

Presidio Heights

Rosmarino, *336*

Richmond District

Alejandro's, *412*
Hong Kong Flower Lounge, *150*
Khan Toke Thai House, *422*
L'Avenue, *40*
Mandalay, *68*
Taiwan Restaurant, *162*

Russian Hill
Hyde Street Bistro, *270*
La Folie, *204*
Tutto Bene, *306*

South of Market (SOMA)
Cadillac Bar, *346*
Cava 555, *226*
Embarko, *38*
Etrusca, *262*
Fringale, *106*
Seltzer City Cafe, *122*
South Park Cafe, *220*

Sunset
Ya Ya Cuisine, *358*

Telegraph Hill
Maykadeh Persian Cuisine, *376*

Union Square
Brasserie Savoy, *82*
Café Mozart, *86*
Campton Place, *32*
China Moon Cafe, *142*
Corona Bar & Grill, *350*
Donatello, *260*
Fleur de Lys, *198*
French Room
    (Four Seasons Clift), *104*
Lascaux Bar & Rotisserie, *332*
Masa's, *212*
Pacific Grill
    (The Pan Pacific), *116*
Postrio, *118*
Trader Vic's, *230*
Victor's (St. Francis), *134*
Vinoteca, *312*

WINE COUNTRY

Geyserville
Chateau Souverain, *92*

Healdsburg
Madrona Manor, *108*

Napa
Napa Valley Wine Train,
    The, *112*
Table 29, *60*

Rutherford
Auberge du Soleil, *76*

Sonoma
Sonoma Mission
    Inn & Spa, *130*

St. Helena
Brava Terrace, *84*
Meadowood,
    The Restaurant at, *180*
Showley's at Miramonte, *126*
Terra, *342*
Tra Vigne, *304*

Yountville
Domaine Chandon, *96*
French Laundry, The, *200*
Mustards Grill, *50*
Piatti, *292*

231 Ellsworth, 72

A
A. Sabella's, 378
Academy Grill, The, 232
Acquerello, 234
Albona, 236
Alejandro's, 412
Alexander Lanzone, 238
Alfreds, 414
Alioto's, 380
Ali's, 356
Amelio's, 186
Angkor Palace, 136
Aqua, 382
Asta, 26
Atrium, 74
Auberge du Soleil, 76

B
Balboa Cafe, 78
Bay Wolf, 320
Beethoven, 172
Bella Voce (Fairmont), 240
Benihana, The Japanese,
    Steakhouse, 362
Bentley's, 384
Bette's Oceanview Diner, 28
Big Four, The, 174
Bistro Clovis, 188
Bistro Roti, 190
Bix, 80
Blue Fox, The, 242
Bontà, 244
Brandy Ho's, 140
Brasserie Chambord, 192
Brasserie Savoy, 82
Brava Terrace, 84
Buca Giovanni, 246
Buck Eye Roadhouse, 30
Buena Vista Cafe, 64

C
Cadillac Bar, 346
Café Jacqueline, 194
Café Mozart, 86
Cafe Oritalia, 316
Café Pastoral, 88
Caffe Esprit, 90
Caffe Macaroni, 248
Caffé Roma, 250
Calzone's Pizza Cucina, 252
Campton Place, 32
Capp's Corner, 254
Carnelian Room, 176
Casa Madrona, 34
Cava 555, 226
Chateau Souverain, 92
Chevys, 348
Chez Panisse, 322
Chez Panisse Café, 324
China Moon Cafe, 142
Cho-Cho, 364
Christopher's Café, 94
Ciao, 256
Circolo, 258
Cliff House, 386
Corona Bar & Grill, 350
Cypress Club, 36

D
Domaine Chandon, 96
Donatello, 260

E
Elite Cafe, The, 70
Embarko, 38
Ernie's, 196
Etrusca, 262

F
Faz, 326
Fior d' Italia, 264
Fishermen's Grotto, 388
Fleur de Lys, 198

Fog City Diner, *98*
Fornelli, *266*
Fournou's Ovens, *100*
Fourth Street Grill, *102*
French Laundry, The, *200*
French Room
   (Four Seasons Clift), *104*
Fringale, *106*

G
Garden Court, The
   (Sheraton Palace), *178*
Gaylord India, *222*
Gira Polli, *268*
Great Eastern, *144*
Greens, *424*
Guaymas, *352*

H
Harbor Village, *146*
Harris', *416*
Hayes Street Grill, *390*
Helmand, The, *24*
Hong Kong East Ocean
   Seafood, 148
Hong Kong Flower Lounge, *150*
House of Nanking, *152*
House of Prime Rib, *418*
Hunan Village, *154*
Hyde Street Bistro, *270*

I
Il Fornaio, *272*

J
Jackson Fillmore Trattoria, *274*
Jack's, *228*
Joe LoCoco's, *276*

K
Kansai, *366*
Khan Toke Thai House, *422*
Khayyam's, *374*
Kyoya (Sheraton Palace), *368*

L
L' Avenue, *40*
L' Entrecôte de Paris, *328*
L' Olivier, *202*
La Fiammetta, *278*
La Folie, *204*
La Pergola, *280*
Lalime's, *330*
Lark Creek Inn, The, *42*
Lascaux Bar & Rotisserie, *332*
Le Castel, *206*
Le Central, *208*
Le Trou, *210*

M
MacArthur Park, *44*
Madrona Manor, *108*
Mandalay, *68*
Mandarin, The, *156*
Masa's, *212*
Masons (Fairmont), 110
Max's Opera Cafe, *46*
Maykadeh Persian Cuisine, *376*
McCormick & Kuleto's, *392*
Meadowood, The Restaurant at, *180*
Milly's, *426*
Miss Pearl's Jam House, *138*
Modesto Lanzone's, *282*
Monsoon, *62*
Mo's, *48*
Mustards Grill, *50*

N
Napa Valley Wine Train, The, *112*
New Asia, *158*
Nob Hill (Mark Hopkins), *114*
North Beach, *284*
North Sea Village, 160

O
Oliveto Cafe, *286*
Oritalia, *318*

P

Pacific Grill (The Pan Pacific), *116*
Pacific Heights Bar & Grill, *394*
Palio, *288*
Pane e Vino, *290*
Paragon, *52*
Pasha, *360*
Piatti, *292*
Piemonte Ovest, *334*
Postrio, *118*
Prego, *294*

R

Remillard's, *214*
Rice Table, The, *224*
Ritz-Carlton Dining Room, *216*
Ritz-Carlton Restaurant, *120*
Rodin, *218*
Rosmarino, *336*
Ruth's Chris Steak House, *420*

S

Salud, *354*
Sam's Grill & Seafood, *396*
Sanppo, *370*
Santa Fe Bar & Grill, *410*
Scoma's, *398*
Scott's Seafood Grill & Bar, *400*
Seltzer City Cafe, *122*
Sherman House, The, *124*
Showley's At Miramonte, *126*
Silks (Mandarin Hotel), *128*
Sonoma Mission Inn & Spa, *130*
South Park Cafe, *220*
Spenger's, *402*
Spiedini, *296*
Splendido, *338*
Spuntino, *298*
Square One, *340*
Stars, *54*
Stars Cafe, *56*
Suppers, *58*
Swan Oyster Depot, *404*

T

Table 29, *60*
Tadich Grill, *406*
Taiwan Restaurant, *162*
Teatro, *300*
Terra, *342*
Tommaso's, *302*
Tommy Toy's, *164*
Tommy's Joynt, *66*
Tourelle, *182*
Tra Vigne, *304*
Trader Vic's, *230*
Trudys, *132*
Tutto Bene, *306*

V

Vanessi's, *308*
Venticello, *310*
Victor's (St. Francis), *134*
Vinoteca, *312*
Vivande Porta Via, *314*

W

Washington Square Bar & Grill, *184*
Waterfront, The, *408*
Wu Kong, *166*

Y

Ya Ya Cuisine, *358*
Yank Sing, *168*
Yoshi's, *372*
Yuet Lee, *170*

Z

Zola's, *344*

Gift Order Form

THE MENU is the perfect gift for every food lover, and is available at bookstores and gift shops everywhere. If you would prefer to order copies by mail, please fill out the form below, and return it to us with your payment. For gift purchases, a personalized card announcing your gift will be enclosed. Bulk discounts are available for corporate giving, conventions, and fund-raising. For more information on bulk discounts, please refer to tear-out card inside back cover.

The Menu, San Francisco Bay Area, 448 pgs. $12.95 x Qty = _____

The Menu, A Restaurant Guide to Oregon, 240 pgs. $9.95 x Qty = _____

Subtotal = $ _____

Postage & Handling (each book) $1.50 x Qty = _____

Total Order = $ _____

❑ I enclose payment of $ _____ payable to David Thomas Publishing.

❑ Please charge this order to my credit card. Total order = $ _____

MasterCard # _____ Exp. Date _____

VISA # _____ Exp. Date _____

Approval Signature _____

Name _____ Phone _____

Address _____

City _____ State _____ Zip _____

Payment must accompany order. Please allow up to four weeks for delivery.
Rush/overnight delivery available. Call for details.

David Thomas Publishing
448 South First Street, Suite 200
Hillsboro, Oregon 97123
(503) 640-6951

(See reverse side for shipping instructions.)

SHIP TO:

Name _____ Phone _____

Address _____

City _____ State _____ Zip _____

Name _____ Phone _____

Address _____

City _____ State _____ Zip _____

Name _____ Phone _____

Address _____

City _____ State _____ Zip _____

Name _____ Phone _____

Address _____

City _____ State _____ Zip _____

Name _____ Phone _____

Address _____

City _____ State _____ Zip _____

Name _____ Phone _____

Address _____

City _____ State _____ Zip _____

❑ Check if additional names attached.

Reader Survey

Your feedback is very important to us! So here's what we'll do to get it — send us your comments and your name will automatically be entered in a random drawing for a $100 gift certificate to *THE MENU* restaurant of your choice. No purchase necessary. Limit one entry per address. Use this form or send a postcard with all of the information below to:
David Thomas Publishing, Dept. SF-01, 448 South First Street, Hillsboro, Oregon 97123

Name _____

Address _____

Phone _____

Sex: ❏ M ❏ F   Age: ❏ 18-25   ❏ 26-34   ❏ 35-55   ❏ 56+

❏ Married   ❏ Single

1. I use *THE MENU* as a reference when dining out:
   ❏ most of the time   ❏ sometimes   ❏ seldom

2. I obtained my copy of *THE MENU* from:
   ❏ Bookstore located in (city, state) _____
   ❏ Airport Gift Shop   ❏ Hotel Gift Shop
   ❏ Received as a Gift   ❏ Restaurant   ❏ Other _____

3. I dine out how many times per week for dinner:
   ❏ 5+   ❏ 3-4   ❏ 2   ❏ 1   ❏ other _____

4. Occupation _____ Job Title _____

5. Household Income: ❏ less than 39,000   ❏ 40-49,000   ❏ 50-69,000
   ❏ 70-89,000   ❏ 90-119,000   ❏ 120-199,000   ❏ 200,000+

6. I am planning to purchase additional copies of *THE MENU* for friends/clients as a gift.

   ❏ Yes ❏ No   If Yes, for what occasion? _____

7. I fly how many times per year: ❏ 20+ ❏ 10-19 ❏ 5-9 ❏ 3-4 ❏ under 3

8. I read the following daily papers: _____

9. I read the following weekly papers: _____

10. I read the following local magazines: _____

11. I read the following national magazines: _____

General Comments/Suggestions: _____

_____

_____

_____

BUSINESS REPLY MAIL
FIRST CLASS MAIL PERMIT NO. 000072 HILLSBORO, OREGON

POSTAGE WILL BE PAID BY ADDRESSEE

David Thomas
Publishing

ATTENTION: TOM DEMAREE
448 SOUTH FIRST STREET, SUITE 200
HILLSBORO, OREGON 97123–9901

Corporate Giving / Fund-raising

Bulk discounts are available for corporate gift giving, sales promotions, conventions and fund-raising. For complete information on Bulk Discounts, please fill out and send in this pre-paid card or call David Thomas Publishing at (503) 640-6951.

Please send information on the following:

❑ Corporate/client gift giving

❑ Fund-raising for (organization) _____

❑ Conventions

❑ Sales promotions/premiums

Product sold: _____

Briefly describe intended promotion/event:

_____

_____

_____

_____

SHIP TO:

Name _____ Phone _____

Address _____

City _____ State _____ Zip _____

BUSINESS REPLY MAIL

FIRST CLASS MAIL PERMIT NO. 000072 HILLSBORO, OREGON

POSTAGE WILL BE PAID BY ADDRESSEE

David Thomas Publishing

ATTENTION: TOM DEMAREE
448 SOUTH FIRST STREET, SUITE 200
HILLSBORO, OREGON 97123-9901